Justin Meggitt is a British Academy Research Fellow in the Faculty of Divinity, and Fellow Commoner of Jesus College, University of Cambridge.

John Barclay and **Joel Marcus** are Lecturers in the Department of Biblical Studies, University of Glasgow.

John Riches is Professor of Divinity and Biblical Criticism, University of Glasgow.

Studies of the New Testament and Its World

Edited by

JOHN BARCLAY
JOEL MARCUS
and
JOHN RICHES

Paul, Poverty and Survival

Paul, Poverty and Survival

JUSTIN J. MEGGITT

T&T CLARK
EDINBURGH

T&T CLARK LTD
59 GEORGE STREET
EDINBURGH EH2 2LQ
SCOTLAND

"Meat Consumption and Social Conflict in Corinth", *Journal of Theological Studies* 42 (1994) 137–141 and "The Social Status of Erastus (Rom. 16:23)", *Novum Testamentum* 38 (1996) 218–223 are reproduced here, with minor alterations, by the kind permission of Oxford University Press and E. J. Brill respectively.

First published 1998

ISBN 0 567 08604 6

British Library Cataloguing-in-Publication Data
A catalogue record for this book is available from the British Library

Typeset by Waverley Typesetters, Galashiels
Printed and bound in Great Britain by MPG Books, Bodmin

Contents

Response

Preface

I should especially like to thank the following institutions: the Ashmolean Library, the Ashmolean Museum, the Bodleian Library, the British Institute of Archaeology at Ankara, the Butler Library of Columbia University, the Cambridge Group for the History of Population and Social Structures, the Cambridge University Library, the libraries of the Classics and Divinity faculties at Cambridge, Conrad Grebel College, Jesus College (Cambridge), the library of the Plunkett Foundation, the Seeley Historical Library, the library of Tyndale House, and, of course, Selwyn College, who kindly provided me with a home for the duration of my doctoral work. The following individuals also deserve my gratitude as they all, in some way, contributed to the creation of this book (although some may not have realised it): Betty Boucher, James Carleton-Paget, Chris Carman, Felicity Collins, Jane Doyle, Deborah Emerson, Peter Garnsey, Morna Hooker, Dave Horrell, Sue Jeffreys, Fazana Khatri, William Klassen, John Leigh, Jane McLarty, Ashley Meggitt, Paul Smith, Don Stebbins, Andrena and Bill Telford, Andrew Wilson, Tina Wilson, and the staff and students of Westminster College (Oxford).

However, four people in particular were vital to the completion of this project: Andrew Chester, my supportive and critical supervisor; Jerry Toner and David Woodhouse, clever and generous friends; and, of course, Melanie Wright – my intellectual, non-violent, sparring partner.

Finally, I should not overlook the debt that I owe to Chris Rowland and John Sweet, who examined an earlier version of this work, and also to the editorial board of *Studies of the New Testament and Its World*: their stimulating and searching questions have improved the manuscript considerably.

This work is dedicated to my parents, in gratitude, for everything, and to Daisy Butler (1901–1987) – καὶ γὰρ αὐτὴ προστάτις πολλῶν ἐγενήθη καὶ ἐμοῦ αὐτοῦ.

JUSTIN MEGGITT
Jesus College
Third Month, 1997

Abbreviations

Ag	Athenian Agora (American School of Classical Studies at Athens)
AA	*American Anthropologist*
AClass	*Acta Classica*
AD	Ἀρχαιολογικὸν Δελτιόν
AE	Ἀρχαιολογική Ἐφημερίς
AHB	*Ancient History Bulletin*
AHR	*American Historical Review*
AIBL	*Académie des Inscriptions & Belles-Lettres*
AJA	*American Journal of Archaeology*
AJAH	*American Journal of Ancient History*
AJPh	*American Journal of Philology*
AM	*Mitteilungen des Deutschen Archäologischen Instituts*
AncSoc	*Ancient Society*
Annales (ESC)	*Annales: économies, sociétés, civilisations*
AntAfr	*Antiquités africaines*
ARA	*Annual Review of Anthropology*
Athm	*Athenaeum*
AW	*The Ancient World*
BA	*Biblical Archaeologist*
BAR	*Biblical Archaeology Review*
BASP	*Bulletin of the American Society of Papyrologists*
BCH	*Bulletin de correspondance hellénique*
BE	*Bulletin Épigraphique*
BGU	Berliner greichische Urkunden
BICS	*Bulletin of the Institute of Classical Studies*
BJRL	*Bulletin of the John Rylands Library*
BR	*Biblical Research*
CA	*Current Anthropology*
CBQ	*Catholic Biblical Quarterly*

CC	*Continuity and Change*
CD	Damascus Document
CIG	Corpus Inscriptionum Graecarum
CIJ	Corpus Inscriptionum Iudaicarum
CIL	Corpus Inscriptionum Latinarum
CJ	*Classical Journal*
CL	*Collection Latomus*
CPh	*Classical Philology*
CR	*Classical Review*
CRBS	*Currents in Research: Biblical Studies*
CSCA	*California Studies in Classical Antiquity*
CSSH	*Comparative Studies in Society and History*
CQ	*Classical Quarterly*
EA	*Epigraphica Anatolica*
EHR	*English Historical Review*
EMC	*Échos du monde classique/Classical Views*
ER	*Epworth Review*
G&R	*Greece and Rome*
GRBS	*Greek, Roman and Byzantine Studies*
HabInt	*Habitat International*
HJAS	*Harvard Journal of Asiatic Studies*
HR/RH	*Historical Reflections/Réflexions Historiques*
HSCP	*Harvard Studies in Classical Philology*
HThR	*Harvard Theological Review*
IEJ	*Israel Exploration Journal*
IG	Inscriptiones Graecae
ILS	Inscriptiones Latinae selectae
JAAR	*Journal of the American Academy of Religion*
JBL	*Journal of Biblical Literature*
JCSRES	*Journal for the Critical Study of Religion, Ethics, and Society*
JHC	*Journal of Higher Criticism*
JHS	*Journal of Hellenic Studies*
JIH	*Journal of Interdisciplinary History*
JMH	*Journal of Modern History*
JÖByz	Jahrbuch der Österreichischen Byzantinistik
JPC	*Journal of Popular Culture*
JQR	*Jewish Quarterly Review*
JR	*Journal of Religion*

JRev	*Juridical Review*
JRA	*Journal of Roman Archaeology*
JRC	*Journal of Rural Co-operation*
JRH	*Journal of Religious History*
JRS	*Journal of Roman Studies*
JS	*Journal des Savants*
JSA	*Journal of Studies on Alcohol*
JSH	*Journal of Social History*
JSNT	*Journal for the Study of the New Testament*
JTS	*Journal of Theological Studies*
Moretti	L. Moretti, *Iscrizioni agonistiche greche*
MNHIR	*Mededeelingen van het Nederlandsch historisch Instituut te Rome*
NovT	*Novum Testamentum*
NSA	Notizie degli Scavi di Antichità
NTS	*New Testament Studies*
OGIS	Orientis Graeci Inscriptiones Selectae
PBSR	*Papers of the British School at Rome*
P. Cornell	Greek Papyri in the Library of Cornell University
PCPhS	*Proceedings of the Cambridge Philological Society*
P. Heid	Veröffentlichungen aus der Heidelberger Papyrussammlung
PIASH	*Proceedings of the Israel Academy of Sciences and Humanities*
P. Merton	A Descriptive Catalogue of the Greek Papyri in the Collection of Wilfrid Merton
P. Mich.	Michigan Papyri
P. Oxy.	Oxyrhynchus Papyri
P. Oxy. Hels	Fifty Oxyrhynchus Papyri (ed. H. Zilliacus et al.)
PP	*Past and Present*
PS	*Population Studies*
P. Sakaon	The Archives of Aurelius Sakaon: Papers of An Egyptian Farmer in the Last Century of Theadelphia.
P. Strasb.	Griechische Papyrus der kaiserlichen Universitäts und Landesbibliothek zu Strassburg
RA	*Revue Archéologique*
Ral	*Rendiconti della Classe di Scienze morali, storiche e filologiche dell'Accademia Nazionale dei Lincei*

RBPh	*Revue Belge de Philologie et d'Histoire*
RIW	*The Review of Income and Wealth*
RSR	*Religious Studies Review*
SB	Sammelbuch griechischer Urkunden aus Aegypten
SC	*Second Century*
SDHI	*Studia et Documenta Historiae et Iuris*
SDQR	*Savings and Development Quarterly Review*
SEG	Supplementum Epigraphicum Graecum
SHA	Scriptores Historiae Augustae
SJAnth	*Southwestern Journal of Anthropology*
SP	*Social Problems*
STh	*Studia Theologica*
SVThQ	*St Vladimir's Theological Quarterly*
Tab. Vindol.	Tabulae Vindolandenses
TAPA	*Transactions of the American Philological Association*
TB	*Tyndale Bulletin*
ThLZ	*Theologische Literaturzeitung*
USQR	*Union Seminary Quarterly Review*
WA	*World Archaeology*
YCS	*Yale Classical Studies*
ZKG	*Zeitschrift für Kirchengeschichte*
ZNW	*Zeitschrift für die neutestamentliche Wissenschaft*
ZPE	*Zeitschrift für Papyrologie und Epigraphik*

1
Introduction

This book aims to examine the economic reality encountered by the churches associated with Paul and the responses that it provoked amongst their members. By such a focus it seeks to provide an extended study of one particular aspect of the social life of early Christians and to contribute, both in terms of method, and in a number of specific questions of detail, to the wider exegesis of the New Testament.

There are, I believe, good reasons for undertaking such an analysis. Although works that address the context and experience of the Pauline congregations are now legion (as a cursory glance through the bibliography will reveal) none have yet focused directly upon their economic life. Indeed, given both the growing interest of contemporary society in economic issues, and the normative quality ascribed to patterns of early Christian behaviour by various faith communities, such a project could be said to be overdue. However, the value of this study, I hope, goes beyond its particular area of focus. Despite the explosion in scholarship in the last couple of decades, the study of the social history of the New Testament has become remarkably self-referential and, as a consequence, a great deal of its output is beset by a debilitating myopia; consensuses have been arrived at too easily and reconstructions too readily accepted because, with one or two notable exceptions, many contributions are now, in essence, derivative. The time has come to reconsider some of the presuppositions and interpretations that have been so foundational to previous analyses and this is best attempted, I believe, by engaging critically, not only with the work of biblical scholars, but also with that of historians (and not solely with those historians who have made it their business to examine the early Church). New Testament scholarship should recognise afresh its place in the broader discipline of history and I hope this work will contribute to this in some way, even though there is much in the following pages at which various specialists (particularly ancient historians) will, no doubt, balk.

Given the concern of this study and the need to avoid unnecessary confusion from the outset, it seems appropriate to begin with some definitions.

1.1 Defining economics

Definitions of economics are as common as economists, ranging from the highly complex to the hopelessly general,[1] but, for the purposes of this book, economics is understood as *that which has to do with the satisfaction of material wants*.[2] I reject the familiar formulation of the neo-classicists, for whom economics was "the study of the allocation of scarce resources between unlimited wants",[3] as unhelpful in this inquiry. Rather, I side with the 'substantivists', such as Polanyi,[4] Dalton[5] and Halperin[6] (albeit with significant qualifications), who, in opposition to the 'formalists', such as Schneider,[7] believe that such a definition is inappropriate for the study of pre-industrial economies, primarily

---

[1] For Alfred Marshall, for instance, 'economics' was, "mankind in the ordinary business of life". *Principles of Economics*, London: Macmillan, 1890, p. 1.

Often definitions are more confusing than illuminating; indeed in recent years the traditional introductory definitions that are to be found at the front of economic text books have become replaced by a series of questions, illustrating the lack of consensus in the discipline (e.g. R. Lipsey, *An Introduction to Positive Economics*, seventh edition, London: Weidenfeld & Nicolson, 1989, p. 2. See John Harrison, "The Crisis in Economics and the Economics of Crisis", *New Movements in the Social Sciences and Humanities*, ed. B. Dufour, London: Maurice Temple Smith, 1982, pp. 32–48). For a very useful critique of the most popular definitions see R. Burling, "Maximization Theories and the Study of Economic Anthropology," *Economic Anthropology: Readings in Theory and Analysis*, ed. Edward E. LeClair and Harold K. Schneider, New York: Holt, Rinehart & Winston Inc, 1968, pp. 168–187, especially pp. 168–179.

[2] Karl Polanyi was perhaps the most famous adherent of this 'materialist' definition (e.g. "The Economy as Instituted Process", *Trade and Markets in the Early Empires*, ed. Karl Polanyi, Conrad Arensberg and Harry W. Pearson, Glencoe: The Free Press, 1958, p. 243).

[3] Harrison, "The Crisis in Economics and the Economics of Crisis", p. 33.

[4] Karl Polanyi, *The Great Transformation*, Boston: Beacon Press, 1944; "The Economy as Instituted Process"; *Primitive, Archaic and Modern Economies: Essays of Karl Polanyi*, ed. G. Dalton, Boston: Beacon Press, 1968; and *The Livelihood of Man*, ed. H. W. Pearson, London: Academic Press, 1977.

[5] G. Dalton, "Theoretical Issues in Economic Anthropology", *CA* 10 (1969) 63–80 and "Peasantries in Anthropology and History", *CA* 13 (1972) 385–407.

[6] R. Halperin, "Conclusion: A Substantivist Approach to Livelihood", *Peasant Livelihood*, ed. R. Halperin and J. Dow, New York: St Martin's Press, 1977, pp. 267–297.

[7] H. K. Schneider, *Economic Man*, New York: The Free Press, 1974 and *Livestock and Equality in East Africa: The Economic Basis for Social Structure*. Bloomington: Indiana University Press, 1979.

because it makes unwarranted, universalising assumptions about the fundamental character of economic decision making[8] (particularly that it always involves calculating rationalism of some kind).[9] We should concur with Oswyn Murray in recognising the 'otherness' of economic life in antiquity. In the first century economics was culturally embedded in the societal whole,[10] and consequently was controlled by assumptions drawn from the entire gamut of human interaction. Specific economic reality, as we would recognise it, was only just in the process of 'conscious differentiation'.[11] One need only look at the etymology of the word 'economics' itself, a word which was forged in a context not far removed in time from that under analysis, in order to see this alienness. The term combines the two words οἰκός (household) and νέμειν (to regulate),[12] and hence reflects the traditional significance of the household in structuring Hellenistic material relationships. Such an idea is in distinct contrast to the contemporary, asocial, concept of the market, in which,

---

[8] For a summary of the formalist/substantivist debate see D. Kaplan, "The Formal-Substantive Controversies in Economic Anthropology", *SJAnth* 24 (1968) 228–255; J. I. Prattis, "Alternative Views of Economy in Economic Anthropology", *Beyond the New Economic Anthropology*, ed. J. Clammer, London: Macmillan, 1987, pp. 14–22 and J. R. Stanfield, *The Economic Thought of Karl Polanyi: Lives and Livelihood*, London: Macmillan, 1986, pp. 26–53.

Above all, I would not agree with the substantivists' belief in the inapplicability of all contemporary economic theory to non-market contexts. Substantivists have tended to work with a caricature of modern economics, as though all forms of analysis require an assent to the axioms of neo-classicalism. Yet theories which deny the validity of the maximisation principle, and argue instead for the significance of alternative goals and motivations in economic behaviour, have made their mark in economics in recent decades (e.g. R. Cyert and J. March, *A Behavioural Theory of the Firm*, Englewood Cliffs: Prentice Hall, 1963). Such perspectives have been employed fruitfully by anthropologists studying 'primitive' and 'peasant' systems (see J. Prattis, "Alternative Views of Economy in Economic Anthropology", p. 17).

We should also be aware of the potential 'universalising' tendencies of the substantivists themselves, something observed by S. Gudeman, *Economics as Culture: Models and Metaphors of Livelihood*, London: Routledge & Kegan Paul, 1986, pp. 30–31.

[9] Oswyn Murray, "Introduction" to Paul Veyne, *Bread and Circuses*, Harmondsworth: Penguin, 1990, p. xv.

[10] Something that remains true, to some extent, throughout human history. As Prattis argues, the great insight of the substantivists, albeit overlooked by their main proponents as a consequence of their polemical context, was that their stress on the embeddedness of economic reality was as pertinent for the study of the market economy as for primitive and peasant systems ("Alternative Views", p. 18).

[11] N. Luhmann, *The Differentiation of Society*, New York: Columbia University Press, 1982, especially pp. 190–225.

[12] M. I. Finley, *The Ancient Economy*, London: Chatto & Windus, 1973, p. 17.

theoretically, economic decisions are determined solely by the economic criterion of the price mechanism.[13]

There are weaknesses in any definition and mine will seem inadequate to many economists. For example, the equation of 'economics' with the processes involved in meeting specifically *material* wants excludes areas of human endeavour which are aimed at satisfying *non-material* wants such as leisure, and also precludes the investigation of the constant choices made between these material and non-material ends.[14] However, the definition is intended to be heuristic and not rigidly restrictive. It is hoped that it functions to indicate my focus and does not inhibit the recognition of the significance of interrelated phenomena.

1.2 Defining the poor

It is also necessary, at this stage, to say something of the definition of the word poor employed in this work, as the term (and various synonyms such as 'indigent' and 'destitute') appears a number of times in the following pages and is central to its overall thesis. The word 'poor' is redolent with a variety of possible meanings and many of these are not strictly 'economic' at all.[15] However, given our particular concern, it is *material* poverty that is indicated by our use of this expression. So how

[13] As a result 'economic' analysis was almost entirely absent from the Graeco-Roman period. The writings of Aristotle and the Mishnah provide the only two possible exceptions. See Finley "Aristotle and Economic Analysis", *Studies in Ancient Society*, ed. M. I. Finley, London: Routledge, 1974, pp. 26–52; J. Neusner, *The Economics of the Mishnah*, Chicago: The University of Chicago Press, 1990; and also, Roman A. Ohrenstein and Barry Gordon, *Economic Analysis in Talmudic Literature: Rabbinic Thought in the Light of Modern Economics*, Leiden: E. J. Brill, 1992. Despite the title of Xenophon's work *Oeconomicus*, it is not evidence to the contrary. As Finley has argued: "In Xenophon . . . there is not one sentence that expresses an economic principle or offers any economic analysis, nothing on the efficiency of production, 'rational' choice, the marketing of crops" ("Aristotle", p. 22). Although "it may involve 'economic' activity, it is misleading, and often flatly wrong, to translate it as 'economics'". (*Studies*, p. 41).

[14] For the classic statement of the non-material concerns of economics see Lionel Robbins, "The Subject Matter of Economics", *An Essay on the Nature and Significance of Economic Science*, second edition, London: Macmillan, 1935, pp. 1–23.

[15] For the meanings attached to the term in antiquity see Gildas Hamel, *Poverty and Charity in Roman Palestine, First Three Centuries CE*, Berkeley: University of California Press, 1990, pp. 164–211 and also E. Bammel, "πτωχός", *Theological Dictionary of the New Testament*, vol. 6, ed. G. Kittel, Grand Rapids: Eerdmans, 1976, pp. 885–915. For the diversity of modern uses see P. Townsend (ed.), *The Concept of Poverty*, London: Heinemann, 1970.

is *material* poverty to be defined? In the contemporary world it may well be feasible to speak of poverty, for the most part, as ". . . a general form of *relative* deprivation",[16] but in the first-century context, given, as we shall see, the nature of the economy of the Roman Mediterranean, poverty is best understood as an absolute rather than relative phenomenon. It is present where the basic essentials necessary for supporting human life are not taken for granted but are a continuous source of anxiety. Therefore the following definition of the 'poor' given by P. Garnsey, is appropriate for our study: "The poor are those living at or near subsistence level, whose prime concern it is to obtain the minimum food, shelter, and clothing necessary to sustain life, whose lives are dominated by the struggle for physical survival."[17] Of course, there were significant differences between members of this group and these would have appeared important to the poor themselves. Some would have lived more precarious lives than others; "among the poor there is always one who is poorer".[18] But in order to emphasise the reality of the economic predicament that was shared by *all* members of this group, it is important that this term is used without lengthy qualifications, wherever applicable. As a consequence, I am aware that much of my subsequent analysis appears at times somewhat undifferentiated but this is, I feel, a necessary price to pay in order to bring out such an important and neglected aspect of the lives of the Pauline Christians.

1.3 A brief *apologia*

Despite having chosen economics as my area of concentration I must make it clear from the outset that I am not working with the assumption that economic factors are the prime determinants of human social life, in some Marxian sense. Such a perspective is perhaps best represented,

[16] P. Townsend, "Measures and Explanations of Poverty in High Income and Low Income Countries: The Problem of Operationalizing the Concepts of Development, Class and Poverty", *The Concept of Poverty*, ed. P. Townsend, London: Heinemann, 1970, p. 2.

[17] Peter Garnsey and Greg Woolf, "Patronage of the rural poor in the Roman world", *Patronage in Ancient Society*, ed. Andrew Wallace–Hadrill, Routledge: London, 1990, p. 153.

   The Graeco-Romans themselves had a slightly harsher understanding of what constituted subsistence. Gaius (*Digest* 50.16.234.2) defined subsistence as meeting the basic requirements of food, clothing and bedding (straw). He made no mention of the necessity for shelter.

[18] A Breton labourer quoted in Hamel, *Poverty and Charity*, p. 3.

for the period under examination, by de Ste Croix's *The Class Struggle in the Ancient Greek World*, in which he argues that the social relations established in the productive process are the most important factors in human life and tend, in the long run, to determine the other factors ("whether social, political, legal, philosophic or religious").[19] Rather, I would side with Brunt in his criticism of de Ste Croix:

> . . . it is simply an article of faith that these and other motives from which men [*sic*] suppose that they act are necessarily dependent on or at any rate secondary to the desire for material satisfaction to which SC argues fundamental importance, and that the fulfilment of this desire is not also conditioned by other cravings, for example the desire for freedom, power, honour, fame, which Greeks and Romans were apt to stress in their explanations of human conduct.[20]

Indeed, although I believe that wealth was a significant element in determining a person's social status in the first-century world[21] (and that the two coincided to such an extent that it is possible, in general terms, to deduce one from knowledge of the other) this does not mean that I claim it to have been uniquely so. It would be foolish to underestimate the part played by the factors Brunt mentions, and others, whether they be, for example, legal, educational, religious or gender related.

There is much to be gained from examining the economic life of the early Christians, as I trust the following chapters will confirm, but I do not wish it to be thought that my focus of attention *in any way presumes to privilege 'economic' reality*.

Some readers may find themselves summarily dismissing what follows because it is at variance with deeply held assumptions about the nature of life in the Roman Empire. This will, I am sure, be particularly true of

---

[19] G. E. M. de Ste Croix, *Class Struggle in the Ancient Greek World*, London: Duckworth, 1981, p. 26. See also W. V. Harris, "On the Concept of Class in Roman History", *Forms of Subordination and Control*, ed. Toru Yuge and Masaoki Doi, Leiden: E. J. Brill, 1988, pp. 598–610.

[20] P. A. Brunt, "'A Marxist View of Roman History.' Review of de Ste Croix, *The Class Struggle in the Ancient Greek World*", *JRS* 72 (1982), p. 162. Even if this is a somewhat harsh reading of de Ste Croix's position it is true that all Marxists, whatever their hue (de Ste Croix included) at the very least privilege economic factors.

[21] Something epitomised by the census requirements for entry into the ordos (see P. Garnsey and R. Saller, *The Roman Empire: Economy, Society and Culture*, London: Duckworth, 1987, pp. 112–115). Juvenal's observation that "a man's word is believed in exact proportion to the amount of cash which he keeps in his strong box" is also telling in this respect (*Saturae* 3.143).

my discussion of its economic stratification, in which I argue that the Empire's economy was essentially pre-industrial in character and incapable of sustaining a mid-range economic group. This finding may prove particularly difficult for New Testament scholars to concede as, for the most part, they seem to take it for granted that there was, in the words of J. Becker, "a self-confident, urban bourgeoisie with entrepreneurial spirit and sizeable wealth".[22] For individuals living in modern economies, such a claim appears to go counter to common sense: as MacMullen observes, it is difficult for a modern reader not to blindly insist that "that there *must* be a middle-class and that it must be sought where we are used to finding it today, in the urban commercial and industrial segments of the population".[23] Even if such scholars do manage to entertain the possibility that the economy was radically different from the model with which their discipline generally works, it will still be hard for many to accept the full implications of this: that in real terms there were few economic differences between those that found themselves outside of the rarefied circles of the élite.

The related case that I make for the existence of widescale destitution throughout the Empire may also prove difficult for some. After all, it conflicts with the prevailing image of a wealthy, successful (if morally problematic) Empire which has been promoted by a variety of élitist and populist discourses in the West (and is visible in an enormous range of phenomena, from colonial school curricula to luxurious film sets).[24] It appears, superficially, to be confirmed by the myriad of impressive archaeological sites that litter the countries of the Mediterranean and beyond. Of course, the work as a whole stands and falls on its own merits but it is important, if progress is to be made in the study of earliest Christianity, that New Testament scholars are aware of their own assumptions and capable of critically justifying them.

---

[22] Jürgen Becker, "Paul and His Churches", *Christian Beginnings: Word and Community from Jesus to Post-Apostolic Times*, ed. Jürgen Becker, Louisville: Westminster/John Knox Press, 1993, p. 168.

[23] Ramsey MacMullen, *Roman Social Relations 50 BC – AD 284*, New Haven: Yale University Press, 1974, p. 89.

[24] See, for example, C. Stray, *Culture and Discipline: The Transformation of Classics in England 1830–1900*, Oxford: Oxford University Press, 1996 and Maria Wyke, "Make Like Nero! The Appeal of a Cinematic Emperor", *Reflections of Nero: Culture, History and Representation*, ed. J. Elsner and J. Masters, London: Duckworth, 1994, pp. 11–28.

1.4 Admissible evidence

Given that this study is concerned with the economic reality of the communities associated with Paul, the assessment of which epistles belong to the authentic Pauline corpus is significant, as is my estimation of the historicity of the Acts of the Apostles, and so it is appropriate that I deal with these questions briefly before beginning my analysis.

Firstly, I accept the following letters as written by Paul and therefore constituting the primary sources for my investigation: Romans, 1 Corinthians, 2 Corinthians, Galatians, Philippians, Colossians, 1 and 2 Thessalonians. Amongst these, my belief in the authenticity of Colossians and 2 Thessalonians will, no doubt, provoke the most surprise. However, I am not alone in my contention that these are also by the apostle.[25] Although this position is perhaps a minority one, I believe it is quite defensible.

Secondly, I reject the Acts of the Apostles as a primary source for my study. By saying this I do not intend to reject it as a historical document *per se*. That would be a simplistic and unnecessarily pessimistic response. The notorious discrepancies between Acts and the letters of Paul over such important issues as chronology and theology[26] should lead us to treat Acts in the manner proposed by Richard Wallace and Wynne Williams: we should distinguish between the historicity of the background 'world' of the work (the historical geography, the institutions, the cities, etc.) and that of its

---

[25] This is the canon, for example, accepted by W. G. Kümmel, *Introduction to the New Testament*, London: SCM, 1975, pp. 250ff. Although the authenticity of Colossians has been questioned since the work of E. Mayerhoff, *Der Brief an die Colosser*, Berlin: H. Schultze, 1838, it continues to have its defenders e.g. P. O'Brien, *Colossians, Philemon*, Waco: Word Books, 1982 and "Letter to the Colossians", *Dictionary of Paul and His Letters*, ed. G. Hawthorne et al., Leicester: InterVarsity Press, 1993, pp. 147–153; R. P. Martin, *Colossians and Philemon*, Grand Rapids: Eerdmans, 1981. The authenticity of 2 Thessalonians has been doubted by many since Johann Schmidt's observations at the beginning of the nineteenth century (for a history of the debate see F. W. Hughes, "Second Thessalonians as a Document of Early Christian Rhetoric", unpublished PhD dissertation: Northwestern University, 1984, pp. 1–74). For its defenders see, for example, I. H. Marshall, *1 and 2 Thessalonians*, London: Marshall, Morgan & Scott, 1983; Ernest Best, *A Commentary on the First and Second Epistles to the Thessalonians*, London: A. & C. Black, 1972; B. Rigaux, *Saint Paul, Les Épîtres aux Thessaloniciens*, Paris: J. Gabalda, 1956; F. F. Bruce, *1 and 2 Thessalonians*, Waco: Word Books, 1982.

[26] See, for example, the summary found in E. Haenchen, *The Acts of the Apostles*, Oxford: Basil Blackwell, 1971, pp. 112–116.

narrative.[27] Recent studies by the likes of Colin Hemer and others have helped confirm the essential accuracy of much of the former,[28] whilst the work of, for example, Philip Esler[29] and John C. Lentz[30] has made us more fully alert to the *Tendenz* of the latter, particularly in respect to its presentation of socio-economic details. Consequently, in this study Acts is treated with the degree of circumspection it deserves.

[27] See Richard Wallace and Wynne Williams, *The Acts of the Apostles*, London: Bristol Classical Press, 1993, pp. 26–27. Their position is very much influenced by M. I. Finley's classic studies of the *Iliad* and *Odyssey* (*The World of Odysseus*, second edition, London: Chatto & Windus, 1967, and "The Trojan War", *JHS* 84 (1964) 1–9).

[28] Colin J. Hemer, *The Book of Acts in the Setting of Hellenistic History*, Tübingen: J. C. B. Mohr, 1989. See also David W. J. Gill and Conrad Gempf (eds), *The Book of Acts in Its First Century Setting. Volume 2. Graeco-Roman Setting*, Carlisle: Paternoster Press, 1994.

[29] P. Esler, *Community and Gospel in Luke-Acts: The Social and Political Motivations of Lucan Theology*, Cambridge: Cambridge University Press, 1987.

[30] John C. Lentz, *Luke's Portrait of Paul*, Cambridge: Cambridge University Press, 1993.

2

The Context of Interpretation: *theory*

In order to examine the economic experiences and responses of the Pauline communities we must first attempt to construct an appropriate economic context within which data from the epistles can be interpreted.

There are two elements to any such construction. Firstly, it requires sketching the broad boundaries within which the economic lives of the Pauline churches took place. Through addressing the question of the 'development' of the first-century Mediterranean economy (or, more accurately, economies) we can go some way to observing and delimiting their economic experience. Although this necessitates entering the ongoing 'primitivist/modernist' debate about the sophistication and scale of the economy of the Empire,[1] this undertaking is, at least on the general theoretical plane, relatively uncontroversial, and does not require any further justification.

Secondly, such a construction needs to investigate the specific economic *realia* of inhabitants of the first-century world. It has to attend to the question of how individuals actually encountered the various elements that constituted their economic life. Without this focus our investigation would have an abstract, detached quality, in glaring contrast to the vital, human world of the epistles. Without such an interest it would remain, in essence, largely alien to its subject of study.

However, this second aspect of our reconstruction presents us with a major dilemma, one that, given that economics is, as we have noted, a socially embedded reality, is present in all studies of the social world of

---

[1] For a summary of the 'primitivist/modernist' debate see J. R. Love, *Antiquity and Capitalism: Max Weber and the Sociological Foundations of Roman Civilization*, London: Routledge, 1991, pp. 60–65. The primitivist position was advocated most famously by Moses Finley in *The Ancient Economy*, whilst the most prominent modernist work is still M. Rostovtzeff, *The Social and Economic History of the Roman Empire*, Oxford: Oxford University Press, 1957.

the New Testament, though it has yet to be substantially addressed by any: *the problem of dependence upon élite sources*. Whenever we attempt to evoke, in any kind of detail, the experiences of the inhabitants of antiquity, we always run up against this same obstacle. Nevertheless, it is not, I believe, insuperable. There are strategies that can be employed for overcoming it and these, of necessity, must be the object of our first study. Our attempt to outline such approaches may appear, on a superficial examination, to take us away from our specific economic focus but given the importance of dealing with this problem, both for our particular concern, and also for all scholars engaged in studying the wider social history of the early Christians, the following section cannot be seen as a digression. It is fundamental for our quest, and it informs all subsequent chapters.

2.1 The need for an appropriate context of interpretation

The literary output of the privileged classes of the Empire provides a large and easily accessible body of evidence. It dominates, almost completely, the remaining record of life in the Graeco-Roman world. It is not surprising therefore that it has been pressed into use so often by students of the New Testament. However, such material is *atypical and unrepresentative*. It is simply erroneous to collect, more or less uncritically, references from prominent classical authors to illustrate the supposed prevalence of some mode of behaviour or other[2] in the early years of the first millennium CE and then assume its relevance to the interpretation of the New Testament. It is, for example, mistaken to trawl through the writings of "Cicero and Seneca, Dio Chrysostom and Plutarch", on such an important phenomenon as that of 'friendship', and assume that they can give us direct and unproblematic insights into the mentality and behaviour that governed Paul's relationship with his fellow Christians (as, for example, P. Marshall has done).[3] And, likewise, it is unjustifiable to take the thoughts of Pliny the Younger, Martial and Juvenal on the subject of dinner as an indication of social practices that were "widespread and customary at

---

[2] Keith Hopkins' remarks on the method of Fergus Millar's *The Emperor in the Roman World* (second edition, London: Duckworth, 1992) are pertinent (see "Rules of Evidence", *JRS* 68 (1978), p. 183). Though, as B. D. Shaw observes, Hopkins is a little unfair in his criticisms (see "Among the Believers", *EMC* 28 (1984) 453–479).

[3] P. Marshall, *Enmity in Corinth: Social Conventions in Paul's Relations with the Corinthians*, Tübingen: J. C. B. Mohr, 1987, p. x.

the time",[4] and therefore crucial for understanding the problems encountered over the eucharist in 1 Cor. 11:17–34. These sources were the products of an extremely small clique[5] and reflect the concerns of a group whose social practices and relationships were quite consciously distinctive, and not in any way normative. Their members were largely ignorant of, and uninterested in, life beyond their rarefied world. Seneca's actions are illustrative of their outlook. When he sought to play at being poor in the countryside (like some kind of classical Marie Antoinette) he took with him "very few slaves; a carriage load",[6] and the frugal meal he ate as part of his act required "not more than an hour to prepare".[7]

The élite literary sources still have some value in New Testament exegesis, as I hope to show, but they can no longer be allowed to dictate our understanding of its social background: *a context of interpretation needs to be constructed that tries to give voice to the lived reality of the other 99% of the population.*[8]

2.2 Constructing an appropriate context of interpretation

Methodological concerns

In attempting to build this more appropriate and plausible 'context of interpretation' we should look to the work of historians concerned with the study of 'History From Below' and 'Popular Culture', utilising the methodologies and perspectives they have developed. Given the general

---

[4] G. Theissen, *The Social Setting of Pauline Christianity*, Edinburgh: T. & T. Clark, 1982, pp. 156–157.

[5] Even at its broadest reasonable definition, numerically its members made up less than one per cent of the inhabitants of the Roman Empire. G. Alföldy, *The Social History of Rome*, London: Croom Helm, 1985, p. 127.

[6] Seneca, *Epistulae* 87.

[7] Seneca, *Epistulae* 87.

[8] The figure is taken from Alföldy and is an estimate of the percentage of those who lay outside the ranks of the aristocracy and its associated groups (*The Social History of Rome*, p. 127).

Of course, in seeking to do this, I do not claim to be thoroughly original. In many ways I see my work as analogous to, and hopefully enriched by, the efforts of a number of feminist classicists, who have attempted to reconstruct something of women's experience in the Graeco-Roman world. See especially, Sarah B. Pomeroy, *Goddesses, Whores, Wives and Slaves*, London: Robert Hale, 1976, and Ross S. Kraemer, *Meanads, Martyrs, Matrons, Monastics: A Sourcebook on Women's Religion in the Greco-Roman World*, Philadelphia: Fortress, 1988 and *Her Share of the Blessings: Women's Religions Among Pagans, Jews and Christians in the Greco-Roman World*, Oxford: Oxford University Press, 1992. I fully recognise, however, that they would question the validity of my broad, homogenising, approach.

lack of impact these approaches have had on New Testament studies (and, indeed, on ancient history in general)[9] it is appropriate to outline briefly their salient features.

'History From Below'

The distinguishing concern of 'History From Below'[10] is its desire, in the words of E. P. Thompson, to rescue the lives of the non-élite from the "enormous condescension of posterity",[11] or, in those of E. Hobsbawm, to reconstruct the "world of an anonymous and un-documented body of people".[12] It has found perhaps its most famous flowering in *Captain Swing*, a history of agrarian revolts in the England of the 1830s, written by Hobsbawm and the founder and leading figure in this school, G. Rudé,[13] though works from this perspective are now legion.

There have been various problems with the 'History From Below' approach: it has been inclined to concentrate upon the life of the non-élite in atypical circumstances, for example in riots, demonstrations, and revolutions;[14] it has also tended, until relatively recently, to be chronologically and geographically limited to eighteenth-century France or nineteenth-century Britain. Rudé's interpretation of 'popular ideology' as the product of the combination of so-called 'mother's milk'[15] and 'derived' ideologies[16] has, in addition, proved a little unwieldy, doing scant justice to the specificity of various movements. But despite its

[9] See J. Toner, *Leisure and Ancient Rome*, Cambridge: Polity Press, 1995, p. 65.

[10] For an introduction to 'History from Below' in general see Jim Sharpe, "History From Below", *New Perspectives on Historical Writing*, ed. P. Burke, Cambridge: Polity Press, 1991, pp. 24–41.

[11] E. P. Thompson, *The Making of the English Working Class*, London: Victor Gallancz, 1963, p. 12.

[12] E. Hobsbawm and G. Rudé, *Captain Swing*, Harmondsworth: Penguin, 1973, p. 12.

[13] For a review of Rudé's work and a comprehensive bibliography see F. Krantz, "Sans érudition, pas d'histoire", *History From Below: Studies in Popular Protest and Popular Ideology in Honour of George Rudé*, Montreal: Concordia University, 1985, pp. 3–40.

[14] See for example *Captain Swing* and G. Rudé, *The Crowd in History: A Study of Popular Disturbances in England and France*, London: Lawrence & Wishart, 1964, and *Ideology and Popular Protest*, London: Lawrence & Wishart, 1980.
But E. Genovese, *Roll, Jordan, Roll: The World the Slaves Made*, New York: Vintage, 1976 (considered by J. Sharpe to be a fine example of this school) does not suffer from this failing and concentrates on the wider experience of slave life.

[15] That which is 'inherent', "based on direct experience, oral tradition or folk memory and not learned by listening to sermons or speeches or reading books" (Rudé, *Ideology and Popular Protest*, p. 28).

[16] That which is appropriated from outside direct experience, e.g. such concepts as 'The Rights of Man'.

14

failings, 'History From Below' has given a significant impetus to historical writing, encouraging, as J. Sharpe maintains, the exploration of the "historical experiences of those men and women whose existence is so often ignored, taken for granted or mentioned in passing in mainstream history".[17]

'Popular Culture'

Historians of 'Popular Culture' have, at least in their most recent phase, developed and enfleshed many of the concerns of the likes of Rudé and Hobsbawm, albeit mostly without the intensity of their ideological interest. In order to pin down this "elusive quarry"[18] I shall have to employ, once again, some definitions.

Firstly: 'Culture'.[19] The often repeated observation of Raymond Williams is worth repeating once again: 'culture' is "one of the two or three most complicated words in the English language".[20] Definitions abound but the concise one offered by Peter Burke is valuable for our purposes: it is ". . . a system of shared meanings, attitudes and values, and the symbolic forms (performances, artefacts) in which they are expressed and embodied".[21] Indeed, it can be conceived of, quite simply (though perhaps simplistically), as all human production.[22]

The term 'Popular' recognises our chief concern, that culture is not homogenous (contrary to the protestations of some New Testament critics, such as F. G. Downing).[23] Despite the truth of the assertion of

---

[17] Jim Sharpe, "History From Below", *New Perspectives on Historical Writing*, Cambridge: Polity Press, 1991, p. 25.

[18] Peter Burke, *Popular Culture in Early Modern France*, London: Temple Smith, 1978, p. 65 and David Hall, "Introduction", *Understanding Popular Culture*, ed. Steven Kaplan, New York: New Babylon, 1984, p. 5.

[19] For an informed overview of the term and its various meanings see Chris Jenks, *Culture*, London: Routledge, 1993.

[20] Raymond Williams, *Keywords*, London: Fontana, 1983, p. 87.

[21] Burke, *Popular Culture in Early Modern Europe*, p. i.

[22] 'Culture' is in my opinion a preferable term to that of 'ideology', given the common pejorative associations of this word. It is often understood as ". . . a mode of thinking thrown off its proper course" (W. Stark quoted in C. Geertz, "Ideology as a Cultural System", *Ideology and Discontent*, ed. D. Apter, London: Macmillan, 1964, p. 49). Even where it is employed with a wider sense, it still remains too restrictive, and fails to recognise the significance of *all* human life, often limiting itself to its more recognisably political expressions. See also D. McLellan, *Ideology*, Milton Keynes: Open University Press, 1986, pp. 1–9.

[23] See F. G. Downing, "A bas les aristos: The Relevance of Higher Literature for the Understanding of the Earliest Christian Writings", *NovT* 30 (1988) 212–230. He maintains that there was "no sign of a culture gap between the highly literate aristocracy and the masses" (p. 229).

Marx that, "the ideas of the ruling classes are in every epoch the ruling ideas",[24] it is not the case that these ideas are the *only* ideas: the non-élite have ways of living that are not just crude and ossified forms of élite culture, that have trickled down or 'sunk'.[25] Nor can popular culture be dismissed as an "often outdated expression of the norms and ideals of city élites", as many suppose, such as the prominent New Testament scholar Bruce Malina.[26] This has been ably demonstrated by Carlo Ginzburg in *The Cheese and the Worms*,[27] Natalie Davis in *Society and Culture in Early Modern France*,[28] and P. Burke in *Popular Culture in Early Modern Europe*.[29]

The concept of 'popular culture' has its problems of which any study should be aware.[30] For example, 'popular culture' is itself clearly not homogenous.[31] We should more accurately speak of 'popular cultures'. As Gramsci observed, "the people is not a culturally homogenous unit, but it is culturally stratified in a complex way",[32] divided along, for

[24] Karl Marx, *The German Ideology*, London: Lawrence & Wishart, 1970, p. 64.

[25] This was the opinion of the early twentieth-century German folklorists (see Burke, *Popular Culture in Early Modern France*, p. 58). For them the *Unterschicht* was an out of date imitation of the upper class *Oberschicht*.

[26] Bruce J. Malina, *The New Testament World: Insights From Cultural Anthropology*, London: SCM, 1983, p. 74.

[27] Carlo Ginzburg, *The Cheese and the Worms: The Cosmos of a Sixteenth Century Miller*, London: Routledge, 1980.

[28] Natalie Z. Davis, *Society and Culture in Early Modern France*, Cambridge: Polity Press, 1975.

[29] Burke, *Popular Culture in Early Modern Europe*, London: Temple Smith, 1978.

All three of these works, I believe, illustrate the inaccuracy of the assumption that popular culture only came into being with the genesis of the industrial revolution, as cultural theorists such as John Storey presume (*Cultural Theory*, p. 16).

[30] See Ginzburg, *The Cheese and the Worms*, pp. xiii–xviii. For a useful introduction to the debates amongst historians of 'popular culture' see Steven Kaplan (ed.), *Understanding Popular Culture: Europe from the Middle Ages to the Nineteenth Century*, New York: Moulton Publishers, 1984 and also W. H. Beik, "Searching for Popular Culture in Early Modern France," *JMH* 49 (1977) 266–281.

These problems have been compounded, at least in a British context, by the legacy of F. R. Leavis. He saw 'popular culture' as a contradiction in terms and something essentially destructive, to be attacked not studied (John Storey, *Popular Culture*, pp. 27ff.).

[31] As Hildred Geertz, for example, appears to believe. See Hildred Geertz and Keith Thomas, "An Anthropology of Religion and Magic: Two Views", *JIH* 6 (1975) 71–109.

[32] Quoted in Peter Burke, *Popular Culture in Early Modern Europe*, p. 29. See also D. Forgacs and G. Nowell, *A. Gramsci: Selections From Cultural Writings*, London: Lawrence & Wishart, 1985, and W. L. Adamson, *Hegemony and Revolution: A Study of Antonio Gramsci's Political and Cultural Theory*, Berkeley: University of California Press, 1980.

example, ethnic, occupational and gender lines. However, this important qualification should not prevent us recognising general patterns between and within these various 'cultures'.[33] Determining what evidence is *authentically* 'popular' also presents problems.[34] In addition, the opaque quality of much of the data,[35] its incoherence,[36] and its

---

[33] As E. P. Thompson maintained against Keith Thomas who believes popular culture to be unintegrated and fragmented (*Religion and the Decline of Magic*, London: Weidenfeld & Nicolson, 1971, pp. 627–628). See E. P. Thompson, "Eighteenth-century English Society: Class Struggle Without Class?" *JSH* 3 (1978), p. 156.

[34] Ostensible manifestations of 'popular culture' may, on closer examination, prove to be nothing of the sort. Riots, for example, far from being pre-political expressions of popular concerns, can be the consequence of external manipulation. The attempted assaults on the young Octavian in 40 BCE (Appian, 5.67) and Claudius in CE 51 (Tacitus, *Annales* 12.43; Suetonius, *Claudius* 18.2) by mobs angered at the possibility of grain shortages may tell us something about the concern of the non-élite over the precariousness of their food supply, but the 'food' riots of CE 235 against the Emperor Maximus seem to have been orchestrated by the nobility (Herodian, 7.10.5); they cannot be seen as the confident assertion of 'popular' rights in the face of his oppressive rule.

I believe though that C. R. Whittaker goes too far in his pessimism about whether we can ever "disentangle genuinely popular causes from political riots stimulated from outside" ("Studying The Poor in the City of Rome", *Land, City and Trade in the Roman Empire*, Aldershot: Variorum, 1993, p. 19). Certainly, the Roman context makes such data especially difficult to categorise. The myth of the *res publica* continued to maintain an important place under the Principate, and thus encouraged political acts to present themselves as popular acts, driven by popular concerns. But the problems are not insurmountable in most cases.

[35] Many key symbols and actions in 'popular culture' appear incomprehensible to the modern scholar. What, to take an example from medieval culture, does the Bundschuh, the boot on a stick, the icon of the German peasant revolts, mean? How can it illuminate their social reality? (Burke, *Popular Culture in Early Modern Europe*, p. 80). Or, to take an instance from the Roman period: what does the Saturnalia tell us about the reality of the subordinate classes? Is it a festival that reconfirms their position in society, in which the inversion acts as a safety valve for social tensions, as Gluckman's famous account of an analogous festival would have it? (M. Gluckman, *Custom and Conflict in Africa*, Oxford: Blackwell, 1955). Or should we reject this functionalist interpretation in favour of a reading closer to that of Dirk, in which the apparent role reversal can actually be explained as the participants acting out, albeit in a highly exaggerated manner, the activities and relationships that were present in the other 364 days of the year? (*The Black Saturnalia: Conflict and its Ritual Expression On British West Indian Slave Plantations*, Gainsville: University Presses of Florida, 1987, p. xi). Or are both these readings misleading?

[36] 'Popular culture' is perfectly capable of, on occasion, giving voice to mutually incompatible concerns. An example recorded by E. Hobsbawm is particularly illustrative: at the height of Garibaldi's wars, a brigand leader issued a declaration which included the following contradictory aspirations: "Out with the traitors, out with the beggars, long live the fair kingdom of Naples, with its most religious sovereign, long live the vicar of Christ, Pius IX, and long live our ardent republican brothers" (*Primitive Rebels*, Manchester: Manchester University Press, 1959, p. 29). For further examples of this phenomenon see Rudé, *Ideology and Popular Protest*, pp. 31–32.

ambivalence,[37] also provides us with bewildering obstacles of interpretation and 'decoding'.[38] What, for example, are we to make of the bizarre 'funeral' the Roman plebs gave an illustrious 'talking' raven during Tiberius' reign:

> . . . the bird's funeral was celebrated with a vast crowd of followers, the draped bier being carried on the shoulders of two Ethiopians, and in front of it going in procession a flute-player and all kinds of wreaths right to the pyre, which had been erected on the right hand side of the Appian Road . . .[39]

Was it a deliberately subversive and mocking act, ridiculing the pretensions of the Roman aristocracy and their ostentatious rituals of death? Or was it merely intended to be ludic? If it was meant to be the latter then the plebs played hard: the Roman citizen who had brought about the bird's premature demise was put to death. Whatever the case, Pliny, from whom we learn of the incident, seems to have been as perplexed by it as any modern reader.

2.3 Sources of evidence

But how, practically speaking, do we go about constructing a plausible context of interpretation for the first-century world of the early Christians? How can we overcome the absence of relevant documentary material that we have already noted? Certainly we are not fortunate enough to have the rich sources to which scholars of other periods have access, such as the inquisition records that have proved so useful for the study of the non-élite in the middle ages,[40] or the fascinating broadsides and chapbooks[41] of the printed period. But, nevertheless, by utilising the imperatives and techniques of 'History From Below' and 'Popular Culture' we can go far. Not only by looking at new sources of evidence

[37] We must be wary of imposing preconceived political interpretations upon cultural acts which may well be 'ludic' rather than subversive. This is especially true of popular parodies. As Burke has observed, the mock trials, wills, and funerals that are so significant in popular culture may not actually 'mock' at all: such acts may not be a "mockery of religious or legal forms but the taking over of these forms for a new purpose" (Burke, *Popular Culture in Early Modern Europe*, pp. 122–123). We need corroborative evidence before we can see such parodies as deliberately derisive.

[38] I use this term after the fashion of Thompson: to 'decode' is to, "recover the significance of these symbols with reference to the wider symbolic universe, and hence to locate their force" ("Class Struggle Without Class?", p. 155, fn. 43).

[39] Pliny, *Naturalis Historiae* 10.122–123.

[40] So effectively exploited by Ginzburg in *The Cheese and the Worms*.

[41] Burke, *Popular Culture in Early Modern Europe*, p. 71.

but also by looking at old sources of evidence in new ways, I believe that we can glean enough information to make our concern more than just a pious hope.

Let us now turn to a brief examination of these 'sources' for non-élite life and discuss the specific benefits and problems attached to utilising each of them.

Literature

Despite their narrow focus, élite texts are still indispensable in our quest. In general, it is a matter of scrutinising such works 'upside-down'.[42] 'Popular culture' makes its presence felt in these writings in two particularly prominent ways. Firstly, at least some aspects of it can be seen in the behaviour and values which the nobility expended so much time condemning in each other: it provides an important constituent of the vocabulary which they employed to fight their continuous wars of identity and exclusion. Moralistic discourse was essential to the definition of the Graeco-Roman élite. As Catherine Edwards has observed: "accusations and descriptions of immorality were implicated in defining what it meant to be a member of the Roman élite, in excluding outsiders from this powerful and privileged group and in controlling insiders".[43] For the most part such discourse was constructed in conscious opposition to the lives of the non-élite, with its notions of 'immorality' being drawn expressly from their everyday conduct. This was because its purpose was not only to be distinct but also distinguishing; to make the boundaries between the two groups clear and impermeable. The moralising over *popinae* (cookshops) provides an example of this. These immensely popular meeting places for the *plebs urbana*[44] were employed as an almost clichéd rhetorical setting in which to place the particular aristocratic victim who was to be the object of a moralising assault. Anthony, for example, was accused by Cicero, in a lengthy character assassination, of having swapped "the dining room for the popinae".[45] Without such criticisms we would know substantially less

---

[42] Thompson, "Class Struggle Without Class?", p. 157.

[43] *The Politics of Immorality*, Cambridge: Cambridge University Press, 1993, p. 12.

[44] See J. J. Meggitt, "Meat Consumption and Social Conflict in Corinth", *JTS* 45 (1994) 137–141.

[45] Cicero, *Orationes Philippicae* 2.28.69. See also 13.11.24.
    That is not to say that they may not have actually chosen willingly to frequent such places. Paradoxically, 'popular culture' is not the preserve of the non-élite alone; it has a very definite cross-social dimension. This is especially well brought out for our period

about these establishments and their more usual, less socially esteemed, patrons (data that I believe is of crucial importance in interpreting the dispute over meat in 1 Cor. 8 and 10). Of course, the activities regarded as being reprehensible are not 'popular culture' *per se*: they often appear in a caricatured form, having fallen victim to the salacious imagination that is common to moralists. But they are invaluable nonetheless.

The second way that 'popular culture' emerges in élite texts is when it, sometimes quite literally, forced its way to a writer's attention. In revolts, riots, games, festivals and markets, the non-élite clamoured for notice and their concerns and interests could not be ignored.

The fully-fledged popular revolts of the Empire come mostly[46] from the centuries after Paul, but they nevertheless give us some useful insights. The early third-century revolt of Bulla which is recorded in Cassius Dio's history[47] is particularly interesting and pertinent. Its success and tenacity seem to have been partly a consequence of its leader's unusual attitude towards artisans (a group central to the Pauline epistles).[48] Any that were captured in the course of Bulla's activities were given work to do for which they were paid a living wage (something of a novelty for this often destitute class).[49] According to Dio, Bulla understood the economic exploitation of non-élite groups by the élite to be a crucial factor in his movement's survival. He is reported as saying to a centurion whom he was releasing: "Tell your masters that if they would put an end to brigandage they must feed

---

in the work of Toner, *Leisure and Ancient Rome*, pp. 65–88. Various élite Romans actually participated in the games, such as the emperors Nero (Suetonius, *Nero* 21–22 and 54); Commodus (Cassius Dio 72.19–22; Herodian 1.14–17); and assorted knights (Cassius Dio 75.87). The chance to engage in gambling or patronise *popinae* no doubt provided many members of the Graeco-Roman élite with 'ludic' opportunities in which they could enjoy the tension of playing not only with dice but also with the perceptions and definitions of *gravitas* and ἀρετή that distinguished their group; taking pleasure not only from the hot snacks, but also from the thrill of transgression.

[46] Excepting the slave rebellions of the Republic, possibly the activities of the sicarii and Zealots in Israel, and the low level revolts that often plagued the empire's frontiers. See K. R. Bradley, *Slavery and Rebellion in the Roman World, 140 B.C. – 70 B.C.*, Bloomington: Indiana University Press, 1989; B. Isaac, "Bandits in Judaea and Arabia", *HSCP* 88 (1984) 169–203; K. Hopwood, "Policing the Hinterland: Rough Cilicia and Isauria", *Armies and Frontiers in Roman and Byzantine Anatolia*, ed. S. Mitchell, Oxford: B. A. R., 1983, pp. 173–187.

[47] Cassius Dio 87.

[48] After all, Paul was himself one. See chapter 4.

[49] Cassius Dio 87.10.

their slaves."[50] The nature of these revolts and their motives are often more complex than has been recognised, and none actually provides us with a clear social programme that would allow us direct access to their supporters' most pressing concerns[51] but, once again, in the literary material we have, we can discern precious and relevant data[52] about non-élite experiences and expectations.

Riots and civil disturbances are of similar worth (though with the qualifications we have already mentioned). There has been a growing recognition that such events are never meaningless, even though their sense may be hard to determine.[53] As Stevenson notes in the introduction to his authoritative study on popular disturbances: they provide ". . . historians with a kind of 'window' on the attitudes and assumptions of otherwise inaccessible sections of the population".[54] A few examples illustrate the value of this material. The tumult that followed the sentencing to death of Pedanius Secundus' slaves,[55] which so impressed itself upon Tacitus,[56] reveals a fleeting (and ultimately ineffective) example of the capacity for sporadic[57] demonstrations of mutual solidarity by the non-élite in the face of glaring examples of their unjust

---

[50] E. A. Thompson, "Peasant Revolts in Late Roman Gaul and Spain", *Studies in Ancient Roman Society*, ed. M. I. Finley, London: Routledge, 1974, p. 310.

[51] An observation made by Zeev Rubin, "Mass Movements in Late Antiquity – Appearances and Realities", *Leaders and Masses in the Roman World*, ed. I. Malkin and Z. W. Rubinsohn, Leiden: E. J. Brill, 1995, pp. 129–187. This is in striking contrast to revolts that took place outside the empire, such as that of the Mazdakites.

[52] All the more valuable because the literary record is virtually all that was left by these movements. Their material remains are sparse: we have only a few coins issued by the slaves in the First Sicilian Slave Uprising and the possible remains of a Bagaudae stronghold (M. Doi, "Methods of Viewing World History From the Perspective of the Ruled", *Forms of Control and Subordination in Antiquity*, ed. Toru Yuge and Masaoki Doi, Leiden: E. J. Brill, 1988, p. 5).

[53] See John Stevenson's remarks on the riots over the introduction of the Gregorian calendar into Great Britain in September 1752. These are often held up as a prime example of the absurdity of mob action. However: "Protest about the 'lost' days was not simply a display of irrational ignorance, but one based on concern about interference and complication of many important transactions" (*Popular Disturbances in England 1700–1870*, London: Longman, 1979, p. 3).

[54] Stevenson, *Popular Disturbances*, p. 4.

[55] Following the murder of Pedanius Secundus by one of his slaves all four hundred were sentenced to death, in accordance with Roman law. See H. Bellen, "Antike Staatsräson Die Hinrichtung der 400 Sklaven des römischen Stadtpräfekten L. Pedanius Secundus im Jahre 61 n. Chr," *Gymnasium* 89 (1982) 449–467.

[56] Tacitus, *Annales* 14.42–43.

[57] A similar incident recorded in Pliny provoked no such demonstrations of support (*Epistulae* 8.14.12–26).

treatment.[58] The bloodthirsty actions of the slaves who rose up and slaughtered their masters in the midst of the political turmoil of CE 70,[59] which disturbed the same historian, is a vivid reminder of the instability of the master–slave relationship for many of its participants within the first-century world.[60] The aggressive demands for the nuptial *sportulae* (hand-outs), about which Apuleius vehmently complained,[61] and the vigorous protests over grain shortages against Claudius, recorded by both Tacitus and Suetonius,[62] and against Octavian, noted by Appian,[63] illustrate the popular and perennial concern of urban populations over food. The regular riots that Tacitus (once again) and others reported accompanying the performance of pantomime artists throughout the Empire also gives us a rare and vital glimpse of common perceptions of group identity that existed amongst such people.[64]

The games and races also provided arenas for expressing the character of non-élite life. These events, amongst other things, supplied a scenario in which the Emperor, or the local civic élites, could reinforce and legitimate their respective positions of authority (most vividly through the famous act of deciding whether a gladiator lived or died), and opportunities for communities to display and enhance their sense of civic status.[65] But they were also, as Cicero observed, the place where the authentic *vox populi* was heard.[66] They were not mere entertainment. The large numbers of people they attracted (a fifth of the Roman population could watch the races at the Circus)[67] meant that they always

[58] See also *Digest* 11.3.5. for behaviour motivated by a similar sentiment.

[59] Tacitus, *Historia* 4.1.

[60] Contrary to the more static, more stable, models of master/slave relations often presented by New Testament scholars. See Dale B. Martin, *Slavery as Salvation*, New Haven: Yale University Press, 1990.

[61] Apuleius, *Apologia* 88.

[62] Tacitus, *Annales* 12.43; Suetonius, *Claudius* 18.2.

[63] Appian 5.67.

[64] E. J. Jory, "The Early Pantomime Riots", *Maistor: Classical, Byzantine and Renaissance Studies for Robert Browning*, ed. Ann Moffatt, Canberra: The Australian Association for Byzantine Studies, 1984, pp. 57–66. See, for example, the reports in Tacitus, *Annales* 1.54.2; Cassius Dio 57.11.6.

[65] Apuleius, *Metamorphoses* 4.13, 10.18. Under Hadrian, Athens, for example, had a gladiatorial show "out of rivalry against Corinth" (Philostratus, *Vitae Sophistarum.* 529).

[66] Cicero, *Oratio Pro Sestio* 106.

[67] According to Josephus, *Antiquitates Judaicae* 19.24-27, in the first century CE, 200,000 could view the chariots, whilst 50,000 could watch the fights in the Colosseum. These relative numbers are paralleled elsewhere in the Empire. The famous amphitheatre at El-Jem in North Africa had a capacity which exceeded the population of the city (illustrating the games' popularity with neighbouring towns, and the chora); it could

brought with them "the risk of subversion and resistance".[68] They were not to be treated lightly: when Augustus missed a show he made a point of sending his apologies.[69] As Tertullian remarked, the Circus was the place "where they spare neither emperors nor citizens".[70] Of course, as with the revolts and the riots, the *vox populi* could be lost amidst the clamour created by conflicting interests and expectations; the victim of mimicry and manipulation. It was rare for the populace to be univocal in its concerns (though the price of wheat provided a common exception).[71] The crowd was often divided: as Dio informs us, it could quite happily enjoy the spectacle of sections of itself being thrown to a bloody fate in the arena.[72]

Other occasions which led to the gathering of people in numbers, whether for markets or fairs,[73] religious or agonistic festivals, or for popular theatrical productions,[74] had similar potential for articulating popular culture and leaving some kind of mark in élite accounts.

Naturally, all of the above, whether a revolt or a riot, a spectacle or a market, contain comparable problems of interpretation but it is perhaps their atypicality which is their chief drawback for our purposes (a common difficulty for sources of 'History From Below'). As Keith Hopkins observes, "ancient sources represented the abnormal more . . . than the normal".[75] The behaviour of a mob is significant, but

hold some 30,000–60,000 spectators. (MacMullen, *Roman Social Relations*, p. 55 and also Hédi Slim, "Les Amphithéâtres d'El-Jem", *AIBL* 3 (1986) 440–469.) Indeed, recent photographic evidence suggests that a stadium existed in the town with an even greater capacity – see Hédi Slim, *El-Jem: Ancient Thysdrus*, Tunis: Alif, 1996, p. 84). A significant number of the poor could attend such events as entrance was often free (the games were paid for out of élite largesse). See Calpurnius Siculus, *Eclogae* 7.26–27.

[68] Keith Hopkins, *Death and Renewal*, Cambridge: Cambridge University Press, 1983, p. 18.

[69] Hopkins, *Death and Renewal*, p. 19. In the Roman context, as Augustus seems to have been aware, with the disenfranchisement of the plebs the games became the only place where the *vox populi* could be regularly heard. "Augustus set the style of overt respect by emperors to the only surviving assembly of citizens" (*ibid.*, p. 19).

[70] Tertullian, *De Spectaculis* 16.

[71] See Hopkins, *Death and Renewal*, p. 17.

[72] Cassius Dio 59.10.

[73] See B. D. Shaw, *AntAfr* 17 (1981) 37–83 and Joan Frayn, *Markets and Fairs in Roman Italy*, Oxford: Clarendon Press, 1993. For the significance of markets in élite/non-élite relations see L. de Ligt, *Fairs and Markets in the Roman Empire*, Amsterdam: J. C. Gieben, 1993.

[74] Jory, "The Early Pantomime Riots", pp. 57–66. Tiberius was, for example, forced to manumit a particularly well-liked comedian by a mob (Suetonius, *Tiberius* 47.1).

[75] Hopkins, "Rules of Evidence", p. 187.

the 'window' it gives us may be shattered. But, nevertheless, by reading an élite literary text 'upside down' we can obtain much of use.

We can also gain some significant data by focusing our reading upon a small number of privileged authors who stand out as more sensitive to the reality experienced by those beyond their clique; individuals who can be termed 'mediators'[76] of 'popular culture'. Juvenal,[77] Martial,[78] Apuleius,[79] Galen[80] and Vitruvius[81] are noteworthy in this respect but the works of Lucian of Samosata[82] and

---

[76] Burke, *Popular Culture in Early Modern Europe*, p. 68.

[77] Juvenal's third satire is an eloquent portrayal of the struggles of the urban indigent. Written in the early second century it is, in the words of Witke, ". . . a great innovation" for ". . . the urban poor are considered seriously, their problematical existence is examined, probed, and painted . . . their lives and tragedies are also valued in and for themselves" ("Juvenal III. Eclogue for the Urban Poor", *Hermes* 90 (1962), p. 247). However, we must be careful not to exaggerate its value. Juvenal's love of the satirical game and his own not inconsiderable wealth mean that the picture that he paints is not authentically one seen from 'below'. As Cloud has so persuasively argued, social historians should treat Juvenal with more circumspection than is traditionally the case ("The Client–Patron Relationship: Emblem and Reality in Juvenal's First Book", *Patronage in Ancient Society*, ed. A. Wallace-Hadrill, London: Routledge, 1990, pp. 205–218).

[78] Martial's epigrams contain valuable materials for our quest. The fact that he evidently commanded a broad readership should alert us to the value of his observations (see E. E. Best, "Martial's Readers in the Roman World," *CJ* 64 (1969) 208–212). However, despite his 'mendicant façade', it should not be forgotten that he was of equestrian rank (A. Hardie, *Statius and the Silvae: Poets, Patrons and Epideixis in Greco-Roman World*, Liverpool: Francis Cairns, 1983, pp. 51, 54–56).

[79] Apuleius, more famous for insights into the world of the mystery religions, likewise provides a significant contribution in this area, not least because his *Metamorphoses* "expresses a rare and distinctive level of sympathy with the lives of the poor" (Fergus Millar, "The World of the Golden Ass", *JRS* 71 (1981), p. 65).

[80] Galen, a prolific medical writer, potentially furnishes us with a plethora of helpful details; indeed, for Garnsey and Woolf he is "the nearest we can get to an observer of lower-class society" ("Patronage of the rural poor in the Roman world", p. 155). A number of his surviving works cast light on the material experiences of the poor and particularly their experience of subsistence, though the medical character of his interest means that "Galen gives us inadequate coverage of social relationships" (Garnsey and Woolf, "Patronage of the rural poor", p. 153).

[81] Vitruvius' *De Architectura*, published sometime in the 20s BCE, tells us a great deal about the living conditions of the urban populations of the Empire.

[82] The sophist Lucian is also notable for his observations about the lives of the impoverished. As Baldwin says, "he had a genuine sympathy for the poor, inspired in part by his own experiences" (*Studies in Lucian*, Toronto: Hakkert, 1973, p. 112): Lucian came from a family of stonemasons and was, briefly, one himself (*Somnium sive Vita Luciani* 3). This makes him, in some respects, more useful than Juvenal, Martial or Apuleius. However, his value should not be exaggerated. As Hall has argued, Baldwin overstates his case by maintaining that Lucian had some kind of revolutionary 'class' consciousness. He lived most of his life in comfort and had no desire to undermine his

Plautus[83] particularly so, as it seems likely that both individuals actually experienced non-élite life at first hand at some stage in their careers. However, as with all literary evidence, we must be aware of the problems of textuality, alert to the concerns and conventions shown by each author, and wary of taking any detail or scenario, however compelling or apparently innocent, at face value.[84]

But our chief emphasis should be upon a handful of literary works which originated outside the confines of aristocratic society. These have tended to be largely neglected by contemporary scholarship. Although such texts are not themselves *direct* transmissions of popular culture, they have much more affinity to it than do the writings of Juvenal or Martial. The handbooks of Graeco-Roman dream interpreters and astrologers, such as Artemidorus and Firmicus Maternus, give us a wealth of direct information about the common preoccupations of the non-élite in the Empire (such as, for instance, their obsession with their precarious experience of employment).[85] Fabular literature is also

---

privilege: when he touched upon the nature of poverty he was merely a "sophist handling a typically sophist theme" (J. Hall, *Lucian's Satire*, New York: Arno Press, 1981, p. 227).

[83] Plautus, of course, belonged to a much earlier period (his death is traditionally given as 184 BCE). He also made much use of material which had its genesis in an even earlier context: "Most or all of the plays themselves derive from Greek originals, adaptations of New Comedy that create grave difficulties in extracting the Roman elements embedded in the Hellenic texture" (Erich S. Gruen, *Studies in Greek Culture and Roman Policy*, Leiden: E. J. Brill, 1990, p. 124). But, nevertheless, he is eminently useful for our purposes. The soliloquies he put in the mouths of such slave characters as Strobilus and Gripus are particularly revealing of the expectations and frustrations of this class (*Aulularia* 587ff. and *Rudens* 906ff. See also Harpax in *Pseudolus* 1103ff.; Phaniscus in *Mostellaria* 859ff.; Messenio in *Menaechmi* 966ff. See K. R. Bradley, *Slaves and Masters in the Roman Empire*, Oxford: Oxford University Press, 1984, p. 39). For the popularity of Plautus' work see Richard C. Beacham, *The Roman Theatre and Its Audience*, London: Routledge, 1991.

Aulus Gellius, writing in the second century CE, believed that Plautus spent some of his life working as a hired hand in a mill (*Noctes Atticae* 3.3.14).

[84] See Richard P. Saller, "Anecdotes as Historical Evidence For the Principate", *G&R* 27 (1980) 69–83.

[85] See Ramsey MacMullen's indispensable essay on this subject, "Social History in Astrology", *AncSoc* 2 (1971) 105–116, and A. J. Pomeroy, "Status and Status-Concern in the Greco-Roman Dream Books", *AncSoc* 22 (1991) 56–105. Artemidorus' *Oneirocritica* is particularly valuable in this respect as it appears to be the product of careful fieldwork undertaken by the author, during which he examined a plethora of popular, oral traditions (1. *praef.*) from throughout the Mediterranean world (5. *praef.* cf. also Ephesus, 1.8, 2.35; Smyrna, 4.4; Cyzicus, 4.1; Laodicea, 4.1; Miletus, 4.24; Pergamum, 4.33; Alexandria, 4.22; Cyllene, 1.45; Corinth 4. *praef.*, 5:1;

significant. A number of Phaedrus' Aesopic fables seem to have arisen from a slave context[86] where they functioned, in the words of Bradley, ". . . as a vehicle of servile protest and indirect criticism of slave-owners",[87] and consequently allow us some access to the world-view and physical reality of the enslaved. The popular biography of the famous fabulist himself, the *Vita Aesopi*, is also invaluable,[88] particularly because of the way its comedy functions to reveal "the truth of the pretensions" behind the master-slave relationship.[89] Collections of jokes, such as the *Philogelos*[90] offer us "invaluable glimpses"[91] into the world of the non-élite, giving us a fuller picture of their day to day concerns, especially those of disease, crime, brutality, starvation and infant mortality. In addition, the literary products of some philosophical and religious movements of the period, such as the Cynic epistles or the

---

Puteoli, 1.26; Rome, 4.42, 5.69–70). The rigorous method Artemidorus applied in compiling his material is strikingly modern. His work has not unfairly been compared by John Winkler to that of a modern anthropologist (*The Constraints of Desire: The Anthropology of Sex and Gender in Ancient Greece*, New York: Routledge, 1990, p. 26).

[86] See *Fab* 3 *Prol* 33–37. Bradley, *Slaves and Masters*, pp. 150–153 and D. Daube, *Civil Disobedience in Antiquity*, Edinburgh: Edinburgh University Press, 1972, pp. 53ff.

[87] Bradley, *Slaves and Masters*, p. 151. As a genre they had this role in other slave communities; see Genovese's study of American chattel slavery, *Roll, Jordan, Roll: The World the Slaves Made*, p. 582.

[88] The value of the *Vita Aesopi* has only very recently been recognised (see Keith Hopkins, "Novel Evidence for Roman Slavery", *PP* 138 (1993) 3–27). According to Hopkins this composite work reached its final form in the first century CE and whilst this shows the influence of an Egyptian provenance, it is "a generic work, related generally, but not specifically, to slaves in the whole of the Roman world" ("Novel Evidence", p. 1).

[89] Hopkins, 'Novel Evidence", p. 17.

[90] There are other collections in addition to the *Philogelos*. For a discussion of these see Barry Baldwin, "The Philogelos: An Ancient Joke Book," *Roman and Byzantine Papers*, Amsterdam: J. C. Gieben, 1989, p. 628. Nevertheless, the *Philogelos* is probably the most useful, in that the anonymous compiler appears less obsessed by the mores of the privileged than is, for example, Plutarch in his *Regum et Imperatorum Apophthegmata*.

Dating the *Philogelos* presents difficulties and whilst Baldwin is probably correct to see the games of Philip in 248 CE (referred to in joke 62) as a *terminus a quo*, and the destruction of the Serapeum in 391 (not mentioned in joke 76) as *terminus ad quem* (*The Philogelos or Laughter-Lover*, trans. B. Baldwin, Amsterdam: J. C. Gieben, 1983, pp. vi-vii) it is likely that the collection contains material that belongs to a much earlier period. Joke 138 is indicative of this. The joke hinges upon the special privileges of a Roman citizen in the face of punishment by a provincial official. This would make little sense if the joke was composed after the granting of citizen rights to most of the Empire's population by Caracalla in 212, and so it must predate this.

[91] Baldwin, "The Philogelos: An Ancient Joke Book", pp. 624–637.

Mishnah, often cross-social in character, also contain important evidence.[92]

Legal texts

Legal texts are also a rich vein for obtaining materials necessary to construct an 'appropriate context of interpretation'. However, the source-critical issues that beset the use of works such as Justinian's *Corpus*[93] are only part of the problem facing someone attempting to use these texts: their relation to social reality, and especially 'popular culture' is invariably problematic. Their content is governed, above all, by legislative conventions. Law, as Watson observes, "is largely autonomous and not shaped by societal needs".[94] Indeed, "despite its practical impact, [it] is above all and primarily the culture of lawyers and especially of law makers. . . . legal development is determined by their culture; and social, economic, and political factors impinge on legal development only through their consciousness."[95]

In the Roman legal tradition, for instance, it was important for the implications of various axioms to be worked out to their logical conclusions, even though this often meant that many 'laws' were little more than elaborate fictions. *Patria potestas* provides an example of this. Despite the boast of the jurist Gaius that "there are virtually no other people who have such power over their sons as we have over ours",[96] the Roman father's control was, in practice, much more limited. He did not have, for instance, the much vaunted powers of life and death. Moral and religious sanctions, combined with the effects of limited life expectancy and high male age at marriage, curtailed his actual authority:

[92] But they carry with them particularly thorny problems of interpretation. For example, the historicity of the Mishnah cannot be taken for granted; see J. Neusner, *The Rabbinic Traditions about the Pharisees Before 70*, Cambridge: Cambridge University Press, 1971. For the difficulties in exegesis of Cynic sources see F. G. Downing, *Cynics and Christian Origins*, Edinburgh: T. & T. Clark, 1993, pp. 26–84.

[93] Barry Nicholas, *An Introduction to Roman Law*, Oxford: Oxford University Press, 1962, pp. 34–36. Even Gaius' *Institutes*, the only work of a classical jurist which has come down to us in something approaching its original form, is beset with textual problems. See *The Institutes of Gaius*, trans. W. Gordon and O. Robinson, London: Duckworth, 1988, pp. 7–8. In particular, the compilatory nature of the *Codex Theodosianus* and Justinian's *Digest* must make us suspicious of their contents. The desire of the creators of these works to remove obsolete legislation, and to impose coherence upon what was retained, has had a significant impact on the data before us.

[94] Alan Watson, *The Evolution of Law*, Oxford: Basil Blackwell, 1985, p. 119.

[95] Watson, *The Evolution of Law*, p. 118.

[96] Gaius, *Institutes* 1.55.

the social reality had little in common with this legal characterisation.[97] The Roman paterfamilias was, even in pre-Imperial days, a significantly less powerful figure than many classical and New Testament scholars presume him to have been.[98]

The symbolic quality of a significant quantity of legislation can also be confusing.[99] Many laws in operation in the Roman Empire were not intended to be applied. Anti-sumptuary legislation and that aimed at restricting the usurpation of status symbols (such as purple clothing) are good examples of this. As the frequency of their promulgation indicates, such laws were largely ineffective.[100] They ". . . did not depend upon successful enforcement for their effect";[101] it was their *existence* that was crucial. For instance, in the case of the two areas of legislation we have just mentioned, the law functioned to reaffirm symbolically élite self-identity; to re-emphasise the distinctions between the rulers and the ruled. Such legislation can give us information about Graeco-Roman society but it may not be the kind of information that we expect, illuminating mentalities rather than practices.

The intense conservatism of Roman legal culture can also create substantial difficulties. The reverence for laws from the past and the subsequent reluctance to revoke or amend them, helped to make Roman law a rarefied system "with little relation to everyday practice or commonly held beliefs about what is right".[102]

---

[97] Richard P. Saller, "Patria Potestas and the Stereotype of the Roman Family", *CC* 1 (1986) 7–22.

[98] For example, John Stambaugh and D. Balch, *The Social World of the First Christians*, London: SPCK, 1986, p. 124, and C. S. Keener, "Man and Woman", *Dictionary of Paul and His Letters*, ed. G. Hawthorne, Leicester: InterVarsity Press, 1993, p. 587. See J. A. Crook's pertinent remarks in "Patria Potestas", *CQ* 17 (1967), p. 114.

[99] J. R. Gusfield, "Moral Passage: The Symbolic Process in Public Designation of Deviance", *SP* 15 (1967) 175–188; S. L. Hills, *Crime, Power and Morality*, London: Chandler, 1971, pp. 8–9. There is, of course, a symbolic quality to the *patria potestas* legislation as well.

[100] For anti-sumptuary laws see Tacitus, *Annales* 3.53–54. For anti status-usurpation legislation see M. Reinhold, "The Usurpation of Status and Status Symbols in the Roman Empire", *Historia* 20 (1971) 275–302. Anti-sumptuary laws are always difficult to enforce – e.g. see F. E. Baldwin, *Sumptuary Legislation and Personal Regulation in England*, Baltimore: Johns Hopkins University Press, 1926, and D. Shively, "Sumptuary Regulation and Status in Early Tokugawa Japan", *HJAS* 25 (1964) 123–164.

A. H. M. Jones' remarks made in the 1960s are as appropriate now as: "Many modern historians . . . have too readily assumed that Roman citizens obeyed the law, and that everything was done as the imperial government directed" (*The Later Roman Empire*, 1964, p. viii).

[101] Toner, *Leisure and Ancient Rome*, p. 119.

[102] S. Dixon, *The Roman Mother*, London: Croom Helm, 1988, p. 42.

Finally, a rather more mundane problem with using these legal sources for an insight into 'popular culture' should also be mentioned as it is particularly germane to New Testament studies. For the most part, the legal sources we have access to are Roman, but Roman law, at least until Caracalla gave the rights of citizenship to most of its inhabitants in 212 CE, was not the only law operating in the Roman Empire. In the first century the situation remained fluid with Roman law vying with the still strong indigenous traditions, most notably those of demotic Egypt and Greece.[103] The law of the *Pax Romana* was characterised by "evolution and compromise".[104]

Papyri

Papyri are also indispensable. The great majority of those that survive are concerned with the fiscal, commercial, legal and social interactions that, for the most part, would be considered too mundane to warrant mention in literary sources. The information they give us is often arid, and fragmented, but with insights drawn from comparative studies we can at least go some way to determining something of the socio-economic *realia* of the non-élite.[105]

However, the value of the papyri should not be overestimated. Despite their impressive quantity,[106] as Dennis Kehoe notes, "the papyri rarely permit the ancient social or economic historian . . . to undertake

---

[103] See Andrew Lintott, *Imperium Romanum: Politics and Administration*, London: Routledge, 1993, pp. 154–160. The *Gnomon of Idios-Logos* from Roman Egypt, and the Babatha archives from Roman Israel, provide excellent examples of the co-existence of parallel legal traditions within the Empire (see R. Taubenschlag, *The Law of Greco-Roman Egypt in the Light of the Papyri 332 BC to 640 AD*, second edition, Warsaw: Panstwowe Wydawnictwo Naukowe, 1958, and N. Lewis, R. Katzoff, and J. C. Greenfield, "Papyrus Yadin 18", *IEJ* 37 (1987) 229–250).

[104] Lintott, *Imperium Romanum*, p. 154. Nevertheless, "it looks as if cases of real importance tended to be handled by Roman magistrates" (p. 160).

[105] In a study of pastoralism in Roman Egypt James Keenan has demonstrated the indispensability of a comparative approach in making sense of the disparate data that a papyrologist faces. It helps to "suggest how circumstantial evidentiary details in the papyri could fit into a larger frame and lead to the right answer. Possibilities raised from comparative materials conjured up images, images of flocks on the move, of shepherds in the field, that were not necessarily visible in the documents themselves or in their editions, or in the standard papyrological literature" ("Pastoralism in Roman Egypt", *BASP* 26 (1989), p. 169).

[106] Italo Gallo estimates that there are about 40,000 edited documentary papyri alone and at least another 40,000 discovered but yet to be edited (*Greek and Latin Papyrology*, London: Institute of Classical Studies, 1986, p. 67).

statistical analyses of data".[107] They are also geographically restricted almost exclusively to the desert areas of upper and middle Egypt, so insights that can be gleaned from their contents must be treated with care, given that country's distinctive place within the Empire.[108]

Epigraphy

But it is perhaps epigraphy that gives us with the clearest 'window' into 'popular culture'. There is often some misunderstanding about the extent of material included in this class of evidence: it is not confined merely to official inscriptions but encompasses the study of virtually all objects that have been written upon. Its great value lies both in its immediacy[109] and its abundance.[110] Although occasionally official inscriptions let us have some clue to non-élite concerns,[111] it is the study of epitaphs, *defixiones* and graffiti that is especially important in this respect.[112]

[107] Dennis P. Kehoe, "Comparative Approaches to the Social History of Roman Egypt", *BASP* 26 (1989), p. 153.

[108] However, the unusual character of Roman Egypt should not be exaggerated, as has often been the case. See N. Lewis, "The Romanity of Roman Egypt: A Growing Consensus", *Atti del XVII Congresso Internazionale di Papirologia*, Naples: Centro Internazionale per lo studio dei papiri Ercolanesi, 1984, pp. 1077–1084.

[109] Which still remains impressive despite being clouded to some extent by recording habit; "the gap between the recording practice and 'social reality' must remain a problem for all work of this kind" (J. Reynolds, M. Beard and C. Roueché, "Roman Inscriptions 1981–1985", *JRS* 76 (1986), p. 142).

Even a graffiti writer is constrained by conventions to some extent, as any cursory reading of contemporary graffiti will confirm.

[110] "It is epigraphy which provides our most direct access to ancient society and culture, and which shows every sign of being able to add indefinitely to the stock of available texts" (Millar, "Epigraphy", p. 135).

[111] For instance, the inscriptional records of grants of citizenship and even bouletic status to various fairground acts (jugglers, tightrope walkers, strongmen) illustrates the occasionally subversive, playful and powerful nature of the *vox populi*: "Such grants, in the gifts of the local authorities, suggest how the urban élites accommodated themselves, in the interests of civic concord, to a certain vulgarisation of the agon under the principate" (A. J. Spawforth, "Agonistic Festivals in Roman Greece", *The Greek Renaissance in the Roman Empire*, ed. S. Walker and A. Cameron, London: Institute of Classical Studies, 1989, p. 197).

[112] Numismatics is now a clearly defined, separate discipline (though this was not always the case – see Arthur E. Gordon, *Illustrated Introduction to Latin Epigraphy*, Berkeley: University of California Press, 1983, p. 3). It can likewise provide a productive quarry for social data. Although coins are, for the most part, tools of élite discourse (see C. Howgego, *Ancient History From Coins*, London: Routledge, 1995, pp. 70–73) they can still contain valuable information about everyday social realities (e.g. see R. G. Penn, *Medicine on Ancient Greek and Roman Coins*, London: Seaby, 1994).

Contrary to common presuppositions, epitaphs were not the preserve solely of the élite in the Empire. As Richard Saller and Brent Shaw convincingly argue, they "cut through the strata of society from top to bottom".[113] Indeed:

> The wish to perpetuate some memory of oneself after death was not confined to the wealthy, just as in many other pre-modern urban centres, where the poor have gone to considerable lengths to avoid the anonymity of the mass graves of paupers and to assure for themselves the basics of burial in a genteel manner.

Although for many of the non-élite anonymity was an inescapable aspect of death, as their corpses were swallowed up by mass burial pits[114] or wild dogs,[115] some managed to leave behind epitaphs, of which even the most rudimentary give us valuable information about lives that would otherwise remain unknown. The barest details of name, occupation, and age can help us reconstruct something of the social relations and experiences of such people.[116] Although the world of epitaphs tends

---

[113] Richard Saller and B. Shaw, "Tombstones and Roman Family Relations in the Principate: Civilians, Soldiers and Slaves", *JRS* 74 (1984), p. 127; *contra* Keith Hopkins' more restricted view ("On the probable age structure of the Roman population", *PS* 20 (1966), p. 246, and "Graveyard for Historians," *La Mort, Les Morts et L'Au-Delà Dans Le Monde Romain*, ed. F. Hinard, Caen: Centre de Publications, 1987, p. 114). Funerary monuments range widely, from the garish splendour of Gaius Cestius' pyramid in Rome, to stones costing only a handful of sesterces. See also Richmond Lattimore, *Themes in Greek and Latin Epitaphs*, Urbana: The University of Illinois Press, 1942, p. 16.

[114] Hopkins, *Death and Renewal*, pp. 208–209.

[115] Whittaker, "Studying the Poor", p. 13.

[116] In this respect the greater formality of Latin epitaphs over those written in Greek makes them more valuable: "we are more likely to be informed about the station and occupation of the subject" (Lattimore, *Themes*, p. 16).

Of course, all epitaphs are governed by certain conventions. In most age-rounding was rife (R. Duncan-Jones, "Age-Rounding, Illiteracy and Social Differentiation in the Roman Empire", *Chiron* 7 (1977), p. 334) and there were also significant regional variations in some, child deaths were deemed worthy of record, whereas in others they were not (B. D. Shaw, "Among the Believers", *EMC* 28 (1984), p. 471). See also Ramsey MacMullen, "The Epigraphic Habit in the Roman Empire", *AJPh* 103 (1982) 233–246, and E. Meyer, "Explaining the Epigraphic Habit in the Roman Empire", *JRS* 80 (1990) 74–96.

As Hopkins notes, unfortunately these 'habits' combine to make the data they contain unreliable as a basis for demographic calculations: "Commemorative practice is useful for analysing Roman commemorative practice; it may or may not be useful for analysing the relative importance of relationships within the Roman family, or for testing the existence of the extended family at Rome. But commemorative practices, I maintain, are useless for understanding Roman patterns of death" ("Graveyard for Historians", p. 115).

Contra J. M. Lassèr, *Ubique Populus*, Paris: Centre National de la Recherche et de Scientifique, 1977.

to be an 'ideal' one, filled with devoted spouses, obedient children, or grateful slaves,[117] and a sense of politeness pervades even the basest examples,[118] nevertheless, what little information we can glean[119] can radically challenge the image of social life that results from relying upon élite sources alone. For example, the work of B. Shaw has brought to light the characteristic structure of the Latin, non-élite family. Their epitaphs show an interest in the 'descending nuclear family', the commemoration of children by parents, in contrast to those of the élite, which emphasised 'horizontal', and more particularly, conjugal, ties.[120]

The access that curse tablets (*defixiones*)[121] allow us to the cultural *koine* is even more immediate, even if John Gager's recent estimation is a little exaggerated (playing down the influence of literary conventions and the input of scribes in their composition):

> . . . they come to us largely unmediated by external filters; unlike ancient literary texts they are devoid of the distortions introduced by factors such as education, social class and status, and literary genres or tradition . . . they are intensely personal and direct.[122]

The study of *defixiones* has been seriously impeded by a number of prejudices, not least of which is the academic antipathy towards the so-called 'superstitious'.[123] There has been an undeniable tendency to speak

---

[117] The tendency for some individuals to compose their own memorials no doubt contributed to this (e.g. Petronius, *Satyricon* 71.12; *Philogelos* 90).

[118] Lattimore, *Themes*, pp. 283, 299.

[119] And, paradoxically, it is often the living rather than the dead about whom we learn most; after all it is often they who erect the tombstones and it is their concerns that govern the wording and form of an epitaph.

[120] B. D. Shaw, "Latin Funerary Epigraphy and Family Life in the Later Roman Empire", *Historia* 33 (1984), p. 474. Although Shaw's study relies on data from the Western Empire it is still of some value. See also Sandra P. Joshel's valuable work, *Work, Identity and Legal Status at Rome: A Study of the Occupational Inscriptions*, Norman: University of Oklahoma Press, 1992.

[121] *Defixiones* were: ". . . inscribed sheets of metal or other material that were used and generally commissioned, at least in the Roman period, by private individuals (clients) in order to influence – against their will and through the agency of spirits, daimones and deities – the behaviour and welfare of personal enemies and rivals (targets)" (John Gager, *Curse Tablets and Binding Spells From the Ancient World*, Oxford: Oxford University Press, 1992, p. 175).

[122] Gager, *Curse Tablets*, p. v.

[123] This intolerance is not new. Lucian of Samosata turned his nose up at them, attacking their "gibberish" (see *Philopseudes* 10). There were periodic attempts, particularly in later years of the Empire, to prohibit their use. See A. A. Barb, "The Survival of the Magic Arts", *Conflict Between Paganism and Christianity in the Fourth Century*, ed. A. Momigliano, Oxford: Oxford University Press, 1963, pp. 100–125, and

of their use as though it was almost entirely confined to the murky age of the late Roman Empire (the repository of so much irrationality to classical scholars)[124] and insignificant and peripheral to the world of antiquity. In fact, they were a consistent part of ancient society and they had an essential role in the dynamic culture of the classical Mediterranean.[125] Their efficacy was rarely doubted.[126] Their 'clients' came from all sexes, ages, statuses, peoples and religions.[127] Not only were they preeminently 'popular' but the circumstances of their use enhance even further their value for gaining an insight into popular culture, and particularly economic culture. They were almost invariably employed at times of perceived difficulty or uncertainty, and whilst for some the adversity being faced concerned such universal dilemmas as love, theft or violence, nevertheless a very significant number of *defixiones* concern specific anxieties over competition and, literally, survival that plagued the non-élite;[128] their world became one of curse and counter curse, a

---

C. R. Phillips, "Nullum Crimen sine Lege: Socioreligious Sanctions on Magic", *Magika Hiera: Ancient Greek Magic and Religion*, ed. Christopher A. Faraone and Dirk Obbink, Oxford: Oxford University Press, 1991, pp. 260–276.

Gager makes a valuable point about the possible deeper motives for the lack of interest by scholars: "One reason for this persistent neglect stems surely from the potentially harmful character of these small metal tablets – not so much the real harm suffered by their ancient targets but the potential harm to the entrenched reputation of classical Greece and Rome, not to mention Judaism and Christianity, as bastions of pure philosophy and religion" (*Curse Tablets*, p. 3).

[124] C. Bonner, "Witchcraft in the Lecture Room of Libanius", *TAPA* 63 (1932) 34–44, and also Peter Brown, "Sorcery, Demons and the Rise of Christianity", *Religion and Society in the Age of Augustine*, London: Faber & Faber, 1972, pp. 119–146.

[125] For a useful discussion of how such 'magical' practices have a central and not marginal role in cultural *Weltanschauungen* see Hildred Geertz, "An Anthropology of Religion and Magic", pp. 71–109.

[126] As Pliny the Elder testifies: "there is no one who is not afraid of curses and binding spells". *Naturalis Historiae* 28.4.19.

[127] We have, for example, instances of Jewish and Samaritan *defixiones*, in which God is invoked as the principal power, and in which sizeable quotations from the LXX are used (shorn of their context) to add weight to the curse (see Gager, *Curse Tablets*, pp. 185–187). The Jewish fear of curses is evident in 2 Macc. 12:34–39 which records that every fallen Jewish soldier wore an amulet (an apotropaic device) to protect himself from the effects of such things. (For a study of apotropaic devices see Christopher Faraone, *Talismans and Trojan Horses*, Oxford: Oxford University Press, 1992.)

[128] As Gager has observed, the "majority of persons belong to the world of marginal labourers – some free and some slaves – tavern keepers, carpenters, metalworkers, potters, prostitutes and so on" (*Curse Tablets*, p. 152). The attacks upon a 'garland weaver' on curse tablets from Roman Corinth may well be an example of this phenomenon (see N. Bookidis and R. S. Stroud, *Demeter and Persephone in Ancient Corinth*, Princeton: American School of Classical Studies at Athens, 1987, pp. 30f.). However, most

battlefield between *defixiones* and apotropaic devices, in the desperate struggle to gain some slight advantage over neighbours, and to attain some security.

Graffiti likewise have not received the attention they deserve. Although many of them have failed to survive (graffiti in any culture are by their nature ephemeral) their prevalence in antiquity and significance in hearing the voice of popular culture cannot be ignored: as one piece from Pompeii reads: "Everybody writes on the walls but me."[129] Above all they often gives expression to the 'ludic' and/or subversive element of popular culture that would otherwise be overlooked: defying the prevailing hegemony and seeking to raise, however gently or bitterly, a different voice. A first-century CE graffito from the walls of a *popina* provides an excellent example of this:

> *xvii k(alendas) Septem(bres), feridius Cereris Dominae. Hic sibi suabiter fecerun(t) tres adulescentes quorum nomina lege: Onesimus et L. Valerius Ersianus et Filumenus. Unus cum mulier(e), extremus. Multis annis, habe, facian(t) [fo]rtunam propitiam.*[130]

The writer libidinously boasted of the deliberate, and public, breaking of the prohibition on sexual relations that was supposed to accompany the festival of Ceres.[131] And by so doing he ridiculed official culture, and openly expressed his dissent from its conventions.

From a slightly later period, a simple menorah scratched on the steps of Celsus' library at Ephesus gives us another instance of this aspect of graffiti. The building is redolent with the symbolism of the dominant Graeco-Roman aristocracy and functioned as one of the primary foci of

---

surviving examples come from the Classical and Hellenistic periods. See also Christopher Faraone, "The Agonistic Context of Early Greek Binding Spells", *Magika Hiera: Ancient Greek Magic and Religion*, ed. Christopher A. Faraone and Dirk Obbink, Oxford: Oxford University Press, 1991, p. 11.

[129] H. H. Tanzer, *The Common People of Pompeii: A Study of the Graffiti*, Baltimore: Johns Hopkins University Press, 1939, p. 6. Indeed Pompeii, because of the almost unique circumstances of its preservation, contains by far the most impressive collection of this form of evidence. Its proliferation has led Millar to assert that it can "allow an attempt to define the elements of a popular culture" ("Epigraphy", p. 91).

[130] G. Manganaro, "Graffiti e Iscrizioni Funerarie della Sicilla Orientale", *Helikon* 2 (1962) 485–501.

[131] As Casson points out: "The adding of the date was important: it showed that they deliberately chose the solemn holiday when women were supposed to observe nine days of chastity to carry on this way" (*Travel in the Ancient World*, London: Allen & Unwin, 1974, p. 217).

the ruling civic clique. It is not unreasonable to see the menorah as a strident and confrontational affirmation of a marginalised culture (albeit by one representative of it).[132]

However, it should be added that in the ancient world, much as today, certain individuals were more prolific producers of graffiti than others. One character in Pompeii, Aemilius Celer, for instance, was an "inveterate graffiti writer"[133] and alone was responsible for at least thirty-five pieces of work throughout the city. Consequently, they cannot allow us unproblematic access to the popular culture of the period as the perceptions of such untypical people may be over-represented in the data that it provides.

Archaeology

Investigation of material product through archaeology[134] (both in its micro, 'artefact', and macro, 'landscape' scale) also provides us with a number of clues to our interpretative context, allowing us unrivalled opportunities for reassessing the picture of ancient life presented by élite-authored texts.[135]

In the area of artefacts the traditional paradigm of the discipline has proved disabling. A positivist approach predominated until relatively recently that "produced literature replete with descriptive studies providing details on artefact identification, typology and chronology";[136] and had little interest in contextual 'meaning'. Its 'cultural' interest was focused upon the "grand and lasting"[137] monuments of the élite (the

---

[132] See Edwin Yamauchi, *The Archaeology of the New Testament Cities in Western Asia Minor*, London: Pickering & Inglis, 1980, p. 110.

[133] James L. Franklin, "Literacy and Parietal Inscriptions of Pompeii," *Literacy in the Roman World*, ed. J. H. Humphrey, Ann Arbor: Journal of Roman Archaeology, 1991, p. 91.

[134] A discipline long familiar to, and long abused by, New Testament scholars. See, for instance, R. E. Oster, "Use, Misuse and Neglect of Archaeological Evidence in Some Modern Works on 1 Corinthians", *ZNW* 83 (1992), 52–73. There are, of course, exceptions to this, such as the work of the Harvard Ephesos Symposium which can be found in Helmut Koester (ed.), *Ephesos, Metropolis of Asia: An Interdisciplinary Approach to its Archaeology, Religion and Culture*, Valley Forge: Trinity Press International, 1995.

[135] See, for example, the remarks of Andrew Wallace-Hadrill, *Houses and Society in Pompeii and Herculaneum*, Princeton: Princeton University Press, 1994, p. 7.

[136] Mary Beaudry et al., "Artifacts and Active Voices: Material Culture as Social Discourse", *The Archaeology of Inequality*, ed. R. McGuire and R. Paynter, Oxford: Blackwell, 1991, p. 151.

[137] R. Paynter, and R. McGuire, "The Archaeology of Inequality: Material Culture, Domination and Resistance", *The Archaeology of Inequality*, ed. R. McGuire and

palaces, the large houses, the temples, the mausoleums), the remnants of 'high' culture.

Nonetheless, new approaches and concerns within archaeology are allowing us to gain substantially more data from the material under investigation. The positivist approach is giving way in many quarters to a position influenced by the pioneering work of scholars such as J. Deetz[138] who recognise that even the most unassuming of domestic artefacts is a cultural message carrier, not "just as a passive product of economic behaviour, but as an instrumental component of symbolic action"[139] which can illuminate the lives of the neglected masses.

Of course, despite this methodological breakthrough, we are faced with a paucity of evidence. Excavation reports carried out with previous assumptions can often have little of value in them. As Susan Alcock has observed, "urban excavations begin, and usually end, with the public centre of the community",[140] leaving unexplored the material culture of the non-élite. The only data we have access to is drawn from excavations of the areas of cities where the material displays of the discourse of the nobility are especially concentrated (and consequently, those of the non-élite are largely absent). Often, not only do we find that the artefacts and buildings connected with the *res populi* have been ignored, but that these fragile records have been destroyed by the excavators. The new, culturally sensitive, egalitarian approach is very much in its infancy but, nevertheless, the fact that it is no longer feasible to presuppose that only the powerful can make statements with artefacts has opened up a potentially revolutionising source of knowledge for constructing the popular context.[141]

R. Paynter, Oxford: Blackwell, 1991, p. 10. Wallace-Hadrill makes a similar methodological point about the excavations of houses in Pompeii ("Houses and Households: Sampling Pompeii and Herculaneum", *Marriage, Divorce and Children in Ancient Rome*, ed. Beryl Rawson, Oxford: Oxford University Press, 1991, p. 198).

[138] See J. Deetz, *In Small Things Forgotten: The Archaeology of Early American Life*, New York: Anchor Press, 1977; "Historical Archaeology as the Science of Material Culture", *Historical Archaeology and the Importance of Material Things*, ed. Leland G. Ferguson, Tuscon AZ: Society for Historical Archaeology, 1977, pp. 9–12; and "Archaeography, Archaeology, or Archeology?" *AJA* 93 (1989) 429–435.

[139] Beaudry et al., "Artifacts and Active Voices", p. 174.

[140] Alcock, *Graecia Capta*, p. 96.

[141] Beaudry et al., "Artifacts and Active Voices", p. 156.

The recognition that 'landscape'[142] provides us with a powerful "social document",[143] allows another source for exploring the character of popular experience (quite literally, expanding our horizons). Particularly in a city the landscape is not just a product of ecological factors but also of ideological and symbolic concerns; it is "differentially charged".[144] The habitation patterns can give us information about, for instance, the perceived relationships between various types of inhabitant and the centres of religious, political or social power. If we look at, for example, the distribution of places of domicile within Pompeii, we find different status groups intermingled to an extent which counters the usual stereotype of the rigidly ghettoised Imperial city.[145] Similarly, the discovery of extensive market gardens and vineyards within city boundaries[146] challenges the usual assumptions about the division and conflict between the πόλις-χώρα[147] which is at the heart of so many analyses of first-century society.[148] In some ways this approach allows us

---

[142] That is, "the arrangement and interaction of peoples and places in space and time" (S. Alcock, *Graecia Capta*, p. 6).

[143] Alcock, *Graecia Capta*, p. 8.

[144] A. Wallace-Hadrill, "Public Honour and Private Shame: The Urban Texture of Pompeii", *Urban Society in Roman Italy*, ed. T. Cornell and K. Lomas, London: UCL Press, 1995, p. 39. For a reading of the urban landscape as a social document (and its public negotiation through the act of ritual procession) see Guy MacLean Rogers, *The Sacred Identity of Ephesos: Foundation Myths of a Roman City*, London: Routledge, 1991. See also Ray Laurence, *Roman Pompeii: Space and Society*, London: Routledge, 1994, and "The Organization of Space in Pompeii", *Urban Society in Roman Italy*, ed. J. Cornell and K. Lomas, London: UCL Press, 1995, pp. 63–78.

For the benefits of attention to the urban landscape for New Testament studies in general, see J. F. Strange "Some Implications of Archaeology for New Testament Studies", *What Has Archaeology To Do With Faith?* ed. J. H. Charlesworth and W. P. Weaver, Philadelphia: Fortress Press, 1992, pp. 23–59.

[145] See Wallace-Hadrill, "Houses and Households", pp. 191–227.

[146] W. F. Jashemski, *The Gardens of Pompeii*, New York: Caratzas Bros., 1979. See also R. A. Raper, "The Analysis of the Urban Structure of Pompeii: a Sociological Examination of Land Use (Semi-Micro)", *Spatial Archaeology*, ed. D. L. Clarke, London: Academic Press, 1977, pp. 189–221, and "Pompeii: Planning and Social Implications", *Space, Hierarchy and Society: Interdisciplinary Studies in Social Area Analysis*, ed. B. C. Burnham and J. Kingsbury, Oxford: BAR, 1979, pp. 137–148. See also *Vita Aesopi* 34.

[147] "The first and longest class struggle history has known." F. Braudel, *Capitalism and Material Life*, London: Fontana, 1974, p. 373

[148] The excavation of urban leisure facilities tells a similar story. It is obvious that they often drew the inhabitants of the countryside to the city on a regular basis. For example, the amphitheatre at El-Jem is so enormous that it could not have been filled by the population of Thysdrus and must have drawn its crowds from beyond its boundaries (see MacMullen, *Roman Social Relations*, p. 55; Slim, "Les Amphithéâtres d'El-Jem", and *El-Jem: Ancient Thysdrus*). The block reservations on behalf of various

to overcome the problem of the destruction of relevant material, working as it does with a broader vision of the 'culture' under examination (and consequently one less vulnerable to the devastation wrought by excavators).

Despite the attractiveness of these new hermeneutical perspectives we should not overlook the fact that a number of more traditional, empirical branches of archaeology, perhaps more common in the archaeology of pre-history, also have a substantial contribution to make to the investigation of popular culture in the first century. Disciplines such as geomorphology, soil science, climatology, palaeobotany, pollen analysis, and paleopathology, can help construct a picture of the material existence and patterns of behaviour amongst the non-élite. Unfortunately classical archaeologists have been concerned primarily with uncovering the architectural record or distinctive artefacts, and so detailed studies of animal bones or plant remains are rare, "scientific precision and thoughtful sampling even rarer".[149] The study of human skeletal remains has received a little more attention for our period[150] and whilst, as Hopkins[151] and Morris[152] have observed, we must qualify any deductions from this source (especially in respect to demographic calculations) nevertheless it has some value for our analysis (it can, for

---

villages found at the amphitheatre at Oenoanda are equally revealing (Reynolds, "Cities", p. 49).

The preservation and idealisation of agrarian life within Roman cities, something that is especially visible in the character of many of their religious festivals, should also make us question the value of assuming a radical dichotomy between the worlds of the πόλις and χώρα in many parts of the Empire (see J. A. North, "Religion and Rusticity", Urban Society in Roman Italy, ed. T. Cornell and K. Lomas, London: UCL Press, 1995, pp. 135–152). Indeed, given that most of the 1,000 or so cities of the Roman Empire had populations of less than 15,000, the world of the countryside remained unavoidably near and familiar (Alföldy, The Social History of Rome, pp. 97–98; see also Joyce Reynolds, "Cities", The Administration of the Roman Empire 241 BC – AD 193, Exeter: Exeter University Press, 1988, p. 19).

[149] K. Greene, *The Archaeology of the Roman Economy*, London: B. T. Batsford, 1986, p. 71.

[150] See, for example, Peter Garnsey, "Mass Diet and Nutrition in the City of Rome", *Nourrir la Plèbe*, ed. A. Giovannini and D. Berchem, Basel: Reinhardt, 1991, pp. 86–88. Though even here "it is not unknown for hundreds of skeletons to vanish after excavations, while associated vases are published in meticulous detail." (Ian Morris, *Death Ritual and Social Structure in Classical Antiquity*, Cambridge: Cambridge University Press, 1992, p. 101.)

[151] Hopkins, "Graveyard", pp. 113–126.

[152] Ian Morris, *Death Ritual and Social Structure in Classical Antiquity*, pp. 41–42.

example, give some indication of the dietary deficiencies and illnesses that were significant amongst non-élite life and interaction).[153]

2.4 Concluding remarks

As I said at the outset, even with all these sources of information, the limitations in the creation of an 'appropriate context of interpretation' must be recognised. The dearth of evidence only allows us partial and limited insight into non-élite reality. Some of the approaches I have outlined are quite new and have yet to be developed sufficiently to contribute greatly to our quest (though they will, I believe, prove invaluable in the near future) and my own lack of competence in others precludes me from exploiting their potential to the full. Certainly, the material available does not allow us to attempt a 'thick description'[154] of non-élite lived experience (to use an anthropological term now fashionable in social history) even if such a project was not in itself hermeneutically problematic. Beyond the relatively recent past, to claim to be able to do such a thing would be misleading.[155]

---

[153] See S. Zivanovic, *Ancient Diseases: The Elements of Palaeopathology*, London: Metheun & Co., 1982; C. Wells, *Bones, Bodies and Disease*, London: Thames & Hudson, 1964; and A. Cockburn, *The Evolution and Eradication of Infectious Diseases*, Baltimore: Johns Hopkins University Press, 1963.

[154] As, for example, Hopkins claims to attempt in his two works *Conquerors and Slaves*, Cambridge: Cambridge University Press, 1978, and *Death and Renewal*. Shaw provides a very good summary of this interpretative perspective: "Thick description operates, to put it crudely, on the assumption that the best description equals the best explanation. It is a phenomenology which seeks to evoke in its readers an understanding of the causes, motives and explanations inherent in a scenario by translating them mentally into the situation" ("Among the Believers", p. 472).

For a description of the methods and motives of 'thick description' see C. Geertz, "Thick Description: Toward an Interpretative Theory of Culture", *The Interpretation of Culture*, New York: Basic Books, 1973, pp. 3–30 and J. Henretta, "Social History as Lived and Written", *AHR* 84 (1979) 1293–1322. For criticism of 'thick description' see W. Runciman, *A Treatise on Social Theory 1: The Methodology of Social Theory*, Cambridge: Cambridge University Press, 1983, pp. 223–300.

[155] The idealistic desire for an 'emic' reading of a situation, from the 'inside out', in contrast to that of an 'etic', may be useful, if elusive, corrective within anthropology, but it is hardly fair to criticise historians for failing to adopt it given the very different and much more limited data to which they have access (for a discussion of the terms 'emic' and 'etic' see M. Harris, "History and Significance of the Emic/Etic Distinction", *ARA* 5 (1976) 329–350). It is unjust to compare Thompson's "Class Struggle Without Class?" unfavourably with Henry Glassie's *Passing the Time in Ballymenone: Culture and History in an Ulster Community*, Philadelphia: University of Pennsylvania Press, 1982, as do Beaudry et al. ("Artifacts and Active Voices," p. 163). The one is about the social reality of the 1700s, the other about life in a contemporary Northern Irish village.

But despite the obvious shortage of relevant materials that we can bring to bear in interpreting the Pauline epistles, and the resulting 'thinness' of the interpretative context we can construct, it must be emphasised that the option of returning to the uncritical use of élite literary texts is not an option at all. The old approach may appear to give us abundant and easily accessible social data but the frustration of limited knowledge is preferable to the delusion and subsequent mis-representations that it entails. An 'appropriate context of interpretation', however poor, must be preferable to one that is inappropriate, however full.

Having examined the means by which we can construct an 'appropriate context of interpretation', we can now return fully to our original area of concentration and attempt to examine the economic reality of the Pauline Christians. That is, we can resume our quest to describe how these individuals experienced and reacted to the economic component of their total social context. We now have at least some indication of how this can be done in a way that is both more authentic and less abstract than would otherwise be the case.

Historical writing which claims to attempt a 'thick description' is, despite its worthy aspirations, little more than historical fiction. With no obvious means of validation the selection of 'paradigmatic instances' invariably becomes governed by the personal aesthetic and ideological concerns of the author. See Shaw's criticism of Hopkins' work in "Among the Believers", pp. 453–479.

3

The Context of Interpretation: *practice*

Let us now attempt to reconstruct the norms of urban economic existence for members of the Pauline churches. There are two parts to this undertaking, as we observed earlier. Firstly, it is necessary to discern the wider structures which delimited the general economic experiences of the communities. Secondly, we must investigate and, at least in a limited sense, try to evoke something of the specific economic realities encountered. Only when this context has been outlined can we constructively turn towards the task of interpreting the specific data that can be gleaned from the epistles.

3.1 The wider context: the economy of the Empire

Before concentrating on the life of the congregations in the Graeco-Roman cities we must first set the wider context and describe the economic system of the Roman Empire as a whole. This will give us an indication of the material circumstances and the patterns of wealth distribution operative within the first-century Mediterranean world.

The character of the Graeco-Roman economy (or rather economies)[1] remains an area of dispute between the 'primitivists', such as Finley and

---

[1] We should be wary of exaggerating the degree of economic integration experienced by the first-century Mediterranean world (see Lintott, *Imperium Romanum*, pp. 188ff.). Inter-regional trade within the Empire was limited and was largely concerned with the import and export of luxury items. The profusion and diffusion of the remains of amphorae throughout the Mediterranean does not provide evidence to the contrary. They give the impression that the Empire had a highly integrated economy but such an impression is, for the most part, deceptive (see, for example, G. Woolf, "Imperialism, Empire, and the Integration of the Roman Economy", *WA* 23 (1992) 283–293 and M. Fulford, "Territorial Expansion and the Roman Empire", *WA* 23 (1992) 294–305; D. P. Peacock and D. F. Williams, *Amphorae and the Roman Economy: An Introductory Guide*, London: Longman, 1986, p. 60). The flow of such goods in the Empire accompanied Roman political and military expansion and was often shortlived.

Bücher,[2] who believe that nothing approaching market or rational capitalism[3] can be seen in antiquity, and the 'modernists', most notably Frank and Rostovtzeff,[4] who find numerous similarities between economic life in the Empire and that today. A cursory survey of the major components of the economy (agriculture, manufacturing, and commerce) reveals, I believe, the veracity of the essentially 'primitivist' position. The economy remained weak and rudimentary, with little or no growth.[5]

Agriculture was central to the life of the Roman Empire. Nearly 90% of its population lived on, or directly from, the land.[6] Nevertheless, the practice of agronomy was not organised along 'rational' lines (that is, farms were not managed to attain *maximum* profits). For example, Cato and Varro were both influenced by non-commercial criteria in their agricultural management. Cato insisted that in addition to profitability, aesthetic factors, such as the beauty and healthfulness of an estate's location, should be significant in determining its value.[7] Similarly, Varro believed that farmers should be motivated by two goals, "'profit' and 'pleasure'; the object of the first is material return, and the second enjoyment".[8] From other sources it is clear that prestige and

---

Alternative interpretations of the Roman economy, of course, abound. For the most integrationist case see A. Carandini, "Il mondo della tarda antichità visto attraverso le merci", *Società romana e impero tardoantico III*, ed. A. Giardina, Rome: Editori Laterza, 1986, pp. 3–19 and "Italian Wine and African Oil: Commerce in a World Empire", *The Birth of Europe. Archaeology and Social Development in the First Millenium AD*, ed. K. Randsborg. Rome: L'Erma di Bretschneider, 1989, pp. 16–24.

[2] Finley, *The Ancient Economy*, and K. Bücher, *Industrial Evolution*, New York: Franklin, 1901.

[3] An economic system in which the demand and supply of products and factors is determined by the unimpeded operation of the price mechanism (it is 'rational' in the sense that capital accounting is crucial to its functioning).

[4] T. Frank, *An Economic History of Rome*, London: Jonathan Cape, 1927. Rostovtzeff, *The Social and Economic History of the Roman Empire*.

[5] For a useful critique of the axioms of both approaches see Scott Meikle, "Modernism, Economics and the Ancient Economy", *PCPhS* 41 (1995) 174–191.

[6] Alföldy, *The Social History of Rome*, p. 98.

[7] Cato, *De Agri Cultura* 1.1–3.

[8] Varro, *Rerum Rusticarum* 1.4. Whilst Varro does go on to say that ". . . the profitable plays a more important role than the pleasurable", it is important to note that his terminology "suggests that the idea of profit in our modern sense cannot be what Varro has in mind. Rather it seems he is indicating a very general notion of usefulness, advantage, or gain" (J. R. Love, *Antiquity and Capitalism*, London: Routledge, 1991, p. 81). Whilst businesslike considerations were present it was not the concept that we would recognise today.

income stability were also important factors in Graeco-Roman agronomy.[9] Although Columella, in his *De Re Rustica*, argued that economic efficiency should be paramount in farming, his views were untypical. Agriculture stayed underdeveloped throughout the history of the Empire,[10] patterns of land use remained largely static,[11] and technology[12] and bookkeeping continued to be, for the most part, crude.

[9] See Dennis P. Kehoe, "Allocation of Risk and Investment on the Estates of Pliny the Younger", *Chiron* 18 (1988) 15–42; "Approaches to Economic Problems in the Letters of Pliny the Younger: The Question of Risk in Agriculture", *Aufstieg und Niedergang der römischen Welt*, vol. 2.33.1, ed. H. Temporini and W. Haase, Berlin: Walter de Gruyter, 1989, pp. 555–590; and *Management and Investment on Estates in Roman Egypt During the Early Empire*, Bonn: Rudolt Habelt, 1992. He makes a strong case for the 'bounded rationality' of agricultural management in the Empire – knowledge available was applied to the full by estate managers and owners to achieve limited, *not* optimal, goals. The Romans were seeking what H. A. Simon terms "satisficing [*sic*] solutions" (*Administrative Behaviour*, third edition, New York: Free Press, 1976). For a more entrepreneurial and acquisitive interpretation of agricultural practice in the Empire see P. W. Neeve, "A Roman Landowner and His Estates: Pliny the Younger", *Athm* 68 (1990) 363–402, and R. H. Mague, "Some Glosses on Ste Croix's 'Greek and Roman Accounting'", *Crux*, ed. P. Cartledge and F. D. Harvey, Exeter: Exeter University Press, 1985, pp. 233–264.

[10] Though it could produce significant quantities of some commodities. T. Frank, for example, estimates that Rome annually consumed 25 million gallons of wine and half a million of olive oil (*An Economic Survey of Ancient Rome*, vol. 5, p. 221).

[11] The creation of the notorious *latifundia* does not indicate the presence of economic rationality in the practice of agriculture. They were not formed in order to obtain economies of scale, but came about largely as a consequence of war and rural depopulation. Indeed, the size and structure of these estates make it highly unlikely that they could have given such benefits. Although it is customary to perceive *latifundia* as large, single, holdings (see, for example, W. E. Heitland, *Agricola: A Study of Agriculture and Rustic Life in the Graeco-Roman World from the Point of View of Labour*, Cambridge: Cambridge University Press, 1927) this picture has been cogently critiqued, and it is likely that the property that constituted a *latifundium* was geographically scattered and not all part of one, vast estate. See Garnsey and Saller, *The Roman Empire*, pp. 66–71 and K. D. White, "*Latifundia*", *BICS* 14 (1967) 62–79. The way the constituent parts of a *latifundium* were managed following their incorporation into the larger estate did not substantially alter as we can see in the famous example from Veteia.

[12] See K. D. White, *Roman Farming*, London: Thames & Hudson, 1970, p. 452. There are, of course, exceptions to this. See, for instance, J. P. Oleson, *Greek and Roman Mechanical Water-Lifting Devices: The History of a Technology*, Toronto: University of Toronto Press, 1984 and A. Wilson, "Water-Power in North Africa and the Development of the Water-Wheel", *JRA* 8 (1995) 499–510. We should also be wary of believing some of the more extreme myths of Roman agricultural incompetence. For example, the assertion that the Romans failed to develop the harness is inaccurate (see Kevin Greene, *The Archaeology of the Roman Economy*, London: Batsford, 1992, pp. 37–39); for a recent restatement of this mistaken opinion, see Hopkins, *Death and Renewal*, p. xiv. For a survey of the current state of the study of Roman technology see K. Greene, "Technology and Innovation in Context", *JRA* 7 (1994) 22–33.

Industry was also largely rudimentary during this period. Contrary to the work of Oertel, Rostovtzeff, and Frank[13] there is no significant evidence of factory production. Their interpretations are based upon misreadings of the sparse, empirical evidence, as Love, for example, notes:

> Unfortunately Frank, like Rostovtzeff, does not recognise that his 'evidence' is perfectly consistent with economic arrangements of a much less sophisticated kind: for example the 40 workers associated with the 'factory' of Cornelius are not known to have been contemporaneous, so it is possible that this 'large enterprise of forty men' was at any one time manned by as little as ten or even fewer workers.[14]

Rather, manufacturing seems to have been entirely characterised by independent artisans running their own, modest, concerns.[15] The proofs provided by Loane of the prevalence of workshop-based industry continue to be convincing despite being formulated over half a century ago.[16] The abundance and prevalence of the remains of *tabernae* throughout the Graeco-Roman world is enough to confirm this picture but other evidence from, for example, tombs, guild records, and street names, also indicates that such a pattern of production held a

---

[13] F. Oertel, "The Economic Unification of the Mediterranean Region: Industry, Trade and Commerce", *The Cambridge Ancient History*, vol. 10, ed. S. Cook et al., Cambridge: Cambridge University Press, 1971, pp. 382–424; Rostovtzeff, *The Social and Economic History of the Roman Empire*; Frank, *An Economic History of Rome*.

[14] Love, *Antiquity and Capitalism*, p. 115.

[15] The 100-plus slaves in the so-called 'shield factory' mentioned in Lysias' *Contra Ertosthenem* 12.8 were, in fact, unlikely to have been employed in the workshop (J. Hasebroek, *Trade and Politics in Ancient Greece*, New York: Biblo & Tannen, 1965, pp. 73–74). The figures given for those employed in two workshops (twenty and thirty-two) run by Demosthenes' father are untypical: "It is probable that these were atypical for Demosthenes speaks of them as though they were unusually large" (Love, *Antiquity and Capitalism*, p. 117). It is unwise to extrapolate from the association of a number of slave names (sometimes between ten and twenty) with one master on production stamps found upon *terra sigillata* (arretine) ware that pottery provides us with clear evidence of large-scale manufacturing industry for our period. The names are unlikely to belong to contemporaries but rather to individuals employed over the course of the existence of one business (Greene, *The Archaeology of the Roman Economy*, p. 161).

Only a small number of mining enterprises (e.g. Pliny, *Naturalis Historiae* 33.73–77) provide exceptions to this rule for our period, although, from the reign of Diocletian onwards, some military equipment became manufactured in large sites which could be accurately termed 'industrial' (Love, *Antiquity and Capitalism*, pp. 122–123).

[16] H. Loane, *Industry and Commerce in the City of Rome* (50 BC–200 AD), Baltimore: Johns Hopkins University Press, 1938, pp. 63–65.

monopoly in our period.[17] Although there is some evidence that manufactured luxury goods were exported over long distances, "the overall structure of the industry was, however, a decentralised one in which small scale industrial units producing exclusively to satisfy local demand predominated".[18] Jongman's recent thorough study of the wealth of information available from Pompeii substantiates this picture.[19]

Trade was also essentially primitive. The transport costs incurred in moving goods by land any significant distance was prohibitively high[20] and so most commerce took the form of sea-borne trade.[21] Although

---

[17] In addition to Loane's proofs it is significant that a wide variety of trades could be practised in even the smallest town. Hopkins, for example, has estimated that there is evidence of 110 being present in the modest town of Korykos, in Asia Minor ("Economic Growth and Towns in Classical Antiquity", *Towns in Societies*, ed. P. Abrams and E. A. Wrigley, Cambridge: Cambridge University Press, 1978, p. 72). If factory production had existed it would be impossible to explain this phenomenon.

[18] Love, *Antiquity and Capitalism*, p. 122.

[19] W. Jongman, *The Economy and Society of Pompeii*, Amsterdam: J. C. Gieben, 1988, especially pp. 155–186, *contra* O. Moeller, *The Wool Trade of Ancient Pompeii*, Leiden: E. J. Brill, 1976.

   The value of manufacturing carried out by cities should not be exaggerated. Cities were essentially centres of consumption and not production. They did not generate significant wealth but were dependent upon the incomes accrued from the land holdings of the élite and from taxation. In essence they remained essentially parasitic. See Finley, *Ancient Economy*, pp. 123–149. For differences between the 'consumer' and 'producer' city see M. Weber, *The City*, New York: The Free Press, 1966, especially pp. 68–70. This interpretation of the economic nature of classical cities has not gone unquestioned (see, for example, Donald Engels, *Roman Corinth: An Alternative Model for the Classical City*, Chicago: Chicago University Press, 1990) but such criticisms have yet to invalidate the model (see Richard Saller's critique of Engel's recent work on Corinth, "Review of Donald Engels, *Roman Corinth: An Alternative Model for the Classical City*", *CPh* 86 (1991) 351–357 See also C. R. Whittaker, "The Consumer City Revisited: The Vicus and the City," *JRA* 3 (1990) 110–118, and "Do Theories of the Ancient City Matter?" *Urban Society in Roman Italy*, ed. T. Cornell and K. Lomas, London: UCL, 1995, pp. 9–26).

[20] Hopkins estimates that it was sixty times more expensive to move commodities by land than by sea ("Introduction", *Trade in the Ancient Economy*, ed. P. Garnsey, K. Hopkins and C. Whittaker, London: Chatto & Windus, 1983, p. xx). See also Richard Duncan-Jones, *The Economy of the Roman Empire*, pp. 367–369, and "The transport of staples in the Roman Empire", *Trade in Staples in Antiquity*, ed. P. Garnsey and C. Whittaker, Budapest: Akadémia Kiadó, 1982, pp. 80–87 for further discussion of the issues involved in making such an estimate.

[21] River transport was also significant in the Empire, though it was of greater importance in the Western provinces. Nevertheless, it was much more costly than that carried out by sea. (For the relative costs of all three modes of transport see Duncan-Jones, *The Economy of the Roman Empire*, pp. 336–339.)

significant quantities of commodities could be moved this way, as we can see from the figures involved in the supply of corn to Rome;[22] this was mostly undertaken by individual ship owners: ". . . in general the small-scale merchant shipper who hawked his wares from port to port was the rule".[23] No wealthy mercantile class seems to have emerged. As Pleket asserts, "In the Roman world an influential ship-owning and trading urban bourgeoisie is unlikely . . . Most epigraphically attested *emporoi* (merchants) are undistinguished".[24]

Although it is difficult to quantify the relevant data with any accuracy, there are no substantial grounds for believing that the economy of the Empire as a whole experienced any significant growth during the first few centuries CE.[25] Although Hopkins has made a concerted effort to demonstrate that there was some increase in the size of the Roman economy in this period,[26] the evidence he adduces in support of his thesis is at best equivocal and on occasion, simply mistaken.[27] For example, the key part he assigns to the increase in the taxation of the

---

[22] Garnsey estimates that the capital had to import approximately 150,000 tonnes of grain a year (mostly by sea) during the late Republican/early Imperial period. ("Grain For Rome", *Trade in the Ancient Economy*, ed. P. Garnsey et al., London: Chatto & Windus, 1983, pp. 118.)

[23] Love, *Antiquity and Capitalism*, p. 156. Of course, there were exceptions. The famous *Isis*, mentioned by Lucian (*Navigium*), was an enormous vessel, with a capacity in excess of 1000 tons (see Lionel Casson, *Ships and Seamanship in the Ancient World*, Princeton: Princeton University Press, 1971, pp. 186–189 for a discussion of the problems in computing the exact figure). However, the *Isis* was very much an exceptional vessel. As Fik Meijer observes, "Lucian's amazement is caused by its uniqueness" (*A History of Seafaring in the Classical Word*, London: Croom Helm, 1986, p. 226). See also L. Casson, "The Isis and Her Voyage", *TAPA* 81 (1950) 43–56.

[24] H. W. Pleket, "Urban Elites and Business", *Trade in the Ancient Economy*, ed. P. Garnsey, K. Hopkins, and C. R. Whittaker, London: Chatto & Windus, 1983, pp. 137 and 139.

Trade carried out with regions beyond the Empire was negligible. See, for example, W. V. Harris, "Between Archaic and Modern: Some Current Problems in the History of the Roman Economy", *The Inscribed Economy: Production and Distribution in the Roman Empire in the Light of Instrumentum Domesticum*, ed. W. V. Harris, Ann Arbor: University of Michigan Press, 1993, p. 13 and L. Casson, *The Periplus Maris Erithraei*, Princeton: Princeton University Press, 1989.

[25] For a recent study which fails to find any evidence of significant growth in the economy see Raymond W. Goldsmith, "An Estimate of the Size and Structure of the Early Roman Empire", *RIW* 30 (1984) 263–288.

[26] Keith Hopkins, "Taxes and trade in the Roman empire (200 BC – AD 400)", *JRS* 70 (1980) 101–125 and "Introduction", *Trade in the Ancient Economy*, ed. P. Garnsey, K. Hopkins, and C. R. Whittaker, London: Chatto & Windus, 1983, pp. i–xxv.

[27] See, for example, Jongman's valuable criticisms in *Economy and Society of Pompeii*, especially pp. 1–28 and 188–191.

provinces in proving the existence of sustained growth is premised upon a faulty interpretation of the notion of balance-of-payments. By asserting that long distance trade *must* have increased over time because, for the necessary balance-of-payments equilibrium to attain, the provincial economies would need to make good the deficit caused by such taxes, he not only confuses an essentially descriptive concept with a prescriptive one but appears unaware of the variety of ways that deficits can be compensated for within an economy: tax flows need not have been matched by increased long distance trade, as he maintains, but could have been accounted for by a number of means such as increased borrowing by provincials, or the transfer of their assets to Roman ownership.[28]

The weakness of the Mediterranean economy we have just sketched is epitomised by the absence of a clear work-ethos necessary, it is often maintained, for the existence of a 'developed' economy. Although a writer such as Cato praised hard work,[29] his praise was not for a powerful, internal, disposition;[30] rather he praised an essentially romantic (and non-motivationary) myth based upon Roman belief in its agrarian, utopian past.

In addition to being 'primitive' the Roman economy can also be described as characterised by what Weber terms *political capitalism*, that is "the exploitation of the opportunities for profit arising from the exercise of political power".[31] In the absence of market mechanisms, wealth could not be accrued by autonomous entrepreneurial activity: profit-making was in the hands of the élite, the aristocracy (the Senators, Equestrians and Decurions) and the pseudo-aristocracy, those arriviste groups such as the *Augustales*,[32] who were created by the aristocracy to

---

[28] Indeed, as Jongman has observed, if we accept a Keynsian model of the economy, and the operation of a downward multiplier, not only would the withdrawal of income from a province lead to a *contraction* of its economy but the contraction would be *greater* than the net value of the taxes extracted (*Economy and Society of Pompeii*, p. 189).

[29] Cato, *De Agri Cultura* 1.1.

[30] As found, for example, in the 'Protestant work ethic'. M. Weber, *The Protestant Ethic and the Spirit of Capitalism*, London: Unwin, 1930.

[31] Love, *Antiquity and Capitalism*, p. 4. See M. Weber, *The Theory of Social and Economic Organisation*, London: The Free Press, 1964, p. 280.

[32] Garnsey, "Grain for Rome", p. 125. His categorisation of the *Augustales* as middle-class is somewhat misleading. For a discussion of the nature of this group see S. E. Ostrow, "The *Augustales* in the Augustan Scheme", *Between Republic and Empire: Interpretations of Augustus and His Principate*, ed. K. A. Raaflaub and M. Toher, Berkeley: University of California Press, 1990, pp. 364–379.

replenish their ranks.[33] In agriculture, for example, any profit from land was controlled almost entirely by the élite.[34] Likewise in commerce, although Senators were legally prohibited from owning ships, and the social élite disparaged involvement in nautical ventures,[35] it was the upper echelons of Roman Imperial society that were the managers of the sea trade: they were both the source of its funding and its chief financial beneficiaries, albeit through the work of dependants and agents acting on their behalf.[36] The often cited example of Trimalchio, the wealthy freedman who made such outstanding profits through trade in Petronius' *Satyricon*[37] does not contradict this picture. *He cannot be taken as typifying a class of bourgeoisie freedmen speculators.* It is often overlooked that he actually *inherited* his initial wealth (by far the most common way of acquiring a fortune).[38] Trimalchio did not gain his riches by

---

[33] The Graeco-Roman aristocracy had to face the phenomenal loss of 75% of its families with each generation that passed (Garnsey and Saller, *The Roman Empire*, p. 125). Such methods as adoption and marriage were therefore employed to create *nouveaux riches*, who, after a period of socialisation, could be accepted into the ranks of the nobility. With freedmen this process would take a generation as the stigma of their enslavement prevented them joining the top three *ordines* personally, though their children would face no such barrier. For a discussion of the benefits of adopting a freedman see J. F. Gardner, "The Adoption of Freedmen", *Phoenix* 43 (1989) 236–257. This "controlled entry of new members into the propertied class was a crucial element in the stability of the Roman system of inequality" (Garnsey and Saller, *The Roman Empire*, p. 125).

[34] Indeed it was their ownership that, Finley believes, led to the arrested development of farming: ". . . large incomes, absenteeism and its accompanying psychology of the life of leisure, of land-ownership as a non-occupation, and, when it was practised, letting or subletting in fragmented tenancies, all combined to block any search for radical improvements" (*The Ancient Economy*, p. 109).

Of course, not all land was directly in their control. In the provinces, the role of the independent, small farmer remained significant until at least the third century and even in Italy, smallholders survived (J. Frayn, *Subsistence Farming in Roman Italy*, London: Centaur Press, 1979). But such farmers had difficult lives. They were open to exploitation, and were politically vulnerable, as we can see in the fate of the market gardener in Apuleius' *Metamorphoses* 9.35.

[35] The *Lex Claudia* of 219/218 BCE prevented senators from owning seagoing vessels (Livy 21.63.3–4). For élite misgivings about involvement in the sea trade see Plutarch's description of Marcus Cato in *Cato Maior* 21.5–6. See John D'Arms, *Commerce and Social Standing in Ancient Rome*, Cambridge MA: Harvard University Press, 1981.

[36] The use of representatives by the élite was common in many areas of business. Most of these *institores* were enslaved. (See Jean-Jacques Aubert, *Business Managers in Ancient Rome: A Social and Economic Study of Institores, 200 BC to AD 250*, Leiden: E. J. Brill, 1994, p. 417.)

[37] Petronius, *Satyricon* 76.

[38] See Firmicus Maternus 3.7.17. M. Hengel, *The Pre-Christian Paul*, London: SCM, 1991, p.15 makes just such a mistake, as do Paul Veyne, "Vie de Trimalchion", *Annales (ESC)* 16 (1961) 213–247 and Chow, *Patronage and Power*, p. 69.

trade but rather by luck. Although not technically a member of the aristocracy he was an example of the *nouveau riche* we have just discussed. His behaviour in engaging in sea commerce is therefore fully in keeping with that typical of this group; he aped the commercial interests and activities of his social superiors, attempting what R. K. Merton terms "anticipatory socialisation".[39]

The profits obtainable from government contracts for tax collection, public building, or supplying the army, were also governed by the élite; they were entirely controlled by the companies of *publicani* who were drawn exclusively from the ranks of the *equites*.[40] The two other major areas of business in the economy, moneylending[41] and the renting of property,[42] also remained virtually entirely the preserve of the élite.

The fact that the economy of the Graeco-Roman world was 'primitive' and governed by *political capitalism* can allow us to make some statements about the patterns of wealth distribution operative within it. There was no mid-range economic group within the Empire of any importance,[43] the structure of the economy, as in all pre-industrial societies, simply did not allow it;[44] in the words of Alföldy, "a . . .

[39] *Social Theory and Social Structure*, London: The Free Press, 1957, p. 265.

[40] So called because they dealt with public property. Ulpian, *Digest* 39.4.1.1. For the development of the *publicani* see E. Badian, *Publicans and Sinners: Private Enterprise in the Service of the Roman Republic*, Oxford: Basil Blackwell, 1972.

[41] Modern banking did not exist in the Empire. As Duncan-Jones asserts, "No effective credit system had evolved, and banks were rarely more than small-scale and isolated institutions" (*The Economy of the Roman Empire*, p. 2). Money lending, for consumption purposes, largely between wealthy individuals, was the norm (Finley, *The Ancient Economy*, p. 142) and as such was ". . . a regular part of the income of the upper classes" (p. 198). See Tacitus, *Annales* 6.16–17; Cassius Dio 58.21.1–5; Seneca, *Epistulae* 17.10; Pliny, *Epistulae* 3.19.8; Petronius, *Satyricon* 53.3. The rudimentary quality of Graeco-Roman banking is discussed in C. Howgego, "The Supply and Use of Money in the Roman World 200 BC to AD 300", *JRS* 82 (1992) 1–31. See also his *Ancient History From Coins*, p. 22.

[42] See P. Garnsey, "Urban Property Investment", *Studies in Roman Property*, ed. M. I. Finley, Cambridge: Cambridge University Press, 1976, pp. 123–132.

[43] Some of those who furnished "military, administrative, and ideological support" (K. Kautsky, *Aristocratic Empires*, p. 328) to the élite did constitute a group that occupied the income range between the aristocrats and the plebs; however, numerically they are insignificant in our study. The army, for example, amounted to little more than 300,000 men (Garnsey and Saller, *The Roman Empire*, p. 88) for the entire Empire of 54 million (Hopkins, "Taxes and Trade", pp. 118f.) and most of these were posted at its borders and so were irrelevant to the world of the Pauline mission. Administrators who were not aristocrats were also extremely thin on the ground: according to Hopkins proportionally twenty times more bureaucrats were employed in the Chinese Empire (*Death and Renewal*, Cambridge: Cambridge University Press, 1983, p. 186).

[44] P. Crone, *Pre-Industrial Societies*, Oxford: Basil Blackwell, 1989, p. 19.

corollary of the nature of the economy was that a true middle order could not evolve for it would have required its own economic function":[45] the commercial and industrial sectors remained too rudimentary for it to be otherwise. Rather, society was split into two distinct groups, with a wide gulf separating them. The Graeco-Romans' own perceptions of their world shows a consciousness of this powerful dichotomy. We can observe it in the persistent theme of antagonism between the rich and poor found throughout their literature,[46] and in the use of the terms *honestiores* and *humiliores* which became so significant by the second century CE and which functioned to clearly label the two groups.[47] The distribution of what little income was available in the Mediterranean world[48] was entirely dependent upon political power: those devoid of political power, the non-élite, over 99% of the Empire's population,[49] could expect little more from life than abject poverty.[50]

[45] Alföldy, *The Social History of Rome*, p. 99. See also Geza Alföldy, "Römisches Staats- und Gesellschaftsdenken Bei Seuton", *AncSoc* 12 (1981) 349-385. Nevertheless, we must bear in mind that Alföldy's schema has some drawbacks. As H. Turanø observes, "Alföldy allows himself to be bound to a surprising extent by the élite's own self-perception" ("Roman Social Structure: Different Approaches for Different Purposes", *Studies in History and Numismatics*, ed. Rudi Thomsen et al., Aarhus: Aarhus University Press, 1988, p. 119). By presuming the validity of Alföldy I do not wish to deny the variety of divisions that can be made amongst the non-élite.

[46] P. Oxy. 2554; Cicero, *De Officiis* 2.24.85; Lucian, *Gallus* 22, *Saturnalia* 31–39; *Navigium* 27; Plutarch, *Moralia* 822; Herodian 7.3.5 provide samples of this persistent motif. See also Alföldy's comments on social categorisation in the work of Aelius Aristides (*The Social History of Rome*, p. 196.)

[47] These categories cut across previous interpretations of social divisions in Graeco-Roman society. The *humiliores* could include citizens and the free born as well as the more traditionally socially stigmatised slaves and freedmen. See Garnsey, *Social Status and Legal Privilege*, pp. 221–233.

[48] "All pre-industrial societies were dominated by scarcity" (Crone, *Pre-Industrial Societies*, p. 14).

[49] Alföldy estimates that there were approximately 600 senators, 20,000 equestrians, and 100–150,000 decurions in the Empire (*The Social History of Rome*, p. 127). In addition to these there were also *Augustales* and comparable individuals who we can term 'proto' or 'pseudo' élite who, whilst not technically full members of the aristocracy, were on their way to becoming such. Although we have no records for the size of this additional group it seems fair to assume that it was equal to that of the Decurion ordo. If this was the case then the élite totalled approximately 300,000 or so. In an empire of 54 million (Hopkins, "Taxes and Trade", pp. 118f.) it is therefore safe to say that over 99% of the population can be classified as non-élite.

R. Rohrbaugh's estimate of the élite constituting 5–10% of the population is a gross overestimate. See "The Pre-Industrial City in Luke Acts: Urban Social Relations", *The Social World of Luke Acts: Models for Interpretation*, ed. J. H. Neyrey, Peabody, MA: Hendrickson, 1991, p. 133.

Perhaps claiming that such a high percentage of the inhabitants of the Empire lived at, or close to, subsistence level, is hard to accept, especially given the "grandeur that was Rome". But evidence from the capital itself indicates that this was the case. Rome provides us with a rare piece of quantitative evidence which confirms the reality of mass *urban* destitution: the *frumentatio* (the grain dole). Throughout the Principate it was considered expedient to maintain a free monthly distribution of grain to 150,000 resident, adult, male, citizens (about one fifth of the population of the city).[51] It was a provision born of necessity and maintained for the same reason. The handing out of a staple, in quantities directly related to consumption, makes any other interpretation of the dole seem rather implausible.[52]

Perhaps a fifth of the population does not sound significant, especially when we have been describing almost the entire urban non-élite as indigent. However, it should be realised that the fifth who received these regular supplements to their income were the most socially advantaged, and therefore the most potentially economically successful of Rome's population (outside of the élite).[53] Women, children, slaves, non-

---

[50] The non-élite could acquire nothing more than that which they earned by their own labours. There were no mechanisms whereby élite wealth could 'trickle down' in the Graeco-Roman economy. The patron-client arrangement did little more than circulate income amongst the affluent (there is sparse evidence of it functioning below the 'sub-élite' level (Garnsey, "Mass Diet", p. 81)) and charity did much the same: its major recipients were members of the élite. See Hands, *Charities*, pp. 91ff. and R. Duncan-Jones, "An Epigraphic Survey of Costs in Roman Italy", *PBSR* (1965) 189–206 and "Wealth and Munificence in Roman Africa", *PBSR* (1963) 160–177.

[51] Garnsey, "Mass Diet", p. 70. This had begun under the tribunate of Gaius Gracchus in 123 BCE as a distribution of subsidised grain. It became free in 58 BCE under P. Clodius.

[52] It was certainly not an attempt to give the populace a share in the spoils of Empire, for, as Hands has observed, "The days in which the common people had played any significant part in legislation or elections had long since passed" (*Charities*, p. 111).

The fact that some of the rich undoubtedly received it (*Digest* 32.35) does not contradict this. Rome did not possess the apparatus of a sophisticated welfare state and was incapable of distinguishing between its populace in terms of private income (although the most wealthy, the Senators, were prohibited from collecting the *frumentatio*).

[53] See Catherine Virlouvet, "La plèbe Frumentaire à l'époque d'Auguste", *Nourrir la Plèbe*, ed. A. Giovannini, Basel: Friedrich Reinhardt, 1991, pp. 43–65.

We should not, however, overestimate the extent of the privilege. Although the *plebs frumentaria* were a special group, set apart from the *plebs urbana* (as we can see from literary sources such as Fronto, *Epistulae* 1.294 and also from their tombstones which proudly recorded their status (Veyne, *Bread and Circuses*, p. 144)) the dole did not allow them to escape a subsistence existence. According to the calculations of Garnsey the *frumentatio* did provide a guarantee against starvation for the recipient and one

citizens, and those citizens only recently domiciled[54] did not receive the grain, and these groups (at the risk of generalisation) were already disadvantaged in the struggle for survival. Despite the city of Rome being the centre of the Empire and the wealthiest city in antiquity,[55] "Most Romans, most of the 750,000[56]–1,000,000[57] residents of the city, were poor."[58]

The *Scriptores Historiae Augustae* corroborates the picture we gain from the *frumentatio*. After describing the dramatic and impressive success of Aurelian in restoring the Empire, the author has the Emperor declare that, amongst all the benefits his reign has conferred upon his people, he considers the feeding of the population of Rome its crowning achievement: "For nothing can be more joyous than the Roman people fed."[59]

If mass urban destitution was the case for Rome we can, with some certainty, assume a similar situation in other Graeco-Roman πόλεις. Indeed, given Rome's situation as the chief focus of the wealth of the Empire it would be fair to assume that destitution was worse elsewhere.[60] Other urban centres appear to have been incapable of financially

---

dependent, but a diet based solely on the dole would have led to serious deficiencies and ultimately death ("Mass Diet", p. 78). As most adult, male, citizens would have had more than one dependent, the situation would have been precarious: ". . . the claims of conservative politicians such as Cicero and Augustus (Cicero, *Pro Sestio* 103 and Suetonius, *Augustus* 40) that the grain dole turned the plebs into fainéants, might have been good propaganda but did not reflect the realities of life in Rome" ("Mass Diet", p. 81). "No man could live on the dole alone . . . much less depend upon it to feed his family, and rent and clothing required money" (T. Africa, "Urban Violence in Imperial Rome", *JIH* 2 (1971), p. 6).

54 A number of citizens who had been domiciled for some time were also excluded by the *numerus clausus* from the list. Despite Juvenal's infamous remarks about "*panem et circenses*" (*Saturae* 10.81), "a substantial proportion of the really poor saw nothing of the blandishments which supposedly corrupted the Roman plebs" (Whittaker, "Studying The Poor", p. 1).

55 Revelation 17 and 18; *Sibylline Oracles* 3.350–380.

56 P. Brunt, *Italian Manpower*, Oxford: Clarendon Press, 1971, p. 383.

57 Hopkins, *Conquerors and Slaves*, p. 98.

58 Garnsey, "Mass Diet", p. 67.

59 *SHA* 47.4. As Reekman has observed, throughout the *SHA* the concept of "prosperity", is understood as "nothing but the satisfaction of fundamental needs" ("Prosperity and Security in the Historia Augusta", *AncSoc* 10 (1979), p. 240).

60 The image of Rome was crucial to the hegemony of the Empire. It was a powerful articulation of the *maiestas imperii* (Vitruvius, *De Architectura* 1. *preaf.* 1, 2) designed to convince its subject peoples of the power and benefits of the rule of the Principate. For the symbolic significance of Rome see M. Griffin, "Urbs Roma, Plebs and Princeps", (*Images of Empire*, ed. L. Alexander, Sheffield: JSOT, 1991, p. 43).

sustaining comparable alimentary schemes, compounding the deprivation of their various populations.[61] A passage from Apuleius' *Metamorphoses* appears to confirm the difficult situation that the 'common people' (*vulgus ignobile*) of a typical small town faced. In describing the fate of some emaciated, diseased bears turned loose by their owner, Apuleius wrote:

> You could see the animal wreckage of their moribund carcasses lying scattered in most of the streets. Then the common people, who were forced by ignorant poverty with no taste in their choice of food to seek the filthiest supplements and free meals for their shrunken bellies, came running up to these banquets lying strewn about.[62]

3.2 The lives of the *plebs urbana*: toil and subsistence

Having briefly seen something of the wider economic structures within which the Pauline communities were located, and recognised the poverty of most of the inhabitants of the Mediterranean world, let us now focus more closely on the economic lives of the *plebs urbana* as they subsisted within this system. What were their experiences of employment? Of food, clothing and shelter? By asking such questions we should be able to make our generalisation about widescale impoverishment both more tangible and also somewhat more plausible.

Employment

Most of the urban population of the Empire was involved in various manufacturing trades or service industries. Some indication of the variety of occupations available in Graeco-Roman cities can be seen in Diocletian's Price Edict of 301 which, amongst other things, set maximum wages for a plethora of jobs. A provision in the *Codex Theodosianus* which exempted certain artisans from public service is also of value.[63] Whether a person was a slave, a freedperson, or free-

---

[61] For the uniqueness of the *frumentatio* see W. Jongman and R. Dekker, "Public Intervention in the Food Supply in Pre-Industrial Europe", *Bad Year Economics: Cultural Responses to Risk and Uncertainty*, ed. P. Halstead and J. O'Shea, Cambridge: Cambridge University Press, 1989, p. 119.

[62] Apuleius, *Metamorphoses* 4.14. For a text which gives a similar impression see Cassius Dio 86.

[63] *Codex Theodosianus* 13.4.2. See also Maxey's thorough (though dated) study of inscriptional evidence, *Occupations of the Lower Classes in Roman Society*, and S. Treggiari, "Urban Labour In Rome: Merecenarii and Tabernarii", *Non-Slave Labour in the Graeco-Roman World*, ed. P. Garnsey, Cambridge: Cambridge Philological Society, especially

born, made little difference in the type of work they engaged in as, apart from certain domestic positions and jobs in mining, which were almost entirely filled by slaves, all three categories of person were employed in the same non-élite occupations.[64] (Though, of course, it is important to recognise that a slave's standard of living was less directly related to their employment, and their working conditions were often rather more basic.)[65]

The skilled artisans were the most wealthy group amongst the *plebs urbana*, yet their trades seem to have only allowed them to live at, or slightly above, subsistence level. In Lucian's *Gallus*, for example, the

---

pp. 61–64 (she finds confirmation of the existence of over 160 non-élite jobs in Rome alone). Plautus, *Aulularia* 505–522 also gives some insight into the diversity of employment.

[64] ". . . in the world of the Greek city-states, as in Italy under both the Republic and the Empire, there were always free men working alongside the slaves, both in the fields and in the workshops in the towns" (Claude Mossé, *The Ancient World of Work*, London: Chatto & Windus, 1969, p. 112). There is no reason for assuming that this pattern of employment did not exist throughout the Empire.

[65] Despite Columella's assertion that urban slaves had an easy life (*De Re Rustica* 1.8.1ff.) the great majority experienced extreme hardship. Certainly, some city slaves did avoid the appalling deprivation and degradation of the mines (Diodorus Siculus 3.12.2–3.13.3) and the agricultural chain gangs (Columella, *De Re Rustica* 1.8.16.). A few even enjoyed some kind of home-life as a result of being employed in wealthy households (Bradley, *Slaves and Masters*, p. 75 and M. B. Flory, "Family in Familia: Kinship and Community in Slavery", *AJAH* 3 (1978) 78–95) but most urban slaves would not have worked in such a setting and so we should not assume their situation to have been significantly easier than their rural counterparts (*contra* Dale B. Martin in *Slavery as Salvation*, New Haven: Yale University Press, 1990, pp. 2–11). The horrendous description of slaves in a bakery in a small hill-town given in Apuleius' *Metamorphoses* (9.12) is a particularly sobering reminder of this:

> The whole surface of their skin was painted with livid welts. Their stripped backs were merely shadowed, not covered, by the tattered patchwork they wore: some had thrown on a tiny cloth that just covered their loins, but all were clad in such a way that you discern them clearly through their rags. Their foreheads were branded, their heads half shaved and their feet chained. They were hideously sallow too, and their eyelids were eaten away by the smoky darkness of scorching murk until they were quite weak sighted; like boxers who fight sprinkled with dust, they were dirty, whitewashed with flowery ash.

Such a picture would have been repeated in city bakeries throughout the Empire. Even in the urban households where Columella believed slaves worked in relative comfort, the lot of the slave could be equally atrocious. Many had dangerous and unpleasant jobs in the houses. For example, a slave could be employed as an *ostiarius*, chained to the door post, with no possessions except the chain that bound him (Mima Maxey, *Occupations of the Lower Classes in Roman Society*, Chicago: Chicago University Press, 1938, p.44).

cobbler Micyllus faces a daily struggle to earn enough to avoid starvation, as we can see from the cock's opening speech upon waking the cobbler up early one morning:

I thought I could do you a favour by cheating the night as much as I could so that you might make use of the morning hours and finish the greater part of your work early; you see if you get a single sandal done before the sun rises you will be much ahead toward earning your daily bread. But if you had rather sleep, I'll keep quiet for you and will be more mute than a fish. Take care, however, that you don't dream you are rich and then starve when you wake up.[66]

A similar picture of his hard life appears in Lucian's *Cataplus*. In this work the same Micyllus tells how he was only too ready to lay down his tools and die when the time came,[67] and sarcastically mourns the things he has lost in death:

Alas my scraps of leather ! Alas my old shoes ! Alackaday, my rotten sandals! Unlucky man that I am, never again will I go hungry from morning to night or wander about in winter barefooted and half-naked, with my teeth clattering from cold.[68]

The situation of Philinus the smith is much the same. Although while alive he was able to support himself, his wife, and his daughter,[69] he did not earn enough to leave any savings behind after his death. Within a few months his widow is forced to make their daughter into a prostitute in order to procure enough money to eat.[70]

Lucian also gives an insight into the subsistence lifestyle of artisans when he attacks the false philosophers in *Fugitivi*. He describes the trades of the cobblers, builders, fullers, and carders as, "laborious and barely able to supply them with just enough".[71]

Evidence of skilled workers lifting themselves out of their subsistence existence is scant. Contrary to Dio Chrysostom's optimistic opinion,

---

[66] Lucian, *Gallus* 1.
[67] Lucian, *Cataplus* 15.
[68] Lucian, *Cataplus* 20.
[69] Lucian, *Dialogi Meretricii* 6.293.
[70] Not an uncommon situation as BGU 1024.7 indicates. Cf. also *Digest*, 23.2.43.5; Plautus, *Cistellaria* 38–45; and Terence, *Eunuchus* 934–940.
[71] Lucian, *Fugitivi* 12–13. Such experiences helped create in first-century artisans a way of viewing the world and themselves at fascinating variance with the assumptions of contemporary Western culture, as an example from Artemidorus illustrates: for a man to dream of having sex with his mother was interpreted as auspicious for business if he happened to be a craftsman or labourer (*Oneirocritica* 1.79).

thrift and hard work did not lead to a life of affluence.[72] Those that
escaped poverty did so as a result of élite largesse, inheritance or
marriage. Micyllus' rich neighbour Simon, for instance, acquired his
wealth by inheritance,[73] and the moneyed barber who was a victim of
Juvenal's vitriol[74] received his wealth from a rich admirer.[75] The
experience of the carpenter in Artemidorus' *Oneirocritica*, who was
forced to flee his country to avoid debts, was much more common.[76]
The regular use of *defixiones* by craftsmen and women in order to achieve
some slight advantage over their competition is illustrative of this
difficult and desperate context.[77] The lives of the artisans were
characterised by extreme privation.

   The large numbers of semi-skilled and unskilled workers present in
the Graeco-Roman cities faced an even more difficult situation. These
people filled the urban settlements, though their existence has traditionally been overlooked. They formed a large pool of casual labour and
were employed in a variety of menial jobs necessary for the day to day
functioning of an ancient town.[78] As Sjoberg has observed in his
description of pre-industrial urban life: "Numerous tasks that in the
highly industrialised environment are accomplished by machines are

---

[72] Dio Chrysostom, *Orationes* 7.109. Some could manage limited relative success. For
   example, Tryphon the weaver accrued enough wealth to buy a loom (P. Oxy. 2.264)
   and a part of a house (P. Oxy. 1.99). However, we cannot be certain that he gained his
   money entirely from weaving (*contra* Ronald Hock, *The Social Context of Paul's Ministry:
   Tentmaking and Apostleship*, Philadelphia: Fortress, 1980, p. 84 and J. D. Crossan, *The
   Historical Jesus: The Life of a Mediterranean Jewish Peasant*. Edinburgh: T. & T. Clark,
   1991, pp. 19–30).

[73] Lucian, *Gallus* 14.

[74] Juvenal, *Saturae* 1.25, 10.225–226.

[75] Courtney believes that the barber mentioned by Juvenal was likely to have been
   Cinnamus who, according to Martial, became an equestrian as the result of patronage
   by a rich woman (*Satires*, p. 90; Martial, *Epigrammata* 7.64).
       The account of the wealthy freedman artisan Gaius Pompeius Diogenes which is
   found in Petronius' *Satyricon* (38) does not contradict this picture: the passage implies
   that he also received his money suddenly – if not from a legacy then from a substantial
   investment by his master.
       For the common fantasy of escaping poverty by marriage see Gager, *Curse Tablets*, p.
   106.

[76] Artemidorus, *Oneirocritica* 4.1.

[77] Gager, *Curse Tablets*, pp. 151–174.

[78] P. A. Brunt, "The Roman Mob", *PP* 35 (1966), p. 17. *Contra* H. W. Pleket, "Labour
   and Unemployment in the Roman Empire: Some Preliminary Remarks", *Soziale
   Randgruppen und Außenseiter im Altertum*, ed. I. Weiler, Graz: Leykam, 1988, p. 268.
   Though it should be observed that there seems to have been a decline in the *plebs
   ingenua* during our period (see Parkin, *Demography*, p. 121).

here fulfilled by humans: the city teems with servants, burden bearers, messengers, animal drivers and others."[79] Diocletian's edict confirms this picture for antiquity. Amongst the occupations we find listed in the edict are those of mule drivers, water carriers, and sewer cleaners; inscriptions record the existence of such occupations as porters and movers.[80] It is likely that most who were lucky enough to find work found it in the building trade. In pre-industrial cities this was a significant source of employment[81] and the Graeco-Roman world was no exception. This is evident from Vespasian's famous remark to a mechanical engineer who promised to transport some heavy columns to the Capitol at small expense, by using a new invention. After giving him a reward he made it clear that it was of no use to him, saying, "You must let me feed my poor *plebs*."[82] Josephus' account of the completion of Herod's rebuilding of the Temple also indicates something of the significance of large scale construction projects for urban employment: it led to 18,000 men being made unemployed in Jerusalem and forced Herod to concoct another project almost immediately (they were put to work paving the city).[83]

The life of such unskilled workers was precarious,[84] in many ways analogous to the experience of the destitute agricultural day labourers

---

[79] G. Sjoberg, *The Pre-Industrial City*, Glencoe: The Free Press, 1960, p. 122.

[80] See Maxey, *Occupations of the Lower Classes in Roman Society*, pp. 67–76 for a detailed discussion of the categories of jobs involved in transportation evidenced from inscriptions. See also Firmicus Maternus, 4.14.2. Petronius, *Satyricon* 117.11–12. See J. Shelton, *As the Romans Did: A Sourcebook in Roman Social History*, Oxford: Oxford University Press, 1988, p. 133.

[81] G. Rudé has estimated that a third of all Parisian wage-earners in pre-industrial, eighteenth-century France were engaged in the building trade. See *The Crowd in the French Revolution*, Oxford: Clarendon Press, 1959, p. 19.

[82] Suetonius, *Vespasian* 18. Despite the objections of Casson ("Unemployment, Building and Suetonius", *BASP* 15 (1978) 43–51) the traditional reading of this text remains the most probable.

[83] Josephus, *Antiquitates Judaicae* 20.219–222. Of course, concern for the fate of wage labourers was not always something shown by governing authorities. In the first century CE, for example, we have evidence of a Roman governor sacking such people and replacing them with public slaves (see Pleket, "Labour and Unemployment", p. 271).

[84] ". . . there is no evidence at all for *regular* hired labour of any kind at Rome . . . We are obliged, therefore to assume the existence of a great deal of *short-term* hiring" (de Ste Croix, *Class Struggle*, pp. 192–193). We certainly should not presume from Vespasian's words and Herod's actions that public works programmes, designed to keep the semi-skilled and unskilled permanently employed, were operative (in this L. Casson is correct, "Unemployment, Building and Suetonius", p. 45). It is important to emphasise that there was no coherent system of public works in the Empire (*contra* Francois Houtart, *Religion et Mode du Production Précapitalistes*, Bruxelles: Université de Bruxelles, 1980, p. 223).

who are familiar figures in the gospels.[85] The Oxyrhynchus papyri, for example, record how a person without a trade (ἄτεχνος) had to flee the town, driven out by his desperate poverty,[86] and the *Didache* assumes that a person similarly unqualified was incapable of providing for himself and would have to rely upon the church for survival.[87]

All free workers, skilled or unskilled, lived in constant fear of unemployment and its consequences.[88] Worry about such an eventuality is prevalent in Artemidorus.[89] If a person was 'lucky', unemployment would eventually lead, via debt,[90] to slavery;[91] if they were unlucky they would become a beggar or starve. Beggars filled the cities of the Mediterranean world[92] and loathing for them filled their

---

Indeed, the situation of such hired labour was even worse than that of slaves as they did not have access to the limited material security slavery afforded (K. R. Bradley, *Slavery and Sociey at Rome*, Cambridge: Cambridge University Press, 1995, p. 92).

[85] Matt. 20:1–16. See L. Schottroff, "Human Solidarity and the Goodness of God: The Parable of the Workers in the Vineyard", *God of the Lowly*, ed. W. Schottroff and W. Stegemann, Maryknoll: Orbis, 1984, pp. 129–147, especially pp. 129–135, for material on the conditions these workers endured. Indeed, many of the *plebs urbana* actually worked on the land, when they could, providing a necessary source of labour for farmers (see Duncan-Jones, *The Economy of the Roman Empire*, p. 260 and P. Garnsey, "Non-slave labour in the Roman world", *Non-Slave Labour in the Graeco-Roman World*, ed. P. Garnsey, Cambridge: Cambridge Philological Society, 1980, pp. 42–43).

[86] P. Oxy. 2.251.

[87] *Didache* 12.4. Two other texts are illustrative of the difficulties in earning a living encountered by those who were not established in a trade: Dio Chrysostom mentions a couple of herdsmen who fled to a city in winter looking for work, but could not find any (*Orationes* 7.11–20), and in Lucian's *Dialogi Meretricii* the widow Crobyle was reduced to a state of starvation after failing to make a success of weaving, an occupation she was forced to take up after the death of her husband Philinus (6. 293).

[88] Underemployment was also an important problem (see L. Casson, *Ancient Trade and Society*, Detroit: Wayne State University Press, 1984, pp. 124–125).

[89] Artemidorus, *Oneirocritica* 1.76, 2.3, 2.22. See also Pomeroy, "Status and Status Concern," p. 63.

[90] For evidence of the harsh experience of debt amongst the non-élite see Artemidorus, *Oneirocritica* 3.41 and Matt. 18:23–34.

[91] Self-sale was common in the Empire as de Ste Croix has argued. This was often motivated by the basic need for an individual to acquire money so that he/she and her/his dependants could eat. 1 Clem. 55.2 provides first-century evidence of this phenomenon (de Ste Croix, *Class Struggle*, p. 170). De Ste Croix has also persuasively argued that debt bondage, which was in many ways indistinguishable from slavery, was also rife during this period (*ibid.*, pp. 165–169). It probably lies behind the events described in Matt. 18:23–34; Matt. 5:25–26; Luke 12:58–59.

[92] Juvenal, *Saturae* 4.116, 5.8; Seneca, *Controversiae* 10.4. In combination with petty criminals and vagrants, beggars probably formed a large 'underclass' in Graeco-Roman cities. This is a common feature of pre-industrial societies: ". . . no less than 10% of the population of seventeenth-century France . . . is believed to have fallen into this category" (Crone, *Pre-Industrial Societies*, p. 19).

inhabitants.[93] To a population in which nearly all lived only a little above subsistence level the beggar embodied their profoundest fears. It is no surprise, therefore, that to dream of one was appallingly inauspicious: even to dream of giving one alms was to have a premonition of personal disaster.[94]

Even those close to the élite and in their direct, personal, employ had little security and would find it hard to escape the fate of the old, broken philosopher in Lucian's *De Mercede Conductis*:

> . . . after garnering all that was most profitable in you, after consuming the most fruitful years of your life and the greatest vigour of your body, after reducing you to a thing of rags and tatters, he (the master) is looking about for a rubbish heap on which to cast you aside unceremoniously, and for another man to engage who can stand the work.[95]

The Graeco-Roman world of work was hard and mercurial for all but those cushioned by political privilege.

Food

Sustenance, the most important aspect of subsistence, remained a continuous cause of concern for most of the *plebs urbana*, whatever their occupation, as we have already observed. It was only obtained, for most, under great duress. Micyllus worked all day, every day, solely to earn his daily meal[96] and even then, in the *Cataplus*, he complains that hunger was his usual experience.[97] Philinus' widow turned her daughter into a prostitute specifically in order to get food.[98] The

---

[93] Artemidorus, *Oneirocritica* 3.53. There were some exceptions, such as Firmicus Maternus (MacMullen, "Social History," p. 115 – before his conversion to Christianity) and, of course, most notably, Jews.

[94] ". . . if beggars receive a coin, it portends great harm and danger and frequently even death either for the man who gives it to them or for one of his associates" (Artemidorus, *Oneirocritica* 3.53).

[95] Lucian, *De Mercede Conductis* 39. This work also gives an insight into the poor remuneration a person could expect when actually employed by a wealthy house. Physical proximity to riches did not necessarily lead to a comfortable life: ". . . there is nothing put by, no surplus to save: on the contrary, what is given, even if it is given, even if payment is received in full, is all spent to the last copper without satisfying their need . . . if a man who is always poor and needy and on an allowance thinks that thereby he has escaped poverty, I do not know how one can avoid thinking that such a man deludes himself" (*De Mercede Conductis* 5).

[96] Lucian, *Gallus* 1.22.

[97] Lucian, *Cataplus* 20.

[98] Lucian, *Dialogi Meretricii* 6.293.

philosopher of Lucian's *De Mercede Conductis*,[99] and the protagonist of Juvenal's fifth satire,[100] endured abuse and ridicule to obtain the meal they so needed. People commonly sold themselves and their families into servitude to avoid starvation.[101] Hunger was the continuous complaint of the *plebs urbana*, as we can see in Lucian's *Saturnalia*.[102] The poor's obsession with it was, tellingly, a common theme in Plautus' comedies.[103]

For the non-élite in particular, with their limited purchasing power, the difficulties in getting enough to eat were compounded by the periodical interruptions of the grain supply that characterised urban life throughout the Empire.[104] The quality of what they managed to obtain was also questionable. In the absence of any real grasp of preservation techniques or hygiene, much food supplied to the inhabitants of the cities of the Empire was contaminated[105] and that accessible to the poor, particularly so: for example, the most widely available fish in Rome was a sickly looking specimen caught in the Tiber, a river which was also home to the untreated sewage of the city's teeming population of approximately a million people.[106]

Cicero's depiction of the non-élite as *misera ac ieiuna* (wretched and starveling) appears to be an accurate, if disdainful, description of their unenviable position.[107]

Clothing

Clothing is an expensive item in pre-industrial economies and the first-century world was no exception to this rule. The stripping of the victim

---

[99] Lucian, *De Mercede Conductis* 5.

[100] Juvenal, *Saturae* 5.1–11, 166–173.

[101] De Ste Croix, *Class Struggle*, p. 573.

[102] Lucian, *Saturnalia* 31.

[103] See the opening speeches of Plautus' characters Gelasimus (*Stichus* 155–170) and Peniculus (*Menaechmi* 77–109).

[104] "Food crises were endemic in the Mediterranean region" (Garnsey and Saller, *The Roman Empire*, p. 100).

[105] This is discernible from literary and archaeological sources: stomach-ache, for example, is by far the most common complaint found in Pliny's *Naturalis Historiae*, whilst it is clear from analysis of Roman sewage that intestinal parasites were widespread (see R. Jackson, *Doctors and Diseases in the Roman Empire*, London: British Museum Press, 1988, pp. 37–38).

[106] Vivian Nutton, "Galen and the Traveller's Fare", *Food in Antiquity*, ed. J. Wilkins, D. Harvey and M. Dobson, Exeter: Exeter University Press, 1995, pp. 359–369.

[107] Cicero, *Epistulae ad Atticum* 1.16.11. See also Dio Chrysostom, *Orationes* 46.11.

in the Good Samaritan provides an indication of its high cost,[108] as does the logion recorded in Matt. 5:40/Luke 6:29 (καὶ τῷ θέλοντί σοι κριθῆναί καὶ τὸν χιτῶνά σου λαβεῖν, ἄφες αὐτῷ καὶ τὸ ἱμάτιον·), and the division of Jesus' clothes amongst the soldiers at the crucifixion in all four accounts of the passion.[109] The existence of numerous second-hand clothes markets throughout the Empire gives us another indication of its relative expense.[110] The importance given to clothing as a means of articulating socio-economic distinctions in antiquity also suggests that it necessitated significant financial outlay.[111]

It is not surprising, therefore, that the expense of clothing was a constant source of anguish for the poor, who tried to get as much as possible out of their vestments by patching[112] and sharing[113] what little they could afford. The experience of having inadequate clothing seems to have been common: Micyllus complains of being "barefoot and half naked" in Lucian's *Cataplus*,[114] and the poor in his *Saturnalia* voice a similar grievance.[115] Lazarus, likewise had little in the way of clothes (as

---

[108] Luke 10:30–37.

[109] Matt. 27:35, Mark 15:24, Luke 23:34, John 19:23–25. For a very informative and thorough discussion of the question of clothing and poverty in Roman Palestine see Hamel, *Poverty and Charity*, pp. 57–93. Garments were more than just clothing, they also had to function as bedding. This can be seen in the parable in Luke 11:5–8. The man fears that he will disturb his children, not just because they are all in the same bed, but because, in order to answer the door properly dressed, he would have to take the bedding (his cloak) with him (*ibid.*, p. 71).

[110] See J. Reynolds and R. Tannenbaum, *Jews and Godfearers at Aphrodisias*, Cambridge: Cambridge University Press, 1987, pp. 117–118. See also Cato, *De Agri Cultura* 35.

[111] See, for example, Luke 16:19–31; Matt. 11:8; Mark 12:38; Luke 20:45; Matt. 23:5. Lucian, *Saturnalia*, 35. Minucius Felix, *Octavius* 8.4. Indeed, to be without clothes, to be naked, was to be outside society: to be insane. In the Lukan version of the Gerasene demoniac the possessed man was naked (8:27), once cured, however, he is described as "clothed and in his right mind" (8:35). His garb signifies and emphasises his complete re-entry into society and the recovery of his sanity. ('Madness' and nudity are also seen as related in Epiphanius, *Panarion* 30.10.3.)

It should be noted that nudity was not only problematic for Jews, as is often observed, but was also equally shameful for Graeco-Romans. Despite the prevalence of the baths and gymnasiums throughout the Hellenistic world, and the love of the nude in its art, we would be mistaken to assume, as for example M. Miles does (*Carnal Knowing: Female Nakedness and Religious Meaning in The Christian West*, Boston: Beacon Press, 1989, pp. 26–29) that it was a familiar and accepted feature of everyday Graeco-Roman culture: it was firmly restricted to socially appropriate contexts (as it is today). See, for example, *Vita Aesopi* 77a.

[112] Matt. 9:16; Mark 2:21; Luke 5:36; *m. Kilaim* 9; Juvenal, *Saturae* 3.151.

[113] R. Judah b. Ilai (mid-second century CE) shared a cloak with his wife (*b. Nedarim* 49b), and six of his students apparently used the same mantle in rotation (*b. Sanhedrin* 20a).

[114] Lucian, *Cataplus* 20.

[115] Lucian, *Saturnalia* 31.

seems to be indicated by the οἱ κύνες ἐρχόμενοι ἐπέλειχον τὰ ἕλκη αὐτοῦ).[116] To dream of short clothing presaged poverty[117] in Artemidorus' *Oneirocritica*.[118]

Juvenal's vivid description of the clothing of the protagonist of his third satire is particularly significant:

> . . . the poor man gives food and occasion for jest if his cloak be torn and dirty, if his toga be a little soiled, if one of his shoes gapes where the leather is split, or if some fresh stitches of coarse thread reveal where not one, but many a rent has been patched.[119]

Juvenal is not here describing the appearance of a beggar but that of a man with sufficient funds to keep a number of slaves:[120] therefore, even allowing for the satirist's comical exaggeration, it is fair to say that the clothing possessed by most of the urban population was meagre. In the area of clothing, as with food, the non-élite city dwellers lived close to subsistence, if not below it.

Housing

Not only are we faced with the usual dearth of evidence from literary sources as we attempt to reconstruct something of the norms of non-élite housing in the first century, but, as MacMullen has observed, "archaeology fails us, for no one has sought fame through the excavation of a slum".[121] The study of Graeco-Roman urban housing has tended to concentrate on prestigious *domus*. This is not entirely the fault of the ideological interests of the excavators as the flimsiness of most non-élite housing militates against its long term survival, but, nevertheless, we must not allow our knowledge of the housing of the affluent few to influence our picture of the housing of the impoverished many.

---

[116] Luke 16:19–31. The affluent attire of the rich man emphasises this. It has been traditional to see this parable as dependent upon Egyptian folklore, however, it may reflect characterisations of the rich and poor common in the Graeco-Roman world (R. Hock, "Lazarus and Micyllus: Greco-Roman Backgrounds to Luke 16:19-31", *JBL* 106 (1987) 447–463).

[117] Short clothing was thought to be such an indicator because the cost of clothing was related, for the most part, to the quantity of material used. See Mark 12:38; Luke 20:46.

[118] Artemidorus, *Oneirocritica* 2.3.

[119] Juvenal, *Saturae* 3.147–151.

[120] Juvenal, *Saturae* 3.167. Slaves were themselves recognised by the inadequate state of their clothing (see Bradley, *Slavery and Society*, pp. 95–99).

[121] MacMullen, *Roman Social Relations*, p. 93.

The poorest had no housing as such and slept in the open air.[122] Those slightly more fortunate lived in tombs,[123] in spaces under the stairs of apartment houses (*subscalaria*),[124] cellars and vaults,[125] below bridges and theatre awnings, or in taverns.[126] Some constructed their own habitations, lean-tos (*parapetasia*) built against the walls of permanent buildings, between the columns of porticoes,[127] or beneath aqueducts,[128] or dwelt in 'shanties' (*turguria*), outside the city proper, "similar to the improvised shacks in slums which skirt the capitals of many developing countries";[129] and like their modern counterparts, those that erected such shelters lived in constant fear of having them torn down by the city authorities.[130] The marginally more economically successful would inhabit a room in an *insula*[131] or a shared house. An *insula* was an apartment block and was common throughout the Empire (though not universal).[132] Whilst the lower floors could be quite spacious and were sometimes rented by members of the élite[133] the

---

[122] Bruce W. Frier, "The Rental Market in Early Imperial Rome", *JRS* 67 (1977), p. 30, fn. 20. Gregory of Nyssa said of urban beggars: "The open air is their dwelling, their lodgings are the porticoes and street corners and the less frequented parts of the market-place" (in MacMullen, *Roman Social Relations*, p. 87). Winter was often lethal for such individuals (Martial, *Epigrammata* 10.5).

[123] Hopkins, *Death and Renewal*, pp. 205f.

[124] "The subscalaria of Ostia show heavy use" (G. Hermansen, "The Population of Imperial Rome", *Historia* 27 (1978), p. 167).

[125] A. Scobie, "Slums, Sanitation and Mortality in the Roman World", *Klio* 68 (1986), p. 403.

[126] Hermansen, "The Population of Imperial Rome", p. 167. Ammianus Marcellinus 14.6.25. Martial, *Epigrammata* 11.328.

[127] Dio Chrysostom, *Orationes* 40.8–9; John Chrysostom, *Homilia XI in Epistolam Primam ad Corinthos*; Ulpian, *Digest* 43.8.2; *Codex Theodosianus* 15.1.39.

[128] O. Robinson, "The Water Supply of Rome", *SDHI* 46 (1980), p. 72.

[129] Scobie, "Slums, Sanitation", p. 402. Also Esler, *Community and Gospel*, p. 178, following Sjoberg's generalisation about the population distribution of pre-industrial cities (*The Pre-Industrial City*, pp. 97–98).

[130] Ramsey MacMullen, "Roman Imperial Building in the Provinces", *HSCP* 64 (1959) 208–209. Martial, *De Spectaculis* 11.

[131] I follow here the convention of assuming that the distinction between the *domus* and *insula* is architectural, whereas, for the Romans themselves, the terms referred to properties in different categories of ownership. See Wallace-Hadrill, *Houses and Society*, p. 132; A. G. McKay, *Houses, Villas and Palaces in the Roman World*, London: Thames & Hudson, 1975, p. 83; and also Ian M. Barton, "Introduction", *Roman Domestic Buildings*, ed. Ian M. Barton, Exeter: Exeter University Press, 1996, pp. 1–5.

[132] The *insulae* of Rome and Ostia are perhaps the most well known and best preserved but they were not unique. The youth Eutychus fell from the third floor of one at Troas (Acts 20:9).

[133] Bruce W. Frier, *Landlords and Tenants in Imperial Rome*, Princeton: Princeton University Press, 1980, pp. 39–47.

higher floors were progressively more subdivided and more densely occupied. The highest floors consisted of tiny wooden *cellae*, which were rented on a daily basis.[134] Such rooms offered little more shelter than the lean-tos, as we can see in Juvenal's description of the hapless Codrus, who lived in the roof of a block.[135] The hellish nature of life in these cramped *insulae*, composed of "chambers piled upon chambers", was proverbial. Tertullian, for example, belittled the Valentinians' conception of heaven by comparing it with such tower blocks.[136] Conflagration[137] and collapse[138] were common. The desire for profit led to the construction of extra, precarious wooden floors,[139] despite the efforts of Emperors to limit the height of such buildings.[140] "Cowboy builders" were rife, as Yahvetz notes: "Great was the number of those who made a fortune by using inferior buildings materials, putting up extra thin walls, or neglecting all the elementary rules of solid building."[141] Shared houses, which were far more common than has traditionally been supposed,[142]

[134] Scobie, "Slums, sanitation," p. 401.

[135] Juvenal, *Saturae* 3.203.

[136] Tertullian, *Ad Valentinianos* 17.

[137] Juvenal, *Saturae* 3.190ff. The combustibility of multiple dwellings was taken for granted by Ulpian, *Digest* 9.2.27.8. Rome did have a fire brigade of sorts (the *vigiles*) but its effectiveness should not be overestimated. See P. K. Reynolds, *The Vigiles of Imperial Rome*, Oxford: Oxford University Press, 1926 and J. S. Rainbird, "The Fire Stations of Imperial Rome", *PBSR* 54 (1986) 147–169.

[138] Cicero, *Epistulae ad Atticum* 14.9.1.

[139] These were made of wood in order to be lighter and put less strain on the foundations. See Z. Yavetz, "The Living Conditions of the Urban Plebs in Republican Rome", *The Crisis of the Roman Republic*, ed. R. Seager, Cambridge: Heffer & Sons, 1969, p. 173.

[140] See, for example, Tacitus, *Annales* 15.43. The repeated legislation tells against the effectiveness of such labours on the part of the Emperors, as does the only almost intact *insula* surviving in Rome today, the Casa di via Giulio Romano, which, as Scobie has observed, exceeds both the Augustan and Trajanic height limits ("Slums, Sanitation", p. 406). Martial (*Epigrammata* 7.20) mentions 200 stairs, "which, if meant literally would indicate six or seven storeys" (Courtney, *Commentary*, p. 181). For a discussion of the attempts to limit the height of *insulae* and the efforts to circumvent such legislation, see O. F. Robinson, *Ancient Rome: City Planning and Adminstration*, London: Routledge, 1994, pp. 34–38.

[141] Yavetz, "Living Conditions", p. 509. The flimsiness of *insulae* provided a useful literary image for Roman authors; "for Seneca apartment houses were insubstantial structures, and his works are full of metaphors drawn from the cracking, collapsing, or burning of these buildings" (Packer, "Housing and Population in Imperial Ostia and Rome", *JRS* 57 (1967), p. 81). For example, see Seneca, *De Beneficiis* 4.6.2, 6.15.7, *De Ira* 3.35.4–5.

[142] The widespread assumption that *domus* were inhabited by wealthy owner occupiers and their households has come under attack by Wallace-Hadrill (*Houses and Society*, pp. 103–108). Archaeological remains and legal sources show that the reality was often far more complex. It is clear from the evidence of structural changes in many such

had many characteristics in common with these *insulae*. Certainly conditions within them seem to have been, on occasion, equally squalid and overcrowding was usual.[143]

The *tabernae* (workshops) of some artisans[144] were also a significant source of housing and within these small units[145] the artisans, their families, and slaves, lived and worked.[146] These buildings tended to be very modest and Hock[147] is definitely inaccurate in assuming that each could hold 6–12 craftspeople; such a high number is unfeasible given the proportions of these "small booths";[148] Packer's estimate of an average of four people per unit seems much more likely.[149]

---

buildings (the addition of external staircases, internal walls, and outside doors), the existence of contracts which detail the subletting of sections of houses, and from wills in which individuals were granted the right to live in part of a house on the death of the testator, that, over time, a number of different, distinct, social groups often came to live in such structures. The occupants of a *domus* were not necessarily a socially cohesive group, and we do better to talk of 'housefuls' rather than 'households' when examining the occupancy of many of these structures (see P. Laslett and R. Wall, *Household and Family in Past Time*, Cambridge: Cambridge University Press, 1972).

[143] Valerius Maximus 4.4.8 records sixteen people sharing one room. Such multiple occupancy is also attested in papyrological records. In BGU 115 we find seventeen adults and seven children living in one-tenth of a town house.

[144] Not all artisans earned enough to own or rent a *taberna*. Many had makeshift pitches where they both made and sold their produce, as can be seen from frescoes and graffiti in Pompeii (see R. Étienne, *La Vie Quotidienne à Pompéi*, second edition, Paris: Hachette, 1977).

[145] Packer has distinguished four types of *taberna*, all of a modest size: those with a single multipurpose room, those with a workshop and a mezzanine, those with a workshop and a back room, and those with a shop, back room and mezzanine ("Housing and Population", p. 85). They were not always found grouped with other *tabernae* in a single structure (although this was common) but could also be built into the ground floor of houses (Wallace-Hadrill, *Houses and Society*, p. 139).

[146] As we can see with Micyllus and in Cicero's description of a *taberna* found in his *Orationes in Catilinam* 4.16–17. The existence of 'night doors' in the shop fronts is conclusive evidence that artisans lived in their workshops (Packer, "Housing and Population," p. 85, fn. 54).

[147] Hock, *Social Context*, p. 33.

[148] Loane, *Industry and Commerce*, p. 61. Hock's mean is largely dependent upon the work of A. Burford (*Craftsmen in Ancient Greek and Roman Society*, Ithaca: Cornell University Press, 1972, pp. 79ff.) who arrived at her estimate chiefly from Attic vase painting of the fifth and sixth centuries BCE. The pictures found on these vases tell us more about the conventions of Attic vase painting than the reality of the workshop. The fact that establishments employing ten and thirteen workers are mentioned respectively by Aeschines (1.97) and Herondas (7.44) does not confirm Hock's estimate of the average: Aeschines was writing in the fourth century BCE and Herondas the third.

[149] Packer, "Housing and Population", p. 85.

Nearly all urban dwellers lived in these lean-tos, 'shanties', *insulae*, *tabernae*, and shared houses, or slept rough in the street.[150] Given the awful conditions of overcrowding,[151] shoddy construction, and lack of facilities[152] we have just sketched, we can say, with some justification, that nearly the entire *plebs urbana* lived in "appalling slums", as Brunt maintains.[153]

And such slums did not come cheap. Most housing in the first-century world was rented and, as Frier has observed in his thorough study of Rome, "almost all the non-privileged mass, if they could afford accommodation, were obliged to dwell in buildings they did not own, in exchange for rent that our sources agree was exorbitantly high".[154] Urban property was owned, virtually exclusively, by the élite to whom it offered a significant source of income.[155]

In their experience of housing, as well as in their access to food and clothing, the Graeco-Roman non-élite suffered a subsistence or near

[150] Frier, "Rental", p. 30, fn. 20. His estimate is very approximate but the close correlation between the quantity of élite housing (chiefly the *domus*) and the size of the élite population (Stambaugh, *The Ancient Roman City*, p. 90) validates his appraisal (though there are difficulties with this as: i) much élite housing seems to have been under multiple occupancy, ii) *insulae* could also house the élite (e.g. Seneca, *Epistulae* 56)).

[151] See MacMullen, *Roman Social Relations*, p. 63.

[152] *Digest* 47.10.44 gives a vivid insight into the anti-social behaviour engendered by the lack of cooking and waste disposal facilities in *insulae*.

[153] Brunt, "Roman Mob", p. 13. McKay has much the same opinion: "Rome undoubtedly remained a slum city in large areas of its sprawling mass" (*Houses, Villas, and Palaces*, p. 98). Though Brunt and McKay say this specifically of Rome, there are no grounds for assuming density of occupation, standards of construction, and the supply of utilities, were any better elsewhere in the urban Mediterranean world. (Although Brunt does not define the word 'slum', Graeco-Roman housing meets the criteria set out by Townsend for determining what can justifiably be termed 'slum' accommodation (*Poverty in the UK*, Harmondsworth: Penguin, 1979, pp. 479–486). See A. Scobie, "Slums, Sanitation", p. 404.)

The optimistic speculations about the quality of non-élite housing found in the work of J. E. Packer ("Middle and Lower Class Housing in Pompeii and Herculaneum: A Preliminary Survey", *Neue Forschungen in Pompeii*, ed. B. Andreae and H. Kyrieleis, Recklinghausen: Anurel Bongers, 1975, pp. 133–142) are flawed. Packer fails to take into consideration the density of occupation of the properties he studied. He also assumes that the urban poor lived only in fixed structures.

[154] Frier, "Rental", p. 27 and C. Whittaker, "Studying the Poor", p. 10. Debts incurred from rents were common amongst the plebs according to Yavetz, "Living Conditions", p. 517.

[155] See P. Garnsey, "Urban Property Investment". His findings are confirmed in Wallace-Hadrill's study of Pompeii and Herculaneum ("Elites and Trade in the Roman Town," *City and Country*, ed. J. Rich and A. Wallace-Hadrill, London: Routledge, 1991, pp. 241–269). See, for example, Cicero, *Epistulae ad Atticum* 12.32.2, 15.17.1, 15.20.4, 16.1.5.

subsistence life. Their labour, if they were lucky enough to actually have any, did not allow them to attain sufficient material resources for their lot to be otherwise. They could all, without exception, be accurately labelled 'poor' according to our earlier definition.

Factors intensifying the experience of poverty

A number of factors intensified the experience of deprivation for many of the *plebs urbana*. If a person was old, or female, or ill, acquiring the means to survive was significantly more problematic.[156]

Old age proverbially brought destitution to the few who were fortunate enough to reach it,[157] as their ability to earn their living diminished.[158] The association of old age with poverty in antiquity is well illustrated by Artemidorus: to dream of baldness in the *Oneirocritica* is to be warned of your impending destitution because, so the logic

---

[156] That these three categories of people suffered economic disadvantage is not surprising as even today a person's age, sex, and health are significant determinants of their economic situation. However, it might be surprising that 'race' was not a factor in the Graeco-Roman world (see F. Snowden, *Blacks in Antiquity: Ethiopians in the Graeco-Roman Experience*, Cambridge, MA: The Belknap Press, 1970, and *Before Color Prejudice*, Cambridge, MA: Harvard University Press, 1983; L. Thompson, *Romans and Blacks*, London: Routledge, 1989; and A. Sherwin-White, *Racial Prejudice in Imperial Rome*, Cambridge: Cambridge University Press, 1967). The hostility occasionally directed towards Jews (see Josephus, *Contra Apionem*; Philo, *De Legatione ad Gaium* and *In Flaccum*) is not evidence to the contrary. For the most part, Jews lived peacefully throughout the Roman world and were distributed evenly through the whole range of statuses and occupations in Graeco-Roman society. (S. Applebaum, "The Social and Economic Status of the Jews of the Diaspora", *The Jewish People in the First Century*, vol. 2, ed. S. Safrai and M. Stern, Amsterdam: Van Gorcum, 1976, pp. 701–727; and G. Hanfmann (ed.), *Sardis From Prehistory to Roman Times: Results of the Archaeological Excavation of Sardis 1958–1975*. Cambridge, MA: Harvard University Press, 1983, pp. 184ff.).

[157] And not many did. Hopkins has shown that there was no difference between the age structure of the Empire and other pre-industrial societies. Life expectancy at birth was approximately 30. K. Hopkins, "On the probable age structure of the Roman population", *PS* 20 (1966–67) 245–264. See also Bruce W. Frier, "Roman Life Expectancy", *HSCP* 86 (1982) 213–251 and K. Hopkins' response, "Graveyard for Historians", *La mort, les morts et l'audel dans le monde romain*, ed. F. Hinard, Caen: Centre de Publications, 1987, pp. 113–126.

[158] For perceptions of old age in antiquity see T. Faulkner and J. de Luce, *Old Age in Greek and Latin Literature*, Albany: State University Press, 1989; M. I. Finley, "The Elderly in Classical Antiquity", *G&R* 28 (1981) 156–171 and J. P. V. D. Balsdon, *Romans and Aliens*, London: Duckworth, 1979, pp. 248ff. Being old and a slave was a particularly dangerous predicament to be in: many appear to have been simply abandoned or killed by their owners (Suetonius, *Claudius* 25).

goes, baldness was regarded as a sure sign of old age,[159] and old age was synonymous with poverty.[160]

To be a woman in the Graeco-Roman world was, in general, far from economically advantageous. Although it is difficult to generalise about the experience of women throughout the Empire,[161] they were almost universally denied the opportunities afforded to men.[162] There was a movement towards women gaining greater autonomy during the period roughly contemporaneous with the New Testament,[163] but it was not

[159] Artemidorus, *Oneirocritica* 1.21. Of course, there were exceptions to this rule. A few elderly, particularly those who belonged to the prestigious *gerusia* (a form of pensioner club) had a more comfortable dotage.

[160] Being young also had its economic disadvantages for many. Child labour was a particularly prominent feature of the Roman Empire (K. R. Bradley, "Child Labour in the Roman World", *HR/RH* 12 (1985) 311–330). However, we should not exaggerate the degree to which children were neglected within the Empire. Whilst it is true that, with the exception of Jews and Egyptians (Tacitus, *Historia* 5.5; Diodorus Siculus 1.80.3; Strabo 17.2.5), the practise of exposing unwanted babies was universal, parental indifference, neglect and cruelty were not "general or distinctive features of Roman society" (P. Garnsey, "Child Rearing in Ancient Italy", *The Family in Italy From Antiquity to the Present*, ed. D. Kertzer and R. Saller, New Haven: Yale University Press, 1991, p. 64). For example, the care evidently lavished by its parents upon a Roman hydrocephalus child, recently discovered in Cambridgeshire, should make us reconsider these common accusations (see A. Taylor, "A Roman Lead Coffin with Pipeclay Figurines from Arrington, Cambridgeshire", *Britannia* 24 (1993) 191–225).

[161] The Empire was not homogenous and contained a number of distinct legal and social cultures. Egyptian women, for instance, along with those of Asia Minor, seem to have had rather more freedom than Roman and Greek. Nevertheless, we should not exaggerate the extent of their emancipation as D. Hobson observes ("The Role of Women in the Economic Life of Roman Egypt: A Case Study from First Century Tebtunis", *EMC* 28 (1984) 373–390); despite the participation of women in property ownership, leasing and the arrangement of loans, "a woman's active economic role was not very extensive" (p. 388).

The position of Greek women was particularly bleak, as can be seen from the architectural record. Whilst Roman women had freedom of movement throughout their dwellings, Greek women were restricted to clearly demarcated quarters (see Wallace-Hadrill, *Houses and Society*, p. 8, confirmed in Nepos, *Praefatio* 6–8).

[162] Of course, there were dissenting voices in this area. Perhaps most significant and thorough-going amongst them was Musonius Rufus, the first-century Cynic-Stoic, who advocated equality in education and in male/female roles (see William Klassen, "Musonius Rufus, Jesus and Paul: Three First Century Feminists", *From Jesus to Paul*, ed. P. Richardson and J. C. Hurd, Waterloo: Wilfrid Laurier University Press, 1984, pp. 185–206). The now non-existent *Republic* of Zeno also seems to have done much the same. However, those who objected to the subjugation of women were in the main Cynics and Epicureans, groups that had little impact on wider society (Pomeroy, *Goddesses, Whores, Wives and Slaves*, p. 132).

[163] The growth in non-manus marriage amongst Romans during the late Republic/early Principate is both indicative of, and partly responsible for, this growth in independence. In non-manus marriage a woman remained under the tutelage of her father, rather than

significant and such autonomy did not lead to material security. For example, evidence of wealthy, entrepreneurial, independent women (of whom Paul's co-workers Phoebe and Lydia are often, incorrectly, held to be examples)[164] is almost impossible to find. Most women were denied access to economic resources; their jobs were chiefly menial and semi- or unskilled, and largely reflected traditional household occupations, whether they were slaves or free.[165] The economic experience of widows was particularly dire. It is not surprising therefore that the widow epitomised extreme poverty in both Graeco-Roman[166] and Biblical

---

coming under the authority of her husband, and consequently kept control of her dowry. In practice, the limited life expectancy within the Empire, and also the (relatively) advanced age of Roman fathers, meant that few lived long enough to exert much power over their married daughters and the male guardian who was supposed to take the father's place on his death was often little more than a legal fiction. Some of Augustus' family legislation also encouraged a degree of emancipation as particularly fecund Roman women were rewarded with a significant increase in their legal capacity. For an extended treatment of these issues see Jane F. Gardner, *Women in Roman Law and Society*, London: Routledge, 1991. Diaspora Jewish women also seem to have benefited from this general cultural shift. See Paul Trebilco, *Jewish Communities in Asia Minor*, Cambridge: Cambridge University Press, 1991, pp. 104–126.

[164] See below, chapter 4, for a detailed discussion of Phoebe. There are no grounds for asserting Lydia was affluent although a number of New Testament scholars assume that she was because: i) she is described as a πορφυρόπωλις (Acts 16:14); ii) she possessed a household (16:40); iii) she was capable of giving hospitality to Paul and his companions. None of these details indicates such a thing. i) Few πορφυρόπωλεις were affluent. She need not have been one of the small number of traders in murex purple (the luxury dye whose use was tightly controlled by legislation e.g. Cassius Dio 49.16.1) but is far more likely to have been one of the numerous producers of material coloured by the use of dyes from other sources, such as vegetable roots or minerals. These dyes were popular, not just amongst those who wished to arrogate an élite symbol but also amongst those who wished to have work clothes dyed a practical, dark, colour. Pliny, for example, recommended that the clothing of slaves should be purple (*Naturalis Historiae* 16.77; cf. also Cicero, *Pro Flacco* 70). The colour was widely used among "all classes" (M. Reinhold, *History of Purple as a Status Symbol in Antiquity*, Bruxelles: Latomus, 1970, p. 51. See also "The Usurpation of Status and Status Symbols in the Roman Empire", *Historia* 20 (1971) 275–302; Lillian M. Wilson, *The Clothing of The Ancient Romans*. Baltimore: Johns Hopkins University Press, 1938, pp. 6–10). Indeed, Thyatira, Lydia's place of origin, was known for its production of cheap vegetable dyes (Horsley, *New Documents*, vol. 4, p. 53). For ii) and iii) see below, chapter 4. For a recent, more extensive, discussion of the economic status of Lydia which reaches similar conclusions, see Ivoni Richter Reimer, *Women in the Acts of the Apostles: A Feminist Liberation Perspective*, Philadelphia: Fortress, 1995, pp. 99–130.

[165] Natalie Kampen, *Image and Status: Roman Working Women in Ostia*, Berlin: Gebr. Mann, 1981, p. 153.

[166] For example Aristophanes, *Thesmophoriazusae* 446–552. Demosthenes, *Orationes* 57.31ff.

traditions.[167] Indeed, what little a widow had was easily taken away from her by others.[168]

Ill-health also increased an individual's deprivation, limiting, or ending, their ability to work and generate an income.[169] It was caused by the interplay of environmental, nutritional, and occupational factors which were, ironically, intensified by poverty.[170] Despite the popular reputation of Roman plumbing,[171] sanitary facilities in the Graeco-Roman cities, particularly for the poor, encouraged and fostered sickness:

> Open cesspits in kitchens, a general lack of washing facilities in latrines, defecation and urination in the streets, the pollution of water basins with carrion and filth, lack of efficient fly control, and inadequate street cleaning, do not provide a basis for health in an urban community.[172]

---

[167] 2 Kings 4:1–7. "The widow of 2 Kings 4:1–7 is a paradigm. She has nothing in her house but a cruse of oil and debts which her husband has left and for which the creditors claim her two sons." G. Stählin, "χήρα", *Theological Dictionary of the New Testament*, vol. 9, ed. G. Kittel and G. Friedrich, Grand Rapids: Eerdmans, 1974, p. 444.

Early Christianity saw the emergence of specific institutions termed 'widows' houses' which seem to have been dedicated to providing a collective home for these women (1 Tim. 5:16, Acts 9:36–42, Acts of Peter 21, 22, 28, 29). Although the 'widows' eventually became an ascetic order, as we can see in Ignatius' *Letter to the Smyrnaeans* 13, we should not be blind to the initial economic reasons for this provision.

[168] P. Sakaon 36. See also Mark 12:40 and Luke 20:47.

[169] The profusion of anatomical ex-votos which depict legs or feet are illustrative of this relationship. As Ralph Jackson notes: "they serve as a reminder that of all diseases and disorders those affecting mobility, and therefore livelihood, were amongst the most feared" (*Doctors and Diseases*, p. 159). See also R. Garland, *The Eye of the Beholder: Deformity and Disability in the Graeco-Roman World*, London: Duckworth, 1995, p. 39 for the association between disability and destitution.

[170] M. Bapat and N. Cook, "The environment, health and nutrition: an analysis of inter-relationships in the city of Poona", *HabInt* 8 (1984) 115–126. It is no wonder that poverty could be perceived as a disease (Pomeroy, "Status," p. 63). Indeed, the two are inextricably linked in Artemidorus *Oneirocritica* 3.22 (dreams of sickness portend destitution).

[171] Pliny, *Naturalis Historiae* 36.24.123. The Romans celebrated and promoted this myth on their coins (see Penn, *Medicine*, pp. 133–140); however, the reality appears to have been rather less impressive. The water supplies were often pilfered (Frontinus, *De Aquis Urbis Romae* 2.65–87) and few had direct access to the benefits they provided. Indeed, many projects failed to come to fruition (Pliny the Younger, *Epistulae* 10.37). Some well established towns lacked any drains whatsoever (Strabo 14.1.37).

[172] Scobie, "Slums, Sanitation", p. 421. See Whittaker, "Studying The Poor", p. 12. The contribution of Roman baths to the hygiene of a town was often negative (Toner, *Leisure and Ancient Rome*, pp. 53–64; cf. also *Philogelos* 113). For an excellent overview of drainage and sanitation in this period see A. Wilson, "Drainage and Sanitation", *Ancient Water Technology*, ed. Örjan Wikander, Leiden: E. J. Brill, *forthcoming*.

The insanitary conditions of urban life can be seen in the numerous surviving inscriptions which warned people not to urinate or defecate in the doorways of houses or tombs.[173]

Acute overcrowding was the lot of most city dwellers and this also magnified the risks from diseases.[174] (Martial's quip, that you could shake hands across streets from opposing balconies is born out from the archaeological records of most Graeco-Roman cities.)[175] The fact that Suetonius could record, without apparent shock, that a stray dog entered Vespasian's quarters and dropped a human hand under the breakfast table,[176] is illustrative of the kind of squalor that accompanied Roman urban living and encouraged sickness. The poor diet, which we have already seen most inhabitants experienced, made it all the more probable[177] that they would suffer from disease (as well as, of course,

---

There were, however, some unusual benefits to be gained from this basic state of affairs. According to Suetonius, the study of rhetoric was introduced to Rome by Crates Mallotes, a Greek who gave classes in the subject whilst stranded in the city recovering from a broken leg obtained by falling into one of its many open sewers (Suetonius, *Grammaticis* 2.1).

[173] See Lattimore, *Themes*, p. 120 and also Petronius, *Satyricon* 71.8 and Juvenal, *Saturae* 1.131. *Philogelos* 85 makes a humorous reference to this phenomenon: "Having moved into a new house, an egghead cleaned up in front of the door and put up a notice saying: ANYONE WHO DUMPS EXCREMENT HERE WILL NOT GET IT BACK."

[174] Population density was very high: it ". . . approached 200 per acre, significantly higher than the range we are used to and moreover distributed much less evenly over the whole city" (MacMullen, *Roman Social Relations*, p. 63). This factor, combined with the poor standard of housing, led to the prevalence of a number of illnesses amongst the poor in Greek and Roman towns and cities, such as pulmonary tuberculosis, something which is visible not only in the literary record but also in skeletal remains (see Jackson, *Doctors and Diseases*, p. 180).

The rapid growth in the population of some cities, for example Rome grew from 400,000 in 120 BCE to over a million under Augustus, accentuated the threat from such diseases (Whittaker, "Studying The Poor", p. 9).

Although the Mediterranean world did suffer from various epidemics (e.g. see Suetonius, *Nero* 39), these reached something of an equilibrium during the period we are studying (its relative isolation helped it achieve this state). However, from the second century onwards it met what McNeill terms "epidemiological disaster" (*Plagues and Peoples*, Harmondsworth: Penguin, 1976, pp. 112ff.).

[175] Martial, *Epigrammata* 1.86.

[176] Suetonius, *Vespasian* 5.4. Suetonius' interest in this story comes from the fact that a hand was an emblem of power and the incident therefore appeared to be an omen confirming Vespasian's imperial aspirations. See also Martial, *Epigrammata* 10.5.

[177] "It is now well established that there is a close relationship between infection and malnutrition" (Jane Pryer and N. Cook, *Cities of Hunger. Urban Malnutrition in Developing Countries*, Oxford: Oxfam, 1988, p. 11).

causing deficiency illnesses).[178] Occupational injuries were also common for many of the *plebs urbana*, whose employment was often dangerous[179] and repetitive,[180] as were disabilities suffered as a result of the endemic violence that filled the cities.[181] The inferior quality of health care available to the poor made the situation even more bleak.[182] The absence of effective methods of birth control for the non-élite compounded the problem for destitute women, who had to face the dangers that accompanied regular childbirth from an early age.[183] Health was obviously

[178] For deficiency diseases see Food and Agriculture Organisation of the United Nations, *Handbook on Nutritional Requirements*, Rome: FAO and WHO, 1974. See also Jackson, *Doctors and Diseases*, p. 38. Scurvy (caused by a lack of vitamin C), rickets (caused by a lack of vitamin D) and night-blindness (caused by a lack of vitamin A) were widely known in the Empire.

[179] Juvenal, *Saturae* 3.249–267.

[180] Xenophon, *Oeconomicus* 4.2. The situation was particularly dire for slaves, who could suffer extreme violence at the hands of cruel masters. See Bradley, *Slaves and Masters*, pp. 113–137 and his interpretation of Phaedrus, *Fabularum Aesopiarum* 1.6 (p. 151). See also *Philogelos* 122.

[181] See Juvenal, *Saturae* 3.249–267; Alfenus, *Digest* 9.2.52. 'Police' forces within first-century cities were notoriously ineffectual and could be quite counterproductive, engaging in wholesale extortion and even looting (Cassius Dio 62.17.1; Tacitus, *Annales* 15.38.7; Josephus, *Antiquitates Judaicae* 19.160): they "might have been more trouble than they were worth" (Reynolds, "Cities", p. 33). Legislation from Hierapolis OGIS 527 confirms this. Though, of course, the 'police' had a different opinion of their value to society (see M. P. Speidel, "The Police Officer, a Hero. An Inscribed Relief From Near Ephesos", *EA* 5 (1985) 159–160). See also W. Nippel, "Policing Rome", *JRS* 74 (1984) 20–29 and *Public Order in Ancient Rome*, Cambridge: Cambridge University Press, 1995.

[182] Graeco-Roman medicine was notoriously ineffectual, at least at the popular level. The medical profession was often the subject of attack as can be seen in Lucian's *Dialogi Deorum* 6, 17; Martial, *Epigrammata* 1.47, 8.74; Pliny, *Naturalis Historiae* 29.5.11 (see Darrel W. Amundsen, "Images of Physicians in Classical Times," *JPC* 11 (1977) 642–655). Avaricious, sadistic and stupid doctors are the butt of many of the jokes in the *Philogelos* (139, 174, 175, 176, 177, 182–186, 221). The New Testament also contains such hostile material: of the six uses of ἰατρός found in the New Testament, only one occurs in a positive context (H. C. Kee, *Medicine, Miracle, and Magic in New Testament Times*, Cambridge: Cambridge University Press, 1986, p. 65). Indeed, the woman in Mark 7:25–34 not only lost all her wealth as the result of the attention of doctors but her condition deteriorated.

Despite legislation aimed at raising the standards of medical practitioners (Ulpian, *Digest* 9.2.7.8; Louise Cilliers, "Public Health in Roman Legislation", *AClass* 36 (1993) 1–10) only the most wealthy could have access to competent doctors (J. Scarborough, *Roman Medicine*, Ithaca, NY: Cornell University Press, 1969, p. 102) and even these seem to have become progressively less skilful during the Roman period (p. 96). For a thorough, recent introduction to this issue see Jackson's excellent study, *Doctors and Diseases*.

[183] Although there was some knowledge of birth control in the first century, the most effective methods (such as abortion) were only available to the affluent (see, for example, Juvenal, *Saturae* 6.592–598). For the non-élite, family limitation was achieved almost

not something that the Roman élite could be certain of, whatever their wealth, but it was particularly elusive for those with limited means.[184]

3.3 Concluding remarks

It is not surprising that the aristocracy, from their comfortable height, viewed all of the *plebs urbana*, artisan and beggar, slave and free, as the *sordem urbis et faecem* and the *misera ac ieiuna*.[185] The under-developed, pre-industrial economy of the Graeco-Roman world created enormous disparities of wealth, and within this inequitable, rigid system the non-élite of the cities[186] lived brutal and frugal lives, characterised by struggle and impoverishment.

---

entirely by exposure (see Bruce W. Frier, "Natural Fertility and Family Limitation in Roman Marriage," *CPh* 89 (1994) 318–333, *contra* J. Riddle, *Contraception and Abortion from the Ancient World to the Renaissance*, Cambridge: Harvard University Press, 1992 and Rodney Stark, *The Rise of Christianity: A Sociologist Reconsiders History*, Princeton: Princeton University Press, 1996, pp. 119–122. See also the contributions of E. Eyben, "Family Planning in Graeco-Roman Antiquity", *AncSoc* 11 (1980) 5–82; Keith Hopkins, "Contraception in the Roman Empire", *CSSH* 8 (1966) 124–151; and Jackson, *Doctors and Diseases*, pp. 86–111).

[184] The desire to give the illusion of health was common to most sectors of Roman society, as can be seen from the profusion of cosmetic containers and perfume jars found in the archaeological record of the period, the contents of which were (amongst other things) used in order to disguise the effects of illness. Jackson, *Doctors and Diseases*, p. 53.

[185] Cicero, *Epistulae ad Atticum* 1.16.11.

[186] We must avoid the mistake of assuming that because wealth was visibly concentrated in the cities, indeed literally in the Imperial architecture (the powerful articulation of *maiestas imperii* – Vitruvius, *De Architectura* 1. *preaf.* 1, 2) the economic life of most city dwellers was, *a priori*, any better than those who inhabited the χώρα (*contra*, for example, Hengel, *Property and Riches*, p. 37). Indeed, the lower life expectancy (John Stambaugh, *The Ancient Roman City*, Baltimore: Johns Hopkins University Press, 1989, p. 89) and higher cost of living (Dio Chrysostom, *Orationes* 7.105ff.) could actually increase the degree of poverty experienced by urban inhabitants.

4

The Economic Location of Paul
and the Pauline Churches

Having described the economic realities of the first-century urban environment we shall now attempt to place Paul and his communities within this world. It is my conviction that when we do this we discover that: *Paul and the Pauline churches shared in this general experience of deprivation and subsistence. Neither the apostle nor any members of the congregations he addresses in his epistles escaped from the harsh existence that typified life in the Roman Empire for the non-élite.*

4.1 The economic location of Paul

Paul the artisan

Detailed evidence of the apostle's life is surprisingly sparse. As J. C. Beker observes, "One of the most remarkable things about Paul is how little we really know about him and how little he tells us about his life."[1] But, although autobiographical material is rare in the authentic letters, one detail of his existence recurs a number of times. Paul repeatedly speaks of engaging in arduous, physical labour (1 Thess. 2:9; 2 Thess. 3:7–8; 1 Cor. 4:11–12; 1 Cor. 9:6; 2 Cor. 11:27). Even allowing for the theological[2] and rhetorical[3] concerns that no doubt influenced the apostle's choice of words in these texts, it seems fair to deduce that he was some kind of manual worker.[4] Indeed, we can go further and say

---

[1] J. C. Beker, *Paul the Apostle: The Triumph of God in Life and Thought*, Edinburgh: T. & T. Clark, 1980, p. 3.

[2] Paul's depiction of his personal suffering was no doubt affected by a combination of his 'apocalyptic' world-view (J. Neyrey, *Paul in Other Words: A Cultural Reading of His Letters*, Louisville: Westminster/John Knox Press, 1990, pp. 167–180) and his *theologia crucis* (see J. S. Pobee, *Persecution and Martyrdom in the Theology of Paul*, Sheffield: JSOT Press, 1985). Suffering was something that "authenticated his ministry" (p. 106).

[3] See, for example, J. T. Fitzgerald, *Cracks in An Earthen Vessel: An Examination of the Catalogues of Hardships in the Corinthian Correspondence*, Atlanta: Scholars Press, 1988.

[4] See Hock, *Social Context*, p. 35. Of course, not all Paul's suffering was a consequence of his economic circumstance; much was the result of his missionary activity (2 Cor. 12:10).

that he was probably an artisan, as Acts maintains.[5] The similarities between what Paul tells us of his situation, and that of Micyllus, discussed in the previous chapter, are compelling. They both suffered the same long hours of labour (and the same feelings of hunger)[6] that characterised artisan life.

Paul's experience was probably all the more arduous given the peripatetic nature of his lifestyle. This would have prevented him establishing himself in one place, surely a significant factor in the success of any artisan. The regular demands upon his time made by the gospel no doubt compounded his economic difficulties. Unlike the Cynic-artisan Simon the Shoemaker, who could engage in discourse with visitors and customers, throughout the day, whilst labouring in his workshop, Paul's *modus operandi* did not allow him to combine his labour fully with his ministry (he was far too interested in pastoral and missionary concerns to spend all day in a *taberna*).[7]

---

[5] Acts 18:3 σκηνοποιός. Contrary to P. Billerbeck and L. Hermann (*Kommentar zum Neuen Testament aus Talmud und Midrasch*, vol. 2, Munich: G. H. Becksche, pp. 746f.) Zahn has shown that the word does not mean weaver (*Apostelgeschichte des Lucas*, Leipzig: A. Deichertsche, 1919, pp. 633–634). Nor is it correct to understand σκηνοποιός too precisely as 'tentmaker'. Rather, it should be read in a broader sense as 'leatherworker', a translation that agrees with "the general thrust of versional renderings and patristic interpretations", as Hock maintains (*Social Context*, p. 21; also F. F. Bruce, *The Acts of the Apostles*, second edition, London: Tyndale Press, 1956, p. 343; and Haenchen, *The Acts of the Apostles*, p. 534). Although these differ about the exact kind of leatherworking Paul was engaged in, they are almost unanimous in their perception of the general character of his occupation. Despite the fact that the word is occasionally absent from early manuscripts (S. C. Williams, *Alterations to the Text of the Synoptic Gospels and Acts*, Oxford: Basil Blackwell, 1951, p. 76) I concur with Hock (*Social Context*, p. 20) and Haenchen (*The Acts of the Apostles*, p. 538), that there are no convincing grounds for doubting its authenticity. (Though see Hemer's criticism of Hock in *The Book of Acts in the Setting of Hellenistic History*, Tübingen: J. C. B. Mohr, 1989, p. 119, fn. 46).

It is inaccurate to deduce from this tradition that Paul had the opportunity to become wealthy. Hengel is being anachronistic when he asserts ". . . his craft . . . need not necessarily of itself indicate poverty . . . Even now, many owners of major businesses are proud of having learned 'on the shop floor'" (*Pre-Christian Paul*, p. 15). The small-scale production units we have examined in chapter 2 preclude almost entirely such a fairytale, rags to riches, scenario.

[6] 1 Cor. 4:11; 2 Cor. 11:27.

[7] Though it is possible that Paul may have used his workshop for preaching on occasion as Hock suggests (*Social Context*, pp. 37–42). For further discussion of Simon the Shoemaker see R. F. Hock, "Simon the Shoemaker as an Ideal Cynic", *GRBS* 17 (1976) 41–53 and "The Workshop as a Social Setting for Paul's Missionary Preaching", *CBQ* 41 (1979) 438–450.

It therefore appears that we can locate Paul firmly amongst the *misera ac ieiunia*. He was a man who lived his life "in poverty".[8]

However, I am aware that this picture of Paul will appear rather implausible to many Pauline scholars. A number of objections have been raised since, in recent times, A. Deissmann first presented such a portrait of the apostle,[9] and it is almost universally accepted today that Paul did not in fact experience *fully* the life of the poor in the Roman Empire. It is argued that: i) even though Paul undoubtedly worked as an artisan during his time as an apostle, his trade did not provide his sole source of income during these years, and so his standard of living was unrelated to his manual work: it was significantly higher; ii) whilst Paul's economic life *after* his call to be an apostle did, to a considerable extent, reflect that of a typical artisan, certain biographical details indicate that his life *before* his call was noticeably more comfortable. But both criticisms fail to stand up to scrutiny.

Paul's additional income

We do know that, on occasion, Paul received financial support from churches (2 Cor. 11:9, Phil. 4:15–16) and individuals (Rom. 16:1–2, 16:23). However, it is unlikely that such funds allowed him to attain a level of income considerably higher than that of an average artisan.

What financial help he received from *churches* appears to have been needs-related as we can see by his use of the words χρεία in Phil. 4:16 and ὑστέρημα in 2 Cor. 11:9.[10] It certainly was not a regular feature of his life as a missionary, as we can see from his proud boast in chapter 9 of 1 Corinthians and his stress upon αὐτάρκεια.[11]

---

[8] Christian Wolff, "Humility and Self-Denial in Jesus' Life and Message and in the Apostolic Existence of Paul", *Paul and Jesus*, ed. A. J. M. Wedderburn, Sheffield: JSOT Press, 1989, p. 145.

[9] A. Deissmann, *Paul: A Study in Social and Religious History*, London: Hodder & Stoughton, 1926.

[10] It is unlikely that the financial help Paul expected from the Pauline communities towards his travelling expenses (indicated by the use of the word προπέμπω in 1 Cor. 16:6; 2 Cor. 1:16 (Rom. 15:24) – see B. Holmberg, *Paul and Power*, pp. 86–87) could have been very large; after all, his Corinthian critics still considered him to be financially independent (1 Cor. 9).

[11] Phil. 4:11. (For a discussion of the term see chapter 5.) His repeated self-designation as a 'slave' might also be evidence of this staunch financial independence (see 1 Cor. 9:19; Rom. 1:1; Phil. 1:1; Gal. 1:10). As Best has observed, "a slave is not paid" (*Paul and His Converts*, Edinburgh: T. & T. Clark, 1988, p. 103).

What material assistance he received from *individuals* such as Phoebe and Gaius[12] was probably also modest: there are no firm grounds for assuming that these benefactors were rich in anything but commitment.[13] What support Paul gained appears to have only just made up the shortfall he suffered as a consequence of his erratic lifestyle: in the sight of others he remained one of the poor (2 Cor. 6:8–10).[14] Any income he received from a source other than his own labours could not have been substantial.[15]

The suggestion, made by E. A. Judge, that Paul gained earnings as a professional lecturer, a sophist, in addition to his income from his trade, is implausible.[16] Although "the word 'sophist' is as splendid as it is imprecise"[17] (and Judge's use of the term is particularly so)[18] it is possible

[12] Phoebe (Rom. 16:1); Gaius (Rom. 16:23).

[13] See below for prosopographic profiles of these two figures.

[14] Even if, as seems likely following the work of D. L. Mealand, the apostle here employs a rhetorical commonplace, with parallels in Cynic diatribe, this is no reason to doubt that it reflected Paul's material situation: most Cynics were utterly destitute upon taking up the philosophic life ("As Having Nothing and Yet Possessing Everything", *ZNW* 67 (1976) 277–279; Epictetus, 4.8.31; Dio Chrysostom, *Orationes* 6.8, 8.30).

The details of the peristasis catalogues cannot be doubted on the grounds that such indignities could not have befallen Paul as a Roman citizen (which Acts records he was – 16:37, 38; 22:25–29; 23:27). The rights of citizens were often ignored (see P. Garnsey, "Legal Privilege in the Roman Empire", *The Social Organization of Law*, ed. D. Black and M. Mileski, London: Seminar Press, 1973, pp. 161ff. See Cicero, *De Fato* 10.32.2; *Actio in Verrem* 5.162ff.; Suetonius, *Galba* 9; Cassius Dio 64.2.3).

[15] The Acts account of his final two years under house arrest at Rome (28:30) does not provide grounds for believing that at least during this period he lived a life of luxury at the expense of others. There are good reasons for assuming that the author of Acts considered Paul to be supporting himself with his own hands: as H. J. Cadbury has observed, "μίσθωμα means money paid . . . and it may refer here to what was paid to Paul as wage for his work rather that what was paid by Paul for his food and lodging" (H. J. Cadbury, "Luke's Interest in Lodging". *JBL* 45 (1926), p. 322).

[16] Edwin A. Judge, "The Early Christians as a Scholastic Community", *JRH* 1 (1960) 4–15, 125–137.

[17] G. Anderson, *The Second Sophistic. A Cultural Phenomenon in the Roman Empire*, London: Routledge, 1993, p. 16.

[18] Judge's category of 'sophist' is extremely vague. For Stowers it is as worthless as the notion of the θεῖος ἀνήρ that has proved so influential in the field of New Testament Christology:

> Judge's tendency is much like that of scholars who use the divine man concept. By lumping together Sophists as diverse as Aristides, Cynics, and Apollonius of Tyana, he has created a class which is so broad and heterogeneous that almost any characteristic can be ascribed to it. ("Social Status, Public Speaking and Private Teaching: The Circumstances of Paul's Preaching Activity", *NovT* 26 (1984), p. 74, fn. 82)

to say, with reasonable certainty, that sophists were members of the socially élite[19] who regaled their audiences with powerful oratory, one of the distinguishing features of which was its self-conscious use of references to classical literature.[20] Paul, as we have just observed, was considered one of the indigent, whose 'oratory' failed to impress (2 Cor. 10:10) and whose references to the Greek canon were virtually non-existent (not for him extensive allusions to the *Phaedrus* or the *Iliad*, just one hackneyed quotation from Menander).[21] Not only was his style of teaching at variance with that of such people but his Jewishness,[22] his labour as an artisan, and his allegiance to Christ, would have precluded him from membership of this prestigious profession and from the financial benefits it would have entailed.[23] It is highly unlikely that Paul lived most of his missionary life as a sophist, attaining the lucrative "patronage of eminent persons"[24] as Judge would have us believe.

We can, therefore, I believe, affirm with some confidence A. Deissmann's contention, that Paul was a craftsman whose wages "were the economic basis of his existence".[25]

---

[19] Stowers, "Social Status", p. 75. See, for example, F. Millar, *The Emperor in the Roman World*, second edition, London: Duckworth, 1992, p. 6; G. Bowersock, *Greek Sophists in the Roman Empire*, Oxford: Clarendon Press, 1969; and E. L. Bowie, "The Importance of Sophists", *YCS* 27 (1982) 29–59.

[20] See Anderson, *Second Sophistic*.

[21] 1 Cor. 15:33. By Paul's day this saying had become almost proverbial. See A. J. Malherbe, "The Beasts at Ephesus", *JBL* 87 (1968), p. 73.

[22] Phil. 3:5; 2 Cor. 11:22; Gal. 1:13–14.

[23] Stowers, "Social Status", p. 81.

[24] Judge understands this patronage to have been substantial enough to allow the apostle to maintain a "retinue of assistants" ("The Early Christians", p. 127).

[25] Deissmann, *Paul*, p. 48. Although Deissmann's speculations are, perhaps, a little fanciful, he observes that incidental details contained in Paul's epistles appear to confirm this picture of his life. The apostle's regular complaint that he feared he was "labouring in vain" (Gal. 4:11; Phil. 2:16; 1 Cor. 15:58) is in Deissmann's opinion, a "trembling echo" of the experience of having work rejected by a client (*Light From the Ancient East*, London: Hodder & Stoughton, 1910, p. 317). Paul's self-conscious reference to his crude handwriting in Gal. 6:11 is, for Deissmann, a possible indication that Paul's hands had been deformed by his arduous labours (*Paul: A Study*, p. 49). Does his choice of words in 2 Cor. 5:1–4 also owe itself, perhaps, in part, to his experience of work?

It should be added that even if we accept the historical detail of Paul paying the expenses necessary for the completion of the Nazirite vows of the four Jerusalem brethren (Acts 21:24), which would have involved a considerable financial outlay (*m. Nazir* 6.6–11; Num. 6:1–21), this does not necessarily indicate that he was wealthy (as, for example, B. Rapske maintains in *The Book of Acts in its First Century Setting. Volume 3: Paul in Roman Custody*, Carlisle: Paternoster Press, 1994, p. 106). It is quite possible that he was attempting to pay these out of the 'collection' he had brought with him, as J. Murphy-O'Connor suggests (*Paul: A Critical Life*, Oxford: Clarendon Press, 1996, p. 350).

The myth of Paul's affluent background

It is often asserted that Paul came from a wealthy background[26] and as a consequence did not share completely the bleak lives of the impoverished. As E. P. Sanders, for example, maintains, "Paul's letters show him to be a man of what we would now call middle-class upbringing",[27] and consequently ". . . his poverty . . . was voluntary, and in Paul's letters we do not hear the voice of the lowest level of Greco-Roman society".[28]

A number of disparate points are adduced as evidence of his prosperous upbringing; in rough descending order of their importance and popularity amongst exegetes these are: his Roman and Tarsan citizenships; his education; his experience of, and attitude to, work; his reaction to social affronts; his ability to socialise with the privileged; the tenor of his ethics (in particular his political ethics); his treatment by the Roman authorities; his lineage; his Pharisaism; and his employment of a secretary. But none, as we shall see, are of any value in determining Paul's economic past.

For many New Testament scholars Paul's Roman citizenship[29] proves conclusively that he enjoyed a privileged life before becoming an

[26] He was "middle-class" (Mommsen in Hengel, *Pre-Christian Paul*, p. 15); "petty bourgeois" (Hengel, *Pre-Christian Paul*, p. 17); "upper middle class" (R. Tidball, *An Introduction to the Sociology of the New Testament*, Exeter: Paternoster Press, 1983, p. 93); "well-to-do" (N. Dahl, "Paul and Possessions", *Studies in Paul*, Minneapolis: Augsburg, 1977, p. 35); "born with a silver spoon in his mouth" (Best, *Converts*, p. 10); "upper class" (Horsley, *New Documents*, vol. 5, p. 19); a member of the "higher strata" (G. Theissen, *The Social Setting of Pauline Christianity*, Philadelphia: Fortress Press, 1982, p. 36); "of the provincial aristocracy" (R. Hock, "Paul's Tentmaking and the Problem of his Social Class", *JBL* 97 (1978), p. 562). Socio-economic descriptions of the apostle vary, and the nomenclatures employed are no doubt intended to describe Paul in terms broader than that of economics alone, but it is fair to say that most imply that he did not have an indigent upbringing.

A few scholars have dissented from this consensus: W. Stegemann, "War der Apostel Paulus ein römischer Bürger?" *ZNW* 78 (1987) 200–229 unequivocally sees Paul as lower class, as do A. J. Saldarini *Pharisees, Scribes, and Sadducees in Palestinian Society*, Edinburgh, 1989, pp. 139 and 141 (though with a little more equivocation), D. Engels, *Roman Corinth: An Alternative Model for a Classical City*, Chicago: University of Chicago Press, 1990, p. 314, and, of course, Deissmann, *Paul*, p. 51 and *Light from the Ancient East*, p. 317.

[27] Sanders, *Paul*, p. 10.

[28] Sanders, *Paul*, p. 11. Dahl also makes such a distinction: during his missionary years Paul probably ". . . knew want more often than plenty", though "there can be little doubt that he came from a rather well-to-do family" ("Paul and Possessions", p. 35).

[29] Acts 16:37, 38; 22:25–29; 23:27 (which he acquired at birth, Acts 22:28). The historicity of this detail, found only in Acts, has been doubted by a few scholars, e.g. most recently, W. Stegemann, "Apostel Paulus". For a discussion of Stegemann's position see H. W. Tajra, *The Trial of St Paul*, Tübingen: J. C. B.

apostle. For C. H. Dodd, for instance, it provides the irrefutable detail that establishes his previous wealth,[30] and most would subscribe to the words of Ramsay without too many qualms, that Roman citizenship ". . . placed Paul amid the aristocracy of any provincial town".[31] The usual assumption is that citizenship was almost entirely monopolised by the powerful and wealthy of the Empire (outside of the city of Rome itself), and, particularly at this early date in the Principate,[32] can be seen as a reliable indicator of a person's high social-economic status. In the words of Mommsen, for example, only "prominent municipal figures" were the recipients of citizenship.[33]

There needs, however, to be considerable change in the perception of the *civitas Romana* amongst New Testament scholars. Roman citizenship must be freed from being thought of as bound up in any direct way with ruling élites of the eastern Empire and recognised as a thoroughly ambiguous signifier of economic power. The small number of Roman citizens that lived outside the capital[34] were not

---

Mohr, 1989, pp. 86–89 and S. R. Llewelyn and R. A. Kearsley, *New Documents Illustrating Early Christianity*, vol. 6, North Ryde: Maquarrie University, 1992, pp. 154–155. Saldarini also doubts the historical reliability of this biographical information (*Pharisees, Scribes and Sadducees*, p. 142), as does H. Koester, *History and Literature of Early Christianity*, vol. 2, Philadelphia: Fortress Press, 1982, p. 98.

For Roman citizenship in general see the thorough study by A. N. Sherwin-White, *The Roman Citizenship*, Oxford: Oxford University Press, 1974.

[30] C. H. Dodd, *The Meaning of Paul For Today*, London: Fontana, 1958, p. 22.

[31] W. M. Ramsay, *St Paul the Traveller and the Roman Citizen*, London: Hodder & Stoughton, 1895, p. 31. See Hock, "Paul's Tentmaking", p. 557; Judge, "The Early Christians", p. 127; Dahl, "Paul and Possessions", p. 36; F. F. Bruce, *Paul: Apostle of the Free Spirit*, Exeter: Paternoster Press, 1977, p. 38.

[32] The number of citizens in the Empire increased dramatically in the following years, culminating in Caracalla's edict of 212 which granted citizenship to almost all the free inhabitants of the Empire (Garnsey and Saller, *The Roman Empire*, p. 115).

[33] Mommsen, in Hengel, *Pre-Christian Paul*, p. 15. Judge says much the same in *Social Pattern*, p. 58. See also R. Longenecker, *The Ministry and Message of Paul*, Grand Rapids: Zondervan, 1971, p. 21; H. J. Schoeps, *Paul: The Theology of the Apostle in the Light of Jewish History*, London: Lutterworth Press, 1959, p. 25; F. F. Bruce, "Paul in Acts and Letters", *Dictionary of Paul and His Letters*, ed. G. Hawthorne et al., Leicester: InterVarsity Press, 1993, p. 682.

[34] One of the major paths of non-élite entry into citizenship, its granting to the veterans of the *auxilia*, was not opened up until the reign of Claudius (Clark, "Social Status", p. 110).

Perhaps the most important source for estimating the number of citizens during Paul's life is Augustus' *Res Gestae* of 14 CE which puts the total at 4,937,000. However, Brunt has made a convincing case for seeing this figure as a significant underestimate and calculates that at the time of the *Res Gestae* the number was in fact somewhere between 5,924,000 and 6,171,000 (*Italian Manpower*, p. 116). Of these approximately 1,870,000 were domiciled outside Italy (pp. 264–265).

aristocrats.[35] The overwhelming majority of them acquired their citizenship by being either manumitted by a Roman citizen or by being a descendant of a person who had been so manumitted. It is probable that Paul's predecessors obtained it in just such a way[36] and thus it can tell us nothing about the apostle's supposed wealth.[37]

Paul's Tarsan citizenship also fails to provide us with evidence of the apostle's wealthy past, although for some it has proved crucial in making just such an assessment. For Theissen, for example, it is the only evidence he deems necessary to be certain that Paul "enjoyed an unusual, privileged status"; conclusive proof that he was one of

[35] There was no *systematic* policy of granting citizenship in the Empire as an aid to the Romanisation of the local élites. As Garnsey and Saller have observed: "In the province of Lycia/Pamphylia in south-west Asia Minor, fewer than half of about a hundred known holders of the provincial high priesthood, the highest local office, were Roman citizens before the turn of the second century AD" (*The Roman Empire*, p. 15).

[36] Perhaps one of his predecessors had been amongst the many enslaved Jewish prisoners of war who had acquired citizenship upon their freedom (Philo, *De Legatione ad Gaium* 155, 157) and had subsequently returned to the eastern provinces of the Empire, following the encouragement of the Imperial authorities, as Hengel proposes (*Pre-Christian Paul*, pp. 6–15). The importance of manumission as a method of obtaining citizenship is demonstrated by the examples of self-sale undertaken solely to achieve this end (Petronius, *Satyricon* 57.4; Livy 41:8–9; P. Oxy. 26.3312). See also Lentz, *Luke's Portrait of Paul*, pp. 43–50.

Citizenship could, of course, also be purchased (see Acts 22:27–28; Cassius Dio 60.17. 6–8; A. N. Sherwin-White, *Roman Society and Roman Law in the New Testament*, Oxford: Clarendon Press, 1963, pp. 154–156); or fraudulently claimed (see Suetonius, *Claudius* 25).

[37] *Contra* M. Hengel who assumes that the bestowal of citizenship upon freedmen virtually guaranteed a person a comfortable life. Having persuasively argued that Paul probably came from a family of freedmen he considers this proof enough that he could not have experienced poverty, maintaining that, ". . . we have quite a number of accounts of very rich freedmen from the period of the early Principate" (*Pre-Christian Paul*, p.15). He substantiates this statement by giving an (inaccurate) account of Trimalchio (Petronius' *Satyricon* 15). The example of Trimalchio and other rich freedmen is hardly typical, and Hengel's assertion that these people constituted "quite a number" in the Graeco-Roman world is misleading. There were millions of freedmen in the Roman Empire at any one time, and the handful of those who obtained wealth (as a consequence almost entirely of selective, élite, patronage) are a statistically irrelevant fraction of this figure, however much they may attract our attention in the surviving sources; they certainly do not provide grounds for Hengel's assurance that Paul's family escaped from the difficult lot experienced by the great mass of the working population.

As de Ste Croix has pertinently observed:

> I feel that too much reliance has been placed on the fictitious *cena Trimalchionis* in Petronius: its inventions have too easily been accepted as facts and its deliberately comic exaggerations treated as if they were typical . . . Many of them (freedmen) must have been poverty stricken wretches who were either allowed to buy their

the "wise, powerful, and of noble birth" (1 Cor. 1:26).[38] It is argued that because, according to Dio Chrysostom, a payment of 500 drachmae was a condition of its attainment[39] then the evangelist must have come from a family of considerable means.[40] However, the question of Tarsan citizenship is rather more complex than has often been realised. A closer reading of Dio Chrysostom is called for. It is apparent that there were varied and sometimes conflicting perceptions of who, amongst the inhabitants of Tarsus, could be considered citizens. In addition to the élite group that could afford the 500 drachmae, there was a much greater body of individuals, born and brought up in the city, drawn from the ranks of the artisans, who were often regarded as enfranchised and acted as such, taking their place in the popular assemblies, the ἐκκλησίαι (participation in which was the symbolic affirmation *par excellence* of a citizen of a πόλις). The élite were equivocal in their assessment of the legitimacy of these 'citizens', and Dio Chrysostom upbraided them for their destructive indecision in this regard, but it is quite clear, from what we can glean of the strident behaviour of these non-élite "citizens" themselves, that they did not have any reservations about their status.[41] It is reasonable therefore to assume that the use of the word πολίτης[42] in οὐκ ἀσήμου πόλεως πολίτης (Acts 21:39) tells us nothing about Paul's economic history – it could have been employed, quite naturally, by a person who was far from wealthy.

Paul's supposed high level of education also fails to provide evidence of a moneyed past. Scholarly assumptions about the extent of schooling

---

freedom with every penny they had managed to accumulate as their peculium during slavery, or were left at their master's death with the gift of freedom and nothing else. (*Class Struggle*, p. 178)

[38] Theissen, *Social Setting*, p. 36. For Hemer, it is evidence that Paul's family were "of standing" in Tarsus (*The Book of Acts*, p. 127). See also Bruce, "Paul in Acts and Letters", p. 681.

[39] A sum approximately equal to two years wages for a day labourer. Dio Chrysostom, *Orationes* 34.21–23. See T. Callander, "The Tarsian Orations of Dio Chrysostom", *JHS* 24 (1904), p. 66.

[40] Hengel, *Pre-Christian Paul*, p. 99, fn. 33. See also Bruce, *The Acts of the Apostles*, p. 399; H. Conzelmann, *Acts of the Apostles*, Philadelphia: Fortress, 1987, p. 184; Haenchen, *The Acts of the Apostles*, p. 620.

[41] See Dio Chrysostom, *Orationes* 34.21–23.

[42] The word is also more ambiguous than is often presupposed. According to Tajra, its use in the LXX, Josephus, and the New Testament gives us grounds for translating it as "inhabitant" rather than "citizen"; for him it is "non-judicial . . . a statement of domicile not a proclamation of citizenship" (*Trial*, p. 79; though see Rapske, *Paul in Roman Custody*, p. 76).

Paul displays in his writings have sometimes been somewhat rash. Betz, for example, presupposes that he reached the tertiary level within the Graeco-Roman system,[43] which would have placed him alongside the likes of Seneca. It is important to remember that his contemporaries and near contemporaries were less glowing in their estimates of his academic training: in 2 Cor. 11:6 Paul implies that he has been called an ἰδιώτης, a technical term which indicates that his opponents considered him "unqualified".[44] But more importantly, the underlying supposition which is key in this particular argument, that education and wealth are immutably bound together, is erroneous. Much of the discussion on this subject has seen New Testament scholars hampered by viewing the question of Paul's education too rigidly in terms of Graeco-Roman schooling (which was indeed expensive);[45] as though he could only have learnt to read and write Greek by paying fees to an elementary teacher,[46] or as if he could have only gained what knowledge

---

[43] H. D. Betz, "The Literary Composition and Function of Paul's Letter to the Galatians", *NTS* 21 (1975) 353–379. C. Forbes, "Comparison, Self-Praise, and Irony: Paul's Boasting and the Convention of Hellenistic Rhetoric", *NTS* 32 (1986), p. 24: ". . . his education reached at least beyond the level of the grammatici, and into rhetorical school". See also A. J. Malherbe, *Social Aspects of Early Christianity*, second edition, Philadelphia: Fortress, 1983, p. 59; Koester *History and Literature*, vol. 2, p. 97; B. Witherington, *Conflict and Community in Corinth: A Socio-Rhetorical Commentary on 1 and 2 Corinthians*, Carlisle: Paternoster Press, 1995, p. 2.

[44] Edwin A. Judge, "Cultural Conformity and Innovation in Paul", *TB* 35 (1984), p. 13. Cf. also Acts 4:13. Origen said much the same of the apostle according to Eusebius in *Historia Ecclesiastica* 6.25.11. The pagan critic Hierocles called him ἀπαίδευτος, devoid of education (Eusebius, *Contra Hieroclem* 2).

[45] Excepting a few lecturers and schools funded by the benefactions of Emperors, client rulers, or municipalities, formal education in the Roman Empire was entirely private and expensive (see H. I. Marrou, *A History of Education in Antiquity*, London: Sheed & Ward, 1956, pp. 284ff.) and so only a small number could afford any formal schooling beyond a primary level. At the extreme end of the scale, we get an insight into the potential costs for the very well educated from Cicero: he wrote to Atticus that his property investments in Rome gave him an annual revenue of 80,000 sesterces which was enough to pay for 160 legionaries, but only just covered the expense of sending his son, Marcus, to be educated in Athens (*Epistulae ad Atticum* 12.32.2; 15.17.1; 16.1.5; 20.4; see also the discussion in Stanley F. Bonner, *Education in Ancient Rome: From the Elder Cato to the Younger Pliny*, London: Metheun & Co., 1977, pp. 91–96).

H. Marsh (*The Rebel Jew*, London: Skilton & Shaw, 1980, p. 25), and Dahl, ("Paul and Possessions," p. 36) assume that Paul's family must have been particularly privileged as they could afford to send him away to Jerusalem to gain his education (they both conjecture that his family remained based in Tarsus), as though Paul was packed off to study in some way akin to Marcus.

[46] Too often the debate about literacy has been frustrated by the presumption that literacy and schooling are inseparable in antiquity, as we can see, for example, in the influential work of William Harris (*Ancient Literacy*, Harvard: Harvard University Press, 1989

he displays of specifically Hellenistic thought and style[47] at the hands of expensive grammarians or rhetors.[48] Not only were there plenty of

and "*Literacy and Epigraphy*", *ZPE* 52 (1983) 87–111). There are many other paths for the transmission of literacy as Nicholas Horsfall has shown in his pertinent criticisms of Harris ("Statistics or State of Mind", *Literacy in the Roman World*, Ann Arbor: Journal of Roman Archaeology, 1991, pp. 59–76; see also M. Beard's criticisms in J. Reynolds et al., "Roman Inscriptions 1981–1985", *JRS* 76 (1986), p. 142). It can be learnt in the context of, for example, the *familia* and the workshop. Religion could also be important in acquisition of this skill. The emphasis, amongst Jews, on the reading of the Torah and attaining the education necessary to accomplish this seems to have been especially significant in their high relative levels of literacy (Josephus, *Contra Apionem* 2.204, *Antiquitates Judaicae* 4.211; Philo, *De Legatione ad Gaium* 115, 210; *T. Levi* 13.2). In Paul's case this was a particularly important factor in his Greek literacy as his use of the LXX indicates. It would be fair to argue that instruction in reading the Septuagint or a similar translation had been a central feature of his childhood.

We should beware of making the deceptively easy but profoundly naive assumption that there is, *a priori*, a direct correlation between socio-economic status and literacy. The prolific examples of graffiti from Pompeii provide us with evidence that makes such a belief problematic: as Tanzer observes, its prevalence seems to indicate that, "everybody could read and almost everybody could, and apparently did, write" (*The Common People*, p. 83; see also Franklin, "Literacy"). The use of placards by emperors and others to communicate to crowds (Cassius Dio 69:16; Hopkins, *Death and Renewal*, p. 24; Paul Veyne, "Titulus Praelatus," *RA* (1983) 281–300), and the adorning of pagan temples with written prayers to the gods (Pliny the Younger, *Epistulae* 8.8.7; see Mary Beard, "Writing and Religion: Ancient Literacy and the Function of the Written Word in Roman Religion", *Literacy in the Roman World*, ed. J. H. Humphrey, Ann Arbor: Journal of Roman Archaeology, 1991, pp. 35–58) indicate the extent of literacy amongst the general population, regardless of wealth. Certainly we have plenty of evidence of literate non-élite groups in Graeco-Roman society, such as slaves (A. Booth "The Schooling of Slaves in First Century Rome", *TAPA* 109 (1979) 11–19 and Clarence A. Forbes, "The Education and Training of Slaves in Antiquity", *TAPA* 86 (1955) 321–360) and soldiers (E. E. Best, "The Literate Roman Soldier", *CJ* 62 (1966) 122–127).

See also the following significant contributions to the debate: James Keenan, "Ancient Literacy", *AHB* 5 (1991) 101–106; J. H. Humphrey (ed.), *Literacy in the Roman World*, Ann Arbor: Journal of Roman Archaeology, 1991; and H. Gamble, *Books and Readers in the Early Church: A History of Early Christian Texts*, New Haven: Yale University Press, 1995.

[47] The study of Paul's rhetorical technique in particular has revealed the extent of his debt to the argumentative, expository and dialogical forms found in the rhetorical tradition of his day. The literature produced by this burgeoning area of enquiry is now considerable. See D. F. Watson, "Rhetorical Criticism of the Pauline Epistles Since 1975", *CRBS forthcoming* and D. F. Watson and A. J. Hauser, *Rhetorical Criticism of the Bible: A Comprehensive Bibliography with Notes on History and Method*, Leiden: E. J. Brill, 1994, pp. 178–201. However, as Stanley E. Porter has oberved, many treatments of the apostle have tended to exaggerate his use of the formal categories of classical rhetoric ("The Theoretical Justification for Application of Rhetorical Categories to Pauline Epistolary Literature", *Rhetoric and the New Testament*, ed. S. Porter and T. Olbricht, Sheffield: JSOT Press, 1994, pp. 100–122).

[48] For Sanders, for example, Paul's Greek is evidence that the apostle was essentially "middle-class" (*Paul*, p. 10).

opportunities for much learning to be picked up informally in the general Graeco-Roman urban environment[49] but Paul's Pharisaic education in Jerusalem[50] and his probable contact with Greek synagogues there[51] would have given him ample access to such knowledge[52]

[49] As George A. Kennedy noted, in his influential work, *New Testament Interpretation Through Rhetorical Criticism*, London: University of Carolina Press, 1984, pp. 9–10; see also Gamble, *Books and Readers in the Early Church*, p. 35. Indeed, this is exactly what Simon the Shoemaker (Diogenes Laertius, *Vitae Philosophorum* 2.122) and Philiscus the Cobbler (*Teles fr.* 4. B) seem to have done. We should not underestimate the opportunities available. Popular philosophical preaching was obviously a common feature of urban life and gave "even the unlettered a chance to gain some philosophical understanding. Thus Jews and Christians could have received a smattering of philosophy without ever having received a formal, Hellenistic, education" (J. T. Townsend, "Ancient Education in the Time of the Early Roman Empire", *Early Church History: The Roman Empire as the Setting of Primitive Christianity*, ed. S. Benko and J. O'Rourke, London: Oliphants, 1971, p. 153). Indeed, they could hardly avoid it. Graeco-Roman culture was widely disseminated and displayed (it was not solely the preserve of the élite): quotations from authors such as Virgil, Ovid, Lucretius, much more complex than the one example we have from Paul, were found scratched on walls in Pompeii. (See Tanzer, *The Common People*, pp. 84–85).

Even if we accept van Unnik's proposal that Paul spent little time at all in Tarsus but passed his formative years in Jerusalem, the potential for coming across Hellenistic ideas was still great (see C. van Unnik, *Tarsus and Jerusalem?* London: Epworth Press, 1962 and also, more recently, Hengel, *Pre-Christian Paul*, pp. 18–39).

[50] Paul clearly enjoyed a high level of Pharisaic education according to his own admission (Gal. 1:14), even if we doubt the evidence from Acts 22:3 that he studied at the feet of Gamaliel (something which is open to question; see Hock, *Social Context*, p. 74, fn. 23 and Hengel, *Pre-Christian Paul*, p. 28 for opposing viewpoints).

[51] These were more common in Jerusalem than we might suppose. 'Hellenists' were an influential group in Jerusalem society, as we can see from the split in the early Jerusalem church between Ἑλληνισταί and Ἐβραῖοι (Acts 6:1). Hengel estimates that between 10 and 15% of the city's population had Greek as their mother tongue (*Pre-Christian Paul*, p. 55). Hence, it is no surprise that our sources indicate a prolific number of Greek synagogues operating in the first century (*Pre-Christian Paul*, p. 56; Acts 6:9) and these synagogues seem to have had as part of their function an emphasis upon teaching (A. F. Zimmermann, *Die urchristlichen Lehrer*, Tübingen: J. C. B. Mohr, 1988, pp. 69–91).

[52] For example *b. Sotah* 49b speaks of 500 students of Greek wisdom and 500 students of Hebrew wisdom in the school of Gamaliel. Whether this tradition is accurate or not it is, at the least, "a symbolic indication of the penetration of Greek culture into rabbinic schools" (A. D. Momigliano, "Greek Culture and the Jews", *The Legacy of Greece*, ed. M. I. Finley, Oxford: Clarendon Press, 1984, pp. 357ff.) demonstrating its availability to a Pharisee such as Paul (for a similar passage see *b. Kamma* 83a). Indeed, it is quite possible that rhetorical handbooks had found their way into Pharisaic education (H. Fischel, "Story and History: Observations on Graeco-Roman Rhetoric and Pharisaism", *American Oriental Society, Mid-West Branch, Semi-Centennial Volume*, ed. D. Sinor, Bloomington: Indiana University, 1969, pp. 78–79). Greek ideas had thoroughly permeated Jewish life in Israel by the time of Paul. (The literature on this subject is extensive but see especially M. Hengel, *Judaism and Hellenism*, London: SCM, 1974).

at little or no cost.[53] Particularly in the setting of Judaism we should beware of the simple equation of education and economic status.

Paul's experience of, and his attitude to, work, has also provided evidence of his former affluence.[54] It is assumed by many that the apostle took up a manual trade at the beginning of his studies in order to follow the rabbinic convention of his day, expressed in the maxim, "Excellent is the study of the Torah together with worldly occupation."[55] As a consequence, for some scholars, he ". . . must not be regarded as having the social status of a manual worker".[56] It is also presumed that his attitude towards his labour "bespeaks a certain social standing".[57] It is maintained that he came from a wealthy background and was never fully at ease with the life of an artisan that the halakah thrust upon him (and which he continued to practise when he became a δοῦλος Χριστοῦ).

However, this popular portrayal of Paul is much more problematic than is often realised. Firstly, it is very arguable whether he would have adopted a trade in adulthood, in accordance with rabbinic practice.

[53] *Contra* Marsh (*The Rebel Jew*, p. 25) and Dahl ("Paul and Possessions", p. 36). Such an education was essentially free: at least some rabbis came from the labouring classes (Abba Hilkiah, Hillel, and Shammai (*b. Ta'anith* 23a-b.; *b. Yoma* 35b; *b. Shabbath* 31a)) and others, with their students, seem to have suffered severe poverty during their studies (see J. Jeremias, *Jerusalem*, pp. 115–116). Hengel, *Pre-Christian Paul*, p. 114, fn. 119 argues that these traditions are not late and legendary, as Hock maintains (*Social Context*, p. 74).

[54] It is necessary to note, at the beginning of this section, that the contributions of Hock ("Paul's Tentmaking", and *Social Context*) to the recent discussion surrounding this issue, are, at least in some respects, contradictory. In his article Hock argues that Paul was an aristocrat and took up manual labour when in need (as a result of his Christian mission); ". . . one of the socially privileged classes who when faced with finding support turned to a trade" (p. 563). However, in his book he maintains that Paul acquired his trade as a youth, from his father (p. 24). Although Hock asserts on page 35 of the same work that Paul was "by birth a member of the social élite" this is hardly consistent with such an opinion.

[55] *m. Aboth* 2.2.

[56] M. Dibelius quoted in Hock, "Paul's Tentmaking", p. 557. Also see Bornkamm, *Paul*, p. 12, and Bruce, *Paul*, p. 108.

Alternatively, Hengel (*Pre-Christian Paul*, p. 16) speculates that he may have taken up manual labour as a missionary in order to be financially independent. Hock suggests that he might have followed the example of such aristocrats as Agathocles of Samos (Lucian, *Toxaris* 17–18) who learnt a trade when he found himself in dire need ("Paul's Tentmaking", p. 563).

[57] Forbes, "Comparison", p. 24. C. H. Dodd, "The Mind of Paul: A Psychological Approach", *BJRL* 17 (1933), p. 95; K. Wengst, *Pax Romana and the Peace of Jesus Christ*, London: SCM, 1987, p. 74; Murphy-O'Connor, *Paul*, p. 40.

This custom[58] developed late in the second century, in response to the economic trauma that followed the Jewish wars.[59] Secondly, the accusation that Paul demonstrates a "snobbish" attitude[60] to his own toil is extremely ill thought out. Whilst for some the evangelist perceived of his work as degrading,[61] others conjecture that he saw it as a source of self-conscious pride,[62] and a few believe that he experienced both of these feelings,[63] it is not the case that any of these views provided evidence that he was member of the élite. In fact, both the disparagement of physical work, and unabashed pride in it, can be found in élite and non-élite Graeco-Roman and Jewish sources.[64] Such sentiments, if indeed they are there at all,[65] tell us nothing about Paul's socio-economic past.[66]

[58] Such a custom was in contrast with the traditional practise of the wider Graeco-Roman world (Burford, *Craftsmen*, pp. 89ff.). Starting a trade in later life was not unknown, as we can see in the example of Corbyle (Lucian, *Dialogi Meretricii* 293), but was rare.

[59] ". . . the ideal of combining Torah and a trade is difficult to establish much earlier than the middle of the second century A.D., that is, long after Paul" (Hock, *Social Context*, p. 23). See E. E. Urbach, "Class-Status and Leadership in the World of the Palestinian Sages", *PIASH* 2 (1968) 38–74. Before this rabbis who worked did so out of necessity not as a consequence of religio-ideological motives.

[60] Hock, "Paul's Tentmaking", p. 562.

[61] R. Longenecker, *The Ministry and Message of Paul*, Grand Rapids: Zondervan, 1971, p. 21.

[62] Dahl, "Paul and Possessions", p. 35, and C. H. Dodd in A. D. Nock, *St Paul*, London: Oxford University Press, 1960, p. 21.

[63] Forbes considers that Paul shows both "shame and paradoxical pride" ("Comparison", p. 24).

[64] Cicero, *De Officiis* 1.150 and Seneca, *Epistulae* 88.21, are illustrative of aristocratic disdain for work, and Lucian, *Fugitivi* 13 gives us clear evidence that the non-élite could express similar opinions. Dio Chrysostom, *Orationes* 7.103–53 demonstrates that the wealthy could also praise manual labour (see also Virgil, *Georgicon* 1.145), and inscriptions on tombstones (MacMullen, *Roman Social Relations*, p. 202, fn. 105, also J. P. V. D. Balsdon, *Life and Leisure in Ancient Rome*, New York: McGraw-Hill 1969, p. 135), the existence of trade *collegia*, and the tendency for many artisans to put their names on their produce (CIL 1.2.2437, 406, 2489) likewise show that at least some of the Graeco-Roman non-élite could take pride in their work (see also Joshel, *Work, Identity and Legal Status*).

The absence of distinct 'zoning' within most Graeco-Roman cities, and the existence of *tabernae* integrated into the fabric of élite housing further demonstrates the equivocal nature of attitudes towards physical labour amongst all elements in first-century society (see Wallace-Hadrill, *Houses and Society*, p. 135–139).

[65] Examples of Paul's supposed 'snobbish' attitude towards labour, read in context, appear to indicate no such thing. When in 1 Cor. 4:12 Paul refers to working with his own hands, Sanders comments: "This is revealing: the poor do not find working with their hands to be worthy of special remark" (*Paul*, p. 12). However, the context is unusual, and his use of the qualifying expression understandable. The apostle is engaged in

Likewise, the apostle's reaction towards social affronts is an ambiguous indicator of his background, although many have seen it as indicative of Paul's previously comfortable life. Judge's comment on 1 Cor. 4:13 typifies this common position:

> This social distinction explains his constant sensitivity to the humiliations he suffered from time to time. 'We are made as the filth of the world, and are the off-scouring of all things unto this day' (1 Cor. 4:13) is certainly not the complaint of a person to whom social affronts were normal. On the contrary, they are felt as indignities that he ought not to have been subjected to.[67]

This kind of logic is, however, extremely dubious. Concepts such as dignity and honour are not the prerogative of the wealthy;[68] it hardly needs stating that all human beings are concerned with their worth in their own eyes and in the eyes of their contemporaries, and the poor of the Graeco-Roman world do not provide an exception to this. They were as sensitive to humiliation and offence as anyone else. The *Satyricon* provides an example of this:

> Corax, the hired man, a constant grumbler in his job, kept putting his bag down, hurling insults at us for hurrying, and vowing that he'd throw away the bags and run off with his load.

---

bringing back down to earth those who have arrogant spiritual pretensions, who have declared themselves rich and kings (1 Cor. 4:8), by describing his own earthly reality of suffering and poverty, a reality in which they also share: it is no wonder that he spells out what is conventionally taken as read. The mention of "hands" is also, to an extent, forced upon him by his usual usage of the words ἐργάζομαι and κοπιάω: he normally employs these terms and their cognates to describe his non-physical, gospel labours (for this use of ἐργάζομαι see 1 Cor. 3:13, 14, 15, 15:58, 16:10; Phil. 1:6, 2:30; 1 Thess. 1:3 (and also Rom. 16:21 for cognate noun ὁ συνεργός) and for κοπιάω Rom. 16:6, 12; 1 Cor. 15:10, 15:58, 16:16; Phil. 2:16; 1 Thess. 5:12, 17).

[66] It is also sometimes maintained that Paul's olive tree analogy in Rom. 11:17–24 is evidence of his affluence, displaying a striking ignorance of everyday agricultural practice. However, such criticisms are misplaced and do the apostle an injustice, as Zielser has shown (see A. G. Baxter and J. A. Ziesler, "Paul and Arboriculture: Romans 11:17–24", *JSNT* 24 (1985) 24–32).

[67] Judge, *Social Pattern*, p. 58. Judge says much the same himself elsewhere: "His catalogues of personal hardships and indignities prove not that he was an insignificant person, but that he was sufficiently important for his misfortunes to afford a valuable lesson in humility" ("Scholastic", p. 136). See also Hock, *Social Context*, p. 35.

[68] See, for example, J. Pitt-Rivers' study of Andulasian peasants, "Honour and Social Status", *Honour and Shame: The Values of Mediterranean Society*, ed. J. G. Peristany, London: Weidenfeld & Nicolson, 1973, pp. 21–77, especially pp. 39ff. Malina makes an equally questionable statement: ". . . an inferior on the ladder of social standing, power, and sexual status does not have enough honour to resent the affront of a superior" (*The New Testament World: Insights from Cultural Anthropology*, London: SCM, 1981, p. 36).

"What is this, you people?" he said. "Do you think that I'm a beast of burden or a ship for carrying stones? I contracted for a man's job, not a dray-horse's. I'm a free man as much as you are, even if my father did leave me poor."

Not content with cursing, every so often he lifted his leg right up and filled the road with obscene sounds and smells.[69]

Even someone engaged in a job considered so demeaning by contemporary aristocratic mores[70] as a bag carrier had his pride and was aware of when he was not being treated with the respect he felt he deserved.[71] The entire society, not just the members of the socially élite, were obsessed with these questions.[72] As we can see in Roman law codes, there was almost an infinite variety of ways a person could suffer insult.[73] It is unlikely that anyone, however low in the social pecking order, would have been content to be treated as "the filth of the world" (περικαθάρματα τοῦ κόσμου), "the off-scouring of all things" (πάντων περίψημα) as Judge seems to imply.[74] To follow Judge's reasoning in this area is ultimately to deny the humanity of the poor in the first century.[75]

[69] Petronius, *Satyricon* 117.11, 12.

[70] Cicero, *De Officiis* 1.150.

[71] For further evidence of the non-élite being conscious of suffering social affronts see Lucian, *De Mercede Conductis* 27 and 30, where a poor philosopher (5, 6) complains of the indignities he has suffered at the hands of his cruel patron. Another work of Lucian's, his *Saturnalia*, shows the poor protesting at similar humiliations being meted out by wealthy hosts (32).

[72] Juvenal's description of a mugging in his third satire is a particularly vivid illustration of this preoccupation with matters of honour and shame. The mugger, who is clearly not a member of the élite, asserts his social superiority over his hapless victim as he assaults him: he ridicules his prey for his desperate poverty (by referring to the poor quality of the victim's recent meal). His behaviour makes it clear that in the first-century world a mugger was as concerned about matters of social status as an aristocrat such as Cicero (*Saturae* 3.268–314).

[73] "Generally the Praetor forbade anything which would make someone infamous so whatever anyone does or says which brings dishonour to someone else may give rise to an action for insult." Ulpian, *Digest* 47.10.15. Despite the élite bias of Roman law, non-élite concerns do sometimes show through, especially in relation to the question of *dignitas*. We find, for example, freedmen complaining about being treated as though they were slaves by their patrons (*Digest* 47.10.7) and even, surprisingly, the sexual self-respect of slaves being a matter of legal concern (*Digest* 47.10.9).

[74] 1 Cor. 4:13.

[75] Such a position is similar to the kind of aristocratic blindness typified by Demosthenes who distinguished between the "free man who dreads adverse opinion and the slave who is motivated only by fear of bodily pain" (*Orationes* 8.51). The slave, as much as the free person, shared a social world with others and was as concerned about his or her position within it.

Paul's ability to socialise with the privileged[76] is equally immaterial in determining his previous economic situation. Much of the evidence adduced to support this contention is in itself irrelevant, displaying nothing of the kind,[77] or can be explained as a product of a particular *Tendenz* of the author of Luke–Acts rather than an accurate reflection of the social reality of Paul's life.[78] But more significantly, such an argument is premised upon the mistaken assumption that the pattern of a person's sociability is a reliable indicator of their social status. This is *not* the case, particularly with a figure such as Paul, who led such an untypical life. The conventional limitations that, at least to a partial extent, governed the categories of people with whom the apostle would expect to associate, were broken down as a consequence of his commission. We get some indication of this in 1 Cor. 9:22 where the apostle says that he has become "all things to all men". His situation was in many ways analogous to that of the Jesus of the gospels who, though a workman (τέκτων),[79] was also capable, according to Lukan tradition, of being on close terms with such a figure as the wife of Chuza, Herod's steward, surely one of the most powerful of the ruling élite.[80] It is hardly an unusual practice for a charismatic figure, such as Paul, working at

---

[76] Or, as Judge puts it: to move freely in "the best circles" (*Social Pattern*, p. 58).

[77] For example, Dahl sees Paul's friendship with Barnabas as confirming his impression that the apostle came from a "well-to-do" background ("Paul and Possessions", p. 36) because, for him, Acts 4:36–37 indicates that Barnabas had substantial personal wealth before joining the Jerusalem church. But all we can legitimately glean from Acts is that Barnabas owned one field which in itself may be proof that he was not completely destitute but it hardly evidence of his affluence. As Hamel has observed, such fields, "could be very small, sometimes involving tiny plots or even single trees without adjacent soil" (*Poverty and Charity*, p. 151).

[78] This *Tendenz* has been recently observed by Lentz (*Luke's Portrait of Paul*).

[79] Mark 6:3 (Matt. 8:55). Certainly the meaning of this word is broader than the English term 'carpenter', and no doubt it includes within its range of meaning the more general idea of a builder, as Bauer suggests (*A Greek-English Lexicon of the New Testament*, second edition, Chicago: Chicago University Press, 1979, p. 809) but it is erroneous to argue that the word may have implied that Jesus was a manager or overseer of building projects, and thus, in Buchanan's view, a member of the "upper class" ("Jesus and the Upper Class", *NovT* 7 (1964–65) 195–209, especially pp. 203–205). Buchanan only produces two examples of this use of the word to support his hypothesis, and both are taken uncritically from the *Iliad*, which is hardly an unproblematic source for determining the normative meaning of a term in first-century Israel. In addition, Buchanan himself admits that the word ἀρχιτέκτων was a common term in the New Testament period for describing exactly such a supervisory figure, and so his weak conjecture appears all the more implausible.

[80] Luke 8:3.

the genesis of a new religious movement, to transcend the social barriers of their day, however rigid.[81]

In addition, Paul's ethics, particularly his political ethics, prove to be irrelevant in determining his past. It is assumed that he was ethically conservative and his conservatism reflected his 'class' allegiance. For Hill and Tidball his political ideas were "the typical attitudes of the establishment towards all existing social institutions".[82] However, it is extremely questionable whether it is really appropriate to characterise the apostle's ethics as 'conservative'. Scholars who have been so quick to label Paul's opinions as essentially "aristocratic" or "middle-class",[83] have often been extraordinarily negligent and unnuanced in their examination of the relevant texts in their social context. It is highly debatable, for example, whether it is fair to see him as unconditionally accepting slavery, the subjugation of women, or total obedience to the Roman state.[84] Nor is it accurate to assume that he unthinkingly reproduced such 'conservative' forms of ethical parenesis as *Haustafeln* (Col. 3:18–4:1)[85] or vice–virtue lists (1 Cor. 6:9–11).[86] And, perhaps most significantly, it is important to recognise that the relation between social location of an individual and the character of her/his ethics is more problematic than these scholars allow. It is incorrect to assume, as do Tidball and Hill, that

[81] William Booth, for instance, provides an example of this phenomenon. His origins, as an apprentice pawnbroker, were modest, but he included amongst his associates the leading industrialists and politicians in Victorian Britain (Richard Collier, *The General Next to God*, London: Fontana, 1985, pp. 194ff.). See also Lucian, *Alexandros*.

[82] C. Hill, "The Sociology of the New Testament", unpublished PhD thesis: Nottingham University, UK, 1972, p. 201. Tidball accepts this, with qualifications (*Introduction*, p. 14, fn. 9).

[83] Dahl, "Paul and Possessions", p. 24.

[84] See Appendix 1: *Paul's Social Conservatism: Slavery, Women and the State*.

[85] For Dibelius, for instance, the *Haustafeln* are examples of such wholesale borrowing: they ". . . show that Christian parenesis preserved for the common ethic of the West both the moral family principles of Greek popular philosophy and those of Jewish halakah" (in Yoder, *Politics*, p. 166).

Whilst analysis of the house-lists has become somewhat more nuanced since Dibelius (see D. L. Balch, "Household Codes", *Graeco-Roman Literature and the New Testament*, Atlanta: Scholars Press, 1988, pp. 25–40), there are still some who see the *Haustafeln* essentially from Dibelius' perspective, as something taken over completely from wider society. For a persuasive argument for the innovative use of this form see Yoder, *Politics*, pp. 163–192.

[86] For vice–virtue lists see Conzelmann, *1 Corinthians*, pp. 100–101. He asserts that the content of the list in 1 Cor. 6:9–11 is essentially Jewish. For a more radical assessment of their adaptation see A. Verhey, *Great Reversal*, Grand Rapids: Eerdmans, 1984, p. 109. The vice–virtue lists may not have been as fundamentally transformed in the hands of Paul and other early Christian writers as the *Haustafeln* but they were certainly not merely taken over *verbatim*. They bear the marks of the Pauline *Weltanschauung*.

social conservatism was necessarily the hallmark of the aristocracy or pseudo-aristocracy. Many of the leading Cynics, the most anti-social, least 'conservative' of all movements in antiquity, came from such exalted circles.[87]

Paul's treatment by the Roman authorities has also provided grounds for maintaining that the apostle had a wealthy background.[88] The fact that his appeal to Caesar (Acts 25:11ff.) was allowed, and that the conditions of his captivity were so lenient, to some appears to be incontrovertible evidence of this. Certainly, Festus was not obliged to grant Paul's appeal despite the fact that he was a Roman citizen, as the work of Garnsey has shown,[89] and the matter was entirely in the hands of the governor himself, but, nevertheless, we cannot deduce from this that it was Paul's elevated social standing that led Festus to allow his case to go to Rome. His notoriety alone could have been sufficient cause as Garnsey suggests: "He was a difficult man to handle, and caused trouble wherever he went. Festus would be glad to be rid of him, especially as he really did not know how to deal with him."[90] The "house arrest"[91] which Paul endured after his first appearance before Felix in Caesarea (Acts 24:23) and whilst he was at Rome (28:16, 30) also fails to provide us with evidence of his distinguished status because, according to Ulpian, the form that *custodia* took for an accused person was dependent not only upon such factors as their wealth and distinction, but also the adjudged severity of their crime, and the likelihood of their guilt:

> Concerning the custody of accused men, the proconsul is accustomed to decide whether in each case the person should be put in prison, or handed over to a soldier, or entrusted to guarantors, or even to himself. He usually makes this decision in accordance with the kind of crime which is charged, or the standing of the person accused, or his great wealth, or his innocence, or his dignity.[92]

---

[87] For example, Crates (in A. J. Malherbe, *The Cynic Epistles*, Missoula: Scholars Press, 1983, p. 103).

[88] As Clark says, his treatment shows that he was "at home in the more prosperous levels of society" ("Social Status", p. 111).

For two excellent, recent treatments of the neglected subject of Paul's imprisonment see Rapske, *Paul in Roman Custody*, and Craig S. Wansink, *Chained in Christ: The Experience and Rhetoric of Paul's Imprisonment*, Sheffield: Sheffield Academic Press, 1996.

[89] P. Garnsey, "The Lex Iulia and Appeal under the Empire", *JRS* 56 (1966) 167–189.

[90] Garnsey, "The Lex Iulia", p. 185.

[91] The term employed by Clark, "Social Status", p. 111.

[92] *Digest* 48.3.1. Translation from Garnsey, *Social Status and Legal Privilege*, p. 147.

In Paul's case it is problematic whether he was actually being accused of any crime under Roman law at all. In Acts 23:29 Lysias writes that the accusations of the Jews concerned questions of their own laws, and Festus seems to hold much the same opinion (Acts 25:19, 26), indeed he had to enlist the help of Agrippa to try to formulate some tangible indictments: "For it seems to me unreasonable, in sending a prisoner, not to indicate the charges against him" (Acts 25:27). Whatever the charges were that Paul was eventually sent to Rome to answer,[93] it is clear that they were not considered very significant, and that, according to Acts, the authorities believed him to be innocent (25:25, 26:31ff.). In the light of the words of Ulpian it is therefore unsurprising that he experienced such a relatively lenient pre-trial captivity. We do not need to speculate about his socio-economic status to account for his treatment at the hands of the Roman authorities.[94]

---

[93] There are problems in determining exactly what these charges would have been as the case against Paul by Tertullus is essentially 'constructive' (H. J. Cadbury and Kirsopp Lake, *Beginnings of Christianity*, vol. 5, London: Macmillan & Co., 1933, p. 306) and followed the *extra ordinem* procedure (see Sherwin-White, *Roman Society and Roman Law in the New Testament*, p. 18, and p. 51). The accusers did not bring specific charges against the apostle but rather sought to present a negative picture of his activities, stressing particularly his politically disruptive behaviour, in order to encourage the governor to respond accordingly as the holder of the *imperium*.

Tajra's excellent recent juridical exegesis of this section of Acts is unfortunately, in some respects, flawed. He has an over-optimistic estimation of Jewish belief in their legal rights under the Roman administration. He says, for example, that: ". . . the charge of profaning the Temple was key in Paul's present indictment because for this crime alone could the Sanhedrin condemn a transgressor to death and entertain a confident hope that the governor would execute the sentence" (Trial, p. 123).

In addition he argues that the accusation that Paul was a λοιμός (24:5, a rebel/conspirator) was an attempt to remind the Romans of the terms of the Romano-Jewish alliance recorded in 1 Macc. 15:16–21 which stated that λοιμοί were to be returned to Judaea and punished, "according to the law of the Jews" (p. 121). The likelihood that Paul's accusers had these things in mind is remote given the absolute power of Roman rule (and the difficulties over the reliability of 1 Maccabees). But more importantly, Tajra's reconstruction suffers from an unwillingness to take seriously the 'constructive' nature of the *extra ordinem* procedure, working with the assumption that at its heart the Acts account is concerned with questions of statute law: "Luke's reconstruction of Tertullus' speech is greatly compressed. The full speech would have certainly been a great deal longer than the account give in Acts *and would presumably have developed the case's legal side in greater detail by reference to the specific laws alleged to have been breached*" (my italics; p. 124).

[94] Felix's belief that Paul might provide him with a bribe to obtain his freedom is not evidence of the apostle's personal wealth (Acts 24:26). It is probable that Felix's hope was stimulated by Paul's previous defence (vv. 10–21) in which he mentions that his purpose in coming to Jerusalem was to deliver "alms and offerings" (v. 17).

The other material adduced from Paul's letters as evidence of his past wealth carry little weight and can be quickly dismissed. The assertion by Hengel that Paul's claim to be a member of the tribe of Benjamin (Phil. 3:5) made him a member of the "lay nobility"[95] is something of an exaggeration. It was an understandable source of pride, as the Benjaminites had an illustrious (if chequered) past,[96] but there is no evidence whatsoever for assuming that such Jews were especially privileged. The fact that Paul was a Pharisee (Phil. 3:5) is also not evidence that he came from the ranks of the affluent. It is notoriously difficult to reconstruct who exactly the Pharisees were in the broadest terms[97] let alone determine with precision their socio-economic location in first-century Israel/Palestine but we should be suspicious of attempts to see them as necessarily wealthy.[98] As a popular movement[99] they seem to have been a trans-class phenomenon as Goodman suggests, drawing their adherents from a wide cross-section of Judaean society,[100] including figures as prestigious as Josephus, an aristocrat,[101] and as humble as Abba Hilkiah, a labourer.[102] Sanders' claim that Paul's letters show that he was trained for "ownership or management"

---

[95] Hengel, *Pre-Christian Paul*, p. 17.

[96] Gerald F. Hawthorne, *Philippians*, Waco: Word Books, 1983, pp. 132–133. Judges 19:1–30.

[97] E. Rivkin goes so far as to say that: "The history of Pharisaism is largely non-recoverable because of the nature of the sources" ("Pharisaism and the Crisis of the Individual in the Greco-Roman World", *JQR* 61 (1970), p. 31, fn. 4). All too often the Pharisees have been seen as synonymous with the later rabbis, about whom, of course, we know a great deal, yet as Bowker has warned: "Nothing could be more misleading than to refer to the Pharisees without further qualification as the predecessors of the rabbis" (*Jesus and the Pharisees*, Cambridge: Cambridge University Press, 1973, p.1). For a discussion of the sources for Pharisees and the daunting problems of interpretation see Bowker, and Neusner, *The Rabbinic Traditions About the Pharisees Before 70*.

[98] F. Belo makes this mistake when he calls them the "lower middle-class of the cities" (*A Materialist Reading of the Gospel of Mark*, New York: Orbis, 1981, p. 74), as does Loisy who terms them "bourgeois" (*L'Evangile Selon Luc*, Paris: Novry, 1924, p. 411), and Saldarini, who refers to them as "retainers" (*The Social World of Formative Christianity and Judaism*, ed. J. Neusner, Philadelphia: Fortress, 1988, p. 70).

[99] Josephus, *Antiquitates Judaicae* 18.15, 17. The fact that they are the main opposition in the gospel narratives confirms their widespread support. Though it should be recognised that there has been a tendency to exaggerate the popularity of the Pharisees (Emil Schürer, *The History of the Jewish People in the Age of Jesus Christ (175 BC – AD 135)*, ed. G. Vermes, F. Millar, and M. Black, vol. 2, Edinburgh: T. & T. Clark, p. 389).

[100] M. Goodman, *The Ruling Class of Judaea*, Cambridge: Cambridge University Press, 1987, p. 84.

[101] Josephus, *Antiquitates Judaicae* 1.22.

[102] *b. Ta'anith* 23a-b.

is peculiarly speculative.[103] The fact that Paul used a scribe is not unequivocal evidence of managerial skill; it was, as it still is in many places, a practice of the indigent who are either illiterate or have a poor script (as Paul appears to have had himself from his words in Galatians 6:11).[104]

Concluding remarks

There are no good grounds for qualifying our earlier estimation of Paul as a man who shared fully in the destitute life of the non-élite in the Roman Empire, an existence dominated by work and the struggle to subsist; someone who from his youth repeatedly experienced toil and hardship, hunger and thirst, exposure, and homelessness.[105] Just as the early Church Fathers recognised him as a "common man" (ἀγοραῖος),[106] and his contemporaries saw him as one of the poor (πτωχός)[107] so we should also place him in this economic context. As I hope I have shown, the evidence against this picture is weak and ill-thought out. A few scholars aside, those who have touched on this area of Paul's biography have done so with an air of complacency, as though it is absurd, since Deissmann fell from academic favour, to think that the apostle was a real leatherworker from the cradle to the grave (and not some kind of financially embarrassed aristocrat or the like). Many of their inferences show a carelessness which would hardly be tolerated if they were examining any other aspect of Pauline studies, and many of their deductions do nothing but reveal the prejudices, biases, and perhaps, the socio-economic contexts of the scholars themselves (for example, the presumptions that only the rich consider work slavish, only the affluent are concerned with questions of self-worth, only the formally educated can display signs of learning, are particularly telling). Undoubtedly Paul was not a 'typical' artisan of the Graeco-Roman world – he would not have left such a mark on history if he had been – but his uniqueness, particularly the uniqueness of his religious genius, should not blind us to the fact that his experience of material existence

---

[103] Sanders, *Paul*, p. 11.

[104] The Iulia Felix paintings of Pompeii depict a scribe touting for business in the forum. Harris, *Ancient Literacy*, p. 265. See also E. R. Richards, *The Secretary in the Letters of Paul*, Tübingen: J. C. B. Mohr, 1991, p. 21.

[105] 1 Thess. 2:9; 2 Thess. 3.7–8; 1 Cor. 4:11; 2 Cor. 11:27.

[106] John Chrysostom *De Laudibus S. Pauli Apostoli* 4.494. For other references see Hock, "Paul's Tentmaking", p. 556.

[107] 2 Cor. 6:10.

was far from unusual: it was nothing less than the arduous and bitter experience of the urban poor.

4.2 The economic location of the Pauline churches

Although we have little evidence that allows us to describe with precision the social composition of the Pauline communities, we can say with reasonable certainty that they included amongst their members free labourers and artisans,[108] the enslaved[109] and recent immigrants[110] – groups that constituted the *plebs urbana, misera ac ieiunia*.[111] These individuals experienced the familiar anxieties over material security that were common among such people[112] (debt was, for example, a feared part of their lives).[113] There are also other possible indicators that they came from this group: when they were riven by factions, they articulated their rivalries in language that evoked the partisan conflicts of the circus and popular theatre,[114] and they also appropriated and subverted the

---

[108] 1 Thess. 4:11; 2 Thess. 3:10; (Eph. 4:28); 1 Cor. 7:31. W. Meeks' assertion that rural labourers are unlikely to have been members of the Pauline churches ("The Social Context of Pauline Theology", *Interpretation* 36 (1982), p. 270) is mistaken given the significant numbers of agricultural workers who were domiciled in urban communities, as we have observed in chapter 3.

[109] 1 Cor. 7:21; Philem.; Col. 3:22–4:1; (Eph. 6:5–9). Prosopographical analysis indicates that amongst the Roman Christians mentioned in Rom. 16:3–16 "more than two thirds of the people for whom we can make a probability statement have an affinity to slave origins" (P. Lampe, "The Roman Christians of Romans 16", *The Romans Debate*, ed. K. Donfried, second edition, Edinburgh: T. & T. Clark, 1991, p. 228), that is, they were either enslaved or freed individuals.

[110] Lampe estimates that a minimum of fourteen of the twenty-six Roman Christians mentioned in Rom. 16 were recent immigrants to Rome ("Roman Christians", pp. 226–227). This would put them at a considerable economic disadvantage compared with those already established in the city, particularly as such people were excluded from the regular grain dole. See also *Die stadtrömischen Christen in den ersten beiden Jahrhunderten*, Tübingen: Mohr, 1987, pp. 117–119, 296–297, 347.

[111] Cicero, *Epistulae ad Atticum* 1.16.

[112] 2 Cor. 9:8. Paul's use of αὐτάρκεια refers, in this context, to the *material* self-sufficiency of the Corinthians (Fredrick W. Danker, *II Corinthians*, Minneapolis: Augsburg, 1989, p. 140). The fact that he has to reassure them that they will, as a consequence of the blessing of God, have the surplus to be able to make a gift to the Jerusalem church, indicates that the members of this congregation did not take such a thing for granted (2 Cor. 9:9–15).

[113] Something exploited to good effect by Paul in his Christology. See Col. 2:14 and also Rom. 13:8.

[114] E.g. 1 Cor. 1:12. For evidence of the intense factional allegiances of the non-élite to pantomime artists see E. J. Jory, "The Early Pantomime Riots", *Maistor: Classical, Byzantine and Renaissance Studies for Robert Browning*, ed. Ann Moffatt, Canberra: The Australian Association For Byzantine Studies, 1984, pp 57–66. Their fervour resulted

ruling discourse of the Empire in ways that are indicative of the ruled (as is visible, for instance, in their hymnody[115] and their use of the symbol of the cross).[116] It is also clear that none of them held political office, something that we would expect if any were members of the élite: Rom. 13:1 (Πᾶσα ψυχὴ ἐξουσίαις ὑπερεχούσαις

---

in incessant unrest and repeated legislation by concerned Emperors (Tacitus, *Annales* 1.54.2; Suetonius, *Nero* 16; Cassius Dio 56.47.2). See also Beacham, *The Roman Theatre*, pp. 129–153.

The popular allegiance to charioteers is perhaps more well known. (The best treatment of the relevant sources remains Ludwig Friedländer, *Roman Life and Manners Under the Early Empire*, vol. 2, London: George Routledge & Sons, 1913, pp. 19–40 though see also Magnus Wistrand, *Entertainment and Violence in Ancient Rome: The Attitudes of Roman Writers of the First Century AD*, Göteborg: Acta Universitatis Gothoburgensis, 1992, pp. 41–47 and Toner, *Leisure and Ancient Rome*, pp. 34–52.) Nero, for example, played at being one in the hope that some of their popularity might rub off on him (Tacitus, *Annales* 14.14.1ff.). Sentiments ran high amongst the fans, as an episode recorded by Pliny the Elder illustrates: one enthusiast was so determined to show the intensity of his loyalty to a recently deceased charioteer that he leapt on to his idol's funeral pyre. (Rival fans down-played the significance of this act by maintaining that he had, in fact, been overcome by the cheap perfume of the other mourners.) Pliny, *Naturalis Historiae* 7.180–186.

[115] The Christ hymn of Phil. 2:5–11 is, at least in part, a subversion of Imperial public propaganda. For the relationship between Imperial ideology and the Philippians' 'Christ-hymn' see David Seeley, "The Background of the Philippians Hymn (2:6–11)", *JHC* 1 (1994) 49–72, and J. J. Meggitt, "Laughing and Dreaming at the Foot of the Cross: Context and Reception of a Religious Symbol," *JCSRES* 1 (1996) 9–14.

For important recent works on the development, articulation, and dissemination of Imperial propaganda in the early Empire see Paul Zanker, *The Power of Images in the Age of Augustus*, Ann Arbor: University of Michigan Press, 1990 and A. Wallace-Hadrill, "Roman Arches and Greek Honours", *PCPhS* 216 (1990) 143–181.

[116] Rom. 6:6; 1 Cor. 1:17, 18, 2:2, 8; 2 Cor. 13:4; Gal. 2:20, 3:1, 5:11, 24, 6:12, 14; Phil. 2:8, 3:18; (Eph. 3:16).

The *mors turpissima crucis*, as Origen rightly called it (*Comm. Matt* 27.22) was central to the culture of oppression which sustained the position of the élite, and was consequently a persistent fear of the non-élite in the Empire. We can see this manifested in their humour (*Philogelos* 121), taunts (Plautus, *Aulularia* 522; *Bacchides* 584; *Casina* 416; *Persa* 795; Terrence, *Eunuch* 383; Petronius, *Satyricon* 126.9; *Vita Aesopi* 19) and even dreams (Artemidorus, *Oneirocritica* 2.53, 4.33, 4.49). It is not surprising that its appropriation and subversion by the Christian communities was regarded as a sign of the new religion's madness (Justin, *Apologia* 1.13.4; Minucius Felix, *Octavius* 9.4; 1 Cor. 1:23). For an excellent summary of the offence of the cross in the context of the first-century world see Martin Hengel, *Crucifixion*, London: SCM, 1977, pp. 1–10. See also Meggitt, "Laughing and Dreaming".

The disturbing and threatening implications of a faith based upon crucifixion to the political powers of his day was certainly not lost on Paul as we can see from 1 Cor. 2:8: ἦν οὐδεὶς τῶν ἀρχόντων τοῦ αἰῶνος τούτου 'ἔγνωκεν, εἰ γὰρ ἔγνωσαν, οὐκ ἂν τὸν κύριον τῆς δόξης ἐσταύρωσαν.

ὑποτασσέσθω) indicates that no Christians (at this stage) were to be found amongst the governing authorities of the first-century world as *all* the believers are told to submit to the power of the ἐξουσίαι. Likewise, Paul's remarks in 1 Cor. 6 demonstrate that Christians did not hold civic magistracies, as the apostle refers to such people as ἄδικοι ("unrighteous" v. 1), ἐξουθενημένοι ("least esteemed" v. 4) and ἄπιστοι ("unbelievers" v. 6) and dis-tinguishes sharply between them and the ἅγιοι ("saints" v. 1) and ἀδελφοί ("brothers" v. 5, v. 8) who constitute the church. It not surprising that the apostle could refer to members of his Corinthian congregation, *without exception*, as τὰ μωρὰ τοῦ κόσμου, τὰ ἀσθενῆ τοῦ κόσμου, τὰ ἀγενῆ τοῦ κόσμου, τὰ ἐξουθενημένα, τὰ μὴ ὄντα.[117]

The Pauline Christians *en masse* shared fully the bleak material existence which was the lot of more than 99% of the inhabitants of the Empire, and also, as we have just seen, of Paul himself. Statistically this is unremarkable. To believe otherwise, without clear evidence to the contrary, given the near universal prevalence of poverty in the first-century world, is to believe in the improbable.

Of course, this characterisation of the Pauline communities is in conflict, to a great extent, with the so-called 'New Consensus',[118] which has been most famously articulated for the Pauline epistles by G. Theissen and W. Meeks.[119] This 'consensus' sees the early churches as incorporating individuals from a cross section of first-century society,[120] including some from the higher strata (who would be,

---

[117] 1 Cor. 1:27–28.

[118] A title given to it by A. J. Malherbe, *Social Aspects of Early Christianity*, Baton Rouge: Louisiana State University Press, 1977, p. 31. My conflict with the 'New Consensus' is, in a sense, indirect, because my focus is only upon one aspect of human social life (the economic) whereas their reconstructions aim to encompass a broader range of descriptive categories.

[119] Theissen, *Social Setting*; Meeks, *First Urban*. There have, of course, been many other advocates of this position: see especially Becker, "Paul and His Churches", pp. 132–210; Chow, *Patronage and Power*; Andrew Clarke, *Secular and Christian Leadership in Corinth: A Socio-Historical and Exegetical Study of 1 Corinthians 1-6*, Leiden: E. J. Brill, 1993; M. Hengel, *Property and Riches in the Early Church*, Philadelphia: Fortress Press, 1974; Judge, *Social Pattern*; Malherbe, *Social Aspects of Early Christianity*; Carolyn Osiek, *What Are They Saying about the Social Setting of the New Testament?* New York: Paulist Press, 1984; Marshall, *Enmity in Corinth*; B. W. Winter, *Seek the Welfare of the City: Christians as Benefactors and Citizens*, Carlisle: Paternoster, 1994; Witherington, *Conflict and Community*.

[120] Positing a model of earliest Christianity similar in many respects to that described in Pliny's famous epistle to Trajan in the early second century: the Bithynian Christian community had a membership which came from "all ranks" (*Epistulae* 10.96).

amongst other things, economically affluent). It is a 'New' consensus in that it is in distinct and deliberate contrast to the previously dominant perception of early Christianity as "a religion of the slaves and the oppressed, made up of poor peasants and workers",[121] a position most persuasively and influentially maintained by A. Deissmann.[122] There is some variety within the 'New Consensus',[123] but the internal debates of its supporters have never appeared to threaten its dominance. It has gone almost entirely unchallenged for the last two decades.[124]

However, not only are many of the reconstructions of the 'New Consensus' dependent upon anachronistic and inappropriate inter-pretations of first-century society[125] but the specific evidence adduced by its followers in support of this interpetation cannot stand up to close scrutiny. Their arguments cannot provide grounds for maintaining that the early communities' experience of life was in any way distinguishable from the common urban experience I have just outlined.

The methodology of the 'New Consensus'

Before we look at the individual pieces of evidence mustered by the proponents of the 'New Consensus', it is appropriate that we first make a few remarks about the logic underlying their position because it suffers from serious weaknesses that have yet to be noted.

The plausibility of the constructions of the 'New Consensus' depends, to a large extent, upon the weight of 'cumulative evidence'.[126] There is nothing intrinsically wrong with this; it is a familiar enough form of argument in New Testament studies and is an understandable response to the fragmentary, random and often opaque nature of the

---

[121] Holmberg, *Sociology*, p. 28. They affirm Celsus' notorious portrait of the early communities as being composed of "wool-workers, cobblers, laundry-workers and the most bucolic and illiterate yokels" (Origen, *Contra Celsum* 3.55).

[122] Deissmann, *Light From the Ancient East*.

[123] For example, Clarke criticises Meeks for being too modest in his estimate of the position of the most socially powerful Pauline Christians: for Clarke members were drawn from the highest levels in Imperial society (Clarke, *Secular and Christian*, p. 45).

[124] Excepting the contributions of Georg Schöllgen, "Was wissen wir über die Sozialstruktur der paulinischen Gemeinden?" *NTS* 34 (1988) 71–82; Luise Schottroff, *Befreiungserfah-rungen: Studien zur Sozialgeschichte des Neuen Testaments*, München: Ch. Kaiser, 1990, pp. 247–256; J. Gager, "Review of Grant, Malherbe, Theissen," *RSR* 5 (1979) 174–180 and also "Shall We Marry Our Enemies? Sociology and the New Testament," *Interpretation* 36 (1986) 256–265.

[125] Such as a presumption of the existence of a middle-class, e.g. Becker, "Paul and His Churches", p. 168.

[126] See, for example, Clarke, *Secular and Christian*, p. 57.

evidence that confronts an exegete interested in the social analysis of these early Christian communities. But such reasoning can quite easily be deceptive. Firstly, it must be recognised that the likelihood of the truthfulness of the consensus is not merely the simple *sum* of the probabilities of the various pieces of evidence marshalled to support it (as so many of its practitioners seem to presume). The relationship between the plausibility of the individual pieces of evidence and the probability of the overall historical reconstruction is more subtle than that.[127] Each additional piece of evidence does not add to the likely veracity of the thesis in the dramatic way often assumed. Secondly, as C. B. McCullagh observes, "the frequency with which descriptions of the world are true increases with the number of *independent* pieces of evidence which render them probable" (my italics).[128] Yet the various pieces of evidence which support the 'New Consensus' are often not *independent* at all, but *interdependent*; they can appear to reinforce one another, and the thesis as a whole, in a way which is superficially reassuring but in essence circular, and, therefore, to a great extent illusory. Within the 'New Consensus' possibilities too readily become probabilities and are too quickly treated as though they were certainties.[129]

The evidence for the 'New Consensus' position examined

The evidence for the 'New Consensus' position can be usefully divided into two categories: I) that which appears to be indicative of the existence of affluent *groups* within the Pauline communities, and II) that which appears indicative of the existence of affluent *individuals* within the communities.

I) Evidence for affluent *groups* within the Pauline churches

Such evidence can again be subdivided into two further categories: a) that which, it is maintained, reveals *explicitly* the existence of affluent

---

[127] For a discussion of the problems of statistical inference in historical method and a critique of some of the models often employed, see C. B. McCullagh, *Justifying Historical Descriptions*, Cambridge: Cambridge University Press, 1984, pp. 45–73.

[128] McCullagh, *Justifying*, p. 59.

[129] There are plenty of examples of the exaggerated and misplaced confidence this kind of reasoning induces. Theissen's work can be criticised in such a respect. Having made an interesting, though debatable (see below) case for the significance of four possible criteria for determining a person's social status (possession of offices, houses, offering of services and travel – see *Social Setting*, pp. 69–119) he seems content to view the coalescence of three or even two of these as sufficient for him to categorise individuals as members of the "upper class" (p. 95). (Indeed, on one occasion, he even allows a single criterion to function as conclusive (p. 95), despite his previously voiced caution (p. 91).)

groups within the Pauline communities, and b) that which, it is maintained, does so *implicitly*.

a) Explicit evidence

1 Cor 1:26 – Βλέπετε γὰρ τὴν κλῆσιν ὑμῶν, ἀδελφοί, ὅτι οὐ πολλοὶ σοφοὶ κατὰ σάρκα, οὐ πολλοὶ δυνατοί, οὐ πολλοὶ εὐγενεῖς·

This is a central text in the sociological interpretation of early Christianity.[130] As W. H. Wuellner quite rightly says: "No other single verse of the entire New Testament was more influential in shaping popular opinion and exegetical judgement alike on the social origins of early Christianity than 1 Corinthians 1:26."[131] However, his use of the past tense is a little premature: it continues to exert a powerful influence on attempts at the social description of the nascent church.

Ironically, the text has been intrinsic to both the 'Old' and 'New' consensuses, providing a keystone for their respective reconstructions of Christian origins.

For example, A. Deissmann observed that, in this verse, Paul's "words about the origin of his churches in the lower classes of the great towns form one of the most important testimonies, historically speaking, that Primitive Christianity gives of itself", demonstrating unequivocally that it was a movement of the poor.[132] The text was equally pivotal for the Marxist, Karl Kautsky. He justified his statement that "die christliche Gemeinde ursprünglich fast ausschließlich proletarische Elemente umfaßte und eine proletarische Organisation war",[133] by reference to its contents.

Proponents of the 'New Consensus' have read the text more closely and drawn a radically different inference from it. For these scholars it is important to "distinguish between 'not many' and 'not any'", and consequently we should recognise that at least some amongst the earliest Pauline Christians came from more exalted circles.[134]

---

[130] For an historical overview of exegesis of this passage, from the earliest patristic writers to the present, see K. Schreiner, "Zur biblischen Legitimation des Adels: Auslegungsgeschichtliche Studien zum 1. Kor 1,26–29", *ZKG* 85 (1974) 317–347.

[131] W. H. Wuellner, "The Sociological Implications of 1 Corinthians 1:26–28 Reconsidered", *Studia Evangelica IV*, ed. E. A. Livingstone, Berlin: Akademie 1973, p. 666.

[132] Deissmann, *Light From the Ancient East*, p. 8.

[133] Karl Kautsky, *Der Ursprung des Christentus*, Hannover: J. H. W. Dietz, 1910, p. 338.

[134] E. von Dobschütz, *Christian Life in the Primitive Church*, New York: G. Putnam & Sons, 1904, p. 14. As can be seen from the date of publication of this work, the position of the 'New Consensus' is not as new as some of its proponents believe.

Although the closer reading by advocates of the 'New Consensus' does invalidate the exegetical use of this text by the likes of Deissmann and Kautsky (Paul clearly does say 'not many' *not* 'not any') the inferences that they draw from this verse are equally problematic. They assume that the terms σοφός, δυνατός and εὐγενής are indicative of high social rank,[135] something which they believe is particularly clear when they are read in their historical context.[136] Indeed, the terminology allows some of its advocates to locate these prosperous individuals more precisely amongst the upper echelons of Corinthian society. For Andrew Clarke, for instance, "Paul's use of these significant terms in 1 Cor. 1:26 clearly implies that there were in the congregation some from the ruling class of society."[137] But despite the reassuring marshalling of parallels from élite literature we cannot presume to know that the semantic value of the terms σοφός, δυνατός and εὐγενής is identical for Paul and, for example, Aristotle or Philo, as Clarke maintains. The 'New Consensus' exegesis is, to a great extent, wedded to an unreflective, crudely denotative view of language.[138] Such words were substantially more equivocal than has been assumed. As emotive

---

[135] Becker, "Paul and His Churches", p. 170; Clarke, *Secular and Christian*, pp. 41–45; Theissen, *Social Setting*, pp. 71–73; Malherbe, *Social Aspects of Early Christianity*, p. 30; Chow, *Patronage and Power*, p. 145; Judge, *Social Pattern*, p. 59; Dale B. Martin, *The Corinthian Body*, New Haven: Yale University Press, 1995, p. 61.

    See also R. Jewett, *The Thessalonian Correspondence: Pauline Rhetoric and Millenarian Piety*, Philadelphia: Fortress, 1986, p. 120; William F. Orr and J. A. Walther, *1 Corinthians*, New York: Doubleday, 1976, p. 161; F. F. Bruce, *1 and 2 Corinthians*, p. 36; D. Sänger, "Die dunatoi in 1 Kor 1,26", *ZNW* 76 (1985), p. 287; H. Conzelmann, *1 Corinthians*, Philadelphia: Fortress, 1975, pp. 49–50; Roman Garrison, *Redemptive Almsgiving in Early Christianity*, Sheffield: Sheffield Academic Press, 1993, pp. 34–35; Antoinette Clark Wire, *The Corinthian Women Prophets*, Minneapolis: Fortress, 1990, p. 63; Horrell, *Social Ethos*, p. 98; F. V. Filson, "The Significance of the Early House Churches", *JBL* 58 (1939), p. 111; B. Winter, *Philo and Paul Amongst the Sophists: A Hellenistic Jewish and Christian Response*, unpublished PhD dissertation: Macquarrie University, 1988, p. 200; Holmberg, *Paul and Power*, p. 103.

[136] Clarke (*Secular and Christian*, p. 43) has drawn attention to the socially precise use of these terms in the works of Aristotle (*Rhetorica* 2.12.2), Plutarch (*Moralia* 58.E), Dio Chrysostom (*Orationes* 15.29) and Philo (*De Virtute* 187). For references to a study of the significance of these terms in Josephus see D. Sänger, "Die dynatoi in 1 Kor 1,26", *ZNW* 76 (1985), p. 289, fn. 30. See also J. Munck, *Paul and the Salvation of Mankind*, London: SCM, 1959, p. 162–163, n. 2.

[137] Clarke, *Secular and Christian*, p. 45. Also Winter, *Philo*, p. 200, and Gill, "Acts and the Urban Elites", p. 110.

[138] For useful remarks on the analogous, though more surprising, failure of social historians in this respect see Peter Burke, "Introduction", *The Social History of Language*, Cambridge: Cambridge University Press, 1987, p. 3.

labels which had a long history of élite use,[139] they were open to ongoing appropriation and "transgressive re-inscription" (the process by which vocabulary can be radically adapted, and even subverted, upon entering the lexical arena).[140] They ceased (if indeed they ever had been) to be lexically monosemous.[141] Each term gathered to it a broad and dynamic range of possible meanings and the designations became essentially *relative*.

We can see this, for example, in the use of the term εὐγενής, apparently the most socially precise of the three words. It was undoubtedly employed to signify noble birth by the élite of the Graeco-Roman world,[142] but there is also quite clear evidence of its arrogation. Epigraphic sources show that in the period under examination, εὐγενής and its cognates became applied to individuals who were clearly not members of the ruling class by any objective criteria.[143] It appeared, for example, on very humble epitaphs.[144] In fact, εὐγενής became such a popularly ascribed quality that it was used as a common appellation, and was evidently employed as a slave name, as we can see from a number of surviving inscriptions.[145]

[139] J. Ober, *Mass and Elite in Democratic Athens: Rhetoric, Ideology and the Power of the People*, Princeton: Princeton University Press, 1989, p. 12.

[140] Burke, *History and Social Theory*, p. 98.
The capacity for Graeco-Roman popular culture to engage in such manipulation of the constitutive elements of élite ideology is well attested. One need only look at the constant war that raged over the non-élite appropriation of the colour purple and other symbols of élite status. See M. Reinhold, "The Usurpation of Status and Status Symbols in the Roman Empire", *Historia* 20 (1971) 275–302.

[141] See F. Braun's remarks on the analogous fate of terms of address (*Terms of Address: Problems of Patterns and Usage in Various Languages and Cultures*, Berlin: Mouton de Gruyter, 1988, p. 260).

[142] "L'eugeneia d'une ville, comme d'un individu c'est noblesse de sa naissance" (Louis Robert, "De Cilicie à Messine et à Plymouth", *JS* Jul-Sep (1972), p. 202).

[143] SEG 33 (1983) 869 and Charlotte Roueché, *Performers and Partisans at Aphrodisias in the Roman and Late Roman Periods*, London: The Society for the Promotion of Roman Studies, 1993, p. 197 (69.9) – an athlete; SEG 35 (1985) 1327 – an actor/dancer; and SEG 28 (1978) 983 – a doctor.

[144] IG 14.192.

[145] In Heikki Solin's study (*Die griechischen Personennamen in Rom: Ein Namenbuch*, 3 vols, Berlin: Walter De Gruyter & Co., 1982 – based mostly on CIL VI), the following names are attested: *Eugenes, Eugenesis, Eugenetor, Eugenetus, Eugenia, Eugenius*. Although it is often difficult to determine the status of individuals named, a number of these appellations quite clearly belong to slaves and/or freedmen (who were, of course, unlikely to have been 'well-born' in the élite sense). For example, *Eugenes* 34271, 24902, 17326, 647.4.6, Moretti 811, NSA 1914 387, Ral 1973, 272 and *Eugenia* 8205, 12822, 7893, 3845a, 35179, Bull.Comm. 73, 178, NSA 1914 – 380, NSA 1915 – 408. Such names were also common in the Greek world, as we can see from P. Fraser and E. Matthews

The meaning that Paul was intending to convey by his use of such terms in 1 Cor. 1:26 is therefore more elusive than has traditionally been assumed.[146] The words are far more imprecise than has been allowed. Whilst they are indeed socially descriptive,[147] it is impossible to be certain what exactly they describe.[148] By itself Paul's words in 1 Cor. 1:26 can tell us nothing concrete about the social constituency of

---

(ed.), *Lexicon of Greek Personal Names* (*Volume 1, Aegean Islands, Cyprus, Cyrenaica*) Oxford: Clarendon Press, 1987, p. 172 and *Lexicon of Greek Personal Names* (*Volume 2, Attica*), Oxford: Clarendon Press, 1994, p. 165, where twelve examples of Εὐγενής and eight of Εὐγενεία are attested, for the Hellenistic and Roman period (no doubt forthcoming volumes will reveal considerably more). There are also papyrological attestations: Εὐγενία, P. Stras. 148 (v), PAR 21c4 (VI); Εὐγενεά B IV, SB II; and Εὐγένιος SB 9511 (VI).

Latin and Greek names derived from σοφός (Sophia/Sophias – Σόφος Σόφια) and δυνατός (Dynamis/Dynamius – Δυνατος Δυναμις) are also far from infrequent (Solin, *Personennamen*, pp. 1253 and 1203; Fraser and Matthews, *Lexicon, vol. 1*, pp. 410 and 144, and *Lexicon, vol. 2*, pp. 402 and 136; F. Preisigke, *Namenbuch*, Heidelberg: Herausgebers, 1922, p. 393).

[146] This should not surprise us. Language, whether written or spoken, is often deliberately imprecise, leaving much of its meaning implicit, not only out of an understandable desire for concision, but also because such equivocal exchanges allow it to perform the important roles of being generative and confirmatory of social reality. See Peter Berger, and Thomas Luckmann, *The Social Construction of Reality: A Treatise in the Sociology of Knowledge*, London: Allen Lane, 1971, pp. 172–173.

[147] Wuellner's arguments against these words having any sociological significance at all are unconvincing. As Fee maintains, his grammatical argument is "shaky at best" (*The First Epistle to the Corinthians*, Grand Rapids: Eerdmans, 1987, p. 81). For Wuellner's position see "Sociological" and also "Tradition and Interpretation of the 'Wise-Powerful-Noble' Triad in 1 Kor. 1,26", *Studia Evangelica VII*, ed. Elizabeth Livingstone, Berlin: Akadamie, 1982, pp. 557–562.

Clarke misrepresents Wuellner when he says that Wuellner's interpretation of the triadic formula leads him to the conclusion that "the Corinthian Christians came by and large from fairly well-to-do bourgeois circles" (*Secular and Christian*, p. 45, fn. 22). Wuellner's opinion of the social status of these Christians is *not* dependent upon his reading of 1 Cor. 1:26 – the whole tenor of his argument is that the verse is inadmissible as sociological evidence; his thoughts on the social constituency of the early Christians are complete conjecture and he gives no grounds whatsoever to support them in this article.

[148] This is all the more probable if we look at an example of the use of πλούσιος, a word which is generically similar to σοφός, δυνατός and εὐγενής. The village 'rich' man in Dio Chrysostom's *Orationes* 7.64 possessed a house that was far from impressive. He was rich in terms of the village community but not in comparison with the local urban élite. His designation is, as Joyce Reynolds observes, "very relative" ("Cities", p. 21).

It should be noted that whoever the σοφοί, ἰσχυρά, and ὄντα are in verses 27 and 28 they cannot be synonymous with the σοφός, δυνατός and εὐγενής church members of verse 26 as the σοφοί, ἰσχυρά, and ὄντα are contrasted with the *whole* of the congregation.

the congregation he addresses except that a small number were more fortunate than the others. How much more fortunate it is impossible to determine. It may be that the few wise, powerful, and well-born were a small group of literate, *ingenui*, artisans – who amongst the urban poor would have appeared relatively more privileged but whose lives would still have been dominated by fears over subsistence. Indeed, it is probable that, in absolute terms, the gap between the σοφός, δυνατός and εὐγενής and the rest of the congregation was not very great: the apostle soon forgets the distinction that he has drawn and refers to *all* of the Corinthian community, *all* of the called, in the subsequent two verses, as foolish, weak, love, despised, nothings.

The problems over discerning the meaning of Paul's words in 1 Cor. 1:26 mean that, contrary to the recent reconstructions of the 'New Consensus', the verse can no longer be taken as unambiguous evidence of the presence of the élite, or near élite, within a Pauline church. It is far too equivocal. Indeed, it would be unwise to assign to it any role, however minor, in describing the social make-up of the Pauline congregations.

1 Cor 4:10 – ἡμεῖς μωροὶ διὰ Χριστόν, ὑμεῖς δὲ φρόνιμοι ἐν Χριστῷ· ἡμεῖς ἀσθενεῖς, ὑμεῖς δὲ ἰσχυροί· ὑμεῖς ἔνδοξοι, ἡμεῖς δὲ ἄτιμοι

For Theissen this verse is a clear indication of the presence of the 'upper classes' amongst the Corinthian congregation:

> . . . these terms have a sociological significance, for Paul contrasted his circumstances with those of the Corinthians in terms bearing indisputable sociological implications. For example, Paul works with his hands, experiences hunger, has no permanent home, and is persecuted. He is the 'refuse of the world, the offscouring of all things' (1 Cor. 4:11–13). Paul puts himself at the bottom of the scale of social prestige but sees the Corinthians as occupying the top: You are clever, strong, honoured.[149]

But the likelihood that Paul is referring to a socially élite group within the Corinthian church by these words is slim. Rather, the apostle appears to be addressing the entire congregation, and is making reference to the Corinthians' sense of spiritual (rather than social) self-importance

149 Theissen, *Social Setting*, pp. 72–73.

(they are, after all, claiming to be wise ἐν Χριστῷ).[150] 1 Cor. 4:10 should be read in the light of the apostle's preceding words in 1 Cor. 4:8 which surely cannot describe his opponents' actual social situation (ἤδη κεκορεσμένοι ἐστέ· ἤδη ἐπλουτήσατε· χωρὶς ἡμῶν ἐβασιλεύσατε· καὶ ὄφελόν γε ἐβασιλεύσατε, ἵνα καὶ ἡμεῖς ὑμῖν συμβασιλεύσωμεν).

In 1 Cor. 4:10 Paul is contrasting the bleak nature of his daily life as an apostle with the Corinthians' exalted, heavenly, pretensions, in order to highlight the absurdity of their claims, and to bring them back to earthly reality.[151] His words do not tell us anything at all about the Corinthians' socio-economic location.

b) Implicit information about groups within the Pauline churches Eating meat offered to idols (1 Cor. 8 and 10)

Theissen's proposal that the conflict between two different socio-economic groups, the indigent 'weak' and the affluent 'strong', lies behind the dispute over meat consumption in 1 Cor. 8 and 10 has proved remarkably influential, significantly bolstering the 'New Consensus' position.[152] If his reconstruction is correct, which I believe it is not, it provides, albeit indirectly, evidence of the existence of an elevated social group within one of Paul's churches. As his work in this area has not been developed to any noticeable extent by his supporters, my discussion will focus directly upon it.

Before we turn to the main body of his argument it is important to make a couple of observations about his initial premises. Firstly, throughout his thesis, he maintains that there are two clearly defined parties involved in the disputes but such an analysis is problematic. Whilst the 'weak' certainly exist as a group,[153] as we can see in Paul's use of the term ἀσθενής,[154] the 'strong' party actually owes its existence to

---

[150] See A. C. Thiselton, "Realised Eschatology at Corinth", *NTS* 24 (1977) 510–526 and R. Horsley, "'How can some of you say that there is no resurrection of the dead?' Spiritual Elitism in Corinth", *NovT* 20 (1978) 203–231.

[151] Such a movement between the mundane and the metaphysical in the course of an argument by the apostle should not surprise us – 2 Cor. 8:9 provides a similar example of this kind of rhetorical shift, as does 2 Cor. 6:10.

[152] Theissen, *Social Setting*, pp. 121–143. See, for example, Meeks, *First Urban*, pp. 69–70 and Martin, *The Corinthian Body*, pp. 75–76.

[153] 1 Cor. 8:7, 9, 10, 11, 12; 9:22.

[154] J. C. Hurd denies the existence of a 'weak' group in 1 Cor. 8 and 10. He maintains that the 'weak' are in fact a hypothetical construction of the apostle, invented "solely as a way of dissuading the Corinthians from eating meat". He bases this interpretation upon

Theissen: words such as δυνατός, ἰσχυρός, and κράτος, that we might expect to find as evidence indicating the presence of such a group, do not in fact appear in chapters 8 or 10. Secondly, he assumes in his opening argument that Paul's words in 1 Cor. 1:26–27 suggest that the 'weak' in 1 Cor. 8 and 10 are a socio-economically defined group. But it is problematic to see the use of ἀσθενής in this first chapter as determinative of its meaning seven chapters later. Not only is Paul capable of using ἀσθενής and its cognates in a number of quite different ways elsewhere in this epistle (e.g. 9:22, 11:30, 12:22), which in itself precludes a simple association between these two sections of the letter,[155] but the term is qualified in both 1 Cor. 1 and 1 Cor. 8,[156] and qualified quite differently: in 1 Cor. 1:27 the apostle refers to τὰ ἀσθενῆ τοῦ κόσμου, whilst in 1 Cor. 8:7, 11, 12 he speaks of ἡ συνείδησις αὐτῶν ἀσθενὴς οὖσα; ἡ συνείδησις αὐτοῦ ἀσθενοῦς ὄντος; τὴν συνείδησιν ἀσθενοῦσαν. Of course, this does not rule out the possibility that the 'weak' of 1 Cor. 1:27 are identical to the 'weak' who appear later in the epistle but it makes the association rather less certain than is often presumed.

But let us now turn to the specific details of Theissen's argument. In his attempt to justify his interpretation of the dispute he focuses upon four "class-specific characteristics" which he believes reveal the social location of the conflicting groups: those of eating habits, patterns of sociability, forms of legitimation, and forms of communication.

Class-specific characteristics in eating habits: For Theissen, class-specific characteristics in the eating habits of the various protagonists can provide, in part, a plausible explanation for the conflict. For him, the 'weak', as members of the "lower strata", "seldom ate meat in their everyday lives", and when they did, "it was almost exclusively as an ingredient in pagan religious celebration"[157] (while attending festivals or meetings of *collegia*).[158] Hence, for them, it possessed a "numinous"

---

the vagueness of Paul's wording in 8:10 and 10:27: ". . . if someone" (*The Origins of First Corinthians*, London: SPCK, 1965, p. 125). But such an argument is unconvincing; the content of the parenesis seems much too practical to be addressed to a theoretical group.

[155] Indeed, as Hurd has observed, the "variety of usage tells against the assumption that the term carried a special connotation either for Paul or for Corinth" (*Origins*, p. 124).

[156] The word does not appear in chapter 10.

[157] Theissen, *Social Setting*, p. 128.

[158] The Greek terms used for *collegia* are quite diverse but the most significant is θίασοι.

character, and its consumption was something that was problematic and cloaked in taboo. However, the wealthy 'strong' had opposing convictions and perceptions. As prosperous individuals they "were more accustomed to consuming meat routinely";[159] thus it had no such quality and no negative associations.

But this aspect of his interpretation is based upon a fallacious understanding of the norms of first-century meat consumption.[160] Certainly cereals were the staple food for most people in the Mediterranean world,[161] and meat stayed relatively expensive during this period,[162] as he argues, but it was more regularly eaten by the non-élite than he allows. It was also frequently consumed by this group in settings which were decidedly unsacral.

The chief evidence supporting these assertions comes from what we know about the *popinae* and *ganeae*, or 'cookshops', whose existence was overlooked by Theissen. Although food was an emotive and vital element in the moral discourse of the Graeco-Roman nobility,[163] and so

[159] Theissen, *Social Setting*, p. 128.

[160] Which he arrives at, at least in part, by some dubious inferences from some questionable evidence. He assumes, for example, that the non-élite could not have had access to meat because incidents recorded by Tacitus (*Annales* 14.24) and Caesar (*Bellum Gallicum* 7.17) show that, "soldiers ate meat only in exceptional circumstances" (Theissen, *Social Setting*, p. 126). However, his argument is wrong: the diets of soldiers are untypical and can tell us nothing about the eating habits of the rest of the Empire (Porphyry, *De Abstinentia*, 2.4.3; P. Garnsey, "Food Consumption in Antiquity: Towards a Quantitative Account", *Food, Health and Culture in Classical Antiquity*, ed. P. Garnsey, Cambridge: Classical Department Working Papers, 1989, p. 39). (Indeed, contrary to Theissen, we have numerous literary references to the Roman army's prodigious meat consumption (see for instance Appian, *Iberica* 85; Frontinus, *Strategemata* 4.1.2), which are corroborated by archaeological discoveries (Theissen, *Social Setting*, pp. 122–142). For the soldier "meat was part of their ordinary diet, during campaigns as well as garrison duty . . . In fact, they could protest when their diet became *exclusively* meat, as often happened to armies of occupation." (Mireille Corbier, "The Ambiguous Status of Meat in Ancient Rome", *Food and Foodways* 3 (1989), p. 229.) The two episodes that Theissen bases his argument upon are taken out of context and actually imply nothing of the sort. See *Bellum Gallicum* 7.56 and also R. Davies "The Roman Military Diet", *Britannia* 2 (1971), pp. 138–141)).

[161] Theissen, *Social Setting*, p. 126. See D. Sippel, "Dietary Deficiency Among the Lower Classes – Rome", *AncSoc* 16 (1987), p. 51 and K. D. White, "Cereals, Bread and Milling in the Roman World", *Food in Antiquity*, ed. J. Wilkins, D. Harvey and M. Dobson, Exeter: Exeter University Press, 1995, pp. 38–43.

[162] Garnsey, "Mass Diet", p. 86 (though in the 270s Aurelian introduced free pork – SHA, *Aurelian* 35.2). It was even more expensive in the eastern Empire according to Hamel, *Poverty and Charity*, p. 25.

[163] See Edwards, *Politics*; E. Gowers, *The Loaded Table*, Oxford: Clarendon Press, 1993; and Nicola A. Hudson, "Food in Roman Satire", *Satire and Society in Ancient Rome*, ed. S. Braund, Exeter: Exeter University Press, 1989, pp. 69–87.

ascertaining anything concrete about its consumption is fraught with difficulties, we can say, with reasonable certainty, that these establishments served prepared meats to the unmoneyed throughout the urban settlements of the empire.[164] The wealthy may have, on occasion, enjoyed the thrill of rubbing shoulders with their clientele,[165] but they were primarily haunts of the "lower strata".[166] For instance, Juvenal describes a *popina* in Ostia as filled with gangsters, runaway slaves, sailors, thieves, coffin-makers, butchers and eunuch priests,[167] and the list Plautus supplies us with is much the same.[168] They were not patronised by just a few of the *plebs urbana*: they were immensely popular, and, "almost proverbially the meeting places of the common people".[169] Their customers spilled out into the streets according to Martial,[170] and emperors fearful of associations of any sort,[171] tried to keep them under firm control (though as their oft-repeated legislation shows, they largely failed in this).[172] Their popularity is also evidenced in the role they acquired in élite rhetoric as a symbol of all that was crude and debauched.[173] They became part of the verbal ammunition

---

[164] See T. Kleberg, *Hôtels, restaurants et cabarets dans l'antiquité romaine*, Uppsala: Almqvist & Wiksells, 1957. It must, however, be noted that they catered largely for *male* members of the non-élite (see Laurence, *Roman Pompeii*, p. 86).

[165] For example, Nero (Suetonius, *Nero* 26.1) and Lateranus (Juvenal, *Saturae* 8.172).

[166] This was apparent in the furniture of many of the *popinae* which consisted of plebian tables and chairs in preference to the more aristocratic triclinia (Martial, *Epigrammata* 5.70.2–4).

[167] Juvenal, *Saturae* 8.173.

[168] Plautus, *Poenulus*, 4.2.1–13.

[169] Corbier, "Ambiguous Status", p. 233. They proliferated throughout the empire (although the literary record is naturally biased towards Rome). Roman Corinth contains many remains which can be ascribed to such establishments.

[170] Martial, *Epigrammata* 7.61. In CE 92 Domitian had to propagate an edict to control this phenomenon.

[171] See Pliny, *Epistulae* 10.34. Trajan was so paranoid of associations that he would not even allow Pliny's request for the founding of a fire brigade in Bithynia.

[172] They were regulated by Tiberius who applied tight antisumptuary laws (Suetonius, *Tiberius* 34.1) and although these were relaxed initially by Claudius (Suetonius, *Claudius* 38.2), he later sought to prevent the selling of cooked meats of any kind (Cassius Dio 60.6.7), as did Nero (Cassius Dio 62.14.2), and Vespasian (Cassius Dio 65.10.3). Interestingly, Suetonius recounts that Nero suppressed Christians, charioteers, and pantomimic actors and their followers, along with the "cookshops" (*Nero* 16). In their own ways these different constituents of first-century Graeco-Roman life were considered equally subversive (though see SHA, *Severus Alexander* 49.6 for a different picture in which Christians are preferred to *popinae*).

[173] They were invariably associated with vice of all kinds, though particularly with that of a sexual nature. Waitresses at such establishments were considered prostitutes under Roman law and any woman entering a *popina* was viewed likewise and consequently

with which this clique sought to fight its wars of identity and exclusion. For example, in Suetonius and the *Scriptores Historiae Augustae*, 'bad' emperors such as Nero, Verus and Commodus either frequented 'cook-shops' or had them installed in their dwellings;[174] and Mark Antony was accused by Cicero in a lengthy character assassination, of having swapped the "dining room for the *popinae*".[175] If we can speak of "lower class culture" in the Graeco-Roman world, the *popinae* and *ganeae* were at the heart of it.

Although these establishments were probably the main sources from which the non-élite could obtain meat, it was also available at many of the *tabernae* or *cauponae* (wine shops) that filled any town, or from the ambulant vendors who plied the streets,[176] and even the baths.[177]

The meat from all these outlets tended to be in forms that have historically been associated with the poor: sausages or blood puddings appear to have been common,[178] as was tripe,[179] and various 'off-cuts' that might appear unappetising to the modern palate.[180] Its quality was certainly questionable: Ammianus Marcellinus, for example, recoiled in disgust at the sight of the less affluent salivating as they watched the preparation of "a morsel of sickening and imperfect meat".[181] But this is not surprising as the atmosphere of the "cookshops" was hardly conducive to hygiene.[182] The actual quantity eaten would also have been

---

had no legal protection against rape (*Digest* 23.2.43.9; see Kleberg, *Hôtels*, pp. 91ff.; Laurence, *Roman Pompeii*, p. 80). Some *popinae* revelled in this vulgar image, covering their walls with scatological slogans (R. Meiggs, *Roman Ostia*, Oxford: Clarendon Press, 1960, p. 429).

[174] Suetonius, *Nero*, 26:1; SHA, *Verus* 4.5; SHA, *Commodus* 2.7. The emperor Elagabalus was even said to have dressed up as a *popinarius*, a cookshop keeper. (SHA, *Elagabalus* 30.1).

[175] Cicero, *Orationes Philippicae* 2.28.69. See also 13.11.24.

[176] Martial, *Epigrammata* 1.41.9.

[177] Seneca, *Epistulae* 56.2.

[178] Martial, *Epigrammata* 1.41.9.

[179] Horace, *Epistulae* 1.15.34.

[180] For example, the chained slave in Juvenal, *Saturae* 11.81 recalls *calidae sapiat quid vulva popinae* (probably from a sow). In fact these cuts often appeared unappetising to many of the Graeco-Roman non-élite themselves, as we can see from Juvenal's third satire: the mugger ridicules the poverty of his victim, before administering his beating, by, amongst other things, accusing him of recently eating *elixi vervecis labra*, literally "boiled lambs lips"; adding, as it were, insult to injury (Juvenal, *Saturae* 3.294).

[181] *nauseam horridae carnis* (Ammianus Marcellinus, 28.4.34).

[182] Horace, *Epistulae* 1.14.21 complains about the "greasy cookshop" and in *Saturae* 2.4.62 moans about "foul pubs". Cicero protested about the "reek and fume" of the *ganearum* (*Oratio in Pisonem* 13). Although such criticisms are most probably exaggerated by the

modest, no doubt in many cases akin to the '*ofella*', the 'bite' of meat mentioned in Juvenal's eleventh satire.[183] But, whatever the form, quality or quantity of the meat, it was meat none the less.[184] Nutritionally insignificant perhaps but, contrary to Theissen, a familiar enough part of everyday life of the non-élite that 'numinous' qualities could not have been ascribed to it.[185] His characterisation of the class-specific eating habits of the protagonists in 1 Cor. 8 and 10 is therefore erroneous and irrelevant.

So, although the 'strong' in the dispute over meat have perceptions clearly at variance with the 'weak' (and indeed these are at the heart of the dispute), there is no reason to assume these perceptions are evidence of different socio-economic status.

Signs of stratification within patterns of sociability: Theissen's explanation of the dispute in terms of class-specific patterns of sociability is likewise untenable. He maintains that a wealthy person would be loath to avoid eating consecrated meat because of the impossibility of fulfilling their public and professional duties, whilst the poor would lose little socially by such abstention for which they could not be compensated by membership of the church. Hence the 'strong', who argue in favour of consuming consecrated meat, must be wealthy, while the 'weak', who oppose it, must be members of the "lower strata".[186]

However, there is one rather obvious flaw in this observation, of which Theissen is himself aware: the pattern of sociability for the 'strong' and the 'weak' in 1 Cor. 8 and 10 appears to be almost identical. 1 Cor. 10:27ff. indicates that both 'strong' and 'weak' Christians were present

---

authors' 'class' animosity, they contain within them more than a grain of truth: chimneys were not common in this period and so the air in such places would have been thick with the smoke and stench from the *focus* (hearth), that had pride of place in the room. (Hermansen, *Ostia*, p. 194).

The conditions in the *cauponae* were hardly more sanitary: Pliny informs us that it was common, in summer, for them to be infested with fleas (*Naturalis Historiae* 9.154).

183   Juvenal, *Saturae* 11.144.

184   Vegetarianism appears, almost exclusively, to have been a practise associated with various élite groups. See C. Osborne, "Ancient Vegetarianism", *Food in Antiquity*, ed. J. Wilkins, D. Harvey and M. Dobson, Exeter: Exeter University Press, 1995, p. 222.

185   Artemidorus' *Oneirocritica* provides important evidence for meat consumption amongst the non-élite: to dream of eating goat's meat presaged unemployment (1.70). Goat's meat was evidently considered a meat of the poor.

186   Theissen, *Social Setting*, pp. 129–132.

at the same meal. Theissen's attempt to explain away this difficulty is unconvincing. He conjectures that the objector of verse 28 is not a believer at all, but one of the ἄπιστοι who hosts the meal, because of this individual's use of ἱερόθυτον to describe the meat, and also because the conscience of the complainant is never described as 'weak' (unlike, for example, 1 Cor. 8:7). However, there are a number of compelling reasons why a Christian may have employed the word ἱερόθυτον (offered in sacrifice) instead of the more pejorative εἰδωλόθυτον (idolatrous sacrifice): it may have been used out of politeness and respect for the host,[187] or out of habit.[188] It is also fallacious to make much of the fact that the conscience of the objector is not described as 'weak'. If we examine the wider literary context within which this section appears we find that the absence of the term 'weak' in verses 28–29 is explicable without assuming that these verses concern the objections of a pagan: Paul does not use the word anywhere in the whole of chapter 10 at all (he abandons using this term after 9:22).[189]

Perhaps more tellingly, the greatest reason for assuming that verses 28ff. refers to the protestations of a Christian and not a pagan, is the difficulty in understanding how (and indeed why) respect for a pagan's conscience could be an issue. What pagan scruples would the Christian have been offending by eating the meat? It is fair to conclude, with Barrett, that, "it is not easy to see how a non-Christian's conscience could enter into the matter."[190]

Class-specific traits in the forms of legitimation: Theissen's argument that the form of legitimation used by the 'strong', their 'gnosis', is also class-specific, and therefore indicative of this group's social elevation, is likewise flawed. The specific characteristics of 'gnosis' he examines (intellectual level, soteriology based on knowledge, and élite self-consciousness combined with taking pleasure in contact with the pagan

---

[187] C. K. Barrett, *The First Epistle to the Corinthians*, London: A. & C. Black, 1971, p. 242, and Reginald St John Parry, *The First Epistle of Paul the Apostle to the Corinthians*, Cambridge: Cambridge University Press, 1926, p. 221.

[188] Archibald Robertson and Alfred Plummer, *A Critical and Exegetical Commentary on the First Epistle of St. Paul to the Corinthians*, New York: Scribners & Sons, 1911, p. 221.

[189] The fact that the 'conscience' of the objector is not qualified in any way by the apostle does not indicate that he must be an unbeliever of some kind. Throughout chapter 10 the 'consciences' (e.g. vv. 25, 27, 28, 29) of a number of different types of individual are discussed and nowhere does Paul qualify the term.

[190] Barrett, *The First Epistle to the Corinthians*, p. 242.

world),[191] are actually, thoroughly ambiguous, and his case is not made any more plausible (if anything it is further confused) by his parallel examination of analogous features of second-century Gnosticism (groups within which also ate meat offered to idols).

Intellectual level: For Theissen, "Gnostic systems of thought demand a high level of intellect. Their speculations are full of ludicrous systems of logic, and as such were not accessible to simple people."[192] And this he finds true also of the Corinthian 'gnostics'. His assumption seems to be that the kind of intellectual level displayed required an élite, and therefore expensive, education. However, his argument is weak. His belief that intellect and education are synonymous is problematic in itself but it is also the case that neither Corinthian 'gnosis' nor later Gnosticism were as intellectually daunting as he presumes. All we know of the theology of the Corinthian 'gnostics' (and even this is debatable) comes to us through the medium of a handful of rather clichéd slogans, such as, "all of us possess knowledge",[193] which are no more mentally challenging than an advertising jingle; and later Gnostic mythologies were no greater a test of a person's intelligence than the salvation narratives present in the canon of the 'orthodox'. (Gnosticism cannot have been too highbrow as it was capable of sustaining quite populist movements such as the Messalians[194] or the Manichees.)[195]

Soteriology based on knowledge: Theissen argues that "a soteriology of knowledge, faith in the saving power of discernment", is also a class-specific factor, quoting Max Weber's analysis of the 'salvation cults' of

---

[191] Theissen, *Social Setting*, p. 134.

[192] Theissen, *Social Setting*, p. 134.

[193] 1 Cor. 8:1.

[194] S. Runciman, *The Medieval Manichee*, Cambridge: Cambridge University Press, 1982, pp. 21–25.

[195] S. N. C. Lieu, *Manichaeism in the Later Roman Empire and Medieval China: A Historical Survey*, second edition, Tübingen: J. C. B. Mohr, 1992. Although the Manichaean strictures against farming meant that its appeal to peasants was rather limited, it certainly attracted members from groups outside the 'upper classes', having particular success amongst individuals who made their living from trade.

That intricate cosmologies can flourish outside aristocratic circles can also be seen in the case of Mennochio, the sixteenth-century Italian miller made famous by the work of Carlo Ginzburg. In fact, his case contradicts Theissen's picture of the bookish nature of Gnosticism: Mennochio's inquisition reports show how oral culture can also foster and transmit complex soteriological myths (Ginzburg, *The Cheese and the Worms*).

the Graeco-Roman world as evidence that this form of religion can be ascribed to the "upper classes".[196] But, once again, this is not the case. Not only is it rather methodologically dubious to use what we know of 'salvation cults' in order to extrapolate about 'gnostic' groups (the two categories are, phenomenologically, quite distinct) but it is also not the case that 'salvation cults' only attracted the affluent. For example, the leaders of the notorious Bacchic conspiracy were, according to Livy, plebeians,[197] and the majority of the followers of Mithras came from the military and merchant classes,[198] hardly members of the aristocracy. The appeal of such forms of paganism went beyond specific élite groups and so we cannot follow Theissen and say anything class-specific about such types of soteriology. In fact, the originator of by far the most successful faith based upon a 'soteriology of knowledge', the prophet Mani, began life as a slave and was brought up in an ascetic community of Elkasaites; a background which was far from affluent.[199] We cannot, therefore, infer anything about the social status of either Corinthian 'gnostics' or second-century 'Gnostics' from their adherence to a soteriology based on knowledge.

Élite self-consciousness within the community: Élite self-consciousness within a community, an undeniable quality of Corinthian 'gnostics' (1 Cor. 3:1), and also of later Gnosticism, is also regarded by Theissen as an unequivocal class-specific trait. But to see perceived spiritual status as a simple reflection of socio-economic status, whilst understandable, is misguided. It is by no means the only plausible interpretation of this relationship. Religion can also be seen as having, for example, a compensatory element to it, in which a person's perception of their spiritual status is in direct conflict with that of their socio-economic position. This is, perhaps, most visible in some contemporary 'sects':[200] European Jehovah's Witnesses, for example, combine a strong sense of spiritual élitism with a decidedly non-élite socio-economic member-

---

[196] Theissen, *Social Setting*, p. 135, using insights from Max Weber, *The Sociology of Religion*, London: Methuen & Co., 1963, p. 123.

[197] Livy 39.17.6.

[198] Though even slaves were admitted (Walter Burkert, *Ancient Mystery Cults*, Cambridge, MA: Harvard University Press, 1987, p. 42).

[199] See Lieu, *Manichaeism in the Later Roman Empire*, pp. 35–50.

[200] For a definition of the term 'sect' and the cultural presuppositions inherent in the use of such a word, see Bryan Wilson, *The Social Dimension of Sectarianism: Sects and New Religious Movements in Contemporary Society*, Oxford: Oxford University Press, 1990.

ship.[201] Sometimes the relationship between spiritual and socio-economic status is even harder to determine as, for instance, we can see with the Paulicians, who combined a strong sense of their spiritual superiority with a membership drawn from a cross section of the society of their day.[202] We should beware of assuming that spiritual identity is always sociomorphic, that it is invariably and simply shaped by social context.

Taking part in the pleasures of the pagan world: In addition, Theissen's proposal that taking part in the pleasures of the pagan world is a sign of elevated social status,[203] is also rather weak: we should not underestimate the degree of attraction which the *popinae*, pantomimes, baths, games and chariot races, held for the non-élite in the Empire.[204]

Class-specific traits in the forms of communication: Theissen's observations about "class-specific traits in the forms of communication" also fail to convince. He regards the letter itself as a "social fact", indicating that some Corinthians enjoyed an elevated position in the society of their day.

However, even if it could be argued that Paul's original *informants* were indeed the 'strong' (which I believe is rather unlikely)[205] and that

---

[201] Wilson, *The Social Dimension of Sectarianism*, p. 153.

[202] The Paulicians are an important example as they also provide evidence that a sense of éliteness can be felt by different social groups living fully *within* a wider religious community; it cannot therefore be argued that such notions must be dependent upon a sectarian exclusiveness. Although the Paulicians did exist as a separate community for some of their history their members also worshipped within the Orthodox church, taking full part in its rites (Runciman, *Medieval Manichee*, p. 51).

[203] Theissen, *Social Setting*, p. 136.

[204] See, for example, Toner, *Leisure and Ancient Rome*, pp. 65–88.

Theissen also exaggerates the degree to which Gnostics felt at home and were accepted by the wider Graeco-Roman world. As John Schütz has observed: "It is plainly difficult to think of gnostics, with their dour cosmologies, and their clannish sense of separate identity, as paradigms of social integration" (quoted in Meeks, *First Urban*, p. 70). Certainly, the Marcionite who was burnt alongside the orthodox martyr Pionius in Smyrna probably took something rather less than pleasure from his contact with the pagan world (Robin Lane Fox, *Pagans and Christians*, Harmondsworth: Penguin, 1986, p. 492).

Theissen also seems to have underestimated the degree to which many 'orthodox' Christians took their place in the culture that surrounded them; early apologists such as Tertullian testify to their presence throughout all areas of Graeco-Roman life (Tertullian, *Apologeticum* 37.4–8).

[205] Although he dismisses the possibility that any other members of the community could have had a hand in the letter, saying: "Other opinions are not reflected, the catch phrase 'all of us possess knowledge' (8:1) leaving little room for that" (*Social Setting*, p. 137) this

the letter was *addressed* "almost exclusively to the 'strong'",[206] this would *not in itself* tell us, as Theissen maintains, that the 'strong' were socially exalted. Even if such people held leadership positions *within* the church it does not follow that they held such positions *outside* it.[207] Nor can we legitimately see in the apostle's attack upon those Corinthians who criticised him for refusing to take any material support from them[208] (a group which Theissen once again sees as identifiable with the 'strong') evidence of the existence of a wealthy group in the congregation. Although Theissen argues that the "critics" cannot have been "materially impoverished" because, "they are at the moment supporting other missionaries",[209] this is not necessarily the case: supporting a missionary is not a sure sign of affluence. It is possible for all except those facing an immediate subsistence crisis.[210]

The disparate arguments Theissen musters under the title of "Class-specific traits in the forms of communication" do not stand up to scrutiny. The same is true of his overall attempt to provide a plausible

---

is a far from conclusive argument: i) The crucial slogan in 1 Cor. 8:1 may not, in fact, be a quotation from a letter at all, given the absence of the expression Περὶ δὲ ὧν ἐγράψατε (1 Cor. 7:1), or a similar phrase. Paul may be quoting a slogan he heard second-hand from an informer – perhaps from Chloe's people (1 Cor. 1:11) or Stephanas (1 Cor. 16:17); ii) Even if it is a quotation, it is not necessarily the case that the letter was written *entirely* by the 'strong'. Elsewhere in 1 Corinthians we have fragments of this initial epistle that do not seem to come from the 'strong' group. The material concerning sexual matters (1 Cor. 7:1ff.) which, from its opening words, was quite clearly written in response to some section of the initial epistle received by Paul, does not contain any indication that it was formulated specifically to deal with questions raised by the 'strong', despite the apostle's fulsome treatment of the issue. (The fact that Paul gives advice on asceticism does not prove that the question was raised by 'gnostics'. Brian Rosner has shown how the apostle's advice on celibacy can be understood as having a thoroughly Jewish, ungnostic provenance. It therefore follows that the initial questions of the congregation in this area may also have emerged from such a background. See *Paul, Scripture and Ethics: A Study of 1 Corinthians 5–7*, Leiden: E. J. Brill, 1994.)

206 Theissen, *Social Setting*, p. 137.

207 Nor is it the case, as he seems to maintain on p. 137, that the use of the letter as a means of communication is in itself socially significant. Letter writing was common amongst all classes in the Graeco-Roman Empire.

208 1 Cor. 9:1–27.

209 Theissen, *Social Setting*, p. 138.

210 See comments below under the heading of 'Hospitality.' In addition, the model of material renunciation which Theissen believes Paul is presenting to the 'strong' in this chapter cannot be seen as indicative of this group's wealth. Material renunciation is relatively as costly and attractive to all. For example, a cursory glance at the gospels shows that this concept was assumed to be applicable to all social groups and not only reserved as a special teaching directed to the rich. See Mark 10:29ff.

sociological explanation of the quarrel over meat consumption in Corinth. Therefore, his reconstruction cannot be used to argue that an élite group existed within one of the Pauline churches.

Argument over the eucharist (1 Cor. 11:17–34)

The dispute over the eucharist in 1 Cor. 11 has long been interpreted as a clash between poor and rich members of the community. The fact that one group involved in the dispute is referred to as τοὺς μὴ ἔχοντας (11:22), a phrase which appears, superficially, analogous to the English expression "the have nots", whilst their opponents quite clearly are "the haves" (they "have" not only their own homes (v. 22)[211] but enough resources to buy "lavish amounts of food and drink")[212] makes such a reconstruction incontrovertible for many.[213]

Recent socio-historical readings which have examined the incident in the light of Graeco-Roman dining conventions have made this interpretation appear all the more credible. Theissen,[214] for example, has argued that the dispute was, at its root, caused by, "a particular habit of the rich"[215] – that of serving different guests with different quantities and qualities of food in accordance with their social status.[216] For Fee[217] the conflict was a consequence of the divisive practice of a small number of wealthy members who followed the custom of their day by eating a private meal in a *triclinium* (v. 21) whilst the poor were forced to eat rather less well and rather less comfortably, outside in the *atrium*.

If class conflict is clearly attested in 1 Cor. 11:17–34 then we have firm evidence that at least some members of the Pauline communities came from the higher levels of first-century society. But, in fact, upon close examination, this dispute reveals nothing about

---

[211] Theissen, *Social Setting*, p. 150; Chow, *Patronage and Power*, p. 111; Fee, *Corinthians*, p. 543; Martin, *Corinthian Body*, p. 73.

[212] Horrell, *The Social Ethos*, p. 95.

[213] Robertson and Plummer, *The First Epistle of St Paul to the Corinthians*, p. 242: "There can be little doubt that, as οἱ ἔχοντες = 'the rich', οἱ μὴ ἔχοντες = 'the poor'."

[214] Though it is important to note that Theissen's argument is not grounded on the common assumption that οἱ μὴ ἔχοντες is a synonym for the poor (for him it refers to those that do not, specifically, have food, see *Social Setting*, p. 148).

[215] Theissen, *Social Setting*, p. 151. His interpretation is followed by Meeks, *First Urban*, pp. 68–69.

[216] Such as we find for example in Martial, *Epigrammata* 1.20; 3.60 and Lucian, *De Mercede Conductis* 26.

[217] Fee, *Corinthians*, p. 534. Followed by Chow, *Patronage and Power*, p. 111.

such social tensions, or the social constitution of the Corinthian church.

Firstly, the key assumption that οἱ μὴ ἔχοντες is a synonym for the destitute is, however superficially attractive, thoroughly unsound. Whilst there are a few possible occasions when the expression may function in some such way in ancient literature,[218] these are actually quite rare; indeed, it is telling that it is completely absent from key texts concerned with relations between the rich and poor in nascent Christianity. *The Shepherd of Hermas*, which contains one of the most lengthy discussions of inter-class behaviour in antiquity, and which uses a broad and rich vocabulary for describing the two different groups, never employs οἱ μὴ ἔχοντες in such a way;[219] nor do we find it present in the synoptic gospels or the epistle of James as a designation for the poor, despite their obvious interest in this class of people.

In fact, in the great majority of relevant parallel uses of οἱ μὴ ἔχοντες, the substantive participle possesses a specified 'object'; there is a clearly discernible 'thing' which a group does not have. This is sometimes directly apparent from the phrase in which the expression appears, as for example in Diogenes Laertius, *Vitae Philosophorum* (6.33.2) – τοὺς μὴ ἔχοντας πήραν;[220] or, on occasion, it is discernible from the wider sentence in which it is used, as we can see in the LXX 1 Esd. 9.51 – Βαδίσαντες οὖν φάγετε λιπάσματα καὶ πίετε γλυκάσματα καὶ ἀποστείλατε ἀποστολὰς τοῖς μὴ ἔχουσιν;[221] or from the broader literary context, as, for instance, we find in Plato's *Euthydemus* – where that which the οἱ μὴ ἔχοντες of 274.b lack is defined earlier as Ἀρετή (273.d). However, the possibility that τοὺς μὴ ἔχοντας in verse 22 could actually take an 'object' seems to

---

[218] Euripides, *Supplices* 240 seems to provide an instance of this.

[219] See Carolyn Osiek, *Rich and Poor in the Shepherd of Hermas*, Washington: The Catholic Biblical Association of America, 1983, pp. 40–41. On the one occasion the expression is used in this work it clearly has little to do with questions of social class: *Mand* 12.1.2 (44).

[220] For other examples see Aristotle, *Politica* 1282a.19 οἱ μὴ ἔχοντες τὴν τέχνην; Aristotle, *Metaphysica* 995a.16, τοῖς μὴ ἔξουσιν ὕλην; 1 John 5:12, ὁ μὴ ἔχων τὸν υἱὸν τοῦ θεοῦ; 1 Thess. 4:13, οἱ μὴ ἔχοντες ἐλπίδα.

[221] It is clear that it is not the poor *per se* that are being referred to but rather a group that lack rich food and sweet wine to eat and drink. See also LXX 1 Esd. 9.54, καὶ ᾤχοντο πάντες φαγεῖν καὶ εὐφραίνεσθαι καὶ δοῦναι ἀποστολὰς τοῖς μὴ ἔχουσιν; LXX 2 Esd. 18.10 (Nehemiah), καὶ εἶπεν αὐτοῖς Πορεύεσθε φάγετε λιπάσματα καὶ γλυκάσματα καὶ ἀποστείλατε μερίδας τοῖς μὴ ἔχουσιν; Luke 22:36, ὁ μὴ ἔχων πωλησάτω τὸ ἱμάτιον αὐτοῦ καὶ ἀγορασάτω μάχαιραν.

119

have eluded many contemporary exegetes. Barrett appears to have been aware of this possibility, suggesting that τοὺς μὴ ἔχοντας might refer to housing (1 Cor. 11:22a)[222] but such sensitive readings are uncommon.[223] And, more importantly, I have yet to discover a New Testament exegete who holds that the 'object' of this expression is actually what I contend to be the dominant concern of this section of the epistle: the Lord's Supper. *Those not having, are, more specifically, those not having the bread and the wine of the eucharist.* (It is quite evident both from the apostle's own words (vv. 27, 28, 29) and from the important unit of tradition he includes in his argument (vv. 23–26) that 11:17–34 is intended, above all, to give advice on the proper consumption of the elements.) Such an interpretation is not in conflict with a credible overall reconstruction of the dispute recorded in 1 Cor. 11:17–34. Indeed, despite its unfortunate novelty, it provides a more cohesive reading than many of the alternatives.[224]

The fact that this section of the epistle coincidentally reveals that certain members of the community had homes (vv. 22, 34) also fails to indicate the wealth of some Pauline Christians. The use of the verb ἔχω is ambiguous; it does not necessarily imply *ownership* of a property but can also imply that it was rented (which, given the extensive rental sector in Graeco-Roman cities,[225] is a very likely possibility). And, in addition, whether this was rented or owned, it was unlikely to have been substantial: both the terms οἰκία and οἶκός can refer to a wide variety of dwellings,[226] not just the peristyle houses that seem to have

---

[222] Barrett, *First Epistle to the Corinthians*, p. 263.

[223] Even where awareness of the possibility is shown, it is rarely preferred. Meeks, *First Urban*, p. 68: "The last phrase hoi me echontes, could be read quite concretely as continuing the oikias ouk echete of the preceding question; that is, those who have houses are blamed for humiliating those who do not. More likely, the phrase is to be taken absolutely, 'the have-nots,' that is the poor."

[224] For a fuller exposition of this interpretation of the dispute see Appendix 2: The Elements of Conflict: a reading of 1 Corinthians 11:17–34.

[225] Almost invariably ignored by New Testament exegetes, though see Georg Schöllgen, "Was wissen wir über die Sozialstruktur der paulinschen Gemeinden?" p. 74. See also chapter 3.

[226] It is not the case, as Fee maintains, that the term οἰκία used in verse 22 indicates a house rather than a dwelling/home (which he sees designated solely by the word οἶκός, which appears in verse 34 – *Corinthians*, p. 543, fn. 60). Although the meanings of οἰκία and οἶκός differed in ancient Greek literature, it impossible to see such distinctions in their use in the New Testament, the LXX and other literature of the period.

monopolised the interest of New Testament scholars,[227] and, as we observed in chapter 3, most habitations in the Roman Empire tended to be far from ostentatious. Even if a Pauline Christian owned his/her own home, it might well be little more than a shack or lean-to.

Given my reconstruction (see Appendix 2), the ability of some Corinthian Christians to purchase lavish amounts of food and drink cannot be seen as an indication of their wealth. Paul's words in verse 21 do not demonstrate that some believers had the capacity to do such a thing, but are rather concerned with ridiculing those congregants who gorged themselves on the elements.

[227] There are a number of reasons for this fascination, not least of which is the dominant ideology of archaeology that we have already discussed (something often compounded by the need for archaeology to respond to interests of tourism): peristyle houses are usually the most impressive forms of domestic architecture on display at most sites associated with the New Testament. However, it is the assumption that earliest Christianity was a popular movement that has done the most to encourage interest in this form of housing. It is argued that the sheer weight of numbers attending meetings of the Pauline churches could only be contained in such expansive and expensive buildings (J. Murphy-O'Connor, *St Paul's Corinth*, pp. 153–159; Ellis, *Pauline Theology*, p. 144). However, this does not seem to have been the case because we would expect such numbers to have made some impact on non-Christian sources but, as Fox rightly notes, ". . . although we have so much incidental material for life in the Empire, the inscriptions, pagan histories, texts and papyri make next to no reference to Christians before 250" (*Pagans and Christians*, p. 269). The tangible evidence *for* the movement's popularity during this early phase is, in fact, sparse and can be easily dismissed: i) The 'three thousand' and 'five thousand' converts referred in Acts 2:41 and 4:4 are little more than a fanciful exaggeration on the part of the author, a consequence of his redactional and apologetic concerns; ii) Tacitus' report that a great number of Christians were killed by Nero is most plausibly seen as another exaggeration motivated by the desire to accentuate the cruelty of this emperor, a common enough theme in his writing (*Annales* 15.44.2–8); iii) The extensive size of the Bithynian church described by Pliny is inflated in an attempt to justify yet another call upon Trajan's time by this famously unconfident official (*Epistulae* 10.96); iv) The adoption of the faith by Constantine cannot be plausibly accounted for by reference to its strength (the only definite figure we have of church membership pre-Constantine allows us to estimate the Christian population of Rome in 251 CE at about 1% of the total – see Eusebius, *Historia Ecclesiastica* 6.43.11), despite Stark's illuminating analysis of the statistical grounds for believing this to be the case (*The Rise of Christianity*, pp. 3–27).
It seems far more probable that the handful of individuals named and alluded to in the Pauline epistles constitute roughly the total number of adherents to his wing of the church during this period. Given that, from what we know of early Christian practise, it seems unlikely that they all met together (Acts 12:17, 20:20; *Acta S. Iustini* 2), there is even less reason to suppose that the hosts needed to have large homes: virtually any habitation would have sufficed. The example of Gaius, ὁ ξένος μου καὶ ὅλης τῆς ἐκκλησίας, does not contradict this. As C. E. B. Cranfield has observed, the expression might indicate that Gaius "gave hospitality to travelling Christians passing through Corinth" (*The Epistle to the Romans*, second volume, Edinburgh: T. & T. Clark, 1979, p. 807).

The socio-historical explanations of the background to the argument over the events in 1 Cor. 11:17–34 also fail to provide support for interpreting these verses as indicative of class conflict. Theissen's proposal that the élite made a habit of varying the quantity and quality of food that they served to guests of different status, does not give us a plausible background to the tensions in the church. He makes the bold assumption that such practise was confined to the élite (presumably because our knowledge of the custom comes from élite literary sources). He does not raise the possibility that those outside such exalted circles were also capable of behaving in such a fashion. As we observed in chapter 2, non-élite culture, whilst including creative and original forms of social practice, also adopted (albeit with varying degrees of transformation and subversion) the conventions of élite culture. The "particular habit of the rich" may be rather more socially widespread than he allows. Fee's ingenious reconstruction also assumes the congregations met in peristyle houses, which, as we have noted, is extremely unlikely (indeed we have evidence, for example, that such eucharists took place in flats without such luxuries as a *triclinium* or *atrium*).[228] Yet this is not indicated by the text.

There are good grounds for seeing 1 Cor. 11:17ff., despite its popularity, as giving the New Testament social historian no direct evidence at all about social divisions in the early Church; and consequently this section provides us with no information about the presence of socially elevated members within the community.

Litigation (1 Cor. 6:1ff.)

The fact that at least some members of the Corinthian church were capable of taking civil actions (1 Cor. 6:1ff.)[229] against one another has been interpreted by a number of commentators as incontrovertible evidence that a few[230] Pauline Christians came from the social élite.

---

[228] Acts 20:9–12; *Acta S. Iustini* 2; see also R. Jewett, "Tenement Churches and Communal Meals in the Early Church: The Implications of a Form-Critical Analysis of 2 Thessalonians 3:10", *BR* 38 (1993) 23–43.

[229] See B. W. Winter, "Civil Litigation in Secular Corinth and the Church: The Forensic Background to 1 Corinthians 6:1–8", *NTS* 37 (1991) 559–572 and *Seek the Welfare of the City*, pp. 106–121. For the difference between civil and criminal law in the Principate see W. Kunkel, *An Introduction to Roman Legal and Constitutional History*, Oxford: Clarendon Press, 1973, pp. 61–80.

[230] Fee's insistence that only one individual is being referred to here is unconvincing (*Corinthians*, pp. 228–230). The use of the second person plural in verses 7 and 8 is best understood as indicating that a number of law suits were taking place, as Barrett

Andrew Clarke has given the most lengthy summary of the evidence for this position, though he is certainly not alone in his conclusions.[231] For Clarke, "the system of civil claims was so clearly a system in favour of those with established status that it is reasonable to assume the disputes discussed by Paul in 1 Cor. 6 were initiated by those from the higher echelons in the society of the colony".[232] But whilst his characterisation of Roman law is accurate,[233] his inference is most decidedly not. The prejudice of a system which prevented the non-élite having much chance of justice if they instigated proceedings against their *social superiors*[234] is irrelevant if the litigation being referred to in 1 Cor. 6 involves cases between *social equals* from the lower echelons of Corinthian society. Clarke does not even seem to have considered this possibility.

We have enough examples of litigation in which both parties came from the ranks of the non-élite to make this a very high probability indeed. Law was never entirely the preserve of the aristocracy,[235] despite being a product and tool of this class. The wide variety of records that we have indicate that the law was regularly used by people who were, socially speaking, a great distance from the rarefied cliques who held power in Graeco-Roman society. Papyrological evidence furnishes us with information about, for example, business contracts between weavers[236] and goatherds;[237] terms of employment for apprentices[238] and

---

maintains (*The First Epistle to the Corinthians*, pp. 135, 139); also Robertson and Plummer, *The First Epistle of St Paul to the Corinthians*, p. 110; Conzelmann, *A Commentary on the First Epistle to the Corinthians*, p. 104; W. Schrage, *Der erste Brief an die Korinther*, Zurich: Benzinger, 1991, p. 404.

[231] Theissen, *Social Setting*, p. 97; David W. J. Gill, "In Search of the Social Élite in the Corinthian Church", *TB* 44 (1993), p. 330; Winter, "Civil Litigation", and *Seek the Welfare of the City*, pp. 106–121; Martin, *The Corinthian Body*, pp. 76–79; A. J. Mitchell, "Rich and Poor in the Courts of Corinth: Litigiousness and Status in 1 Corinthians 6.1–11", *NTS* 39 (1993) 562–586; Witherington, *Conflict and Community*, pp. 162–169; Chow, *Patronage and Power*, pp. 76–79.

[232] Clarke, *Secular and Christian*, p. 68.

[233] See Garnsey's classic work, *Social Status and Legal Privilege*.

[234] Though this was occasionally possible, despite the slave only being a *res* under Roman law. Slaves could, for example, take their masters to the magistrate to complain of mistreatment – see Bradley *Slaves and Masters*, pp. 123ff. and 153 (Phaedrus, *Fabularum Aesopiarum* 4.4).

[235] Crook, *Law and Life of Rome*, p. 11.

[236] P. Mich. 5.355.

[237] P. Strasb. 1.30.

[238] P. Oxy. 4.724

even castanet dancers;[239] disputes between camel drivers over equipment;[240] builders over wooden beams;[241] occupants of a house over the
furniture.[242] Some of the rulings of the classical jurists concern, for
instance, a shopkeeper fearing litigation from a thief whose eye he had
damaged[243] and disputes between neighbours over waste disposal in
blocks of flats.[244] As Suzanne Dixon observes, "Not all cases in Justinian's
Digest are necessarily historical but many which are attended with
apparently authentic circumstantial detail indicate that significant legal
decisions could be based on cases involving litigants of relatively modest
means."[245] *Defixiones* also testify to litigation amongst the non-élite:
one 'binding spell', for instance, seems to have been used by a slave in
an attempt to prevent other slaves initiating proceedings against him.[246]

The opportunity to go to law to settle a dispute was not something
monopolised by the élite classes.[247] Paul's comments in 1 Cor. 6 are
therefore quite possibly addressed to people who could be termed 'poor'

---

[239] P. Cornell 9.

[240] P. Oxy. Hels. 23.

[241] P. Mich. 5.230.

[242] P. Oxy. 8.1121.

[243] *Digest* 9.2.52.1. For another example of the concern of a shopkeeper over prosecution by a criminal see *Digest* 9.1.2.

[244] *Digest* 9.3.1.

[245] Suzanne Dixon, *The Roman Mother*, London: Routledge, p. 42. Clarke is therefore wrong to presume that the litigants in 1 Cor. 6:1ff. were necessarily men (*Secular and Christian*, p. 68): women could also instigate litigation under most of the legal systems that held sway within the Empire. (For Roman evidence see *Digest* 40.12.13; Suetonius, *De Grammaticis* 7.21; Petronia Iusta's dossier found at Herculaneum (Crook, *Law and Life*, p. 16); for Greek, see Pomeroy, *Goddesses, Whores, Wives and Slaves*, pp. 126–129; for Egyptian, see Deborah Hobson, "The Impact of Law on Village Life in Roman Egypt", *Law, Politics and Society in the Ancient Mediterranean*, ed. Baruch Halpern and Deborah Hobson, Sheffield: Sheffield Academic Press, 1993, p. 209.)

[246] John Gager, *Curse Tablets*, p. 137. See also J. M. Cormack, "A Tabella Defixionis in the Museum of the University of Reading, England", *HThR* 44 (1951) 25–34.

[247] Figures for the actual cost of litigation are hard to come by and no doubt varied tremendously from region to region. We do however have a price list from Timgad in Numidia for 362/3 CE which indicates that the sums involved "were not beyond the reach of a small farmer" (Ramsey MacMullen, *Corruption and the Decline of Rome*, New Haven: Yale University Press, 1988, p. 151) – and this for a period which saw a substantial increase in the fees required by court officials. For a more pessimistic interpretation of the cost of litigation in the fourth century see Chris Kelly, *Corruption and Bureaucracy in the Later Roman Empire*, Cambridge: unpublished PhD dissertation, 1993, p. 105.

For further evidence of non-élite litigation see *Philogelos* 109, 178: the fact that such legal jokes found their way into a popular collection is, in itself, revealing.

according to our definition. Given the apostle's description of the cases as κριτήριον ἐλάχιστον this, I believe, is a distinct probability. So it is untenable to assume that 1 Cor. 6 can be of any value in determining the elevated socio-economic status of a group of individuals in the Pauline communities.

The use of male head coverings (1 Cor. 11:4)

David Gill has suggested that Paul's reference to men covering their head during worship (1 Cor. 11:4) is yet further evidence of the presence of the élite amongst Pauline Christians.[248] In the context of *Roman Corinth*,[249] he maintains, such an act would have clear status implications as only the most socially powerful male Romans traditionally behaved in such a way, as the portraiture and sculpture of the period appears to indicate (we find, for example, numerous representations of Augustus depicted *capite velato*, perhaps most famously on the *Ara Pacis* in Rome but also in a prominent statue from Corinth itself).[250] As he remarks: "The issue which Paul is dealing with here seems to be that members of the social élite within the church – the dunatoi and the eugeneis (1:26) – were adopting a form of dress during worship which drew attention to their status in society."[251]

However, Gill's reading is fundamentally flawed. It is true that élite Roman males did behave in such a way but they were not the only ones to do so: whilst they did indeed cover their head while officiating at major public sacrifices (and public monuments such as the *Ara Pacis* record exactly this kind of practice) less prestigious Roman males were used to doing likewise on a regular basis, whilst undertaking domestic religious rites (as can be seen, for example, depicted on the *lararia* of Pompeii).[252] Indeed, during private prayer (surely a closer parallel to the events described in 1 Cor. 11:4 than that depicted on the *Ara Pacis*)

---

[248] See David W. J. Gill, "The Importance of Roman Portraiture for Headcoverings in 1 Corinthians 11:2–16", *TB* 41 (1990) 245–260 and "In Search of the Social Élite".

[249] During Paul's day, Corinth was still dominated by the Roman culture of its refounders (see J. Wiseman, "Corinth and Rome I: 228 BC – AD 267", *Aufstieg und Niedergang der römischen Welt*, vol. 2.7.1, ed. H. Temporini and W. Haase, Berlin: Walter de Gruyter, 1979, pp. 438–548).

[250] Cynthia L Thompson, "Hairstyles, Headcoverings and St Paul", *BA* 51 (1988), p. 105.

[251] Gill, "Headcoverings", p. 250. See also Gill, "In Search", p. 331.

[252] Orr, D. G. "Roman Domestic Religion: The Evidence of Household Shrines", *Aufstieg und Niedergang der römischen Welt*, vol. 2.16.2, ed. H. Temporini and W. Haase, Berlin: Walter de Gruyter, 1978, pp. 1557–1591.

capite velato was the common apparel of *all* Romans, whatever their social standing, as noted, amongst others, by Plutarch in his *Quaestiones Romanae*.[253] As Oster remarks ". . . the repetition of those Greek authors who characterise *capite velato* as a 'Roman rite' demonstrates that it was the conventional pattern of the pious Roman, whatever his or her station and vocation in daily life".[254] The problem Paul is dealing with in 1 Cor. 11:4 cannot be seen as an indication that the congregation contained socially privileged members, as Gill would have us believe.

Reference to Caesar's household (Phil. 4:22)

The fact that some early believers are identified as members of the Imperial household (οἱ ἐκ τῆς Καίσαρος οἰκίας) has given a number of commentators reason to argue for the presence of socially prestigious individuals amongst the congregations. But such an extrapolation is unwarranted. The *Familia Caesaris* encompassed a wide variety of individuals, whose experiences of life were far from universally positive.[255] Whilst high level bureaucrats enjoyed a prosperous existence, the overwhelming majority of members of the Imperial household were employed in menial domestic or agricultural occupations. Most had little directly to do with the Emperor himself or his court, finding themselves in the rather less prestigious situation of being freedmen or slaves of Imperial freedmen (or even, indeed, of Imperial slaves).[256] The comfortable life of members of the *Familia Caesaris* is a fiction produced by the literary and inscriptional sources, which are biased towards recording the lives and deaths of the affluent (as we have observed). Certainly, those individuals who risked their lives in open revolt against Caesar, by joining Bulla's rebellion, did not do so because they found

---

[253] Plutarch, *Quaestiones Romanae* 266D (10) – a text of which Gill appears to be aware. There is no evidence here that Plutarch is referring only to the most socially significant Romans. As he demonstrates elsewhere in the text, he is sensitive to the differences between the practices of élite and non-élite Romans. See, for example, 267 (18).

[254] R. E. Oster, "When Men Wore Veils to Worship: The Historical Contexts of 1 Corinthians 11:4", *NTS* 34 (1988) 481–505.

[255] Indeed, contrary to Meeks' assertion (*First Urban*, p. 63) it is, in fact, untrue to say that members had greater opportunities for upward mobility than any other non-élite group. Although he refers to R. P. C. Weaver's study to justify this statement (*Familia Caesaris*, Cambridge: Cambridge University Press, 1972), Weaver's findings are only true of those members of the household who were higher level administrators.

[256] For a useful, if now somewhat antiquated, description of the various occupations that might be filled by members of the *Familia Caesaris*, see J. B. Lightfoot, *St Paul's Epistle to the Philippians*, London: Macmillan & Co., 1879, pp. 171–173.

their lives in the Imperial household comfortable: low or virtually non-existent pay made them desperate and the appalling risk of sedition one worth taking.[257]

Supposed references to Pauline civic benefactors

According to B. W. Winter[258] Rom. 13:3 (οἱ γὰρ ἄρχοντες οὐκ εἰσὶν φόβος τῷ ἀγαθῷ ἔργῳ ἀλλὰ τῷ κακῷ. θέλεις δὲ μὴ φοβεῖσθαι τὴν ἐξουσίαν; τὸ ἀγαθὸν ποίει, καὶ ἔξεις ἔπαινον ἐξ αὐτῆς) refers to the Graeco-Roman practice of honouring civic benefactors (those that do good works) and, given that such acts of euergetism[259] did not come cheap, it therefore indicates the presence of a number of rich Christians amongst the Pauline churches

> The cost of a benefaction was very considerable . . . [it] included supplying grain in times of necessity . . . forcing down the price by selling it in the market below the asking rate, erecting public buildings or adorning old buildings with marble revetments . . . , refurbishing the theatre, widening the roads, helping in the construction of public utilities . . .[260]

However, Winter's interpretation of the apostle's words is implausible on a number of grounds[261] but perhaps its most obvious flaw is its failure to take into account the fact that these remarks are specifically addressed to Christians in the city of Rome. Rome was not a Greek polis, as Paul would know. The culture of euergetism had found its way into the capital city but,[262] given Rome's ideological significance as the 'shop-window' of the Empire,[263] it took a very different form to that

---

[257] See Cassius Dio 77.10.5.

[258] "The Public Honouring of Christian Benefactors, Romans 13:3–4 and 1 Peter 2:14–15", *JSNT* 34 (1988) 87–103, reproduced in *Seek the Welfare*, pp. 26–60.

[259] For a discussion of euergetism see below, chapter 5.

[260] Winter, *Seek the Welfare*, p. 37.

[261] For example, i) The use of ἔπαινος and its cognates was not restricted solely to praising the wealthy. See, for example, Dio Chrysostom's ἔπαινος for the poor who occupied themselves with jobs which he considered worthy rather than dissolute (*Orationes* 7.110ff.). (Dio Chrysostom was certainly one of the ἄρχοντες (Rom 13:3) of his home town of Prusa.) ii) The use of the second person singular in 13:3 cannot be seen as an indication that Paul's words were addressed to a small number of wealthy congregants financially capable of making public benefactions ("Public Honouring," p. 94). Paul moves easily, and even quite arbitrarily, between the second person singular and plural when giving counsel aimed at the *whole* church (see, for example, Rom. 14:15 and 16).

[262] For the importation of the Greek language of honours into the Roman context, and its appropriation under the Principate see Wallace-Hadrill, "Roman Arches and Greek Honours".

[263] Veyne, *Bread and Circuses*, p. 385.

found in the eastern Mediterranean. The Emperors curtailed opportunities for private individuals to act as civic benefactors and virtually
monopolised such activity themselves.[264] Benefactions not undertaken
by the Emperor, were made by members of his family or, with severe
restrictions, the chief magistrates.[265] Private benefactors were seen as a
threat to the Emperor's power, as the case of Egnatius Rufus, executed
by the jealous Augustus, demonstrates: "The Emperor could not
tolerate any *euergetes* in his capital other than himself."[266] Rom. 13:3–4
therefore cannot be taken as evidence of élite membership of the Pauline
churches as the verse cannot be interpreted against the background that
Winter proposes.

II) Information about individuals within the Pauline churches

Having established that we have no solid grounds for assuming the
elevated economic status of *groups* within the Pauline churches we
now turn to the question of the economic identity of *individual* congregants. Certain named figures, such as Aquila, Crispus, Erastus, Gaius,
Nympha, Philemon, Phoebe, Priscilla, Sosthenes, and Stephanas, have
been located firmly by followers of the 'New Consensus' amongst the
more prosperous of first-century society, as has one unnamed Christian,
the man guilty of incest in 1 Cor. 5. Such characterisations are, for
the most part, grounded in common, though I believe mistaken,
assumptions about the social significance of certain recurring biographical details that are given in the Pauline epistles. So it is appropriate,
before we turn to the examination of *specific* individuals, that we engage
with these assumed indicators of prosperity. By so doing we avoid much
needless repetition.

Once again Theissen's[267] work has proved perhaps the most influential
in this area. He argues that four common forms of prosopographical
data, "statements about holding office, about 'houses', about assistance
rendered to the congregation, and about travel", provide us with
evidence of elevated social status.[268] We will leave aside his first category
for the moment, that of statements about offices (the significance of
each office needs to be examined upon its own merits, and it is

---

[264] Veyne, *Bread and Circuses*, pp. 386–390.
[265] Individuals who would clearly be considered as amongst the ἄρχοντες, the group of
which Paul evidently considers the Christians not to be members.
[266] Veyne, *Bread and Circuses*, p. 388.
[267] Theissen, *Social Setting*, pp. 69–119.
[268] Theissen, *Social Setting*, p. 73.

inappropriate to generalise about their importance) and turn our attention to the other three.

a) References to 'houses': For Theissen, statements about specific individuals having 'houses'[269] (in this case, more precisely, *households*) refer to extensive domestic units which included slaves; and as slaves were expensive to own (in his opinion) we can take such information as evidence that some Pauline Christians were affluent.

But there are problems with Theissen's position. It is true that the terms οἶκός-οἰκία could be used of households that included slaves,[270] and, from Acts 10:7 and Philem. 2, it is quite clear that some Christian ones certainly did contain them, but we should not be quick to assume that this was always the case. Households could vary in size tremendously. The 'household' of a poor person, for example, could be as small as two family members[271] and the majority were no doubt equally modest in size.[272]

And even if a household did include a slave or slaves amongst its members this is not, in fact, indicative of a householder's exalted social status. Contrary to the apparent consensus amongst New Testament exegetes, a slave could be obtained in the first-century Graeco-Roman world without incurring substantial expenditure. Although costs for an adult slave on the open market *may* have required a significant outlay (and it is difficult to tell whether this was the case)[273] slave *ownership* was not beyond the means of the non-élite,

---

[269] See 1 Cor. 1:16, 1 Cor. 16:15 (Stephanas); Acts 18:8, 1 Cor. 1:14 (Crispus); 1 Cor. 1:11 (Chloe?); Col. 4:15 (Nympha); Philem. 2 (Philemon).

[270] Strobel is wrong to argue that οἶκός-οἰκία correspond only to the Latin word *domus*, something which he maintains referred only to a narrow family unit which could not have included slaves (in contrast to the much broader social group denoted by, in his opinion, the use of the term *familia*). His arguments are flawed: i) οἶκός-οἰκία, as Theissen rightly notes (*Social Setting*, pp. 83–87) could also be used for the Latin word *familia*. ii) Strobel's restricted understanding of the term *domus* is inaccurate: it was quite commonly used to designate a household that included slaves: ". . . *domus* covered a larger group than is usually associated with the family today, encompassing husband, wife, children, slaves and others living in the house . . ." (Garnsey and Saller, *The Roman Empire*, p. 128). See A. Strobel, "Der Begriff des 'Hauses' im griechischen und römischen Privatrecht", *ZNW* 56 (1965) 91–100.

[271] Ovid, *Metamorphoses* 8.635.

[272] As Brent Shaw observes ("The Cultural Meaning of Death. Age and Gender in the Roman Family", *The Family in Italy From Antiquity to the Present*, ed. D. Kertzer and R. Saller, New Haven: Yale University Press, 1991, p. 72).

[273] We only have a handful of records of slave prices for our period and most of these are, frankly, irrelevant. For example, manumission prices recovered from a shrine at Delphi for the last two centuries BCE appear to demonstrate that market costs

in fact it is quite widely attested.[274] Not only artisans[275] but soldiers,[276]

---

were substantial and rising (Hopkins, *Conquerors and Slaves*, pp. 108ff.). However, there are severe problems with the nature and size of this sample of prices (see R. P. Duncan-Jones, "Problems of the Delphic Manumission Payments 200–1 BC", *ZPE* 57 (1984) 203–209) and, even more significantly for us, this evidence is actually inadmissible for estimating the *market* cost of slaves: manumission prices do not give us a straightforward indication of the actual purchase price of a slave on the open market (p. 208; see also W. L. Westermann, *The Slave Systems of Greek and Roman Antiquity*, 1955, p. 36, fn. 7). The manumission price provided masters with an excellent opportunity for profit as the slave had no choice but to agree to whatever inflated figure was set by their owner, regardless of commercial forces. It seems to have been quite common practice of owners to attempt to gain as much profit as possible from their positions of power, upping these prices or reneging on previous agreements as they saw their slave's *peculium* gradually approaching the agreed figure. Just such behaviour was suggested by Tacitus to lie behind the famous murder of the prefect Pedanius Secundus (Tacitus, *Annales* 14.42.1. See also, Bradley, *Slaves and Masters*, p. 99. According to Bradley the same behaviour may lie behind Phaedrus, *Fabularum Aesopiarum* 1.8 (p. 152)).

For a summary of what little can be gleaned about prices of slaves in Italy and Rome see Richard Duncan-Jones, *The Economy of the Roman Empire*, Cambridge: Cambridge University Press, 1974, pp. 348–350. Most of these are obviously exaggerated and untypical.

It is often argued that changes in supply must have forced up slave prices during our period. The views of de Ste Croix (*Class Struggle*, p. 228) and Hopkins (*Conquerors and Slaves*, p. 110) are typical of the prevailing wisdom: they hold that, with the onset of the Principate and the end of the expansionist wars, the supply of slaves decreased, pushing up their cost. However, William Harris has demonstrated that no such dramatic change in supply occurred, as the exposure of children *within* the expanded Empire went a long way to meeting demand ("Towards a Study of the Roman Slave Trade", *The Seaborne Commerce of Ancient Rome*, ed. J. D'arms and E. Kopff, Rome: American Academy in Rome, 1980, pp. 117–140; see also R. Motomura, "The Practice of Exposing Infants and its Effects on the Development of Slavery in the Ancient World", *Forms of Control and Subordination in Antiquity*, ed. T. Yuge and M. Doi, Leiden: E. J. Brill, 1988, p. 413). The constant importation of slaves from peoples outside the boundaries of the Empire was also more than sufficient to make up for the shortfall (M. Crawford, "Republican Denarii in Romania: The Suppression of Piracy and the Slave Trade", *JRS* 67 (1977) 117–124; see also Brunt's criticisms of de Ste Croix in "A Marxist View of Roman History").

It is important to note that foundling slaves were equally likely to have been of either sex (see D. Engels, "The Problem of Female Infanticide in the Graeco-Roman World", *CPh* 75 (1980) 112–120 *contra* Pomeroy, *Goddesses, Whores, Wives and Slaves*, pp. 46, 69–70, 140, etc.).

[274] As Beryl Rawson observes, "it is striking . . . how often epitaphs attest slaves belonging to humble people" (*The Family in Ancient Rome*, Ithaca: Cornell University Press, 1986, p. 12).

[275] Ownership of a slave or two by an artisan seems to have been quite common (Reynolds, "Cities", p. 48). See also Ulpian's words in *Digest* 9.2. 27.9.

[276] See M. P. Speidel, "The Soldier's Servants", *AncSoc* 20 (1989) 239–247. Josephus, *De Bello Judaico* 3.125; Tacitus, *Histores* 2.87; CIL 3.8143. Not only legionaries and praetorians but even auxiliaries seem to have owned such slaves.

peasants,[277] and even other slaves,[278] owned slaves. It was the lot of many slaves to be, in the words of C. Mossé, "companions in the frugal lives of their masters".[279] Such slaves were often acquired for a fraction of their full market cost. Anyone capable of feeding an extra mouth could bring up an exposed child[280] (a practice which offered attractive profits).[281] For those with a little bit more cash to spare, there were also opportunities to buy an infant.[282] Both alternatives offered the chance for an individual to obtain (eventually) a fully grown slave for a small proportion of the sum required to purchase an adult outright. Indeed, for many of those just above subsistence level it was not only an economically viable but also a sensible thing to do.

The inclusion of a slave in a person's household can therefore indicate little about the householder's socio-economic status. A Christian having

---

[277] The poor peasant in the pseudo-Virgilian poem *Moretum* (117f.) still had Scybale, a woman slave, to order about. See also the poor woman with one slave mentioned in P. Oxy. 50.3555.

[278] The *peculium* of a slave could include another slave. See Bradley, *Slaves and Masters*, p. 108 and the classic study of Erman N. Epp, *Servus vicarius: L'esclave de l'esclave romain*, Lausanne: F. Rouge, 1896. See also *Vita Aesopi* 12.

[279] Mossé, *The Ancient World of Work*, p. 112.

[280] The cost of rearing an exposed child was significantly lower than that of purchasing an adult – as we can see from Columella, *De Re Rustica* 1.8.19, which encouraged masters to give rewards to enslaved women for bearing children. Rearing such slaves also had a distinct advantage for the non-élite whose economic situation would make it difficult for them to accumulate the kind of capital lump sum required to purchase an adult outright.

[281] The owner would receive not only the slave's labour (something which they began quite early in life – see I. Biezunska-Malowist, "Les Enfants-esclaves à la lumière des papyrus", *CL* 102 (1969) 91–96 and *L'Esclavage dans l'Egypte Gréco-Romaine: Période Romaine*, Warsaw: Zakkadnarodowy Imienia Osslínskich, 1977) but also the money that would accrue from the slave's sale, either to a third party or the slave her/himself. Given the liquidity of the slave market (see, for example, M. H. Crawford and J. M. Reynolds, "The Aezani Copy of the Prices Edict", *ZPE* 34 (1979), p. 177) there also seems to have been opportunity for "short term speculative advantage" (Keith Bradley, "The Age at Time of Sale for Female Slaves", *Arethusa* 11 (1978), p. 247). This feature made slave ownership particularly attractive for those on lower incomes whose mercurial economic situation demanded that the capital invested in rearing a slave (and the profits accrued over time) should be able to be quickly realised in an emergency. Slaves were (financially speaking) commodities whose value increased with time, from birth up to maturity. Indeed, for any person living close to subsistence level and capable of feeding one extra mouth for even the shortest of periods, bringing up a slave represented an excellent, flexible, investment opportunity which was in many ways preferable to raising a child of his/her own.

[282] Prices were considerably lower for a child than an adult, and there were substantial savings to be made even when the cost of maintaining the slave after purchase until they reached maturity was taken into account – see Bradley, "Female Slaves", p. 247.

a 'household' cannot serve as a *probable*[283] indicator of elevated social status at all.

b) References to services rendered: For a number of New Testament exegetes, references to services rendered by various members of the Pauline communities mark them out as affluent.[284] The kind of activity undertaken by Phoebe and Stephanas, who offered material help to various individuals associated with the church,[285] and Gaius, Aquila, Priscilla, and Philemon, who gave hospitality to the meetings of the saints, is understood as a clear indication of their wealth.

If we suppose that services rendered *in any way* demonstrate élite status we fail to recognise that all exchange (whether hospitality or gift-giving) is redolent with compelling symbolic significance for all sectors of society and is not purely motivated by 'economic rationality';[286] it does not require, for example, a comfortable surplus on the part of the giver. The capacity and desire for the indigent to give to others (by making quite ruthless personal sacrifices) must not be ignored.[287] Hospitality, for instance, cannot be seen as a prerogative of the élite, though some New Testament scholars seem to assume this to be the case.[288] Even those in antiquity who lived lives only just above subsistence level practised it, as we can see from a number of ancient sources. For example, the poor market gardener (*hortulanus*) in Apuleius' *Metamorphoses*[289] extended hospitality to a traveller despite not being able to afford even a straw mat or blanket for himself.[290]

The limited, contemporary Western perception of hospitality is, historically, quite unusual, and a barrier to recognising its predominance and centrality in other cultures, past and present. As Felicity Heal perceptively remarks:

---

[283] Theissen, *Social Setting*, p. 87.

[284] Theissen, *Social Setting*, pp. 87–91.

[285] For Phoebe, see Rom. 16:1 and for Stephanas, 1 Cor. 16:15.

[286] The classic study of the symbolic dimension to exchange is M. Mauss, *The Gift. Forms and Functions of Exchange in Archaic Societies*, London: Cohen & West, 1954, though for a very useful introduction to the subject see John Davis, *Exchange*, Buckingham: Open University Press, 1992.

[287] See, for example, Hermas, *Similitudines* 5.3.7; *Sententiae Sexti* 267; Origen, *Homiliae in Leviticum* 10.2 and Athenagoras, *Legatio pro Christianis* 11.4, which provide evidence of early believers fasting in order to be able to give alms.

[288] It is not necessary, for example, for a person giving Paul and his co-workers hospitality to possess a plethora of "guest rooms and servants" as John Polhill assumes (*The New American Commentary: Acts*, Nashville: Broadman Press, 1992, p. 349).

[289] Apuleius, *Metamorphoses* 9.32–33.

[290] See also Ovid, *Metamorphoses* 8.631 (Philemon and Baucis).

> For modern Western man [*sic*] hospitality is preponderantly a private form of behaviour, exercised as a matter of personal preference within a limited circle of friendship and connection. As such it is also considered a social luxury, to be practised when circumstances are favourable but abandoned without serious loss to status when they prove adverse.[291]

We should be wary not to let our narrow experience of hospitality lead us to draw unreasonable conclusions about what it signifies about the economic status of an individual who practised such behaviour in antiquity.

c) References to travel: References to travel are another popular criterion for "elevated social status".[292] Although Theissen expresses some caution, recognising the ambiguity of such data, and seems to show an awareness of the fact that travel was undertaken by a variety of classes of individuals in the first-century world,[293] nevertheless it still remains, for him, evidence of the likelihood of a person's wealth; it can still play a part in the "coalescence of several criteria".[294] However, such an association between travel and wealth is untenable in the *Pax Romana* which afforded its inhabitants the unrivalled (until recently) opportunity to move about the Mediterranean and its environs, largely unhindered by the wars and brigandage that had restricted their predecessors.[295] There were many motivations for undertaking a journey: as well as business or work,[296] people travelled for reasons of health,[297]

---

[291] Felicity Heal, *Hospitality in Early Modern England*, Oxford: Clarendon Press, 1990, p. 1. See also J. Pitt-Rivers, "The Law of Hospitality", *The Fate of Shechem*, Cambridge: Cambridge University Press, 1977, pp. 94–112.

[292] Theissen, *Social Setting*, p. 73. See also Meeks, *First Urban*, p. 57.

[293] Theissen: "We must necessarily be cautious in drawing conclusions about the social status of people who travel. Business trips can be made by dependent workers; others who travel are simply sailors, companions of the wealthy and so forth" (*Social Setting*, p. 91). Meeks makes similar qualifications (*First Urban*, p. 57).

[294] Theissen, *Social Setting*, p. 91.

[295] Aelius Aristides' famous words may be a "rhetorical effusion" (E. Hunt, "Travel, Tourism and Piety in the Roman Empire: A Context for the Beginnings of Christian Pilgrimage", *EMC* 28 (1984), p. 391) but they seem to be accurate: "Now indeed it is possible for the Hellene or non-Hellene, with or without his property, to travel wherever he will, easily, just as if passing from fatherland to fatherland" (*Orationes* 26.100–101).

[296] Naphtali Lewis has observed that labour mobility in Graeco-Roman Egypt (often forced) accounted for the bulk of the 20–30% of adult males that were absent at any one time from Egyptian villages (*Life in Egypt Under Roman Rule*, Oxford: Clarendon Press, 1983, p. 77).

[297] Lionel Casson, *Travel in the Ancient World*, London: Allen & Unwin, 1974, pp. 130–134.

religion,[298] sport,[299] tourism[300] or to avoid debt or taxation.[301] There was also a wide variety of methods of travel, from expensive to the inexpensive; from, for example, the costly and prestigious horse,[302] or covered wagon with suspension,[303] to the rather more humble Shanks's pony. Certainly, the experience of travel differed tremendously[304] but, nevertheless, travel *per se* cannot be regarded as a class indicator. All but the enslaved or the sick could journey at their own volition.

Given the weakness of these three criteria we can immediately rule out the possibility that a number of individuals mentioned by Paul in his epistles can be reasonably classed with the élite or prosperous in society. If references to households, services rendered to the church, and travel, are not sustainable grounds for regarding an individual as wealthy, then we have no indication that Aquila,[305] Gaius,[306] Philemon,

---

[298] To visit the oracles, or to see the latest wonder worker (Casson, *Travel*, pp. 134–136).

[299] Casson, *Travel*, p. 136–137. Such international events as the Olympic festival (see Lucian's *De Morte Peregrini* 1, 35) or the Pythia at Delphi (Gellis, *Noctes Atticae* 12.5.1; Philostratus, *Vita Apollonii*, 4.17) drew enormous crowds.

[300] Casson, *Travel*, pp. 137–148 and 229–329. See also Friedländer, *Roman Life and Manners*, vol. 1, pp. 323- 428. This was much more common than is often supposed. Tour guides are, for instance, mentioned in Lucian, *Philopseudes* 4; Verrius Flaccus, *Historiae* 2.31. Pausanias' famous *Graeciae Descriptio* is, in fact, virtually a guide book, written by a Greek for a Roman audience interested in visiting the sites of antiquity (Hunt, "Travel", p. 398). For the popular draw of regional markets, see Joan M. Frayn, *Markets and Fairs in Roman Italy*, Oxford: Clarendon Press, 1993.

[301] See P. Oxy. 1477.

[302] Stuart Piggott, *Wagon, Chariot and Carriage: Symbol and Status in the History of Transport*, London: Thames & Hudson, 1992, p. 74.

[303] Greene, *Archaeology of the Roman Economy*, p. 38. See also C. W. Röring, *Untersuchungen zu römischen Reisewagen*, Koblenz: Numismatischer Verlag Forneck, 1983.

[304] For example, in the area of sea travel, the experience could vary from one of complete luxury (see Suetonius, *Caligula* 37; Plutarch, *Lucullus* 7.5 (implied in the critique of Mithradates – see also Lionel Casson, *Ships and Seamanship in the Ancient World*, Princeton: Princeton University Press, 1971, pp. 191–197)) through to the somewhat more basic one of the great mass of voyagers who "camped on deck, living either in the open or under tiny, temporary shelters" (Casson, *Ships and Seamanship*, p. 181; see Achilles Tatius 2.33.1; Petronius, *Satyricon* 100.6; Lucian, *Toxaris* 20). Most passengers endured crowded conditions (Casson, *Ships and Seamanship*, p. 172; Josephus, *Vita* 15; Acts 27:37) – and also, on occasion, were forced to pull their weight (Acts 27:19, 38). At the bottom end of the market some shipping operations were distinctly dubious – see Synesius' Voyage, *Epistulae* 4 (Casson, *Travel*, pp. 160–162). Popular jokes reflected the precariousness of many voyages in antiquity (see *Philogelos* 25).

[305] Rom. 16:3; Acts 18:2, 18, 26; 1 Cor. 16:19.

[306] Rom. 16:23; 1 Cor. 1:14.

Priscilla,[307] or Stephanas[308] differ in their economic status from the rest of the church members or society at large.

However, there still remain five other individuals, namely Erastus,[309] Crispus,[310] Sosthenes,[311] Phoebe,[312] and the unnamed man guilty of incest (mentioned in 1 Corinthians)[313] about whom we have information about offices held and/or further details that, regardless of the invalidity of the other criteria, have been taken as indicative of wealth. They require more detailed, separate, analysis.

Erastus (Rom. 16:23)

Erastus is perhaps the most significant figure for followers of the 'New Consensus'. He appears to give us the firmest evidence for the spread of Pauline Christianity amongst the urban élite of the Empire. For Clarke, for example, he is "one of the most important links with the secular leadership of Corinth".[314]

There are a number of reasons for believing that Erastus came from such exalted circles. Firstly, from the New Testament alone, the description of this individual as ὁ οἰκονόμος τῆς πόλεως (Rom. 16:23) appears unequivocally to indicate this. Whilst the expression is, by itself, socially somewhat ambiguous (it could be used both for high ranking municipal officers and also for low ranking public slaves)[315] the fact that Rom. 16:23 is the only occasion in which Paul mentions the secular status of a member of the congregation is taken as an indication of its social significance.[316] But such an argument is less than convincing. It presupposes that Paul would take special pride in having a powerful convert – yet the apostle, if anything, shows antipathy to the notion of secular prestige in his epistles.[317] The title may, in fact, be used by

---

[307] Rom. 16:3; Acts 18:2, 18, 26; 1 Cor. 16:19.
[308] 1 Cor. 1:16, 16:15, 17, 24 (Theissen, *Social Setting*, p. 95).
[309] Rom. 16:23.
[310] 1 Cor. 1:14; Acts 18:8.
[311] 1 Cor. 1:1; Acts 18:17.
[312] Rom. 16:1–2.
[313] 1 Cor. 5:1ff.
[314] Clarke, *Secular and Christian*, p. 46.
[315] Theissen, *Social Setting*, pp. 76–79; Clarke, *Secular and Christian*, pp. 49–54. For an example of the full title ὁ οἰκονόμος τῆς πόλεως being used during our period of a slave (and clearly, from the brevity of the inscription, a far from wealthy one) see AD 35 (1980) B369.
[316] Theissen, *Social Setting*, p. 76. Followed by Clarke, *Secular and Christian*, p. 56.
[317] For instance, 1 Cor. 1:27–28; 1 Cor. 6:1.

Paul to distinguish between the several Erastuses mentioned in the New Testament on a number of occasions as associated with the Pauline mission (Rom. 16:23; Acts 19:22; 2 Tim. 4:20 – if we assume, as many exegetes do, that they are separate individuals).[318] Or, perhaps (though somewhat more speculatively) it could be argued that this is not a reference to a secular title at all. Rather, Paul may be referring to an office *within* the church: Erastus may be *the* steward or treasurer, overseeing, for example, the financial contributions towards the 'collection', a significant element in the life of the Pauline congregations (Rom. 15:25–32; 1 Cor. 16:1–4; 2 Cor. 8 and 9; Gal. 2:10). This is quite possible given the literary context of Rom. 16:23,[319] and also the propensity for *collegia* (which have many parallels to the early communities)[320] to employ the terminology of civic government for their own offices.[321]

Secondly, in addition to the New Testament evidence there is also a famous piece of epigraphical datum marshalled to support this reading. An inscription from Corinth refers to a figure called Erastus who held the important civic office of *aedile*, and had the resources to pay for the paving of part of the city's marketplace.[322] If he is the same individual referred to in Rom. 16:23 then evidently Paul's Erastus would have been amongst the most socially powerful of his day. Some scholars have

---

[318] For example, Hemer, *Acts*, p. 235. It is surely not enough to protest, as Theissen does, that "Paul himself, however, never mentions any other Erastus" (Theissen, *Social Setting*, p. 76).

[319] Rom. 15:26ff. refers to the collection and the description of Erastus follows immediately from that of Gaius, who, though not holding a specific office, clearly has a distinct role in the church, as its 'host'.

[320] Superficially, of course, there were significant similarities between the Christian churches and these institutions, as we can see both from pagan and Christian commentators (see Pliny, *Epistulae* 10.96; Origen, *Contra Celsum* 1.1, 8.17.47; SHA, *Vita Alexander* 49; Tertullian, *Apologeticum* 38–39). See R. L. Wilken, "Collegia, Philosophical Schools and Theology", *Early Church History: The Roman Empire as the Setting of Primitive Christianity*, ed. S. Benko and J. O'Rourke, London: Oliphants, 1971, pp. 268–291, and *The Christians as the Romans Saw Them*, New Haven: Yale University Press, 1984, pp. 31–47. See also John S. Kloppenborg, "Collegia and *Thiasoi*: Issues in Function, Taxonomy and Membership", *Voluntary Associations in the Greco-Roman World*, ed. John S. Kloppenborg and Stephen G. Wilson, London: Routledge, 1996, pp. 16–30.

[321] J. P. Waltzing, *Étude historique sur les corporations professionelles chez les Romains depuis les origines jusqu'à la chute de l'Empire d'Occident*, 4 vols., Louvain: Charles Peteri, 1885, vol. 4, pp. 323–430 and Kloppenborg, "Collegia and *Thiasoi*", p. 26.

[322] J. H. Kent, *Inscriptions 1926–1950: Corinth viii. Part Three*, Princeton: The American School of Classical Studies at Athens, 1966, p. 99.

been quite bold about making this identification[323] whilst others have been somewhat more cautious,[324] but few, if any, resist assuming an association between the two characters.

There are a number of grounds posited for assuming that the Erastus of Rom. 16:23 and that of the inscription are one and the same: a) the dating of the inscription; b) the possibility that the expression ὁ οἰκονόμος τῆς πόλεως is synonymous with or closely related to that of 'aedile'; c) the relative rarity of the name 'Erastus'. However, on closer inspection, it is evident that these arguments are much more unsafe than has hitherto been recognised.

a) Dating: The dating of the inscription to "sometime near the middle of the first century after Christ",[325] by J. H. Kent (in the fullest excavation report) appears to support such an identification, given the likelihood that Paul wrote the last chapter of Romans from Corinth sometime in the early 50s.[326] However, Kent's claim is somewhat too precise. Palaeography alone can only give us the roughest approximation of a date.[327] When the crucial central slab was discovered in 1929[328] it was initially rather more vaguely dated to the second half of the first century[329] and some subsequent commentators have placed it even later.[330] A *terminus ad quem* is provided by the fact that the inscription

---

[323] Otto F. A. Meinardus, *St. Paul in Greece*, Athens: Lycabettus Press, sixth edition, 1992, p. 75; Engels, *Roman Corinth*, p. 108; V. P. Furnish, "Corinth in Paul's Time. What Can Archaeology Tell Us?" *BAR* 15 (1988), p. 20; Kent, *Corinth*, p. 99; O. Broneer, "Corinth, Center of St Paul's Missionary Work in Greece", *BA* 14 (1951), p. 94; T. L. Shear, "Excavations in the theatre district and tombs of Corinth in 1929", *AJA* 33 (1929), p. 526; Winter, *Seek the Welfare of the City*, p. 192; Witherington, *Conflict and Community*, pp. 33–34; Murphy-O'Connor, *Paul*, p. 269.

[324] Clarke: ". . . the present information does not allow us to make a certain identification between the Erastus of Romans 16:23 and that of the first century Corinthian inscription" (*Secular and Christian*, p. 55). Gill, "The link between the two Erastoi cannot be certain" ("In Search", p. 325).

[325] Kent, *Corinth*, p. 99.

[326] See, for example, Barrett, *First Epistle to the Corinthians*, p. 5 and Fee, *Corinthians*, p. 15. Even Gerd Lüdemann's chronology does not differ substantially from this date (*Paul: Apostle to the Gentiles: Studies in Chronology*, London: SCM, 1984, p. 363).

[327] Writing ". . . may be conjecturally datable within a century or two" (Gordon, *Latin Epigraphy*, p. 40).

[328] Of the three pieces that make up the inscription as we have it, the central slab was found in 1929, almost intact, and the two pieces that constitute the somewhat less preserved right-hand slab, in 1928 and 1947 respectively.

[329] F. J. Waele, "Erastus, Oikonoom van Korinthe en Vriend van St. Paulus", *MNHIR* 9 (1929), p. 43.

[330] According to Henry J. Cadbury's account of the history of relevant scholarship, "Erastus of Corinth", *JBL* 50 (1931), p. 46.

seems to have been used in repair work to a pavement that was undertaken some time in the middle of the second century,[331] but as H. Cadbury noted: "The original inscription is therefore older than that, but whether one generation older or more cannot be determined."[332] The dating of the inscription is much more problematic than has often been assumed[333] and therefore the correlation between the date of its dedication and that of the composition of the apostle's words about Erastus in his letter to the Romans is considerably less impressive than is normally maintained.

b) ὁ οἰκονόμος τῆς πόλεως: This phrase has also encouraged the association of the two Erastuses. Scholars have been somewhat divided upon the exact relationship of this office to that of 'aedile' mentioned in the inscription. For some they are identical. As Kent remarked "Saint Paul's word οἰκονόμος describes with reasonable accuracy the function of a Corinthian aedile."[334] For others, such as Theissen, the term indicates a position that "one held prior to the office of aedile".[335] But whichever option is the more plausible, the link between the office referred to by Paul and that

---

[331] R. Stillwell, *The Theatre: Corinth ii*, Princeton: The American School of Classical Studies at Athens, 1962, p. 4.

[332] Cadbury, "Erastus of Corinth", p. 46. Theissen observes that, out of respect, the inscription would only have been reused after the passage of "some considerable time" which would bring the date "back to the mid-first century C.E." (*Social Setting*, p. 80). However, even allowing for this delay in recycling the inscription (and this is not by any means certain, as it was not uncommon for officials to fall from grace and find their memorials quite quickly taken down and found another use, as we see in Roman *damnationes*) we should not push the date back so far (and therefore need not see it as contemporary with Paul's remarks about the Erastus of Rom. 16:23). The amount of time that elapsed between the erection of the inscription and Erastus' death is unlikely to have been long. Public office was something a person could only hold if they were over the age of 25 (E. Eyben, *Restless Youth in Ancient Rome*, London: Routledge, 1993, p. 69) and the office of aedile was one attained, on average, some years after someone began such a public career. Given the low life expectancy, even for the élite in the Empire (see above), it is probable that Erastus did not live much more than a decade or so after the inscription was made. Even allowing for a full generation to elapse from Erastus' death before the inscription was reused, this would still only give us an approximate date in the tail-end of the first century CE for its original dedication (and it could, of course, have been put up much later than that).

[333] It certainly is not the case that, "The dating of the inscription to the middle of the first century AD is not widely disputed" (Clarke, *Secular and Christian*, p. 49).

[334] Kent, *Corinth*, p. 99.

[335] Theissen, *Social Setting*, p. 81. See also Chow, *Patronage and Power*, pp. 93, 155.

mentioned in the inscription appears (on first sight) compellingly close.

But whilst ὁ οἰκονόμος τῆς πόλεως may indeed be used to indicate a powerful civic functionary, we should not forget, as we have observed above, that it does not necessarily do so at all; there are numerous examples of the phrase being used of individuals who held much more menial roles and were of far less social standing.[336] For example, Longeinos, an οἰκονόμος τῆς πόλεως of Thessalonica, whom we know of from a simple epitaph he erected to his wife, was unlikely to have been socially very exalted: the brevity of the inscription, cut into recycled stone, is hardly indicative of wealth or position. Indeed, the fact that he refers to himself with a single name, and one particularly common to the enslaved at that, confirms his modest status.[337]

c) The relative rarity of the name: The assumed relative rarity of the name Erastus has also invited this identification.[338] For example, V. P. Furnish asserts that "since the name itself is not common, it would appear that this Erastus is the same one whom Paul and the author of 2 Timothy mention".[339] However, we have substantially more epigraphic attestations of the name than has hitherto been realised. I have discovered fifty-five examples of the use of the Latin cognomen Erastus[340] and twenty-three of the Greek Ἔραστος,[341] making it, in

---

[336] Cadbury, "Erastus of Corinth", p. 50. See also Fox, *Pagans and Christians*, p. 293.

James Dunn makes the pertinent point that we should not interpret the definite article as evidence that Erastus held high public office: "The definite article does not necessarily indicate that there was only one oikonomos; it could just mean the oikonomos who was a Christian" (*Romans 9–16*, p. 911).

[337] The full inscription reads: ΛΟΝΓΕΙΝΟΣ ΟΙΚΟΝΟΜΟΣ ΤΗΣ ΠΟΛΕΩΣ ΑΡΤΕΜΙΔΩΡΑ ΤΗ ΣΥΜΒΙΩ Μ(ΝΕΙ)ΑΣ ΧΑΡΙΝ. (AD 35 (1980) B369 (Thessalonika)). See also H. W. Pleket's comments on SEG 38 (1988) 710.

[338] Kent, *Corinth*, p. 100.

[339] Furnish, "Corinth in Paul's time," p. 20.

[340] CIL III 2840, 9052; IV 179, 4614, 4641, 5820; V 6821, 7232; VI 695, 1300, 1914 (379), 1934 (219), 5232, 5858, 7513, 8518 (twice), 8875, 9865 (12), 9759, 9915 (6), 11178, 13501, 14040, 14457, 15031, 15325, 15439, 15483, 15492, 15728, 17253, 24452, 24776, 24739, 27452, 33109, 33614, 36364; IX 3418; X 527, 1878, 2002, 2519, 6144; XI 227, 1620, 3613 (12), 6700 (320), 6712 (133); XII 128; XIV 1255, 4032, 4562 (4); XVI 33. AE 1984, 625.

[341] AM 95 (1970) p. 212 nos. 149–150; SEG XI 622, 994; XXIV 194; XXV 194; XXVIII 1010; XXIX 301; XXXV 1259. CIG 1241; 1249; 6378. IG II² 1945 (4), 1968 (7), 1973 (76), 1985 (3), 1990 (12, 22), 2030 (20), 2059 (93), 2067 (90), 2323 (221), 3762 (10); IG IV 1488 (39); P. Heid Bi 7 (IIa). There are also a number of literary references – Plato, *Epistulae* 6.322d, 323a; Diogenes Laertius, *Vitae Philosophorum* 3.46; Strabo 13.608.

fact, a relatively common name for our period,[342] and the identification of the inscriptional Erastus with that in Rom. 16:23 therefore much less likely.[343] Finally, we have another reason for doubting the relevance of the Corinthian inscription for determining the socio-economic status of Paul's Erastus. It might well be the case that the inscription was actually set up by an individual who was not called Erastus at all but rather *Eperastus*,[344] a widely attested, if somewhat less popular, cognomen.[345]

This is not quite as improbable as it might at first sight seem. The inscription that we have is not complete. A left hand section has yet to be recovered.[346] What remains is broken on the E of ERASTUS and so, by itself, we have no reason to assume that ERASTUS is actually a complete word (except ignorance of the possible alternative EPERASTUS).

The chief objection to the name Eperastus being present in the inscription is the problem of space. Most scholars have followed Kent's assumption that line 2 (which appears complete) was placed symmetrically below the partially complete line 1, allowing us to estimate that the number of letters that were on the left hand missing section must have amounted to about seven[347] – enough room for an abbreviated praenomen and short nomen of five or six

---

[342] The most recent study by Clarke has produced eleven attestations. See Clarke, *Secular and Christian*, pp.54–55 and also "Another Corinthian Erastus Inscription", *TB* 42 (1991) 146–151.

[343] Interestingly, as Clarke has pointed out, the assertion that no other Erastus is attested for Corinth, made by Kent (*Corinth*, p. 99) and Theissen (*Social Setting*, p. 83), is, in fact, inaccurate. See Clarke, "Another Corinthian Erastus Inscription", pp. 146–151.

[344] H. van de Weerd, "Een Nieuw Opschrift van Korinthe", *RBPh* 10 (1931) p. 91.

[345] I have found fifteen attestations of the Latin *Eperastus* (CIL III 14.195, 14.0; VI 1879, 7381, 12816, 16262, 16403, 17195, 21834, 22397, 24267a (twice); X 1403 (d, 1, 13); XI 982; I. Ephesus 860; and eighteen of the Greek Ἐπέραστος: IG II² 1996 (21), 2086 (49, 120), 2094 (70), 2119 (27), 2123 (19), 2123 (25), 2191 (61), 11278, 11449; IG IV 1230; VII 2434; IX 1121 (3); Ag xv 307, 6; SEG IX 917; XI 1274; XVIII 53; XXI 639, 2; XXVIII 166 (7).

[346] *Contra* Witherington who seems to think that the inscription as we have it is complete, and that it only had room for the donor's cognomen, despite the excavation reports and all subsequent scholarship (*Conflict and Community*, p. 34). He is also wrong to claim that the other inscription found at Corinth which mentions an 'Erastus' refers to the same individual. Despite his reference to Clarke's article on this other inscription ("Another Corinthian Erastus Inscription") he appears unaware of its conclusions (see also Clarke, *Secular and Christian*, p. 55).

[347] Kent, *Corinth*, p. 100.

letters[348] but not for the two additional letters EP that the Eperastus option would require. However, it is quite possible that the inscription is, in fact, *not* symmetrical and more than seven letters might be missing. There are plenty of examples of even prestigious inscriptions being badly executed,[349] and difficulties in spacing were quite a regular occurrence. Indeed, the inscription belongs to a type that was particularly susceptible to error. Its long width and short height encouraged problems of spacing that were less common on narrower *stelae*. Certainly, the irregular gaps between the letters in the complete second line are hardly indicative of precision. It is therefore quite possible that there was room for these two letters. A margin of error of two letters is not in itself substantial.[350]

But this is only a possibility. Regardless of the veracity of the Eperastus option, it is still improbable that the Erastus of Rom. 16:23 is identifiable with the figure mentioned in the Corinthian inscription. Erastus' economic situation was most likely indistinguishable from that of his fellow believers.

Crispus and Sosthenes (οἱ ἀρχισυνάγωγοι)

The possible (though not certain) identification of the Crispus mentioned in 1 Cor. 1:14 with the Κρίσπος ὁ ἀρχισυνάγωγος of Acts 18:8,[351] and the Sosthenes[352] referred to in 1 Cor. 1:1 with Σωσθένης ὁ ἀρχισυνάγωγος of Acts 18:17, has also provided proof, for many exegetes, of the presence amongst the Pauline churches of wealthy individuals: for not only were holders of this office in Jewish communities highly esteemed (even by the non-Jews)[353] but, it is often

---

[348] Clarke (*Secular and Christian*, p. 48) and David W. J. Gill ("Erastus the Aedile", *TB* 40 (1989), p. 295, fn. 4) follow Kent in assuming centring (*Corinth*, p. 100).

[349] See G. C. Susini, *The Roman Stonecutter: An Introduction to Latin Epigraphy*, Oxford: Basil Blackwell, 1973, pp. 39–49.

[350] The available space on the original inscription, which can be estimated from the surviving fragments, would certainly allow room for these extra letters.

[351] For Fee, it is "almost certain" (*Corinthians*, p. 62; see also Barrett, *First Corinthians*, p. 47; Theissen, *Social Setting*, pp. 73–75; Conzelman, *Corinthians*, p. 36).

[352] For Barrett, for example, it is "at least possible, and perhaps more than possible" (*First Corinthians*, p. 31). See also A. Schlatter, *Die Apostelgeschichte*, Stuttgart: Cawler, 1948. However, for the two Sosthenes to be one and the same we must assume that: i) the Sosthenes of Acts 18:17 became a Christian; ii) he migrated from Corinth to Ephesus. Given the additional popularity of the name we should, perhaps, agree with Conzelmann, who deems such speculation "idle" (*Corinthians*, p. 20).

[353] Theissen, *Social Setting*, p. 74. Though against this we should note that when *Alexander Severus* was called the "Syrian archisynagogos" it was not in order to flatter him (SHA, *Alexander Severus* 28).

argued, they were responsible for the upkeep of the synagogue building,[354] clearly something that required access to considerable funds.[355]

But, in fact, such reasoning is based upon a rather inadequate understanding of the term. The prestige of an ἀρχισυνάγωγος does not, *a priori*, indicate that an ἀρχισυνάγωγος was a wealthy person. Prestige and wealth do not necessarily go hand in hand within religious communities, and especially within Judaism (as we see, for instance, with Abba Hilkiah, the labourer).[356] Nor is it the case that Crispus and Sosthenes, as ἀρχισυνάγωγοι, would be expected to have sufficient wealth to fund maintenance and construction work in the synagogue. Certainly, there is inscriptional evidence that a *few* ἀρχισυνάγωγοι had this responsibility[357] but we cannot extrapolate from this that *all* ἀρχισυνάγωγοι did so.[358] To make such a deduction is to fall into the trap of assuming that the position of ἀρχισυνάγωγος was uniform both throughout all the diaspora communities and also throughout all six centuries from which our meagre knowledge of the office comes,[359] an assumption which the fragmentary nature of the literary and epigraphic evidence hardly warrants. Indeed, significantly, much of the evidence of ἀρχισυνάγωγοι undertaking such tasks comes from *after* the 'Christianisation' of the Empire, an event which appears to have actually led to a distinct increase in their social importance as they became the official channels through which the Imperial authorities dealt with their Jewish populations.[360] To think that ἀρχισυνάγωγοι

---

[354] Theissen, *Social Setting*, p. 74–75. See also Clarke, *Secular and Christian*, p. 46.

[355] This detail leads the following scholars to say, about Crispus: "He was probably a person of wealth" (Chow, *Patronage and Power*, p. 89); "probably well-to-do" (Meeks, *First Urban*, p. 57); a person of "distinction" (Judge, "The Early Christians", pp. 129–130). See also Theissen, *Social Setting*, p. 75, and Wayne Meeks and Robert L. Wilken, *Jews and Christians in Antioch in the First Four Centuries of the Common Era*, Missoula: Scholars Press, 1978, pp. 53f., 56.

[356] *b. Ta'anith* 23a-b. Indeed, interestingly, from the few pagan uses of the term ἀρχισυνάγωγος that we possess we have evidence that non-élite individuals could hold this position. A yoke-maker named Aretmon is described as an ἀρχισυνάγωγος in one such source (see *BE* 7 (1972), p. 203, fn. 263).

[357] See the famous Theodotos inscription from Jerusalem (CIJ 1404) and that from the Julia Severa synagogue at Akmonia (CIJ 766).

[358] A mistake that I believe Rajak and Noy make ("Archisynagogoi", p. 88).

[359] See Bernadette J. Brooten, *Women Leaders in the Ancient Synagogue*, Chico: Scholars Press, 1982, pp. 28–29 for an example of this.

[360] Rajak and Noy note that nine ἀρχισυνάγωγοι are recorded as donors out of a total of forty mentioned in the surviving inscriptional records, and in comparison with the numbers of donors holding other offices in the synagogue (such as the gerousiarchs)

had to pay for the construction and maintenance of synagogues is to be deluded, to some extent, by the peculiar nature of epigraphic evidence itself, which invariably has a bias towards recording involvement in funding building work:[361] the handful of inscriptions that we have that refer to such responsibilities are not necessarily as typical of the behaviour of actual ἀρχισυνάγωγοι as is so often assumed.

The generalisations about ἀρχισυνάγωγοι, which form the basis of 'New Consensus' estimates of the socio-economic situation of Crispus and Sosthenes, are unjustified. The case for seeing them as affluent individuals is based upon rather weak foundations.

Phoebe (Rom. 16:1–2)

Phoebe has often been thought of as a wealthy member of a Pauline church. With some small variation in terminology New Testament scholars have placed her firmly amongst the affluent of her day. For Caroline Whelan, for example, she was "a member of the upper classes",[362] for Elizabeth Schüssler Fiorenza she was "rich",[363] for Wayne Meeks, she was a woman of "some wealth",[364] and for H. Lietzmann she was "well-to-do".[365]

There are three major arguments proposed for asserting that she possessed such economic power:

a) From Paul's words she is clearly an independent woman and, it is argued, independence was something obtained only by women from privileged backgrounds.

---

they consider this proportion suggestive. But of these nine, between five and seven inscriptions belong to the post-Constantine era ("Archisynagogoi", p. 80).

Indeed, given the evidence that more than one ἀρχισυνάγωγος was often found in a synagogue (Mark 5:22; Acts 13:15; CIJ 766; Brooten, *Women Leaders*, p. 29; Horsley, *New Documents*, vol. 4, pp. 218–219) it is quite possible that the title ἀρχισυνάγωγος incorporated both those with the facilities to make benefactions and also those whose strengths lay in contributing to the wider religious life of the community (Acts 13:15, 42; Justin, *Dialogos Tryphone* 137).

[361] As Brooten observes (*Women Leaders*, p. 24).

[362] Caroline F. Whelan, "Amica Pauli: The Role of Phoebe in the Early Church" *JSNT* 49 (1993), p. 84. See also Theissen, *Social Setting*, p. 95.

[363] Fiorenza, *In Memory of Her*, p. 182.

[364] Meeks, *First Urban*, p. 60. Fox, *Pagans and Christians*, p. 293; Dunn, *Romans 9–16*, pp. 888–889; Chow, *Patronage and Power*, p. 101.

[365] H. Lietzmann, *A History of the Early Church*, vol. 1, London: Lutterworth, 1963, p. 149; see also Hugo Montgomery, "Women and Status in the Greco-Roman World", *STh* 43 (1989), p. 120.

b) She is described as a patron (προστάτις) of Paul and many Christians.

c) She had the resources to travel.

But when we re-examine this evidence of her exalted position, and in particular when we re-examine it 'from below', this characterisation appears rather unconvincing.

a) Phoebe's position as an independent woman: Phoebe was most definitely an independent woman. She is not mentioned with any reference to a male (unlike, for example, Priscilla[366] and Junia).[367] She evidently made the journey from Cenchreae to Rome,[368] and also conducted her business in Rome, alone. But this autonomy is not, as is so often assumed, an indication of her wealth. There were successful, independent, élite women in the Empire[369] and by following the

---

[366] Rom. 16:3; Acts 18:2, 18, 26; 1 Cor. 16:19.

[367] Rom. 16:7. See Richard S. Cervin, "A Note Regarding The Name 'Junia(s)' in Romans 16.7", *NTS* 40 (1994) 464–470.

[368] I reject the destination of Ephesus, which is sometimes maintained (initially by D. Schulz, "Einleitung in das neue Testament", *Theologische Studien und Kritiken*, 2 (1829), pp. 609ff., but also subsequently by others such as J. Goodspeed, "Phoebe's Letter of Introduction", *HThR* 44 (1951) 55ff.; T. W. Manson, "St. Paul's Letter to the Romans – and Others", *BJRL* 31 (1948) 224ff.; T. M. Taylor, "The Place of Origins of Romans", *JBL* 67 (1948) 281ff; Munck, *Paul*, p. 198; G. Bornkamm, "Der Römerbrief als Testament des Paulus", *Geschichte und Glaube*, vol. 2, München: Chr. Kaiser, 1971, pp. 120–139; Schmithals, *Paul and the Gnostics*, p. 237.

For the more widely accepted destination of Rome: C. E. B. Cranfield, *The Epistle to the Romans*, pp. 5–11; C. H. Dodd, *The Epistle to the Romans*, London: Hodder & Stoughton, 1942, p. xvii; K. P. Donfried, "A Short Note on Romans 16", *The Romans Debate*, Edinburgh: T. & T. Clark, 1977, pp. 44–52; Dunn, *Romans 9–16*, pp. 884–885; H. Gamble, *The Textual History of the Letter to the Romans*, Grand Rapids: Eerdmans, 1977; Meeks, *The First Urban*, pp. 16–17; Francis Watson, *Paul, Judaism and the Gentiles: A Sociological Approach*, Cambridge: Cambridge University Press, 1986, pp. 98–102; U. Wilkens, *Der Brief an die Römer*, Zürich: Benziger, 1978, vol. 1, pp. 24–27.

[369] Such as, for example, the various prominent female members of the Imperial family (see J. P. V. D. Balsdon, *Roman Women: Their History and Habits*, New York: J. Day, 1963, pp. 68–130, 140–164) or figures such as Iunia Theodora of Corinth (D. I. Pallas, S. Charitonidis, and J. Venencie, "Inscriptions Lyciennes Trouvées à Solômos près de Corinth", *BCH* 83 (1959) 496–508; also H. W. Pleket, *Epigraphica II: Texts on the Social History of the Greek World*, Leiden: E. J. Brill, 1968, pp. 20–25 – see SEG XVIII, 143, XXII, 232, XXIII, 176 and R. A. Kearsley, "Women in Public Life", *New Documents Illustrating Early Christianity*, vol. 6, ed. S. Llewelyn and R. A. Kearsley, North Ryde: Macquarrie University Press, 1992, pp. 24–27); Eumachia of Pompeii (Pomeroy, *Goddesses, Whores, Wives, and Slaves*, p. 200), or Plancia Magna of Perge (see Mary T. Boatwright, "Plancia Magna of Perge: Women's Roles and Status in Asia

example of certain female members of the Imperial family[370] (as well as drawing upon indigenous traditions)[371] such individuals made a distinct impact on society at the time of the Principate[372] (provoking the eloquent, if hysterical, scorn of Juvenal and Martial, who railed against the threatening figure of the assertive, wealthy woman).[373] But it is quite simply erroneous to argue that such autonomy was limited to the most affluent women in first-century society, as Kearsley does:

> In noting the fact that certain women played a notable and individual role in a variety of fields within the Greek cities of the early Imperial period, the lack of evidence that women of all strata of society could or did attain such independence from their domestic context must be emphasised. It was only by virtue of their wealth and their family connections that some women stepped beyond the conventions of social anonymity and domestic fidelity.[374]

We should not let the visibility of *élite* women blind us to the existence of *non-élite* women, who also attained some measure of independence during this period,[375] as we can see from a plethora of inscriptions.[376]

Minor", *Women's History and Ancient History*, ed. S. Pomeroy, Chapel Hill: University of North Carolina Press, 1991, pp. 249–272). Such figures contradict the picture that was propagated by the classical jurists who baldly asserted, despite evident reality, that women did not hold offices or give testimony (Paulus in *Digest* 5.1.12.2).

[370] See Boatwright, "Plancia Magna", p. 260.

[371] For example, in Asia Minor the culture had long given women a prominence that was lacking elsewhere in the Mediterranean (a point first made by O. Baunstein, *Die politische Wirksamkeit der griechischen Frau: eine Nachwirkung urgriechischen Mutterrechts*, Leipzig: unpublished dissertation, 1911).

[372] See Eva Cantarella, *Pandora's Daughters: The Role and Status of Women in Greek and Roman Antiquity*, Baltimore: Johns Hopkins University Press, 1987, pp. 135–170.

[373] Juvenal's invective is the most acidic (*Saturae* 6.25–32 or 6.115–135). As Cantarella notes, "Juvenal expresses an aversion to the female sex which borders on the pathological" (*Pandora's Daughters*, p. 147). Martial's is rather more restrained (*Epigrammata* 4.24).

[374] Kearsley, "Women in Public Life", p. 27.

[375] As Averil Cameron has observed: "As in many societies, the inferiority of women did not prevent them from leading active lives . . . Already, in fact, in late Republican and early Imperial Rome large numbers of women of lower- and middle-class status must have lived relatively active lives" ("Neither Male Nor Female", *G&R* 27 (1980), p. 62).
   She makes these remarks in the context of a valuable critique of Meeks. Nevertheless, it must be noted that Cameron works with the assumption that there was a significant entrepreneurial middle-class in the Empire and so concludes that a figure such as Phoebe was, "if not upper-class, certainly of substantial means" (p. 63).

[376] See, for example, the female shop owners cursed in the *defixio* IG III.iii.68, 69; the four freedwomen who collaborated in running a food franchise at a sanctuary near the Via Latina (AE 1980.216); the female fishmonger (CIL 9801); female clothing menders (CIL VI 3988, 4468, 9876, 9877b, 33907); female flagon seller (CIL VI 9488); female

Their lives and experiences are much less easy to reconstruct[377] but were no less real.

This is not surprising as the coalescence of cultural and environmental factors (high male age at marriage and low life expectancy) dictated that many women, from *all* sectors of society, would be left, like Crobyle in Lucian's *Dialogi Meretricii*, widowed and independent.[378]

Indeed, it is possible that autonomy was actually more often the possession of non-élite women. An independent élite woman had significant personal financial and social resources which encouraged men to attempt to exert authority over her. A non-élite woman had less to offer. Her independence was both less of a threat and less of an opportunity for males, and thus a status more likely to be maintained.[379]

b) *The term 'patron' (προστάτις) as an indication of wealth:* The term προστάτις has attracted a great deal of debate. The fact that it literally means 'patron' or 'benefactor' has traditionally caused difficulties for commentators who, disliking the idea that Paul could speak about a woman in such an exalted fashion, have preferred to use expressions such as 'helper' when translating Rom. 16:1.[380]

---

resin worker (CIL VI 9855); female lime burner (ILS 7663); female spinners (P. Oxy. 948, 1647); female porter (CIL VI 6326). See John K. Evans, *War, Women and Children in Ancient Rome*, London: Routledge, 1991, pp. 119–130; Kampen, *Image and Status*.

[377] Pomeroy makes some valuable observations about the problems inherent in attempting to undertake such a task (*Goddesses, Whores, Wives and Slaves*, pp. 190–191).

[378] Lucian, *Dialogi Meretricii* 293. Crobyle kept herself and her daughter alive by weaving and spinning.

[379] We should, however, beware of generalising about the opportunities available to women in the first-century world. The different cultural and legal traditions that operated in the early Empire helped shape women's lives in such a way that their experiences varied quite dramatically. For instance, the women of Roman Egypt seem to have had some role in owning property but in comparison with the women of Rome, where the concept of a lifelong *tutela* (guardian) was already significantly eroded by the first century, their ability to act as independent agents was severely restricted (see Deborah Hobson, "Women as Property Owners in Roman Egypt", *TAPA* 113 (1983) 311–321 and "Women in the Economic Life of Roman Egypt"). The importance of the different cultural contexts within the first-century world has been admirably highlighted by W. Cotter, "Women's Authority Role in Paul's Churches: Countercultural or Conventional?" *NovT* 36 (1994) 350–372.

[380] The RSV, NAB, NJB, Moffatt, NIV, Vulgate, and NKJV follow this rendering. The NRSV has restored the original force of the term, translating it as: "a benefactor of many". A point also made by Caroline Whelan, "Amica Pauli: The Role of Phoebe in the Early Church", p. 68, with a concise summary of reasons for rejecting the term 'helper' as an adequate translation of προστάτις.

(Phoebe's other designation, as a διάκονος, has, for similar ideological reasons, encouraged scholars to undertake comparably strained exegesis).[381]

But the fact that modern commentators have now restored the more literal sense to the term should not lead us to presume that the word προστάτις unequivocally indicates that Phoebe was wealthy. It is one thing to say that Paul referred to Phoebe as a patron, it is another thing entirely to argue that she must have been in some sense an *élite* patron who enjoyed a position similar, for example, to that of the celebrated Iunia Theodora in first-century Corinth[382] (as, for instance, R. A. Kearsley seems to suppose),[383] or the upper-class patrons of *collegia* (as Caroline Whelan suggests).[384] Such interpretations ignore the fact that patronage ties extended throughout the different strata of Roman society and its language could be applied to relationships between a wide variety of classes.[385]

Indeed, there are good grounds for doubting that the apostle intended to denote by his use of προστάτις that Phoebe held a position of social superiority. His use of the term is, frankly, too unconventional.

Firstly, the language of patronage was incredibly potent in the Roman world and, as a consequence, as Saller has observed, its vocabulary was severely restricted; patrons and clients were implied rather than identified, at least in letters.[386] To assert baldly before others that

---

[381] See Fiorenza, *In Memory of Her*, p. 47, for an illuminating discussion of the misogynism that has led exegetes to try and obscure the full sense of this title.

Despite the debate over the exact meaning of this term we can concur with Keener that it demonstrates that ". . . at the very least Phoebe held a position of considerable responsibility, prominence, and authority within her congregation" (*Paul, Woman and Wives: Marriage and Women's Ministry in the Letters of Paul*, Peabody, MA: Hendrickson, 1992, p. 239). However, for our purposes, it gives us no clue as to Phoebe's socio-economic position. As Meeks has correctly noted, the term διάκονος "cannot, however, tell us anything directly about Phoebe's status in macrosociety" (*First Urban*, p. 60).

[382] She was regarded as a patron by the members of the Confederacy of Greek Cities and also Myra, Patara, and Telmessos. For a discussion of Iunia Theodora see Kelly, *Corruption and Bureaucracy*, p. 25 and MacMullen, *Corruption and the Decline of Rome*, pp. 100ff.

[383] Kearsley, "Women in Public Life", p. 25.

[384] Whelan, "Amica Pauli", pp. 75–77.

[385] Tab. Vindol. II 250 provides an example of such lower-level patronage. See Alan K. Bowman, *Life and Letters on the Roman Frontier*, London: British Museum Press, 1994, p. 31.

[386] Richard P. Saller, *Personal Patronage under the Roman Empire*, Cambridge: Cambridge University Press, 1982, pp. 1 and 10.

someone was your patron, as Paul does, would have sounded decidedly odd to Graeco-Roman ears, if that had been the case.

Secondly, patrons required certain returns from their clients for their assistance, such as political or social support, but they did not ask for the kind of material help suggested by the terms χρῄζῃ πράγματι in Rom. 16:2.[387] One of the most telling (and nauseating) features of the patronage system for contemporaries of Paul was precisely the open financial support patrons gave their clients: the *sportulae* they deigned to distribute.[388] An act which could in any way appear to reverse this convention (something which Paul was encouraging by his words here) would have been quite unthinkable and distasteful within the traditional understanding of the patronage relationship.

Thirdly, the recommendee was usually socially inferior to the patron and certainly was never superior;[389] yet, in Rom. 16:1–2, Paul sends a letter of recommendation on behalf of his 'patron'. This, once again, is almost the exact inverse of the custom of his day.

These departures from the conventions of patronage should alert us to the fact that Phoebe did not actually fulfil the traditional role of a patron. The apostle's words do not therefore say anything about her social status, either directly or indirectly. It is much more likely that in Rom. 16:1–2 the apostle is engaged, as he so often is elsewhere in his letters, in manipulating socially emotive language[390] (rather than using it in a straightforward, descriptive sense). It is quite probable that by his choice of words he intended to pay Phoebe a powerful, public, compliment, and to indicate to the Roman Christians something of her importance to the church at Cenchreae.

c) Travel as an indicator of wealth for Phoebe: The fact that Phoebe was capable of travel also fails to tell us anything, as should be clear from our discussion above.[391] Journeys by sea[392] are not especial indicators

---

[387] See Matt. 6:32/Luke 12:30; Luke 11:8. Though it should not be forgotten that πρᾶγμα can have a very wide range of meanings; it could even be used to refer to law suits (cf. 1 Cor. 6:1), a possibility that Dunn is quite right not to rule out (see *Romans 9–16*, p. 888).

[388] See Juvenal, *Saturae* 1.119 and Martial, *Epigrammata* 2.14.4.

[389] Pliny, *Epistulae* 10.5; P. Merton 62; Tab. Vindol. II. 250; P. Oxy. 32; Cicero, *Epistulae ad Familiares* 13.76. Though it can also be the case that the recommendee is an approximate social equal (see P. Oxy. 743).

[390] As we see, for instance, in his use of the term δοῦλος. See Martin, *Slavery*.

[391] Theissen, *Social Setting*, p. 95.

[392] Whether she was travelling to Rome or Ephesus she would have undertaken the journey by ship from Cenchreae.

of élite status.[393] Clearly Phoebe was a crucial figure in the early Pauline communities.[394] The apostle's vocabulary makes this unequivocal but her significance cannot be assumed to be a consequence of her wealth.[395]

The Man Guilty of Incest (1 Cor. 5:1–13)

In a recent work Andrew Clarke has also put forward a reconstruction of the situation in 1 Cor. 5 which contends, amongst other things, that the man living with his stepmother (ὥστε γυναῖκά τινα τοῦ πατρὸς ἔχειν), probably belonged to the "élite class".[396]

For Clarke there are a number of reasons for drawing this inference. By examining the legal background to the issue of incest he maintains that the man's action can be most plausibly explained if he is understood to be wealthy. Clarke believes that there was a significant financial incentive for such behaviour as it prevented the man's patrimony from passing to another family through his stepmother's remarriage.[397] The fact that the congregation left him alone to pursue his immoral relationship seems to confirm his elevated social status. Clarke suggests that this may have been the consequence of his role as a key benefactor in the church:[398] not only would it have been expedient for the community to allow his behaviour to go unchallenged but most members would have considered themselves bound by social conventions to leave him, as a 'patron', to his own devices. Laws that prevented a client from proceeding against a patron would also, in Clarke's eyes, have encouraged their com-

---

[393] For example, Flavius Zeuxis, a Hierapolis merchant, who sailed seventy-two times to Italy, did not leave a very prestigious monument behind him (CIG 3920; see F. Meijer, *A History of Seafaring in the Classical World*, London: Croom Helm, 1986, p. 176). His personal fortune could not have been great.

[394] She remained a figure of some significance for later generations as we can see from a fourth-century inscription to Sophia ἡ δευτέρα Φοίβη. See Horsley, *New Documents*, vol. 4, pp. 239–244 and also Kraemer, *Maenads, Martyrs, Matrons, Monastics*, p. 221, and *Her Share*, p. 183.

[395] And therefore theories, such as that of Jewett, which are posited upon her apparent wealth, are flawed ("Paul, Phoebe and the Spanish Mission", *The Social World of Formative Christianity*, ed. J. Neusner, Philadelphia: Fortress, 1988, pp. 142–161).

[396] Clarke, *Secular and Christian*, p. 130. See also pp. 73–88. See also Chow, *Patronage and Power*, pp. 140–141. We cannot say for certain whether the stepmother was also a member of the church, though Paul's focus on the man in the text probably indicates that she was not.

[397] Clarke, *Secular and Christian*, pp. 81–84.

[398] Clarke, *Secular and Christian*, pp. 85–86.

plicity,[399] as would the more general legal obstacles of the day that made it impossible for members of the élite to be taken to court by their social inferiors.[400] In addition, the notorious boasting (v. 6) of the Corinthians is viewed by Clarke as corroborating his reconstruction: he interprets it as the community taking pride in the exalted social status of the immoral man[401] (rather than, for example, their own strident antinomianism).

But, in fact, 1 Cor. 5 tells us nothing more about the incestuous man other than that he lived with his stepmother. Despite Clarke's interesting discussion of the social and legal background, his arguments are ultimately erroneous. We cannot say that this man was a member of the socially élite from the information we possess in this chapter.

Firstly, the financial incentive to commit incest was not class specific. Certainly, "some children might well have feared for their patrimony upon their mother's remarriage",[402] as we can see, perhaps most notoriously, in the example of Apuleius, who was forced to write his *Apologia* as a consequence of a case brought by just such a concerned stepson. However, fear over the fate of patrimony was common to all classes, and although the sums involved no doubt varied tremendously, it would be difficult to claim that the worries were relatively greater for the élite than the non-élite. Taking his stepmother as a concubine,[403] as Clarke suggests, could not, in any case, have prevented its loss. Concubinage was a *de facto* marriage relationship that was entered into by couples where at least one partner was technically ineligible to undertake *matrimonium iustum*.[404] (Soldiers, for example, were barred from legally marrying but they were allowed to take concubines, and Romans of senatorial rank could not marry freedmen or freedwomen but could likewise take them as concubines.)[405] However, *some categories*

---

[399] Clarke, *Secular and Christian*, p. 86. See Garnsey, *Social Status and Legal Privilege*, p. 181 and *Digest* 4.3.11.1.

[400] Clarke, *Secular and Christian*, p. 86.

[401] Clarke, *Secular and Christian*, p. 87.

[402] Dixon, *The Roman Mother*, p. 49.

[403] Clarke, *Secular and Christian*, p. 84.

[404] This is the convincing position put forward by Beryl Rawson, "Roman Concubinage and Other De Facto Marriages", *TAPA* 104 (1974) 279–305 *contra*, amongst others, J. Plassard, *Le concubinat romain sous le Haut Empire*, Paris: Librairie de la Société du Recueil Sirey, 1921 who maintained that those who legally could enter into marriage also often chose concubinage.

[405] Such a marriage was prohibited according to Augustus' *Lex Julia de maritandis ordinibus*. For the various restrictions on marriage see J. A. C. Thomas, *Textbook of Roman Law*, Oxford: North Holland Publishing Company, 1976, pp. 422–423.

of people remained ineligible for both legal marriage and also all forms of de facto marriage, including concubinage,[406] *and this was true for relationships between stepsons and stepmothers.* Any kind of association with the stepmother would, far from guaranteeing the retention of the man's patrimony, have left him open to a charge of *stuprum*[407] or *incestum*[408] which would have, at best, resulted in a heavy fine, though probably something much worse.[409] It is actually difficult to think of a course of action *more* likely to result in the loss of the father's inheritance than the flagrant breach of such a legal and social taboo.[410]

The so-called financial incentive for the incestuous relationship, when examined against the social and legal background, appears somewhat improbable, to say the least.[411]

---

[406] Concubinage "could be created with any woman other than one with whom marriage would be impossible on grounds of kinship or with a ward" (Thomas, *Textbook of Roman Law*, p. 433 – see *Digest* 23.2.56; 25.7.1.3). The Roman idea of kinship stressed not just relationships of consanguinity but also affinity as a bar to marriage and was particularly emphatic that ascendants/descendants (rather than collaterals) could not marry (*ibid.*, p. 422). Stepmother/stepson marriage is explicitly banned in Justinian's *Institutes* 1.10.7 for this reason.

[407] *Stuprum* (debauching) was comprehensively defined by Augustus' *Lex Iulia de adulteriis*. It denoted prohibited sexual relations *knowingly* entertained with a widow or unmarried female person. P. Csillag, *The Augustan Laws on Family Relations*, Budapest: Akadémiai Kiadø, 1976, p. 180 and *Digest* 48.5.13.

[408] Paul, *Sententiae* 63, 64. See Csillag, *Augustan Laws*, pp. 183–184. As Patricia Watson remarks, ". . . a sexual union between a stepson and stepmother was in Rome (as distinct from classical Athens) not merely adulterous but incestuous" (*Ancient Stepmothers: Myth, Mysogyny and Reality*, Leiden: E. J. Brill, 1995, p. 137; see also Gardner, *Women in Roman Law and Society*, p. 126 and S. Treggiari, *Roman Marriage*, Oxford: Oxford University Press, 1991, p. 281). It should be emphasised that it made no difference if the father was now dead, or if he had since divorced the stepmother: in Roman law, once a step relationship was established it was considered permanent and could not be affected by any subsequent changes in circumstances (O. Robinson, *Roman Criminal Law*, London: Duckworth, 1995, p. 55; see also Gaius, *Institutes* 1.58, 63–64; *Digest* 23.2.68, 23.2.14, 23.2.56). Given the Roman nature of Corinth in this period, these remarks about Roman law are applicable to the situation described in Paul's letter.

[409] The heavy fine was a penalty for *stuprum* (Csillag, *Augustan Laws*, p. 198). Traditionally those guilty of *incestum* found themselves "precipitated from the Tarpeian rock", though, by the Principate, *deportatio, relegatio* and the confiscation of property were practised (p. 199).

[410] For evidence of the widespread disgust and rigorous punishment of the incestuous see Cassius Dio 58.22; Pliny, *Epistulae* 4.11.6; *Digest* 48.9.5 and James T. South, *Disciplinary Practices in Pauline Texts*, Lewiston: Edwin Mellen Press, 1992.

[411] Clarke's suggestion that the woman may have been motivated to engage in such a relationship in order to avoid the financial penalties that she would incur under Augustan family legislation for not producing enough children is also unconvincing. As he says himself, any children of such a relationship would be considered illegitimate (*Secular and Christian*, p. 85).

Secondly, the failure of the church to move against the immoral man cannot be taken as evidence of his status. It is problematic whether church members would have any notion of themselves as 'clients' of a benefactor to the church, as Clarke assumes, but even if they did, it is still highly questionable whether they would have felt socially restrained from making criticisms of their patron.[412] It certainly is not the case, as Clarke maintains, that 'clients' in the church (if we accept his terminology) were legally prevented from taking action against the incestuous man if they so wished. It was only the freedmen of patrons who were legally restricted in this way – the relationship between patrons and voluntary 'clients' (as would be at least the bulk of the church members) was not governed by any legal restraints whatsoever.[413] Nor can it be argued that the exalted social status of the immoral man would have been a barrier to the church moving against him. The laws on morality that had been instigated under Augustus did not require an individual to initiate litigation against another, they merely had to act as a (well paid) informer[414] and so the notorious social inequity of the Roman legal system is irrelevant in cases such as this (the 'state'

It is likely the incest was motivated by mutual attraction, something which Clarke points out was "by no means without precedent in the contemporary literature" (*Secular and Christian*, p. 84). See Apuleius, *Metamorphoses* 10.2–12 and Cicero, *Oratio pro Cluentio* 5.12–6.16; indeed the theme of the "amorous stepmother" appears to have been quite popular in Roman literature of the period (see Watson, *Ancient Stepmothers*, pp. 135–136). Recent work on the respective ages of men and women at marriage indicates that men tended to marry in their late twenties whilst women did so in their mid to late teens (although there is some dispute over class variation in estimating the approximate figure, see Parkin, *Demography*, p. 124. See also Brunt, *Italian Manpower*, pp. 137–140 and W. Den Boer "Demography in Roman History: Facts and Impressions", *Mnemsoyne* 26 (1973) 29–46). The stepmother, as at least a second wife, would probably have been considerably younger than her husband, and therefore quite close in age to his son, as is often the case in literary examples of the phenomenon.

[412] Clarke's reconstruction assumes too rigid an interpretation of the concept of patronage: it was a much more variegated phenomenon than he allows, filled with ambiguities and contradictions. It was far from being the static, stabilising social form that is often presupposed by scholars attracted by the alluring simplicity of structural functionalism and encouraged by the mythology of ancient authors such as Dionysius of Halicarnassus (*Antiquitates Romanae* 2.9–11; see also Seneca, *De Vita Beata* 2.4). The experience and expectations of both patrons and clients varied tremendously.

[413] The various pieces of evidence Clarke collects (*Secular and Christian*, p. 86, fn. 61) to support his argument all refer specifically to the prohibition on freedmen taking their patrons (ex-masters) to court.

[414] Richard I. Frank, "Augustus' Legislation on Marriage and Children", *CSCA* 8 (1975) 41–52. See Tacitus, *Annales* 3.28.4.

undertook the prosecution).[415] Indeed, the congregation could have moved against the incestuous man in a *quasi legal* manner if they had so wished. When Roman populations were alerted to sexual mis-demeanours (real or imagined) in their midst, they often dispensed popular justice (with the connivance of the authorities) irrespective of the status of the accused. [416]

The economic status of the immoral man cannot be determined from the information given to us in 1 Cor. 5. There is no reason to believe that he should be located amongst the secular élite of the city.

4.3 Concluding remarks

The various pieces of evidence presented by proponents of the 'New Consensus' to substantiate their belief in the presence of affluent groups or individuals in the Pauline churches are not convincing. Our initial economic characterisation of the Pauline communities therefore still stands: *they shared fully in the bleak material existence that was the lot of the non-élite inhabitants of the Empire.*[417]

---

[415] This assumption is found in J. D. M. Derrett, "'Handing Over to Satan': An Explanation of 1 Corinthians 5:1–7", *Studies in the New Testament*, Leiden: E. J. Brill, 1986, p. 172.

　　The troublesome failure of the Corinthian Christians to move against the immoral man is likely to be a consequence of their belief in the abrogation of marriage bonds, past or present, contracted outside the church (see J . D. M. Derrett, "Handing", p. 173).

[416] Nippel, *Public Order*, pp. 39–46.

[417] It should also be added that there are no grounds in the letters for maintaining that there were any sharp differences between the general wealth of the respective Pauline churches (the reference to the Macedonians' poverty in 2 Cor. 8:2 (ὅτι ἐν πολλῇ δοκιμῇ θλίψεως) cannot be taken as indicative of the affluence, in real terms, of the Corinthians: Paul's remarks in 2 Cor. 9:8–15 indicate that the Corinthians also lived economically precarious lives, as we have observed above). Nor can it be argued that any one community, by virtue of its context alone, must have enjoyed a substantially higher level of material prosperity than any other. Although there were some variations in wealth between cities these were not great (it is, for example, inaccurate to suppose that Corinth was some kind of Graeco-Roman boom town – see Saller, "Review of Donald Engels") and had little effect on the standard of living of the mass of their populations. By the first century the cities of the eastern Empire shared *approximately* the same political and social structures and consequently the same patterns of income distribution, and this precluded the non-élite from benefiting from a city's affluence: little wealth trickled down from élite circles in any polis. (A. H. M. Jones, *The Greek City from Alexander to Justinian*, Oxford: Clarendon Press, 1940, pp. 170–182, and A. N. Sherwin-White, *Roman Society and Roman Law in the New Testament*, Oxford: Clarendon Press, 1963, pp. 84–86.)

　　In making such a statement about the economic experiences of the various churches I must stress that I do not wish to imply that their *social* experiences were identical.

153

Barclay has quite rightly drawn attention to the radical differences between Corinthian and Thessalonian communities in this respect; the former were integrated into the wider community and the latter evidently quite alienated from it (J. M. G. Barclay, "Thessalonica and Corinth: Social Contrasts in Pauline Christianity", *JSNT* 47 (1992) 49–74; as he notes, these differences in socialisation cannot, in isolation, be taken as evidence of economic differences (see pp. 56 and 68)).

5

Survival Strategies

5.1 Economic relationships in the Pauline churches

A number of different economic relationships were practised amongst the members of the apostle's churches within this subsistence context. Broadly these can be seen to fall into four categories: those of αὐτάρκεια, almsgiving, hospitality, and 'mutualism'.

The first category is really not a 'relationship' at all. Αὐτάρκεια, which can be roughly translated as 'self-sufficiency', was a common theme in many branches of Hellenistic thought contemporary with Paul, though it had its genesis much earlier.[1] It was particularly widely disseminated by the Cynics,[2] who, alone amongst the different strands of Greek philosophy, seem to have had a genuinely popular appeal.[3] At

[1] Democritus 246; Plato, *Philebus* 67a; Aristotle, *Ethica Nicomachea* 1.7.6; 5.6.4; 10.7.4. The term had been especially associated with Stoic thought but by the apostle's day it has become "widely used, by people of many persuasions, most frequently without the intellectual or psychological baggage of Stoicism" (A. J. Malherbe, "Paul's Self-Sufficiency (Phil. 4:11)", *Friendship, Flattery, and Frankness of Speech: Studies on Friendship in the New Testament World*, ed. J. Fitzgerald, Leiden: E. J. Brill, 1996, p. 135.)

[2] For examples of the use of αὐτάρκεια by Cynics see PsDiogenes 28.8; 46; PsCrates 11a; Diogenes Laertius, *Vitae Philosophorum* 6.104, 6.37, 6.38; Clemens Alexandrinus, *Stromateis* 6.2; Porphyry, *Ad Marcellam* 28.

[3] One only has to look at the kind of individuals who claimed to adhere to Cynicism in Lucian's *Demonax*. Its popularity probably lies at the root of the common accusation, levelled by élite Graeco-Roman writers, that pure Cynic philosophy had been corrupted (Julian, *Orationes* 6.200c–202c; Lucian, *Demonax*; Maximus of Tyre, *Discourse* 36; Epictetus, *Discourse* 3.22).

There are, of course, difficulties in trying to categorise Cynics. Diogenes Laertius' description of Cynicism as a way of life rather than a philosophical school (*Vitae Philosophorum* 6.103) seems to have been accurate for its later history: Cynicism could include adherents who had philosophical allegiances that were widely divergent, if not mutually exclusive – for example Peregrinus Proteus was a neopythagorean (see H. M. Hornsby, "The Cynicism of Peregrinus Proteus", *Hermathema* 48 (1933) 65–84) whilst the author of the Pseudo-Socratic Epistles combined Cynic ideas and Socratic thought. See A. J. Malherbe's study of self-definition amongst the Cynics in *Paul and the Popular Philosophers*, Philadelphia: Fortress Press, 1989, pp. 11–24 and Downing, *Cynics and Christian Origins*, pp. 26–56.

least one aspect of this somewhat amorphous concept can be understood to refer specifically to material self-sufficiency.[4] But, for our purposes, it should be observed that the term αὐτάρκεια is only mentioned on a few occasions in the Pauline epistles (2 Cor. 9:8; Phil. 4:11) and self-sufficiency is therefore not a key theme in Pauline Christian economic behaviour.[5]

Almsgiving features even less in the epistles. Only Paul's advice in Gal. 6:9 can be considered as clear evidence that almsgiving was practised (or at least prescribed) in the Pauline communities. This is the sole text that refers to an act of material interaction which presumes the kind of economic distance between the giver and the recipient which is, for the most part, a distinguishing characteristic of almsgiving *per se*[6] (perhaps a surprising fact given the significance that such behaviour acquired in later Christian[7] and Jewish[8] traditions).

Hospitality was somewhat more prominent though not markedly so. As we observed, we have evidence that it was present in a number of the

---

[4] See A. N. Rich, "The Cynic Conception of AYTARKEIA", *Mnemosyne* 9 (1956) 23–29.

[5] See also 1 Tim. 6:6–10. It is also important to note that Paul differs from his contemporaries in understanding how αὐτάρκεια is achieved: it is not accomplished through personal struggle but by the believer's relationship with Christ: πάντα ἰσχύω ἐν τῷ ἐνδυναμοῦντί με (Phil. 4:13)

[6] Rom. 12:13 is not unequivocally concerned with the issue of almsgiving. Although some interpreters have maintained that Paul is here referring to acts of material charity (Cranfield, *The Epistle to the Romans*, vol. 2, pp. 638–639), it is possible that he is, in fact, specifically discussing the collection for the poor of Jerusalem (see, for example, Dunn, *Romans 9–16*, p. 743). The language is ambiguous and open to both readings as Karl Barth discovered (in his *Epistle to the Romans*, Oxford: Oxford University Press, 1933, p. 450, he maintained that Rom. 12:13 concerned the collection, whilst in his later work, *A Shorter Commentary*, London: SCM, 1959, p. 154, he opted for the alternative position).

[7] Almsgiving is a significant element in the ethical parenesis of the early church. For example, Mark 10:21; Matt. 5:42, 19:21; Luke 6:30, 38, 18:22; Acts 10:4, 20:35; James 1:27; Heb. 13:16; 1 John 3:17; 2 Clem. 6:9; 16:4; *Didache* 4.5–6; *Barnabas* 19.10; Hermas, *Sim.* 1 and 2; *Sententiae Sexti* (52); Tertullian, *De Patientia* 7.13; Justin, *Apologia* 13. For a discussion of this theme in early Christian history see especially Garrison, *Redemptive Almsgiving*; L. W. Countryman, *The Rich Christians in the Church of the Early Empire: Contradictions and Accommodations*, New York: Edwin Mellen Press, 1980, pp. 103–121; and Osiek, *Rich and Poor*.

[8] Interest in almsgiving was rooted in the Hebrew Bible (e.g. Lev. 19:9ff./Deut. 24:19ff.; Psalm 41:1–3; 112:9; Prov. 21:26; 31:8–9, etc.) but seems to have undergone major development in later years, especially in those immediately after the destruction of the second Temple, when it began to function, in a limited way, as a replacement for the lost system of atonement – see *m. Peah*). See Garrison, *Redemptive Almsgiving*, pp. 46–59. For almsgiving amongst the Essenes, Josephus, *De Bello Judaico* 2.8,6. See also CD 14.12–16.

Pauline congregations: certain individuals practised hospitality towards whole communities by allowing churches to meet in their dwellings (such as Gaius,[9] Philemon,[10] Aquila and Priscilla,[11] Nympha[12]) and some also extended such behaviour towards individual congregants.[13] Paul went out of his way to encourage this kind of conduct (Rom. 12:13b: τὴν φιλοξενίαν διώκοντες). But the evidence we have for 'hospitality' amongst the Pauline Christians is not as striking as that which we have from other early Christian communities.[14]

However, it is those economic relationships within the Pauline churches which I believe can be described as exhibiting the characteristics of 'mutualism' which are by far the most prominent in the letters of the apostle[15] and seem most clearly related to the specific conditions that his communities faced.

'Mutualism', as a term, might strike the modern reader as inappropriate and perhaps anachronistic for describing a first-century practice. After all, as a concept, it has been associated inexorably since the nineteenth century with the thought of either anarchists, such as Kropotkin and Proudhon,[16] or the proponents of the co-operative movement. In both cases the term became indicative of wide-ranging political, economic and social aspirations[17] alien to the world of the first century.

[9] Rom. 16:23.
[10] Philem. 2
[11] Rom. 16:3–5; 1 Cor. 16:19.
[12] Col. 4:15.
[13] Philemon probably practised hospitality towards Paul (Philem. 22) and other Christians (Philem. 7). Individuals in the church of Rome almost certainly extended hospitality towards Phoebe (Rom. 16:2).
[14] *Didache* 11–12; 1 Tim. 5:10; Heb. 13:2; 1 Peter 4:9; 2 John 10; cf. Matt. 10:11–14; Mark 6:10; Luke 6:4, 10:5–7. For a significant study of this issue see John Koenig, *New Testament Hospitality: Partnership With Strangers as Promise and Mission*, Philadelphia: Fortress Press, 1985.
[15] Indeed, it quite possibly underlies the hospitality theme. Probable practitioners of hospitality such as Phoebe (Rom. 16:1–2) and Stephanas (1 Cor. 16:15) seem to have expected, in return, to receive it (Rom. 16:1–2; 1 Cor. 16:17) – it is likely that Stephanas and his associates were lodging, accompanied by Paul, with Aquila and Priscilla (16:19) or some other Christian group.
[16] See, for example, Peter Kropotkin's *Mutual Aid*, London: Freedom Press, 1987 (first published in 1902) and the works of P. J. Proudhon such as *Qu'est-ce que la propriété?*, Paris: Garnier-Flammarion, 1966 (first published 1840).
[17] Although this is generally recognised to be the case with anarchists (when they are not confused, rather sloppily, with nihilists) there is widespread ignorance of the world-shaping claims of the co-operative movement, at least in the UK. Its largest proponents, such as CWS or CRS, have mostly abandoned this aspect of their tradition (Stephen Yeo, "Rival Clusters of Potential: Ways of Seeing Co-operation", *New Views of*

Nevertheless, it is an appropriate term to employ in our study if it is defined as the implicit or explicit belief that *individual and collective well-being is attainable above all by mutual interdependence.*[18] It cannot be seen as synonymous with 'reciprocity' as this word can be applied to a wide variety of human material relations, many of which, under close examination, are far from equitable and therefore cannot be understood as promoting the *well-being* of all those involved.[19] For instance, 'vertical reciprocity' (that which occurs between individuals of different economic status, such as, for example, patronage) is, by its nature, thoroughly inequitable.[20] (If mutualism has to be understood in the language of 'reciprocity' then it can be said to be, in a rough sense, a form of horizontal reciprocity.)

The 'economic mutualism' of the early Christian communities is found principally in the so-called 'collection', something which absorbed a great deal of Paul's attention during his life as a missionary and appears in nearly all his major epistles.[21] A cursory glance at these texts allows us

---

Co-operation, ed. Stephen Yeo, London: Routledge, 1988, p. 6). The decay of the revolutionary dimension to the co-operative movement is encapsulated in the title of Sidney Pollard's essay: "Nineteenth-Century Co-operation: From Community Building to Shopkeeping", *Essays in Labour History,* ed. Asa Briggs and John Saville, London: Macmillan, 1967, pp. 74–112.

[18] The *Oxford English Dictionary* definition is not completely appropriate for our purposes as it assumes mutualism to be essentially a political philosophy of Proudhon, and consequently it is rather too dogmatic. 'Mutualism" is "The doctrine that individual and collective well-being is attainable only by mutual dependence."

[19] See Marshall Sahlins, *Stone Age Economics,* London: Tavistock, 1974, pp. 195–196. His recognition of 'negative' reciprocity is a useful corrective to the equitable reciprocity presupposed, for example, in the classic study of Marcel Mauss, *The Gift.* Interestingly, the *Oxford English Dictionary* assumes that mutuality and reciprocity are synonymous terms.

[20] For such a differential between two people to be established in the first place, and continue to exist over time, in an economy in which reciprocity is a major form of exchange relationship, the reciprocity must work to the disadvantage of the person in the subordinate position. See the work of Pierre Clastres, *Society Against the State,* Oxford: Basil Blackwell, 1977 and Harold Barclay, *People Without Government,* second edition, London: Kahn & Averill, 1990, pp. 134–135. For more on the inequitable nature of many reciprocal relationships see E. Colson, *Tradition and Contract: The Problem of Order,* London: Heinemann, 1975, pp. 45–51.

[21] Rom. 15:25–32; 1 Cor. 16:1–4; 2 Cor. 8 and 9; Gal. 2:10. According to the Acts narrative Paul's so-called 'third missionary journey' was, to a great extent, dominated by this project. As P. Vassiliadis quite accurately observes, ". . . there is no aspect of his missionary endeavour that occupies more space in Paul's thought and activity than the collection, a fact manifestly reflected in his epistles" ("Equality and Justice in Classical Antiquity and in Paul: The Social Implications of the Pauline Collection", *SVThQ* 36 (1992), p. 52).

to distinguish a number of components of the 'collection' that justify such a classification.

Firstly, it was aimed at promoting *material well being*. It was initially undertaken to achieve a tangible end: *the relief of the economically poor in the Jerusalem church*;[22] and this remained a significant motivating factor in its execution (though, of course, eschatological,[23] ecumenical,[24] and other[25] concerns also became important in this respect).

Secondly, it was thoroughly *mutual* in its character. *It was in no sense an individual or unilateral undertaking for any of those involved.* Paul emphasises that *all* the members of the churches were contributors[26] as, indeed, were *all* the communities (we hear of no exceptions). It was not intended to be the work of a few wealthy members or congregations.[27] And it was premised on the assumption of *mutual interdependence*. It was not a one-off act of charity. *The material assistance given was understood as something that would, in time, be returned, when the situation was reversed.* 2 Cor 8:14 gives us an indication of this: ἐν τῷ νῦν καιρῷ τὸ ὑμῶν περίσσευμα εἰς τὸ ἐκείνων ὑστέρημα, ἵνα

---

[22] Gal. 2:10. Despite the broader use of 'poor' in Jewish tradition (it could refer to the people of Israel in general, as well as the economically destitute – see Prov. 19:22; Pss. Sol. 5:2, 10:6; 1; QM 11; 1QH 2, 3; 1QpHab 12); the poor of Jerusalem are clearly the economically poor (2 Cor. 8:14, 9:12; Rom. 15:26 – the genitive in the expression εἰς τοὺς πτωχοὺς τῶν ἁγίων τῶν ἐν Ιερουσαλήμ is more naturally understood as partitive rather than epexegetic, as Dunn maintains in *Romans 9–16*, p. 875).

[23] Paul may have understood the collection in terms of fulfilment of the vision of Isa. 2:2–4 and Mic. 4:1–3 (the gentile nations journeying to Jerusalem), as something that presaged the conversion of all Israel (Rom. 10:19; 11:11–16) in his end-time scheme. For a useful summary of the eschatological argument, and indeed all the major arguments put forward for interpreting the meaning of the collection, see David Horrell, "Paul's Collection: Resources For A Materialist Theology", *ER* 22 (1995) 74–83. See also Nickle, *The Collection*, London: SCM Press, 1966, pp. 129–132.

[24] It is quite possible that the collection was also intended as an attempt to heal the rift between Paul and the Jerusalem Church (Gal. 2:12), an act designed to gain acceptance and further legitimation for the gentile mission, something which was certainly not a foregone conclusion (Rom. 15:30–31). Dahl, "Paul and Possessions", p. 31, and Nickle, *The Collection*, pp. 111–129; Watson, *Paul, Judaism and the Gentiles*, p. 175.

[25] Such as that over the apostle's disputed authority. Paul's power was often questioned (2 Cor. 10–12 – see Holmberg, *Paul and Power*), and it is not unreasonable to posit that the success of the collection was important for the apostle because, for him, it was indicative of the extent of the authority he exerted within his congregations.

[26] 1 Cor. 16:2; Rom. 12:13; 2 Cor. 9:7.

[27] See 2 Cor. 8:1–5, 9:1–4.

καὶ τὸ ἐκείνων περίσσευμα γέηται εἰς τὸ ὑμῶν ὑστέρημα, ὅπως γένηται ἰσότης.[28]

Of course, this interpretation might strike some commentators as problematic. 2 Cor. 8:14 is often seen as indicating that the Jerusalem church will respond to the Corinthians' material gifts with *spiritual* ones. Such readings tend to dismiss out of hand the possibility that Paul could have envisaged the Corinthian congregation as being in material need at some future date. As H. D. Betz says, "It is hard to imagine that Paul would ever have expected a material shortage in Corinth to be relieved by the material affluence of the church in Jerusalem."[29] In addition, such scholars tend to read the text in terms of Rom. 15:27 (εὐδόκησαν γὰρ, καὶ ὀφειλέται εἰσὶν αὐτῶν· εἰ γὰρ τοῖς πνευματικοῖς αὐτῶν ἐκοινώνησαν τὰ ἔθνη, ὀφείλουσιν καὶ ἐν τοῖς σαρκικοῖς λειτουργῆσαι αὐτοῖς).[30]

But, in fact, given that the problem facing the Jerusalem church was almost certainly brought about by a localised food shortage,[31] it is quite

[28] Alfred Plummer's words express this well: "There is to be reciprocity, mutual give and take, so that in the end each side has rendered the same kind of service to the other" (*A Critical and Exegetical Commentary on the Second Epistle of St Paul to the Corinthians*, Edinburgh: T. & T. Clark, 1915, p. 245). See also C. K. Barrett, *A Commentary on the Second Epistle to the Corinthians*, London: A. & C. Black, 1973, pp. 226–227.

[29] H. D. Betz, *2 Corinthians 8 and 9: A Commentary on Two Administrative Letters of the Apostle Paul*, Philadelphia: Fortress Press, 1985, p. 68.

[30] H. D. Betz, *2 Corinthians 8 and 9*, pp. 68–69; Koenig, *Hospitality*, pp. 77–78; Dieter Georgi, *Remembering the Poor: The History of Paul's Collection for Jerusalem*, second edition, Nashville: Abingdon Press, 1992, p. 92.

[31] Of course, the cause of the Jerusalem Christians' poverty is not actually given by Paul in his epistles but it is likely to have been a localised food shortage because:
1) The future reversal of fortunes that Paul envisages precludes the cause being atypical. It is, for instance, unlikely that it could have been induced by the utopian short-sightedness of the Jerusalem church found in Acts 2:44–45 and 4:32–35 – see J. A. Ziesler, *Christian Asceticism*, Grand Rapids: Eerdmans, 1973, p. 110 and G. H. C. Macgregor, in *The Interpreter's Bible*, vol. 9, p. 73; Hengel, *Property and Riches*, p. 34; Nickle, *The Collection*, p. 24; C. H. Dodd, *The Epistle to the Romans*, London: Hodder & Stoughton, 1942, p. 230; Jackson and Lake, "Primitive Christianity," *Beginnings 1*, p. 306; Dunn, *Romans 9–16*, p. 876 (a myopia which is, in any case, open to question – see Justo L. Gonzalez, *Faith and Wealth: A History of Early Christian Ideas on the Origin, Significance and Use of Money*, San Francisco: Harper & Row, 1990, pp. 79–82). And food shortages were common in the first-century world (see below).
2) Acts 11:28: ἀναστὰς δὲ εἷς ἐξ αὐτῶν ὀνόματι Ἅγαβος ἐσήμανεν διὰ τοῦ πνεύματος λιμὸν μεγάλην μέλλειν ἔσεσθαι ἐφ᾽ ὅλην τὴν οἰκουμένην· ἥτις ἐγένετο ἐπὶ Κλαυδίου. Although this refers to another, earlier, collection by the Antioch church for Jerusalem, independent of Paul's later commission to undertake the wider collection in the gentile churches (Gal. 2:10; Acts 24:17) it seems to provide a plausible explanation for this larger, more thorough, act of mutualism as the present tense of the verb μνημονεύω in Gal. 2:10 suggests the continuation of a course of

SURVIVAL STRATEGIES

feasible that Paul would have had such economic reciprocation in mind: food shortages were a common problem for all urban populations throughout the Roman Empire.[32] It is quite plausible that the apostle foresaw a time when the situation would be reversed. Reading 2 Cor. 8:14 in terms of Rom. 15:27 also raises such enormous difficulties that it appears much more reasonable to treat the text on its own terms: after all, the Corinthians are not actually viewed by Paul as suffering from any spiritual want (1 Cor. 1:7) and, whereas in Rom. 15:27 the respective blessings are qualified as spiritual (πνευματικοί) and physical (σαρκικοί), no such qualifications appear in 2 Cor. 8:14 where the plain meaning discernible from the context is that the various abundances and wants are *material* abundances and wants. As it stands, 2 Cor. 8:14 says nothing about the *spiritual* quality of the Jerusalem church's response to the Corinthians' aid. By meeting the needs of the Jerusalem congregation, the communities were contributing to their own, long-term, economic stability.[33]

Economic mutualism was not something confined to the collection alone. A similar, inter-community mutual ethic may also lie behind Paul's words in 1 Thess. 4:9–10 depending upon how the verb ἀγαπάω is to be understood: ⁹Περὶ δὲ τῆς φιλαδελφίας οὐ χρείαν ἔχετε γράφειν ὑμῖν, αὐτοὶ γὰρ ὑμεῖς θεοδίδακτοί ἐστε εἰς τὸ ἀγαπᾶν

---

action already begun (see Nickle, *The Collection*, pp. 23–32, 59–60). The two collections are not as unrelated as they might at first appear.

3) Food shortages tended, for the most part, to be localised, perhaps, to modern eyes, surprisingly so (as we can see from Acts 11:28, despite the wording, Antioch obviously was not expected to suffer from this famine – see B. W. Winter "Acts and Food Shortages", *The Book of Acts in its First Century Setting: Volume 2: Graeco-Roman Setting*, ed. David W. J. Gill and Conrad Gempf, Carlisle: Paternoster Press, 1994, pp. 67–69). There was, for instance, a food shortage in Antioch in 362–363 CE which was relieved when the Emperor Julian sent a large quantity of wheat from Chalcis and Hierapolis, cities only 50 and 100 km away (see Julian, *Misopogon* 369c).

[32] For the most detailed study of the erratic nature of food supply in antiquity see Peter Garnsey, *Famine and Food Supply in the Graeco-Roman World: Responses to Risk and Crisis*, Cambridge: Cambridge University Press, 1988.

[33] Some have suggested that the collection failed (see C. H. Buck, "The Collection for the Saints", *HThR* 43 (1950) 3–9). Such an interpretation rests on the assumption that 2 Cor. 10:1–13:10 (the so-called 'angry letter') belongs chronologically to a period later than chapters 8–9 and is, in part, a consequence of the collection's lack of success. But this is somewhat speculative. The textual history of 2 Corinthians is confused to say the least (see, for instance, G. Bornkamm, "The History of the Origin of the So-Called Second Letter to the Corinthians", *The Authority and Integrity of the New Testament*, London: SPCK, 1965, pp. 73–81) and such an inference is therefore rather tenuous.

161

ἀλλήλους·[10] καὶ γὰρ ποιεῖτε αὐτὸ εἰς πάντας τοὺς ἀδελφοὺς τοὺς ἐν ὅλῃ τῇ Μακεδονίᾳ. παρακαλοῦμεν δὲ ὑμᾶς, ἀδελφοί, περισσεύειν μᾶλλον. For the early Christians to 'love' a person often implied rendering her/him material support,[34] and the context seems to imply just such a concrete aspect to the behaviour Paul expected of the Thessalonians.[35]

2 Thess. 3:6–12 provides evidence that mutualism was a guiding assumption of economic relations, not only *between* but also *within* the communities. The expression ὅτι εἴ τις οὐ θέλει ἐργάζεσθαι μηδὲ ἐσθιέτω (v. 10) is not a truism but an "ethical imperative",[36] and indicates that the idlers were, in fact, being supplied with food by other church members, something which is also clear from the historical context (as we have noted, there was an almost complete absence of alimentary schemes outside of Rome).[37] We should not see these troublemakers as the recipients of alms as they obviously did not belong to the category of people who traditionally received such charity, that is those individuals who were prevented by age or infirmity from earning their own keep (e.g. Acts 3:2ff.): Paul's words in v. 12 indicate that they are capable of earning their own living but have chosen not to. Clearly, therefore, the members of the Thessalonian church were practising a form of economic mutualism,[38] albeit one that was being abused by some.[39] It should be stressed that such mutualism need not imply that

[34] Rom. 12:9–13; 1 John 3:17; 2 Clement 4:1–3.

[35] 1 Thess. 4:11: καὶ φιλοτιμεῖσθαι ἡσυχάζειν καὶ πράσσειν τὰ ἴδια καὶ ἐργάζεσθαι ταῖς ἰδίαις χερσὶν ὑμῶν, καθὼς ὑμῖν παρηγγείλαμεν.

[36] James Everett Frame, *A Critical and Exegetical Commentary on the Epistles of St Paul to the Thessalonians*, Edinburgh: T. & T. Clark, 1912, p. 304.

There is therefore little value in interpreting this expression in terms of proverbial sayings based upon Gen. 3:19 (such as Prov. 10:4; *Genesis Rabbah* 2).

[37] Evidence for alimentary schemes outside Rome during the Imperial period is virtually non-existent (Garnsey, *Famine*, pp. 262–266).

[38] A fact often overlooked in most commentaries but picked up, from time to time, by various Christian groups, who, as a consequence of their distinct ecclesiologies, are more hermeneutically sensitive to the implications of these words. E.g. see W. Trilling, *Der zweite Brief an die Thessalonicher*, Zürich: Benziger, 1980, pp. 148–150 for a history of the interpretation of this text in monastic communities, and *The Chronicle of the Hutterian Brethren: Volume 1*, Rifton NY: Plough Publishing House, 1987, pp. 273–274, for its significance in this branch of Anabaptism.

[39] The consequence of a rather intense eschatological fervour. For a recent restatement of this common view see Menken, *2 Thessalonians*, p. 141. This interpretation has, of course, come under some criticism in recent years, most notably from R. Russell, "The Idle in 2 Thess. 3:6–12: An Eschatological or a Social Problem", *NTS* 34 (1988) 105–119 and B. W. Winter, "'If a man does not work . . . ,' A Cultural and Historical Setting

they had a communal lifestyle similar to the picture we find in Acts 2:44–45 and 4:34–35 (though this is a possibility).[40]

We should not be so surprised to find this form of behaviour in the Pauline epistles. Economic mutualism appears to have been present in other early Christian communities. The *Didache*, for example, contains the admonition that the believer should be ". . . not one who stretches out his hands to receive, but shuts them when it comes to giving".[41] Such a command is predicated on the notion that the same individual may be both a giver and a recipient. The idea is a central characteristic of economic mutualism.

5.2 Mutualism as a survival strategy

The fact that mutualism emerges as a significant form of economic relationship practised by the Pauline communities is not, I believe, completely accidental. It is understandable if we examine it against the prevailing situation of economic deprivation experienced by the early believers: it performed the valuable function of a *survival strategy*.

Such an interpretation of early Christian mutualism is, perhaps, surprising, and requires both explanation and justification. Firstly, a

---

for II Thessalonians 3:6", *TB* 40 (1989) 303–315 (in the former the idleness of some of the congregation is seen as a consequence of urban unemployment, in the latter, it is a result of patronage relations). However, Menken's criticism of these explanations of the situation at Thessalonica is apposite: they leave unclear the motive for the idle not being *willing* to work (2 Thess. 3:10c).

It is unlikely that 2 Thess. 3:10–12 is evidence that certain Thessalonian Christian teachers came under the influence of Cynic ideas which demeaned labour (a suggestion made by A. J. Malherbe, *Paul and the Thessalonians*, Philadelphia: Fortress Press, 1987, pp. 99–101. See also Downing, *Cynics and Christian Origins*, p. 11). Given Paul's high estimation of Christian teachers in the Thessalonian correspondence (1 Thess. 5:12–13) it seems unlikely that they could actually be amongst the idle group he criticises so severely (a point made by Winter, "If a man", p. 304).

[40] E. Earle Ellis' inability to contemplate the possibility of non-communal mutual aid contributes to his implausible theory that the idle are not normal members of the congregation, but rather Paul's co-workers ("Paul and His Co-workers", *NTS* 19 (1977), p. 450).

Although we should be suspicious of the historicity of Acts, as I observed at the outset, the practise of the Jerusalem church described in these two passages need not be ficticious. The idealised language used by the author of Luke-Acts does not mean that the account is unhistorical, as is often argued (see S. Scott Bartchy, "Community of Goods in Acts: Idealization or Social Reality," *The Future of Early Christianity*, ed. B. A. Pearson. Minneapolis: Fortress Press, 1991, pp. 309–318).

[41] *Didache* 4.5.

definition of a survival strategy is required: *a survival strategy is a coping mechanism whereby a person living close to subsistence attempts to ensure adequate access to the necessities of existence*. It may take the form of a conscious and calculated action directly and clearly related to need, such as, for example, the sale of assets to buy grain, but it also includes embedded strategies which are just as crucial to survival, such as membership of an extended kinship group (one consequence of which, but obviously not the only consequence, is that it allows an individual a call on resources in times of crisis). Early Christian mutualism can be quite reasonably understood as just such an embedded strategy. It provided a means whereby individuals in precarious economic circumstances could attain some measure of material stability.[42]

Indeed, if we look at the other survival strategies available to the urban poor in the first century we can go further and say that the value of Christian economic mutualism was, in fact, considerable, and that the other survival strategies open to the *plebs urbana* were extremely limited and largely ineffectual. Early Christian mutualism fulfilled a very real need.

5.3 Urban survival strategies in antiquity

Unfortunately the study of survival strategies in the ancient world is a relatively recent pursuit and so there is a dearth of secondary material.

---

[42] The efficacy of mutualism amongst those living close to subsistence level should not be underestimated: contemporary and historical evidence abounds. For example, the recent debate in development economics over the failure of co-operatives enforced by governments and agencies alien to indigenous communities, has led to the recognition of a plethora of pre-existing forms of economic mutual aid in developing societies (which, it is argued, might be employed creatively as foundations for the creation of more complex and effective co-operative structures). See, for example, H. Abatena, "The Potential Contribution of Indigenous Self-Help and Mutual Aid Organisations to the Socio-Economic Development of Ethiopia", *JRC* 15 (1987) 89–106; F. J. A. Bouman, "Indigenous Savings and Credit Associations in the Third World: A Message", *SDQR* 4 (1977) 181–214; A. Okorie and M. E. Obeta, "Nigerian Traditional Mutual Aid Societies and Their Compatibility with Modern Cooperatives", *JRC* 14 (1986) 107–118; P. De Camarmond and D. Soen, "Saving Associations Among the Bamileke: Traditional and Modern Cooperatives in South Western Cameroon", *AA* 74 (1972) 1170–1179.

There are numerous historical studies of mutualism but of particular note is the recent work by Eric Hopkins (*Working-Class Self-Help in Nineteenth-Century England*, London: UCL Press, 1995). The classic study of mutualism by Kropotkin (*Mutual Aid*) remains significant in this respect.

The two relevant treatments that have appeared to date, those of Peter Garnsey[43] and Thomas Gallant,[44] have only limited direct application to our concern.[45] But, nevertheless, despite the paucity of work in this area, we can legitimately go some way to sketching the various forms that survival strategies took amongst the urban masses.

The poor who lived in cities could take only very limited *direct* action in the face of subsistence risk.[46] For the most part they were reliant upon markets and market dependent shops for their foodstuffs and were therefore passive victims of problems of supply (whereas peasants had a number of adaptive agricultural mechanisms – risk buffering techniques – which could allow them to maintain better some kind of consumption stability).[47] The *plebs urbana* were also unable to fall back upon food stockpiles in the way that the rural poor seem to have been able to do,[48] or supplement their diet by exploiting the resources of the wild[49] (what little of worth there might be within reach of the inhabitants of a *polis* would be spread rather thinly given the population density of such communities).[50]

The only *direct* responses available to an urban dweller faced with a subsistence crisis seems to have been the removal of dependants from

[43] Garnsey, *Famine*.

[44] Thomas Gallant, *Risk and Survival In Ancient Greece*, Cambridge: Polity Press, 1991.

[45] Garnsey's work, for example, is not concerned primarily with the response 'from below' to subsistence risk but concentrates mostly upon the systemic macro responses of Athens and Rome. Gallant's study concentrates upon the domestic economy of Greek peasantry from the Classical and Hellenistic periods.

[46] Above all, we should avoid the assumption that variations in the food supply, and indeed famines themselves, can be understood solely as the consequence of climatic difficulties. Subsistence risk can be the product of a wide range of both macro and micro factors, both systemic and personal, as well as climatic. See Amartya Sen's classic work, *Poverty and Famines: An Essay On Entitlement*, Oxford: Oxford University Press, 1981.

This is not to underestimate the importance of adverse weather in creating such situations. Garnsey's work on the influence of climate on the rate of crop failure in the Greek world shows, for example, that the wheat crop in Attica would be expected to fail one year in four (*Famine*, p. 11) and on the island of Samos, the main subsistence crops of wheat and barley would fail one year in two (*ibid.*, p. 13).

[47] Peasants could make significant choices in both the form of agricultural production undertaken (they could for instance, engage in crop diversification, intercropping, land fragmentation, variable sowing rates, etc.) and in their method of processing. See Gallant, *Risk and Survival*, pp. 34–59.

[48] Gallant, *Risk and Survival*, p. 94. Most pre-industrial peasants maintained food stores that could last for a year to eighteen months.

[49] Though we should not overestimate their importance for peasantry: for example, the energy needed to gather wild flora, and its general low calorific intake, limited its value (Gallant, *Risk and Survival*, p. 118).

[50] See Galen, *Comm. in Hipp. Epid II*.

the household (through exposure, ejection or sale),[51] emigration,[52] begging, crime or asset stripping (which could take a number of forms, from the sale of clothing, household utensils, furniture, stock[53] or tools).[54] None of these options were particularly effective in the first-century urban world[55] and most suffered from the obvious drawback that, if practised in a context where others were doing likewise (in the face of a systemic rather than purely personal subsistence crisis), they lost much of their value (as markets responded to gluts of, for instance, furniture or slaves, or criminals faced stiff competition).

But, of course, the urban poor's access to food went beyond that which they could obtain as a consequence of their *direct* ownership of realisable assets. They were also involved in a number of wider vertical and horizontal social relationships which theoretically also provided them with opportunities to secure some material provisions, to maintain some call upon resources in times of crisis. But these, in fact, provided little security.

Given the absence of any direct governmental (imperial or local) intervention in an individual's welfare, outside the institution of the dole in Rome, the most significant form of vertical relationship which should have provided access to food was the association that a person had with one of the great élite benefactors, the εὐεϱγέται, who were found in small numbers in all the cities in the Empire. These wealthy figures had potential access to vast resources. Unfortunately, the ideology of euergetism was one created and practised for the benefit of the élite, and not for the poor: the élite sought by public acts to acquire prestige

---

[51] For sale see de Ste Croix, *The Class Struggle*, p. 170.

[52] See Robert Dirks, "Social Response During Severe Food Shortfall and Famine", *CA* 21 (1980) 27–30.

[53] Which, given the small, workshop basis of both production and retail in the first-century economy, was never extensive.

[54] See, for example, *The Chronicle of Joshua the Stylite* 39. For selling tools see Lucian, *Dialogi Meretricii* 293. Though it is important to remember that for individuals living close to subsistence in the first place, asset stripping is invariably a question of short term survival over long term viability, and therefore hardly an optimal strategy. The dangers inherent in being forced to behave in such a way were recognised by later Jewish communities who gave out funds specifically to prevent somebody facing destitution from being forced to sell the tools of their trade (see *m. Peah* 8:8).

[55] Crime, as a survival strategy, was more effectively pursued from a rural base in this period (see Apuleius, *Metamorphoses* 4.6ff.).

Begging was also of only limited value. Almsgiving was not sanctioned by any prevalent form of morality in the Graeco-Roman period though it was practised to a limited extent (see Veyne, *Bread and Circuses*, p. 31).

and confirm their status, and sometimes to gain a handsome profit from a local crisis,[56] not to alleviate destitution. It was almost always the case that they lavished their benevolence upon the most prosperous in their communities – little, if anything, trickled down from such acts.[57] Their behaviour certainly was not philanthropic and since the destruction of the autonomy of the Greek *poleis*, by the Hellenistic and then Roman Empires,[58] the sense of civic obligation had all but died, and so had the related feeling of responsibility towards the less fortunate city dwellers. The plebs had little ability to demand anything of substance from these individuals (though through brute force they sporadically had some satisfaction).[59]

Nor did the vertical relationship between an élite patron and a poor client provide a useful source of support in time of crisis. Firstly, as we have suggested elsewhere, it is in fact questionable whether élite patronage ties really functioned at all for any but a minority of the non-élite in the Graeco-Roman world.[60] As Garnsey observes:

> . . . ordinary citizens did not emerge in the sources as clients of the rich and powerful. In Rome the typical client was someone of moderate means or better, a Martial or a Juvenal. Despite Horace's charming story about a Roman senator, Philippus, who picked up a man of genuinely humble station called Mena, made him a regular guest at his

---

[56] A fine example of this comes from the Hellenistic period. A member of the élite of the Greek island of Amorgos was publicly honoured for his prompt action in the face of a subsistence crisis. Despite the enthusiasm of the inscription his assistance had, in fact, amounted to lending money at an interest rate of 20% APR to members of the island's population to enable them to buy his grain which he was selling at ten times the normal price. See Léopold Migeotte, *L'emprunt public dans les cités Grecques: Recueil des documents et analys critique*, Quebec: Les Éditions du Sphinx, 1984, pp. 192–194.

[57] See, for example, Duncan-Jones, "An Epigraphic Survey of Costs in Roman Italy", and "Wealth and Munificence in Roman Africa". See also Justin Goddard, "The Distribution of Money and Food in the Towns of Italy in the early Empire", *Food, Health and Culture*, ed. P. Garnsey, Cambridge: Department of Classics Working Papers, 1989, p. 130; Hands, *Charities*, p. 91. The chief recipients of public benefactions were almost invariably the wealthiest members of a community.

[58] A point well made by Thomas Gallant, "Crisis and Response: Risk Buffering Behaviour in Hellenistic Greek Communities", *JIH* 19 (1989) 408–409. See John K. Davies, "Cultural, Social and Economic Features of the Hellenistic World", *Cambridge Ancient History*, vol. 7, ed. F. W. Walbank et al., Cambridge: Cambridge University Press, 1984, pp. 304–320.

[59] See, for example, Apuleius, *Apologia* 88; Tacitus, *Annales* 6.13; Dio Chrysostom, *Orationes* 46; Philostratus, *Vita Apollonii* 1.15.

[60] Tacitus, *Historiae* 1.4.

table and gave him money and land, it would be absurd to suggest that the gap between the rich and the poor in Rome was regularly bridged in this way.[61]

Quite simply, a client had to have something to offer, and as is made clear again and again in Roman literature, the poor had nothing the rich wanted.[62]

Patronage certainly was not the all pervasive phenomenon so often assumed by Classical[63] and New Testament scholars.[64] They have been rather too easily attracted to it as a catch-all explanation for the assumed social cohesion of most of the Empire, believing rather too uncritically in the mythology which élite writers such as Dionysius of Halicarnassus,[65] Seneca[66] or Plutarch[67] sought to disseminate[68] (and finding this picture confirmed in rather naive readings of Martial and Juvenal).[69]

---

[61] Garnsey, *Famine*, p. 84. For Greek cultures Garnsey observes: "Apart from Sparta, where patronage primarily served the function of recruiting the élite, as in Rome, the evidence for patronage from the Greek world is very thin" (p. 84).

[62] Plautus, *Menaechmi* 571ff; Cicero, *De Officiis* 2:69–71.

[63] See, for example, de Ste Croix, *Class Struggle*, p. 364.

For a critic of such a perspective see P. A. Brunt, *The Fall of the Roman Republic*, Oxford: Clarendon Press, 1988. He reacts against the "modern fashion of superimposing clientship on the evidence" (p. 432) and makes the telling and accurate observation that, "clientship appears infinitely more often in modern than in ancient writings" (p. 391). The sheer number of plebs, in contrast to the small number of élite, must have precluded patronage ties from being significant for all but a small minority of the non-élite (a point made by Nippel, *Policing*, p. 33).

[64] For New Testament scholars, see for example, Crossan, *The Historical Jesus*, p. 65; Whelan, "Amica Pauli", p. 82; Chow, *Patronage and Power*, p. 83. Its all pervasive quality is hardly surprising given the loose definition of the concept by some – see for example Malina, *The New Testament World*, pp. 80–81. For Malina any vertical exchange relationship appears to qualify (rather bizarrely, for instance, Matt. 9:27 is seen to be an example in which Jesus is represented as a patron to the blind men whom he heals).

Problems of definition have beset the use of patronage in analysing the first-century world (see, for example, J. D'Arms, "Review of Richard Saller, *Personal Patronage under the Roman Empire*", *CPh* 81 (1982) 95–98).

[65] Dionysius of Halicarnassus, *Antiquitates Romanae* 2.9–11.

[66] Seneca, *De Brevitate Vitae* 2.4

[67] Rom. 13.

[68] Out of class self-interest, or pure ignorance of the experience of those beyond their class. Indeed, far from being the cement that held the Empire together, as such élite authors presumed, it contained tensions and contradictions which actually encouraged social instability – see Tacitus, *Annales* 13:26; Suetonius, *Claudius* 25. One epitaph rather tellingly reads: "Antonina. I never injured my patron Cyricus" (Lattimore, *Themes*, p. 281).

[69] See N. Rudd, *Themes in Roman Satire*, London: University of Oklahoma Press, 1986; D. Cloud, "The Client–Patron Relationship: Emblem and Reality in Juvenal's First Book", *Patronage in Ancient Society*, ed. A. Wallace-Hadrill, London: Routledge, 1990,

Secondly, the asymmetry of the relationship, the implications of which are often overlooked,[70] did not necessarily endear it to the urban poor. The "steep premiums" that they had to pay for their "subsistence insurance policy"[71] meant that its value was extremely questionable for the few non-élite who might have been caught up in its web. No doubt it led many who could have had access to it, to avoid such a relationship.[72]

The only form of patronage that had any impact on the life of the urban plebs was that of patronage by some members of the élite of *collegia*, and even here the upper-class largesse seems to have been limited to providing the funds for an occasional meal and little else.[73]

The vertical relationships of the urban masses were of small value in securing consumption stability and cushioning against subsistence risk. Quite frankly such relationships were at best non-existent and at worst exploitative. They afforded no real opportunities to engender effective strategies for survival.

The horizontal interpersonal support networks that could be drawn upon to ensure stability were also of only limited value.[74] The first recourse in time of need, the kinship group, was a structure that, for many urban dwellers, was neither extensive nor intensive enough for it to be particularly beneficial. Such important Pauline cities as Rome, Corinth and Ephesus were, in many ways, cities of immigrants, populated to a great extent by individuals, such as Aquila and Prisca,[75] whose peripatetic lifestyles had stretched their consanguine ties con-

---

pp. 205–218; and see also Brunt, *The Fall of the Roman Republic*, p. 391. For an example of New Testament scholars using, uncritically, evidence from these satirists to construct a model of patronage see Bruce J. Malina and Richard R. Rohrbaugh, *Social-Science Commentary on the Synoptic Gospels*, Minneapolis: Fortress Press, 1992, pp. 74–75.

[70] See James Scott, "Patronage or Exploitation?", *Patrons and Clients*, ed. E. Gellner and J. Waterbury. London: Duckworth, 1977, pp. 21–39.

[71] Gallant, "Crisis and Response," p. 405.

[72] For a treatment of patronage which highlights the attractiveness of remaining outside such ties see P. Millet, "Patronage and its Avoidance in Classical Athens", *Patronage in Ancient Society*, ed. Andrew Wallace-Hadrill. London: Routledge, 1990, pp. 15–27.

[73] See Waltzing, *Étude Historique Sur Les Corporations Professionelles Chez Les Romains*, pp. 426–446.

[74] The "economics of affection", in Hyden's terminology (see *Beyond Ujama in Tanzania: Underdevelopment and an Uncaptured Peasantry*, London: Heinemann, 1980, pp. 18–19). Affective ties are those based, for example, upon common descent, common residence, etc.

[75] The couple appear to have lived in Ephesus (1 Cor. 16:19), Rome (Rom. 16:5) and probably Corinth (Acts 18:2, 18, 26).

siderably, rendering them ineffective as survival strategies (kinship suffers from 'distance decay', the further apart relatives reside, the less obligated they feel).[76] Friends and neighbours were perhaps more valuable than kin, providing a readily expandable and also, to a certain extent, controllable support network, but they suffered from the drawback that they shared the same economic context as the person who might require help. With a somewhat rootless urban population, it is rather questionable as well how deeply such ties of friendship could go. As Gallant has observed, "the extent and the assurance of assistance in times of trouble was directly proportional to the degree and the intimacy of the connection between individuals".[77] Unlike static rural communities, where there was a great deal of continuity in a person's experience of friends throughout their life cycle, the urban environment, at least for many, did not allow the fostering of such strong bonds. The effectiveness of neighbour-based support networks is also questionable. Many neighbours were neighbours because they shared the same occupation (given the Graeco-Roman propensity for trades to be located in the same areas) and the resulting fierce competition, which we can see, for example, in *defixiones*,[78] could be anything but beneficial for a person's attempt to ensure her/his economic stability. In a time of crisis, to rely upon a neighbour could be to rely upon an enemy.

The horizontal links that an individual had with *intentional* groups were also of marginal value in guaranteeing economic security. The *collegia*[79] may have provided many of the urban non-élite with a means of articulating a sense of social location and social significance,[80] but

---

[76] See S. J. Woolf, *The Poor in Western Europe in the Eighteenth and Nineteenth Centuries*, London: Methuen, 1986.

[77] Gallant, *Risk and Survival*, p. 144.

[78] Gager, *Curse Tablets*, pp. 151–174.

[79] Superficially, of course, there were significant similarities between the Christian churches and these institutions, as we can see both from pagan and Christian commentators (see Pliny, *Epistulae* 10.96; Origen, *Contra Celsum* 1.1; 8.17.47; SHA, *Vita Alexander* 49; Tertullian, *Apologeticum* 38–39). See R. L. Wilken, "Collegia, Philosophical Schools and Theology", *Early Church History: The Roman Empire as the Setting of Primitive Christianity*, ed. S. Benko and J. O'Rourke, London: Oliphants, 1971, pp. 268–291 and *The Christians as the Romans Saw Them*, New Haven: Yale University Press, 1984, pp. 31–47.

[80] Attained, for example, through public acts such as group attendance at the theatre and group participation in triumphs and religious festivals. The architectural and epigraphic displays of the *collegia* were also significant in this respect. See Ramsey MacMullen, *Enemies of the Roman Order: Treason, Unrest and Alienation in the Roman Empire*, Cambridge, MA: Harvard University Press, 1967, p. 175. For the imposing architecture of some *collegia* buildings see Hermansen, *Ostia*, p. 74.

offered little in terms of material support. Despite the obvious attractiveness of assuming an analogy between the trade *collegia*[81] and modern unions or trade associations, such bodies were economically all but impotent.[82] In fact the trade *collegia* rarely took any corporate action to defend their members' economic interests;[83] nor did they have a system for providing assistance from joint funds to members facing financial difficulty.[84] Indeed, nor were they as all-pervasive as is often assumed.[85] The funeral clubs, the *collegium funeraticium* or *collegium tenuiorum*, although substantially more popular, particularly amongst

---

Most members of associations would have been excluded from holding civic office because of their social status (there are few examples of holders of *collegia* magistracies who also held posts in the municipal adminstration – H. L. Royden, *The Magistrates of The Roman Professional Collegia in Italy From the First to the Third Century A.D.*, Pisa: Giardini, 1988, pp. 232–235) and so the *collegia* provided an important alternative arena for accruing and displaying honours for those unable to take part in the civic *cursus honorum* (a point also made by Kloppenborg, "Collegia and *Thiasoi*", p. 26).

Indeed, the sense of fraternity engendered by such clubs can be seen in the degree to which emperors sought to repress them (see Hermansen, *Ostia*, pp. 244–245 for a survey of the evidence of this and also W. Cotter, "The Collegia and Roman Law: State Restrictions on Voluntary Associations, 64 BCE–200 CE", *Voluntary Associations in the Graeco-Roman World*, ed. John S. Kloppenborg and Stephen G. Wilson, London: Routledge, 1996, pp. 74–89); they represented threatening alternative clusters of allegiance, ripe for rebellion.

[81] It is important to distinguish between the different forms of *collegia* – the trade, funerary, religious and household *collegia*. Waltzing's thorough study (*Étude Historique*) is flawed by failing to do this, as Royden has observed (*Magistrates*, p. xiv).

[82] An historically common mistake: see, for example, Karl Kautsky, *The Foundations of Christianity*, New York: Russell & Russell, 1953, pp. 357–359. For the sparse evidence of collective action see Kloppenborg, "Collegia and *Thiasoi*", pp. 19–20.

[83] See MacMullen, *Enemies*, p. 176. MacMullen has found evidence of only a dozen strikes spread over a period of four centuries. Though see also W. H. Buckler, "Labour Disputes in the Province of Asia", *Anatolian Studies Presented to Sir Michael Ramsey*, ed. W. H. Buckler and W. M. Calder, Manchester: Manchester University Press, 1923, pp. 27–50.

[84] They did occasionally provide assistance to members in need but reciprocal assistance was not a clear feature of such organisations until the Byzantine period (A. E. R. Boak, "The Organization of Gilds in Greco-Roman Egypt", *TAPA* 68 (1937), p. 218).

[85] By the second century MacMullen estimates that their membership must have included up to a third of the male urban population (*Enemies*, p. 174). But this may be rather exaggerated. As J. Pearse has observed, the cost of the regular subscriptions was probably prohibitive for many (see *The Organisation of Roman Building During the Late Republic and Early Empire*, Cambridge: unpublished PhD dissertation, 1974, p. 123 and S. L. Dyson, *Community and Society in Roman Italy*, London: Johns Hopkins University Press, 1992, p. 166). Certainly, the epigraphic evidence is rather less impressive

those at the bottom of Graeco-Roman society, did not offer anything more to their members than the occasional meal and the eventual fulfilment of the purpose of their creation, a decent burial.[86] Even the religious associations of the 'mystery cults'[87] lacked any real social welfare, despite the intense religiosity which bound together their adherents.[88]

Nor can it be said that membership of the numerous diaspora Jewish communities in the Empire provided access to an effective system of material support. Although *ad hoc* almsgiving was undertaken by Jews more frequently than by their non-Jewish contemporaries,[89] there is no clear evidence of the existence of systematic forms of poor relief amongst Jewish groups outside Israel.[90] The institutions of the *quppah* (basket) and *tamhui* (plate) amongst the communities discussed in the Mishnah[91] do not contradict this: the

---

than MacMullen assumes (see Pearse, *The Organisation of Roman Building*, p. 122). Finley's assertion that the "collegia played an important part in the social and religious life of the lower classes, both free and slave" (*The Ancient Economy*, p. 121) is no longer sustainable.

[86] A point made by Dyson, *Community and Society*, p. 166 and Hands, *Charities*, p. 60.

[87] A problematic category given the heterogeneity of the groups often included within it. See Walter Burkert, *Ancient Mystery Cults*, Cambridge, MA: Harvard University Press, 1987.

[88] The shared ritual experiences and regular cultic meals did not create any sense of an organized and stable community (Burkert, *Ancient Mystery Cults*, p. 43). Despite the common assumption of certain leading figures in the *religionsgeschichtliche* school, such as R. Reitzenstein, it is inaccurate to speak of "Mysteriengemeinden" (*ibid.*, pp. 30–53). The 'cults' remained essentially socially conservative despite their potential for symbolically sanctioning new forms of social organisation and solidarities between their initiates. As White has observed about those involved with the worship of Mithras: "The so-called seven grades of initiation characterised in our literature on Mithras were perhaps more socially determined than has generally been recognised" (*Building God's House*, 1990, p. 58).

[89] Interestingly, Bolkestein suggests that Jewish influence actually caused something of a change in conventional Graeco-Roman perceptions and encouraged a more positive appreciation of such activities (*Wohltätigkeit und Armenpflege im vorchristlichen Altertum*, Utrecht: Oosthoek, 1939, pp. 435ff., 471).

[90] Although this is not to deny the existence of common chests amongst diaspora synagogues, an institution which they appear to have shared with pagan *collegia* (see J. Albert Harrill, *The Manumission of Slaves in Early Christianity*, Tübingen: J. C. B. Mohr, 1995, pp. 129–157, 172–178). We have no clear evidence that the funds were used to meet the material needs of their members.

[91] Emil Schürer, *The History of the Jewish People in the Age of Jesus Christ*, vol. 2, revised edition, ed. Geza Vermes et al., Edinburgh: T. & T. Clark, 1979, p. 437.

information from this source is beset by too many critical problems of dating[92] for it to be admissible.[93]

Christian mutualism therefore emerged to meet a very real need. Given the difficult economic experience of most inhabitants of the first-century Graeco-Roman world, coupled with the near absence of other effective survival strategies for urban populations living close to subsistence level, we can say that it represented an understandable response. Indeed, we can go further: it seems to have met a very real need extremely well. The mutualism that was practised appears to have been especially powerful. Two of its features in particular are indicative of its considerable strength. Firstly, the explicitness of the relationship. Amongst the most important factors that affect the likelihood and extent of material reciprocation is the degree to which a relationship is visible for the parties involved.[94] From the apostle's lengthy discussions of the subject of the collection (2 Cor. 8 and 9), and the open[95] and effective[96] response that the churches made to his appeals, it is clear that Christian mutualism was indeed a prominent and distinct component of the lives of the Pauline communities.

Secondly, the enmeshment of the theme of economic mutuality in the theological, and in particular Christological, language of the community, also gave substantial weight to this form of exchange relationship. The theme of mutualism was inseparably bound up with

---

[92] See E. P. Sanders' pertinent criticisms of the works of Schürer and Jeremias (*Judaism: Practice and Belief 63 BCE–66 CE*, London: SCM, 1992, pp. 10–11). However, it should be noted that the patterns of Christian charity presented in Acts 6:1–5 and 1 Tim. 5:3–16 might be a witness to the existence of such systematic procedures amongst the first-century diaspora synagogues as they bear a striking resemblance to the institution of the *quppah* and *tamhui*.

[93] Even the existence of organised charity in Jerusalem in the first century CE has become rather debatable. See, for example, D. Seccombe's attack on J. Jeremias's *Jerusalem at the Time of Jesus*, pp. 116–117 in "Was There Organized Charity in Jerusalem Before the Christians?" *JTS* 29 (1978) 140–143, though his analysis is contentious. Of course, more sectarian groups within Israel appear to have fostered ties of close economic interdependence. See, for example, Brian Capper, "The Palestinian Cultural Context of Earliest Christian Community of Goods", *The Book of Acts in its First Century Setting. Volume 4: The Book of Acts in its Palestinian Setting*, ed. R. Bauckham, Carlisle: Paternoster Press, 1995, pp. 323–356.

[94] Gallant, *Risk and Survival*, pp. 150–152.

[95] Such as the appointment of delegates to travel with the collection (1 Cor. 16:3; 2 Cor. 8:19).

[96] E.g. 2 Cor. 8:2. Though this is not to say that they did not need considerable encouragement, on occasion, as we can see from Paul's words to the Corinthians in 2 Cor. 9.

Paul's participationist, corporate, Christology. For the believers that had salvation ἐν Χριστῷ[97] were inexorably joined together not only with their Lord but also with each other, as we can see in the famous body imagery;[98] an idea complemented and amplified by Paul's pneumatology.[99] A similar notion is found in the recurring Pauline theme of κοινωνία – the believers' fellowship with Christ[100] also presumes fellowship with others.[101] This intense theological solidarity was given regular ritual emphasis through the practice of baptism and the eucharist, which were interpreted as expressions of the unity of the congregation[102] by the apostle, and, no doubt, were accompanied by liturgy that emphasised this theme.

Indeed, I believe that we are justified in going further: Christian economic mutualism not only provided a valuable survival strategy for early believers but it probably improved the situation of the

[97] ἐν Χριστῷ has proved something of a contentious phrase. As Ziesler has observed, "the main difficulty in examining this language is that nowhere does Paul explain himself, but assumes his readers will readily understand it" (Ziesler, *Pauline*, p. 51). But nevertheless, despite some difficulties, this expression, which saturates most of Paul's writings, can be legitimately understood as, for the most part, a shorthand way of expressing the experience of participation in the body of Christ. Albert Schweitzer's (*The Mysticism of Paul the Apostle*, New York: H. Holt, 1931, pp. 122ff.) initial championing of this interpretation has remained ascendant and attempts by Bultmann and others to deny a connection between this phrase and the body imagery are ill-founded and unduly atomistic. (For a summary of the debate see Sanders, *Paul and Palestinian Judaism*, pp. 453ff.).

[98] 1 Cor. 6:15; 10:16; 12:27; Rom. 12:4–6 – which J. A. T. Robinson quite accurately calls "the lynch pin of Paul's thought . . . the very pivotal point on which the whole of his theology turns" (*The Body: A Study in Pauline Theology*, London: SCM, 1953, p. 48). Though see also the recent contribution by Gosnell Yorke, *The Church as the Body of Christ in the Pauline Corpus: A Re-examination*, Lanham NY: University Press of America, 1991 who argues against the identification of the body of Christ with the body of believers.

[99] 1 Cor. 12:13.

[100] 1 Cor. 1:9; 10:16; Phil. 3:10.

[101] Philem. 17; 2 Cor. 8:23; Rom. 15:27. See also Gal. 2:9. See also F. Hauck, "κοινός, κοινωνός, κοινωνέω, κοινωνία, συγκοινωνός, συγκοινωνέω, κοινωνικός, κοινόω", *Theological Dictionary of the New Testament*, vol. 3, ed. G. Kittel, Grand Rapids: Eerdmans, pp. 797–809 and J. Y. Campbell, " Κοινωνία and its Cognates in the New Testament," *JBL* 51 (1932) 352–380.

It is quite possible that in using this language we see Paul creatively exploiting the language of *societas* (concensual contract) as Sampley maintains ("Societas Christi: Roman Law and Paul's Conception of Christian Community", *God's Christ and His People*, ed. W. Meeks and J. Jervell, Oslo: Oslo University Press, 1977, pp. 158–174 and *Pauline Partnership in Christ: Christian Community and Commitment in the Light of Roman Law*, Philadelphia: Fortress, 1980).

[102] Gal. 3:27–28; 1 Cor. 10:16–17.

early Christians, not only through the positive construction of a new form of economic relationship, but also by freeing the small number of congregants that might have been involved in patronage ties from exploitative relationships with members of the élite classes.[103]

5.4 Concluding remarks and *apologia*

My conclusions in this section and indeed my whole focus will be contentious to many New Testament commentators. To some they might raise the disturbing spectre of economic reductionism, the denial, in general terms, of a "transcendent referent"[104] in the construction and maintenance of these interactions. To others it might appear to trample on the validity of both interpretations given by the early Pauline Christians themselves, and also those produced by recent exegetes. It is therefore appropriate that I include here something of an *apologia*. I have no intention of committing such a catalogue of sins. In saying that economic relations of mutualism can be characterised as a form of survival strategy, I am not intending to be crassly reductionist.[105] I have no desire to deny the possibility of a "transcendental referent" contributing to the genesis and morphology of these mutual relationships.

---

[103] Indeed, interestingly, the ethos of economic mutualism no doubt contributed to the lack of élite membership within the Pauline communities: the conventional public honouring of benefactors, a crucial element in the ideology of euergetism, seems to have been completely absent from the churches. It was irrelevant in the face of a new ideology which saw all, and not just the affluent few, as morally responsible for providing economic support to the needy (1 Cor. 16:2). No lengthy 'honours' are found in the New Testament texts nor in early Christian archaeological records (Countryman, *Rich Christians*, pp. 164–165 makes a similar observation). Other New Testament traditions are also hostile to euergetism and its heirarchical implications, as we can see in Luke 22:24–26: ²⁴ Ἐγένετο δὲ καὶ φιλονεικία ἐν αὐτοῖς, τὸ τίς αὐτῶν δοκεῖ εἶναι μείζων.²⁵ ὁ δὲ εἶπεν αὐτοῖς, Οἱ βασιλεῖς τῶν ἐθνῶν κυριεύουσιν αὐτῶν καὶ οἱ ἐξουσιάζοντες αὐτῶν εὐεργέται καλοῦνται.²⁶ ὑμεῖς δὲ οὐχ οὕτως, ἀλλ᾿ ὁ μείζων ἐν ὑμῖν γινέσθω ὡς ὁ νεώτερος, καὶ ὁ ἡγούμενος ὡς ὁ διακονῶν.

[104] To borrow an expression from Philip Esler, *The First Christians in their Social Worlds: Social-Scientific Approaches to New Testament Interpretation*, London: Routledge, 1994, p. ix.

[105] The relationship between economic practice and religious ideas is never one of simple causality. This point was made by Max Weber in the final paragraph of his influential *The Protestant Ethic and the Spirit of Capitalism* (p. 183) though, ironically, this work has often been read as arguing for just such a simple association (albeit in reverse – religious ideas shaping economic practice). See Michael Hill, *A Sociology of Religion*, London: Heinemann Educational Books, 1973, pp. 98–139.

Nor do I intend to compromise the conceptual autonomy of these interactions, by presuming that the articulation of them by the original actors is in any sense superficial or subservient to a deeper economic explanation.[106] The *emic* interpretations must still stand, to employ an apposite term from anthropology. I am not, for example, denying the eschatological, ecumenical or other motivations for the collection which can be clearly discerned in Paul's correspondence, as I have already said. It would, for example, be ludicrous to maintain that such an important notion to the Pauline Christians as that of their participationist and corporate Christology, which I believe contributed so significantly to the rhetoric of material interdependence, functioned as mere theological icing on an essentially economic cake.

Nor, by my economic focus, do I intend to commit the related sin of dismissing *a priori* the validity or significance of other contemporary explanations of these transactions produced by those who have examined the material from their different, though, for the most part, equally valid perspectives. I make no claims that my *etic* reading is the only one that is appropriate or valuable for investigating this area of early Christian behaviour. To do so would be to obliterate the complexity of human *cultural* life – in essence to deny the embedded quality of economic reality which I stressed at the outset of this work. We could, for example, quite fruitfully look at the evidence for the collection in the terms of its role in community formation amongst these early Christians, its reciprocity both signifying, establishing and re-establishing the necessary solidarities and distinctions that went to create and sustain the various Pauline churches;[107] functioning in a way analogous to the rituals,[108]

---

[106] For a valuable argument in favour of respecting conceptual autonomy in interpreting exchange relations see Davis, *Exchange*.

[107] For the significance of economic interaction in these processes see S. N. Eisenstadt and Louis Roniger, "The Study of Patron-Client Relations and Recent Developments in Sociological Theory", *Political Clientism: Patronage and Development*, ed. S. N. Eisenstadt and René Lemarchand, London: Sage Publications, 1981, pp. 271–295; S. N. Eisenstadt, *Patrons, Clients and Friends: Interpersonal Relations and the Structure of Trust in Society*, Cambridge: Cambridge University Press, 1984; also G. MacCormack, "Reciprocity", *Man* 11 (1976) 89–104. Neyrey makes just such a suggestion in *Paul in Other Words*, p. 78.

[108] Such as baptism (Rom. 6:1–11, Gal. 3:27–28) and the eucharist (1 Cor. 10:14–22 and 11:17–34; see Meeks, *First Urban*, pp. 140–163 and Neyrey, *Paul in Other Words*, pp. 75–101). For the importance of the holy kiss in this respect see W. Klassen, "The Sacred Kiss in the New Testament: An Example of a Social Boundary Line", *NTS* 39 (1993) 122–135. (Rom. 16:16; 1 Cor. 16:20; 2 Cor. 13:12; 1 Thess. 5:26 (1 Pet. 5:14)); see also Stephen Benko, *Pagan Rome and the Early Christians*, London: B. T. Batsford, 1985, pp. 79–102).

discipline,[109] general parenesis,[110] literary innovations,[111] special terms applied to insiders/outsiders,[112] and perhaps fundamental metaphors[113] that were employed within these communities.

My explanation of this form of economic relationship is *not intended to be the consequence of methodologically privileging economic causation*. It is not the case, as I hope was clear from the beginning of this study, that I view economy as base and all other forms of social life, both those recognised by the actors, and those revealed by the work of other commentators, as superstructural.[114]

Indeed, a thoroughgoing reductionist interpretation of this aspect of early Christian social life would be absurd. After all, the economic

---

[109] 1 Cor. 5 (see G. Harris, "The Beginnings of Church Discipline: 1 Corinthians 5", *NTS* 37 (1991) 1–21) and also 1 Thess. 5:14; Rom. 15:14; Gal. 6:1. Note the use of the plural in Paul's advice about admonitions (Gerhard Lohfink, *Jesus and Community*, London: SPCK, 1985, pp. 104–105).

[110] Especially the parenesis which is characterised by the apostle's use of the term ἀλλήλων (one-another): Rom. 12:5,10,16; 13:8; 14:13; 15:5,7,14; 16:16; 1 Cor. 12:25; 16:20; 2 Cor. 13:12; Gal. 5:13; 6:2; (Eph. 4:2,25,32; 5:21); Col. 3:9,13; 1 Thess. 3:12; 4:9,18; 5:11,15; 2 Thess. 1:3. Lohfink usefully terms such parenesis the "Praxis of Togetherness" (*Jesus and Community*, pp. 99–105). Despite its prominence, it has been neglected in the study of early Christian ecclesiology (there is no entry in *Theological Dictionary of the New Testament* under ἀλλήλων).

[111] We should not underestimate the role in the formation of the Pauline Christians' sense of community of the dramatic breaks with the rigid epistolary conventions that they regularly encountered in the letters of the apostle. These departures would have emphasised the distinctiveness of the contents of the letters. For the conservative nature of epistolary forms of the period see Stanley K. Stowers, *Letter Writing in Greco-Roman Antiquity*, Philadelphia: Fortress Press, 1989 and W. G. Doty, *Letters in Primitive Christianity*, Philadelphia: Fortress Press, 1973.

[112] Paul uses a variety of unusual and distinctive terms for those who belong to his communities and those who do not. For example, in Romans alone we find ἅγιοι (Rom. 1:7; 8:27; 15:25, 26, 31; 16:2,15); ἀδελφοί (Rom. 1:13; 7:1, 4; 8:12, 29; 10:1; 11:25; 12:1; 15:14, 30; 16:14); ἐκλεκτοί (Rom. 8:33); κλητοί (Rom. 8:28) used for members of the church (the positive terminology cannot be dismissed as mere epistolary convention, it is used far too frequently and far too self-consciously for this to be the case). Those outside the church are described in a variety of negative ways, for example see Rom. 1:29–31. Such use of language naturally engendered a strong sense of location amongst church members. See Meeks, *First Urban*, pp. 85–88 and Neyrey, *Paul in Other Words*, pp. 41–43.

[113] See, for instance, S. Barton, "Paul and the Cross: A Sociological Approach", *Theology* 85 (1982) 13–19. Paul's appropriation of emotive language associated with the temple (e.g. Rom. 12:1 cf. also Rom. 3:25, 8:23) must have also proved particularly significant in the construction of the community.

[114] But nor do I believe that economy is a subordinate subsystem, in some Parsonian fashion, at the mercy of other factors of social life, a passive product of other forms of human activity (T. Parsons and N. Smelser, *Economy and Society*, Glencoe, New York: The Free Press, 1964, pp. 8–13).

mutualism that emerged was not universal but, I believe, largely specific to early Christian communities, despite the roughly universal experience of subsistence risk that faced inhabitants of the first-century world. Clearly other factors, discernible from both *emic* and *etic* perspectives, must have been both active and distinct (either in themselves, or in combination) if we are to explain this difference between the life of the Pauline communities and their non-Pauline neighbours.

Rather, my characterisation is intended to highlight the essential significance of economic context in understanding the coming to be of this distinct form of exchange relationship. I do not hold that economic reality is the determinative reality in human life, in all places and in all times, but, in this particular historical case, in this particular area of human social life, I believe it has a visible and prominent role to play. This is not unsurprising: at moments of subsistence difficulty, I contend, economic factors can cease to be fully embedded, surface, and, in a way that is much more obvious than is normally the case, actively shape the wider cultural life of a community.[115]

---

[115] There are plenty of examples of the emergence of economic reality as *temporarily* determinative of other aspects of human cultural (including religious) life. The Cokelers, or Society of Dependents, a Non-Conformist movement founded in the 1850s in Sussex, largely amongst the agricultural labourers and related groups, and still (though barely) alive today, provides us with just such an instance. Although initially indistinguishable from many other Non-Conformist groups of the time, they appear to have been forced into economic mutualism as a consequence of persecution and poverty; and this in turn seems to have given birth to their distinct theology of 'combination' (based upon 1 Cor. 1:10). They developed, for instance, a unique hymnody, which both justified and perpetuated their unusual economic relationships. See Mick Reed, "'The Lord Does Combination Love': Religion and Co-operation Amongst a Peculiar People", *New Views of Co-operation*, ed. S. Yeo. London: Routledge, 1988, pp. 73–87.

Anabaptist experience provides another example of this phenomenon (see P. J. Klassen, *The Economics of Anabaptism 1525–1560*, The Hague: Mouton & Co., 1964 and J. M. Stayer, *The German Peasants War and Anabaptist Community of Goods*, Montreal: McGill-Queen's University Press, 1991).

6

Conclusion:
The Poverty of Our Quest

Our investigation of the economic reality of the Pauline epistles is at an end. In the preceding pages I have argued that Paul and his followers should be located amongst the 'poor' of the first century, that they faced the same anxieties over subsistence that beset all but the privileged few in that society. In addition, I have sketched something of their rather distinctive response to this predicament. And, I hope, in the process of this study I have offered some solutions to important issues of method, data and explanation that face any similar undertaking.

Of course, I recognise some significant failings in my approach. Chief amongst these, I believe, is the sheer quantity of space that I have had to dedicate to refuting a number of aspects of the 'New Consensus' position. Consequently my work may, on occasion, appear rather more destructive than constructive. But, given the contemporary scholarly climate, and the ascendancy of the 'New Consensus', to have ignored, or treated superficially, those elements of it that impinged on my study would have been foolhardy.

To speak of a 'conclusion' to our quest is a little premature. I certainly believe in the fundamental veracity of my thesis, but if one thing has emerged from this study that I think might be of general, and I hope, lasting, value for other scholars examining *any* aspect of the social reality of the early Christians, it is that all such projects must take seriously the need to construct and apply an 'appropriate context of interpretation', one that, as E. P. Thompson so eloquently put it, rescues the non-élite from the "enormous condescension of posterity".[1] And of necessity, they must recognise the provisional quality of the reconstructions such a context will generate. The 'condescension' has been too great, and the effort exerted to overcome it too small for us to think otherwise.

---

[1] Thompson, *Making*, p. 12.

In a way, this study and its subject matter share a sense of 'poverty'. But just as the early Christians produced the means from amongst themselves of alleviating, at least to some degree, *their* poverty, I hope that this thesis contains within it the potential for overcoming *its* poverty, providing the resources for future, richer, expositions of its theme by those seeking to take its concerns further.

Apppendix 1

Paul's Social Conservatism: Slavery, Women and the State

The apostle's attitude towards the institution of slavery, the role of women and the Roman state have often been seen as indicative of his essential social conservatism. However, an examination of the relevant evidence, in its appropriate social context, reveals Paul to be more radical than is usually supposed.

i) Slavery

If we take a brief look at the primary texts in the Pauline epistles that deal with slavery (Philem.; Col. 3:22–4:1; 1 Cor. 7:21) it becomes clear that the eschatological reunification formulas (Gal. 3:28; 1 Cor. 12:13; Col. 3:11) that are at the heart of the Pauline kerygma are of more than "spiritual significance";[1] they had a very real effect, functionally dissolving the institution within the community.

In the letter to Philemon, which provides us with our most detailed knowledge of the apostle's treatment of the subject of slavery, this is spelt out particularly vividly. In verse 16 Philemon is told that he is no longer to treat Onesimus as a slave but as a "beloved brother . . . both in the flesh and in the Lord". To emphasise that Paul expects the relationship between the two men to have altered physically ("in the flesh") and not just on some abstract 'spiritual' level, Paul says that the master is to treat the slave as though he were the apostle himself. By addressing the letter to the whole church (v. 2) and by mentioning that he will himself soon be visiting the two Christians involved (v. 22), it is clear he expects the change in the relationship to be a visible one. Within the eschatological community, the realm within which Paul's radical ethical precepts operated fully, slavery was *functionally* (if not technically) at an end. Of course, legally, the slave remained a slave but manumission

---

[1] Kyrtatas, *Early Christian Communities*, p. 30; G. E. M. de Ste Croix, "Early Christian Attitudes to Property and Slavery", *Church, Society, and Politics*, Oxford: Basil Blackwell, 1975, p. 19.

was not entirely in the hands of the master or mistress, its wider social impact had caused the whole process to be severely restricted, particularly under Augustus, so it is no surprise that Paul nowhere demands this.[2]

The part of the Colossian *Haustafel* (Col. 3:18–4:1) concerned with master-slave relations does not appear as revolutionary as Philemon yet it does contain many innovative features common to all Christian houselists such as its unusual conscientisation of the slave, and the recognition of her/him as a moral agent in their own right (not merely a '*res*' as under Roman law). In fact, the demands laid upon the master do echo, to some extent, the teaching in Philemon when they are examined in detail: the words δίκαιον (justly) and ἰσότης (fairly)[3] in 4:1 carry more force than their English equivalents and indicate that Paul expects the master–slave relationship to be one marked by a functional equality.[4]

It is unfair to interpret the apostle's words in 1 Cor. 7:21 as evidence that he was such a vigorous supporter of the institution of slavery that he counselled slaves to remain in their condition even if offered freedom. Contrary to Kyrtatas' interpretation[5] the apostle does not unquestionably tell the slave to remain enslaved. The debate concerning the exegesis of this difficult verse is much more substantial than he allows but, following the work of Harrill, it seems clear that the balance is now tipped in favour of those who see v. 21cd as directing slaves to take manumission if it were offered to them.[6] It is worth noting that it is no surprise that nowhere does Paul advise slaves openly to break the law and run away. Although on occasion this policy did work,[7] the existence of *stationarii* throughout the Empire (troops who had a number of policing functions, amongst which was the apprehension of such

[2] S. Scott Bartchy,*ΜΑΛΛΟΝ ΧΡΗΣΑΙ*: *First Century Slavery and the Interpretation of First Corinthians 7:21*, Missoula: Scholars Press, 1973, p. 83; Bradley, *Slaves and Masters*, pp. 87ff.; Suetonius, *Augustus* 40.4.

[3] E. Lohse, *Colossians and Philemon*, Philadelphia: Fortress Press, 1971, p. 162, fn. 74.

[4] For a reading of the Colossian houselist which emphasises its radical innovations see J. H. Yoder, *The Politics of Jesus*, first edition, Grand Rapids: Eerdmans, 1972, pp. 163–192.

[5] Kyrtatas, *Early Christian Communities*, p. 33, following M. Goguel, *The Primitive Church*, London: Allen & Unwin, 1964, pp. 554–555.

[6] Harrill, *Manumission*. Harrill's work gives a valuable summary of the vast literature that this difficult verse has generated.

[7] Apuleius, *Metamorphoses* 8.15–23.

slaves),[8] the prevalence of slave catchers,[9] and the brutal punishment such a runaway would face (such as impalement)[10] would have rendered such advice foolhardy.[11]

ii) Women[12]

The reunification formula (Gal. 3:28) which denies the division of the sexes within the eschatological community was taken seriously by Paul, as can be seen in, amongst other things, the powerful presence of such women as Phoebe the deacon and 'patron' (Rom. 16:1), Junia the apostle (Rom. 16:7),[13] and Priscilla, leader of three house churches (Rome [Rom. 16:3–5], Corinth [Acts 18:2] and Ephesus [1 Cor. 16:19]) and tutor of Apollos in the faith (Acts 18:26).[14] It is also visible in the apostle's didactic method: in 1 Cor. 7, for example, he is so determined to address both sexes equally that his style descends into "tautologousness and awkwardness".[15] This sexual egalitarianism is, at least in part, corroborated by the presentation of the apostle and his associates

---

[8] M. Corbier, "Fiscus and Patromonium: The Saepium Inscription and Transhumance in the Abruzzi", *JRS* 73 (1983) 126–131. See CIL 9. 2438. Pliny, *Epistulae* 10.74.

[9] Alan Watson, *Roman Slave Law*, Baltimore: Johns Hopkins University Press, 1987, p. 64. See also D. Daube, "Slave Catching", *JRev* 64 (1952) 12–28. Such mechanisms were far from ineffectual, as Augustus' boast in his *Res Gestae* illustrates (4.25).

[10] Cassius Dio 49.12.5.

[11] Bradley's recent assertion that Paul was instrumental in creating a "spiritual image that bolstered the acceptability of slavery in the real world and increased the ammunition of those who wished to regard it as a human institution" (*Slavery and Society*, p. 153) through his use of the metaphor of slavery to express the believer's relationship to God (Rom. 1:1; Phil. 1:1, etc.) and also Christ (Phil. 2:7) is erroneous. The relationship between social reality and spiritual metaphor is rather more complex. For example, it can hardly be said that Paul's use of the metaphor of crucifixion (Rom. 6:6) bolstered the acceptability of crucifixion in the 'real world'.

[12] The literature on the role of women in the Pauline churches is vast though the following studies are particularly notable: Fiorenza, *In Memory of Her*, pp. 205–241; B. Witherington, *Women in the Earliest Churches*, Cambridge: Cambridge University Press, 1988, pp. 1–127; R. Jewett, "The Sexual Liberation of the Apostle Paul", *JAAR* 47 (1979) 55–87 and Klassen, "Musonius Rufus, Jesus, and Paul", pp. 185–206.

[13] See Cervin, "A Note Regarding The Name 'Junia(s)' in Romans 16.7", and John Thorley, "Junia, A Woman Apostle", *NovT* 38 (1996) 18–29.

[14] Indeed, women may well have been the dominant gender in the Pauline churches if the information given to us by the apostle in Rom. 16:3–16 is accurate and representative of the other churches. Although more men than women are named in this greeting (17 to 9), substantially more women than men are singled out as especially active in the church. See Lampe, "Roman Christians", pp. 222–224.

[15] R. Scroggs, "Paul and the Eschatological Woman", *JAAR* 40 (1972), p. 234.

in the popular second-century apocryphal book, *The Acts of Paul and Thecla*.[16]

Against this picture of Paul "the first century feminist" (to employ the somewhat anachronistic label of W. Klassen)[17] stands, in particular, the apostle's hierarchical argument for male superiority in 1 Cor. 11:1–16, his demand for wives to be silent in churches found in 1 Cor. 14:34, and his counsel that wives should be subject to their husbands in Col. 3:18. Read in context, and without exegetical presuppositions drawn from the undeniably sexist teaching of the pastorals (such as 1 Tim. 2:12–14), this material fails to contradict such a picture of Paul.

Paul's patriarchal argument in 11:3ff. is balanced by his statement of eschatological equality "in the Lord" in 1 Cor. 11:11, a radical assertion that may have been included by the apostle out of fear that his earlier arguments, which are aimed entirely at the question of head covering, might be taken as a general principle for oppressing women in the church.[18]

1 Cor. 14:34–35[19] is an admonition to one particular group of women, wives, to stop talking during the worship at Corinth, and is part of his concern to curb some of the more chaotic excesses of that community's behaviour: the reprimand is found between Paul's assertion that "God is not a God of confusion but of peace" (14:33a) and "All things should be done decently and in order" (14:40). It is not a basis for the subjugation of women *en masse* (nor, as Fiorenza argues, a prescription against the active participation of wives, as opposed to single 'holy' women in worship).[20]

The advice in Col. 3:18 is part of Paul's call to mutual obligation and submission within the Christian marriage. He demands from the husband, by his use of the word ἀγάπαν, an utter powerlessness (see

---

[16] The apostle's inclusion of women in the ἐκκλησία might also be an indication of his radical egalitarianism, given the association this term would have had for gentile converts: as the usual title for the voting assembly of a city in the Hellenistic world, it generally referred to a powerful and exclusively male institution. Paul's ἐκκλησία was therefore a subversion of one of the key elements of the patriarchal culture of his day. See Cotter, "Women's Authority".

[17] Klassen, "Musonius Rufus, Jesus, and Paul".

[18] Fiorenza, *In Memory*, p. 229.

[19] I assume here that this section is authentic. However, such an assumption is contentious. See, for example, J. Murphy-O'Connor, "Interpolations in 1 Corinthians", *CBQ* 48 (1986) 81–94.

[20] *In Memory*, p. 231.

1 Cor. 13:1ff.) which reverses traditional expectations of his role and (ideally) destroys oppression within the relationship.[21]

iii) The State

It is true that Rom. 13:1–7 became "the most influential part of the New Testament on the level of world history"[22] and, unfortunately, it is also true that its influence has been almost entirely negative, encouraging, as it appears to do, uncritical support for any form of government, however unjust. With the benefit of hindsight, de Ste Croix is quite right to refer to Paul's words here as "disastrous".[23] However, it is unfair to presuppose that in writing these verses the apostle *himself* believed that it was a Christian obligation to obey all political authority, without exception, as ordained by God. Read in the context of Rom. 12 and the rest of chapter 13 it is clear the Christian's chief responsibility was to the community which subverted the claims of such authority: they are told not to be conformed to the world (12:2) and their obligations are in distinct and deliberate contrast to those of the state.[24] In addition, the terminology he employed to name such powers, and to express the relationship of God and the Christian to them, does not invest them with anything approaching this kind of blanket legitimisation that has often been assumed. By using the word ἐξουσίαι for the authorities he indicated both their transient nature and their essential inferiority: they are part of the old world order, soon to come to an end (1 Cor. 2:6) and to be

---

[21] See Yoder, *The Politics of Jesus*, pp. 180–182.

[22] E. Bammel, "Romans 13", *Jesus and the Politics of His Day*, ed. E. Bammel and C. Moule. Cambridge: Cambridge University Press, 1984, p. 365.

[23] De Ste Croix, *Class Struggle*, pp. 398, 439, and "Property and Slavery", p. 36.

[24] Christians give honour and material assistance *freely* to one another (12:10, 13), wheras honour and taxes are something that is *due* to the authorities (13:7 – ἀπόδοτε πᾶσιν τὰς ὀφειλάς, τῷ τὸν φόρον τὸν φόρον, τῷ τὸ τέλος τὸ τέλος, τῷ τὸν φόβον τὸν φόβον, τῷ τὴν τιμὴν τὴν τιμήν). Whilst the Christians are told not to take vengeance (12:19– μὴ ἑαυτοὺς ἐκδικοῦντες), the state is described as being able to do so (13:4– ἐστιν ἔκδικος). Christians must not repay evil with violence (12:17 – μηδενὶ κακὸν ἀντὶ κακοῦ ἀποδιδόντες; 12:18 – τὸ ἐξ ὑμῶν μετὰ πάντων ἀνθρώπων εἰρηνεύοντες), the state can repay evil by such means (13:4 – ἐὰν δὲ τὸ κακὸν ποιῇς, φοβοῦ), the Christian cannot kill (13:9 – Οὐ φονεύσεις) the state can (13:4 – οὐ γὰρ εἰκῇ τὴν μάχαιραν φορεῖ). The Christian order is one of interdependence and equality (12:3–9), the state order is characterised by authoritarianism and deference (13:3). This parallelism is too thorough to be accidental.

judged by the saints (1 Cor 6:1ff.).[25] God *orders* them (τεταγμέναι 13:1) he does not *ordain* them:[26] they are merely the tools for working out his wrath, much as are the Assyrians in Isa. 10. Most importantly, the Christian is told to be subject ὑποτάσσω to them, *not* to obey them (ὑπακούω, πειθαρχέω, πείθεσθαι).[27] In his own life Paul was not frightened of breaking the laws of the Empire, as we can see in his action in taking in the runaway slave Onesimus and not returning him at once to his master (Philem. 10),[28] almost certainly in direct violation of Roman legislation (Ulpian, *Digest* 11.4.1). His flight from Aretas, a Roman vassal (2 Cor. 11:32) also demonstrates his uncomfortable relationship with the governing authorities. He paid a high cost for his defiance on various occasions (2 Cor. 11:25 – the beating by rods here is an explicitly Roman punishment);[29] and his disregard for the Empire's rule almost certainly led to his death (Eusebius, *Historia Ecclesiastica* 25.5). It is, therefore, unlikely that in Rom. 13:1 Paul "enjoined strict obedience to the civil authorities",[30] rather his attitude can be more aptly characterised as one of "non-resistance"[31] – a position perhaps owing much to Jewish ideas that resulted from "living for centuries under foreign imperialism".[32]

But, of course, Rom. 13 does not provide us with our only information about Paul's understanding of the Empire. Elsewhere the apostle

---

[25] See the classic study by O. Cullmann, *The State in the New Testament*, second edition, London: SCM, 1963 which, in my opinion, stands, despite the thorough criticism of it by W. Carr, *Angels and Principalities*, Cambridge: Cambridge University Press, 1981, especially pp. 115ff.

[26] Yoder, *Politics*, pp. 203ff.

[27] See C. E. B. Cranfield, "Some Observations on Romans XIII. 1–7", *NTS* 6 (1960) 241–249.

[28] This traditional interpretation of Onesimus as a runaway slave has come under attack, particularly in recent years but also earlier. See J. Knox, *Philemon Among the Letters of Paul*, London: Collins, 1960; Sara Winter, "Methodological Observations on a New Interpretation of Paul's Letter to Philemon", *USQR* 39 (1984) 203–212 and "Paul's Letter to Philemon", *NTS* 33 (1987) 1–15; Clarice Martin, "The Rhetorical Function of Commercial Language in Paul's Letter to Philemon (Verse 18)", *Persuasive Artistry*, ed. D. F. Watson. Sheffield: JSOT Press, 1991, pp. 321–337. However, the assumption this was the case still seems plausible. See J. G. Nording, "Onesimus Fugitivus: A Defense of the Runaway Slave Hypothesis in Philemon", *JSNT* 41 (1991) 97–119 and J. M. G. Barclay, "Paul, Philemon and the Dilemma of Christian Slave Ownership", *NTS* 37 (1991), p. 164.

[29] Grant, *St Paul*, p. 26.

[30] De Ste Croix, "Early Christian Attitudes", p. 14.

[31] For this interpretation see especially Yoder, *Politics*, pp. 193–214.

[32] Elaine Pagels, "Christian Apologists and 'The Fall of the Angels': An Attack on Roman Imperial Power", *HThR* 78 (1985), p. 308.

appears far more critical. Perhaps most famously he mocked the slogan "*Pax et Securitas*" in 1 Thess. 5:3, an expression regularly employed in Imperial propaganda.[33] It was, after all, the Romans who had literally "enslaved" Jerusalem (Gal. 4:25) and, as Grant has speculated, his pessimistic perception of the present world order, a theme that permeates his writings, must in some respect reflect his negative assessment of the *Pax Romana*.[34] In fact, in many ways Paul was openly hostile to Roman sovereignty. It is often overlooked just how far his thoughts in the epistles were in direct conflict with Roman hegemony and would be interpreted by his contemporaries as downright seditious. His Christology was, for example, thoroughly treasonous. The Philippians Christ-hymn, for instance, in its assertion that Jesus was Lord of all the earth (Phil. 2:9–11) which, by implication, meant that Caesar was not,[35] and also that Christ would receive universal reverence, something normally reserved for the Emperor (Phil. 2:9),[36] would be disturbing enough for any Roman official, but the claim, in a striking subversion of Imperial ideology, that the cross, one of the symbols *par excellence* of the Empire's power to exert its force, was the means by which Jesus attained this pre-eminence (Phil. 2:8), would have been especially so.[37] Indeed, in Colossians, Paul argued that the cross became the means by which the ruling authorities were transformed into a public spectacle (2:15), appropriating and reversing the imagery of the Imperial triumph, the

---

[33] See Holland Lee Hendrix, "Archaeology and Eschatology at Thessalonica", *The Future of Early Christianity*, ed. Birger A. Pearson, Minneapolis: Fortress Press, 1991, pp. 107–118. He effectively demonstrates the significance of this slogan in the culture of Thessalonica. See also E. Bammel, "Ein Beitrag zur paulischen Staatsanschauung", *ThLZ* 85 (1960) 838–839. Elliott suggests that even the Pauline interest in δικαιοσύνη and πίστις may, in part, owe itself to the significant roles that *ius* and *fides* played in the language of Imperial ideology (see Elliott, *Liberating Paul*, pp. 190–195).

[34] Grant, *St Paul*, pp. 28f. Not an unusual outlook for a Jew of this period (see N. de Lange, "Jewish Attitudes to the Roman Empire", *Imperialism in the Ancient World*, ed. P. Garnsey and C. Whittaker, Cambridge: Cambridge University Press, 1978, pp. 255–281, especially pp. 261–262).

[35] See Acts 16:7. The introduction to the *Res Gestae* provides an indication of how such an affirmation would appear to conflict with the Imperial claims (*Res Gestae Divi Augusti*, ed. P. Brunt and J. M. Moore, Oxford: Oxford University Press, 1967, p. 19). See also Velleius Paterculus, *Historiae Romanae* 2.126.2–5.

[36] Imperial ritual was still in its formative stages (see S. R. F. Price, "From Noble Funerals to Divine Cult: The Consecration of the Roman Emperor", *Rituals of Royalty, Power, and Ceremonial in Traditional Societies*, ed. D. Cannadine and S. Price, Cambridge: Cambridge University Press, 1987, p. 97), and προσκύνησις was regarded with distaste, but obeisance of some kind undoubtedly took place and was expected, particularly of non-Romans.

[37] See above, chapter 4.

most celebrated articulation of the rule of the Emperors. Indeed, as Elliott remarks, "As soon as we recognise the centrality of the cross of Christ for Paul, the common view that Paul was uninterested in political realities should leave us perplexed."[38]

His assault on paganism, a persistent theme in his letters (Rom. 1, 1 Cor. 10:21, etc.), was just as brazen. It was an onslaught not just upon what we would call 'religious' sensibilities but rather, given that paganism was so immutably bound up with the Rome's understanding of its strength and destiny, and indeed the authority of the *Pontifex Maximus* himself, it was an attack upon the heart of the Empire. Even his espousal of celibacy, politically innocuous to us, was in direct conflict with Augustus' marriage legislation which encouraged fecundity and matrimony within the Empire.[39] According to Dio, Augustus graphically equated "the unmarried life with the immoral way of life" (56.6.6–7.2). As Fiorenza has noted: "Paul's advice to remain free from the marriage bond was a frontal assault on the institutions of existing law and the general cultural ethos, especially since it was given to people who lived in the urban centres of the Roman Empire."[40]

As a Roman citizen, a man who lived his entire life within the boundaries of the Empire, it would be ludicrous to assert that Paul would not have been aware of the subversive dimension to his teaching and the political implications of his words. If we follow Yoder as characterising Paul's attitude as one of non-resistance we can fairly say that his non-resistance had a fiery, critical, aspect to it. We should not exaggerate the nature of Paul's radicalism. It was, at least to some extent, a development of ideas already present in the society of his day.[41] But from our brief survey of these three important areas of ethical interest, it is apparent that to label the apostle, as most New Testament scholars do, as socially conservative, is to do both him, and the evidence we have before us, a grave injustice.

---

[38] Elliott, *Liberating Paul*, p. 93. See, for example, 1 Cor. 2:2.
[39] See K. Galinsky, "Augustus' Legislation on Morals and Marriage", *Philologus* 125 (1981) 126–144, P. Csillag, *The Augustan Laws on Family Relations*, Budapest: Akadémiai Kiadó, 1976 and Dixon, *The Roman Mother*, pp. 71–103. Although these laws were limited in their direct application to the élite, they were clearly intended to, and did, have a significant impact upon the wider population of the Empire. We can see this, for example, from the discernible changes in group portraiture during the early decades of the first century (see D. E. E. Kleiner, *Roman Group Portraiture: The Funerary Reliefs of the Late Republic and Early Empire*, London: Garland, 1977).
[40] Fiorenza, *In Memory of Her*, p. 225
[41] A point made by Cotter in respect to the role of women (see "Women's Authority").

Apppendix 2
The Elements of Conflict:
A Reading of 1 Corinthians 11:17-34

¹⁷Τοῦτο δὲ παραγγέλλων οὐκ ἐπαινῶ ὅτι οὐκ εἰς τὸ κρεῖσσον ἀλλὰ εἰς τὸ ἧσσον συνέρχεσθε.¹⁸πρῶτον μὲν γὰρ συνερχομένων ὑμῶν ἐν ἐκκλησίᾳ ἀκούω σχίσματα ἐν ὑμῖν ὑπάρχειν, καὶ μέρος τι πιστεύω. ¹⁹δεῖ γὰρ καὶ αἱρέσεις ἐν ὑμῖν εἶναι, ἵνα⁻ καὶ οἱ δόκιμοι φανεροὶ γένωνται ἐν ὑμῖν.²⁰Συνερχομένων οὖν ὑμῶν ἐπὶ τὸ αὐτὸ οὐκ ἔστιν κυριακὸν δεῖπνον φαγεῖν, ²¹ἕκαστος γὰρ τὸ ἴδιον δεῖπνον προλαμβάνει ἐν τῷ φαγεῖν, καὶ ὃς μὲν πεινᾷ, ὃς δὲ μεθύει. ²²μὴ γὰρ οἰκίας οὐκ ἔχετε εἰς τὸ ἐσθίειν καὶ πίνειν; ἢ τῆς ἐκκλησίας τοῦ θεοῦ καταφρονεῖτε, καὶ καταισχύνετε τοὺς μὴ ἔχοντας; τι εἴπω ὑμῖν; ἐπαινέσω ὑμᾶς; ἐν τούτῳ οὐκ ἐπαινῶ.

²³Ἐγὼ γὰρ παρέλαβον ἀπὸ τοῦ κυρίου, ὃ καὶ παρέδωκα ὑμῖν, ὅτι ὁ κύριος Ἰησοῦς ἐν τῇ νυκτὶ ᾗ παρεδίδετο ἔλαβεν ἄρτον ²⁴καὶ εὐχαριστήσας ἔκλασεν καὶ εἶπεν,Τοῦτό μού ἐστιν τὸ σῶμα τὸ ὑπὲρ ὑμῶν· τοῦτο ποιεῖτε εἰς τὴν ἐμὴν ἀνάμνησιν. ²⁵ὡσαύτως καὶ τὸ ποτήριον μετὰ τὸ δειπνῆσαι, λέγων,Τοῦτο τὸ ποτήριον ἡ καινὴ διαθήκη ἐστὶν ἐν τῷ ἐμῷ αἵματι· τοῦτο ποιεῖτε, ὁσάκις ἐὰν πίνητε, εἰς τὴν ἐμὴν ἀνάμνησιν· ²⁶ὁσάκις γὰρ ἐὰν ἐσθίητε τὸν ἄρτον τοῦτον καὶ τὸ ποτήριον πίνητε, τὸν θάνατον τοῦ κυρίου καταγγέλλετε, ἄχρις οὗ ἔλθῃ.

²⁷Ὥστε ὃς ἂν ἐσθίῃ τὸν ἄρτον ἢ πίνῃ τὸ ποτήριον τοῦ κμρίου ἀναξίως, ἔνοχος ἔσται τοῦ σώματος καὶ τοῦ αἵματος τοῦ κυρίου. ²⁸δοκιμαζέτω δὲ ἄνθρωπος ἑαυτόν, καὶ οὕτως ἐκ τοῦ ἄρτου ἐσθιέτω καὶ ἐκ τοῦ ποτηρίου πινέτω· ²⁹ὁ γὰρ ἐσθίων καὶ πίνων κρίμα ἑαυτῷ ἐσθίει καὶ πίνει μὴ διακρίνων τὸ σῶμα. ³⁰διὰ τοῦτο ἐν ὑμῖν πολλοὶ ἀσθενεῖς καὶ ἄρρωστοι καὶ κοιμῶνται ἱκανοί. ³¹εἰ δὲ ἑαυτοὺς διεκρίνομεν, οὐκ ἂν ἐκρινόμεθα· ³²κρινόμενοι δὲ ὑπὸ⁻ τοῦ κυρίου παιδευόμεθα, ἵνα μὴ σὺν τῳ κόσμῳ κατακριθῶμεν. ³³ὥστε, ἀδελφοί μου, συνερχόμενοι εἰς τὸ φαγεῖν ἀλλήλους ἐκδέχεσθε. ³⁴εἴ τις πεινᾷ, ἐν οἴκῳ ἐσθιέτω, ἵνα μὴ εἰς κρίμα συνέρχησθε. Τὰ σὲ λοιπὰ ὡς ἂν ἔλθω διατάξομαι.

The community treated the elements of the Lord's Supper (v. 20) as though they were constituents of a normal meal (v. 21)[1] with the consequence that when the church came together to eat (vv. 20, 33) some consumed all the bread and wine quickly (v. 33), leaving others, who were less fast on the uptake, with nothing (v. 22) (something quite plausible given the limited quantity of the elements).[2] Paul regarded the bread and the wine as eaten in an unworthy manner (v. 27) because by such behaviour the body (the church as a whole) was being ignored (v. 29): what should have been a unifying communal rite (10:17) was transformed into a display of divisiveness and selfishness. Paul therefore gave the practical advice (v. 34) that, in order to avoid the elements being treated as food, those that were tempted to do so should consume a real meal before coming together, so that their hunger was sated before the rite began.

I foresee that the main ground for criticising this reconstruction is the commonly held belief that Paul is dealing here with problems over a real meal and not over the consumption of the elements alone. There are two major reasons why some exegetes assume this: 1) the language Paul uses, "one goes hungry, another is drunk" (v. 21), appears to say as much (as Conzelmann observes, "It is plain that we have here not merely a sacramental proceeding but a real meal");[3] 2) the supposed tradition of a common meal accompanying the eucharist (the so-called ἀγάπη).[4]

But these objections do not stand up to criticism: 1) The use of terms associated with a real meal is not in itself surprising if we understand that Paul regards the Corinthians' behaviour as indistinguishable from that which would be expected at a normal meal: his choice of terms is

---

[1] Given the popularity of meals in Jewish and pagan religious contexts such a presumption is hardly surprising. See Peter D. Gooch, *Dangerous Food: 1 Corinthians 8–10 in Context*, Waterloo: Wilfrid Laurier University Press, 1994, and W. L. Willis, *Idol Meat at Corinth*, Chico, CA: Scholars Press, 1985.

[2] The mechanics of eucharistic practice in the Pauline churches, as far as we can determine, supports this reading. The notion that some people could go without consuming any of the elements is quite possible if one loaf (10:17) and one cup (10:21) were used. The unrestrained and selfish consumption of the limited elements envisioned in verse 21 would lead to the deprivation of others, humiliating those who missed the opportunity to take part in this core ritual of the early church.

[3] Conzelmann, *A Commentary on the First Epistle to the Corinthians*, p. 195. See also Meeks, *First Urban*, p. 158.

[4] "The practice of assembling for common meals seems without question implied" (Fee, *Corinthians*, p. 532); Felix L. Cirlot, *The Early Eucharist*, London: SPCK, 1939, p. 24; J. Keating, *The Agape and the Eucharist in the Early Church: Studies in the History of the Christian Love Feasts*, London: Methuen & Co., 1901, p. 47.

part of his display of displeasure, and he wishes to remind them that they are behaving as though they are eating τὸ ἴδιον δεῖπνον and not the Lord's supper. That Paul complains of some being drunk does not necessarily indicate that there must have been more wine present than the single cup of the Lord would allow: his description may be a caricature, part of the "biting rhetoric"[5] that is characteristic of this particular section of the epistle, and a feature of his style which is familiar from elsewhere in the letter.[6] Indeed, in the first century this term was used not only of individuals who were in a state of physical intoxication but also of anyone who exhibited the kind of unrestrained behaviour which accompanied the consumption of alcohol, even if they had, in fact, imbibed very little,[7] something which makes this reading appear all the more possible. πεινάω, as well as evoking a normal meal, can still refer to the absence of the eucharist elements: it has a wide breadth of meaning and can refer to the hunger for something other than actual physical sustenance (see, for instance, Matt. 5:6). Given that the Corinthians lived in a culture in which both the consumption of food and drink were areas of acute moral concern, it is impossible to take the apostle's words at face value, as is so often done.

2) The supposed prevalence of the common meal or love-feast in the early church is doubtful when the evidence from the New Testament is examined.[8]

The phrase τῇ κλάσει τοῦ ἄρτου and related expressions are often taken as indicative of a love feast.[9] But we cannot assume that they had any such implications. Although, within the New Testament,

---

[5] Fee, *Corinthians*, p. 531.
[6] See for example, his sarcastic caricature of his opponent's pretensions in 1 Cor. 4:8–11.
[7] Philo, *De Plantatione* 35 (142f.). In a culture in which drink signified the transition from work to play, such behaviour was common (for the symbolic potency of alcohol see Mary Douglas, *Constructive Drinking: Perspectives on Drink from Anthropology*, Cambridge: Cambridge University Press, 1987).

The correct consumption of alcohol was a subject of significant moral concern in the first-century world. Much was written concerning the manner, location, and quantity of drink that was acceptable to different groups. See, for example, J. D'Arms, "Heavy Drinking and Drunkenness in the Roman World: Four Questions for Historians", *In Vino Veritas*, ed. Oswyn Murray and Manuela Tecusan, London: The British School at Rome, 1995, pp. 304–317; E. M. Jellinek, "Drinkers and Alcoholics in Ancient Rome", *JSA* 37 (1976) 1718–1741 (though this article is conceptually somewhat imprecise); Toner, *Leisure and Ancient Rome*, pp. 77–78.

[8] The scarcity of references was noted by Keating, *The Agape*, p. 36.
[9] Fee seems to assume this when he refers to Acts 2:42, 20:7, 11 as evidence of such a meal (*Corinthians*, p. 532).

breaking bread can refer to the regular Jewish practice of blessing the food before a meal began (Luke 24:30; Acts 27:35),[10] the expression had a distinct eucharistic meaning quite early in the lives of the Christian communities (1 Cor. 10:16; 11:24; Mark 14:22; Matt. 26:26; Luke 22:19).

There is only one occasion in the New Testament when normal food appears to be eaten alongside the eucharist (Acts 2:46)[11] but it is hardly evidence to support the existence of a regular church practice: it forms part of the idealised description of the intensely communitarian life of the Jerusalem church in which, not only meals, but properties as well, were shared (2:43–45): in such an (atypical and short-lived) arrangement it is not surprising therefore that the breaking of bread would coincide with a common meal.

Only Jude verse 12 provides evidence of the regular practice of a love feast and even this is questionable. We have no idea what exactly was meant by the ἀγάπαι referred to here; ἀγάπαι could quite possibly be a synonym for the eucharist.

Exegetes who have found the Agape in the New Testament have indeed, in the words of Batiffol, "l'on veut tirer des textes plus que leur contenu".[12] They have invariably allowed subsequent church traditions, deduced from patristic and pagan sources, to govern their interpretation.[13] Such practice is not only methodologically dubious in itself, assuming a rather simple correlation between liturgical practice in the primitive and later churches, but when the corroborative evidence gleaned from patristic and pagan sources is examined it is often found to be the product of quite clearly tendentious readings.[14] A few interpreters also seem to have fallen victim to the related problem

---

[10] See Bruce, *Acts*, p. 132.

[11] Acts 20:11 ἀναβὰς δὲ καὶ κλάσας τὸν ἄρτον καὶ γευσάμενος ἐφ' ἱκανόν τε ὁμιλήσας ἄχρι αὐγῆς, οὕτως ἐξῆλθεν is not another example. γεύομαι does not have the force of ἐσθίω and should be translated "tasted" rather than, as the RSV has it, "eaten". Tasting is much more likely to be a reference to taking the communion element rather than eating a meal.

[12] P. Batiffol, *Études d'Histoire et de Theologie Positive*, third edition, Paris: Librairie Victor Lecoffre, 1904, p. 283.

[13] See, for example, Keating, *The Agape and the Eucharist in the Early Church*, p. 36.

[14] Amongst our sources for church practice in the second century there are no distinct references to the existence of an ἀγάπη. Tellingly, the writings of Justin Martyr and Irenaeus do not contain any possible allusions to such meals despite the copious information they give us about other aspects of early Christian liturgy (see, for example, Justin Martyr's lengthy description of a church service in *Apologia* 65–67).

of seeing antecedent traditions as occupying a similarly dominant role. The identification of influential meals in both Jewish[15] and pagan[16] traditions contemporary with the earliest Christian communities should not be treated as determinative of early Church practice.

The meal mentioned in Pliny's letter to Trajan (10.6) is not necessarily an ἀγάπη at all, as is commonly assumed. The picture that Pliny paints is a plausible description of a eucharist through the eyes of a Roman governor who had received his information from apostates. Such people would have been, understandably, keen to present their previous activities as relatively harmless, and the eucharist as a normal meal, rather than a rite in which they ate the body and blood of a man (see Batiffol, *Études*, p. 299 and C. C. Coulter, "Further Notes on the Ritual of the Bithynian Christians", *CPh* 35 (1940) 60–63).

The *Didache*, chapter 9 and 10, also often taken as evidence of an ἀγάπη, need not be a reference to such a practice at all. The chapters can make perfect sense if a eucharist rather than an agape is the object of the liturgy: 10:1 can refer to the elements, and 10:6 need not be seen as anticipatory (and therefore may not be evidence that the custom was to follow a eucharist with an ἀγάπη). The discovery of textual and structural parallels between the *Didache* and Jewish liturgies does not, *a priori*, prove that these chapters indicate the existence of a full meal. As John W. Riggs notes, "Establishing the text and source texts does not necessarily imply the context for the actual use of the prayers. For example, showing that the prayers have a literary basis in Jewish meal blessings does not mean that they could only have been used at a Christian meal gathering and not at a formal celebration of the Eucharist." ("From Gracious Table to Sacramental Elements: The Tradition History of Didache 9 and 10", *SC* 4 (1984), p. 83.)

The Epistle of Ignatius to the Smyrnaeans (8) also fails to provide us with unequivocal evidence. See Batiffol, *Études*, p. 297.

15   For example, the Passover (Seder), the Sabbath Meal, regular Jewish meals of fellowship, the eschatological meal in Isa. 25:6–8; and the community meal in Qumran 1QS 6.4–6 have all been adduced as influential parallels. See Hans Lietzmann, *Mass and the Lord's Supper: A Study in the History of Liturgy*, Leiden: E. J. Brill, 1979, pp. 165–171; K. G. Kuhn, "The Lord's Supper and the Communal Meal at Qumran", *The Scrolls and the New Testament*, ed. K. Stendahl, New York: Harper & Brothers, 1958, pp. 65–93.

16   See Gooch, *Dangerous Food*, and Willis, *Idol Meat at Corinth*.

Bibliography

Primary Sources

All ancient sources and translations are from the *Loeb Classical Library* editions except:

Aesopica. Ed. B. Perry. Urbana: University of Illinois Press, 1952

Apulei Apologia. Ed. H. E. Butler and A. S. Owen. Oxford: Clarendon Press, 1914.

Artemidorus. *Oneirocritica: The Interpretation of Dreams*. Trans. R. J. White. Park Ridge: Noyes Press, 1975.

Claudii Galeni Opera Omnia. Ed. C. Kühn. Hildesheim: Georg Olms, 1964–1986.

Maternus, Firmicus. *Mathesos Libri VIII: Ancient Astrology in Theory and Practice*. Trans. J. R. Bram. Park Ridge: Noyes Press, 1975.

Maximus of Tyre. *Maximi Tyrii*. Ed. H. Hobein. Leipzig: B. G. Teubner, 1910.

Res Gestae Divi Augusti. Ed. P. Brunt and J. M. Moore. Oxford: Oxford University Press, 1967.

The Apocryphal Old Testament. Ed. H. F. D. Sparks. Oxford: Clarendon Press, 1984.

The Babylonian Talmud. Ed. I. Epstein. London: Soncino Press, 1935–1952.

The Chronicle of Joshua the Stylite. Ed. W. Wright. Cambridge: Cambridge University Press, 1882.

The Cynic Epistles. Ed. A. J. Malherbe. Missoula: Scholars Press, 1977.

The Digest of Justinian. Ed. T. Mommsen and P. Krueger. Trans. A. Watson. 4 Volumes. Philadelphia: University of Pennsylvania Press, 1985.

The Greek Magical Papyri in Translation. Volume One: Texts. Ed. Hans Dieter Betz. Second edition. Chicago: Chicago University Press, 1992.

The Institutes of Gaius. Trans. W. Gordon and O. Robinson. London: Duckworth, 1988.

The Mishnah. Trans. Herbert Danby. Oxford: Clarendon Press, 1938.

The Nag Hammadi Library. Ed. James M. Robinson. San Francisco: HarperCollins, 1990.

The Panarion of Epiphanius of Salamis: Book 1 (Sects 1–46). Trans. Frank Williams. Leiden: E. J. Brill, 1987.

The Philogelos or Laughter-Lover. Trans. B. Baldwin. Amsterdam: J. C. Gieben, 1983.

The Sentences of Sextus. Ed. R. A. Edwards and R. A. Wild. Atlanta: Scholars Press, 1981.

Secondary Sources

Abatena, H. "The Potential Contribution of Indigenous Self-Help and Mutual Aid Organisations to the Socio-Economic Development of Ethiopia". *Journal of Rural Co-operation* 15 (1987) 89–106.

Abbott, F. F. *The Common People of Ancient Rome.* New York: Scribner & Sons, 1911.

Achtemeier, P. J. *Romans.* Atlanta: Scholars Press, 1985.

Adamson, W. L. *Hegemony and Revolution: A Study of Antonio Gramsci's Political and Cultural Theory.* Berkeley: University of California Press, 1980.

Adkins, A. W. "Problems in Greek Popular Morality". *Classical Philology* 73 (1978) 143–158.

Africa, T. "Urban Violence in Imperial Rome". *The Journal of Interdisciplinary History* 2 (1971) 3–21.

Agrell, G. *Work, Toil and Sustenance: An Examination of the View of Work in the New Testament, Taking into Consideration Views Found in Old Testament, Intertestamental, and Early Rabbinic Writings.* Lund: Håkan Ohlssons, 1976.

Alcock, Susan. *Graecia Capta: The Landscapes of Roman Greece.* Cambridge: Cambridge University Press, 1993.

Alföldy, Géza. "Römisches Staats- und Gesellschaftsdenken Bei Seuton". *Ancient Society* 12 (1981) 349–385.

———. *The Social History of Rome.* London: Croom Helm, 1985.

Amundsen, Darrel W. "Images of Physicians in Classical Times". *Journal of Popular Culture* 11 (1977) 642–655.

Anderson, G. *The Second Sophistic. A Cultural Phenomenon in the Roman Empire.* London: Routledge, 1993.

Applebaum, S. "The Social and Economic Status of the Jews of the Diaspora", *The Jewish People in the First Century.* Volume 2. Ed. S. Safrai and M. Stern. Amsterdam: Van Gorcum, 1976, pp. 701–727.

Archea, D. C. "Who Was Phoebe?" *The Bible Translator* 39 (1988) 401–409.

Argetsinger, Kathryn. "Birthday Rituals: Friends and Patrons in Roman Poetry and Cult". *Classical Antiquity* 11 (1992) 175–193.

Aschhoff, Günther and Eckhart Henningsen. *The German Co-operative System: Its History, Structure and Strength.* Frankfurt am Main: Fritz Knapp, 1986.

Aubert, Jean-Jacques. *Business Managers in Ancient Rome: A Social and Economic Study of Institores, 200 BC–AD 250.* Leiden: E. J. Brill, 1994.

Avila, Charles. *Ownership: Early Christian Teaching.* Maryknoll: Orbis, 1983.

Badian, E. *Roman Imperialism in the Late Republic.* Second edition. Oxford: Blackwell, 1968.

——. *Publicans and Sinners: Private Enterprise in the Service of the Roman Republic.* Oxford: Basil Blackwell, 1972.

——. "Figuring Out Roman Slavery". (Review of Keith Hopkins, *Conquerors and Slaves.*) *Journal of Roman Studies* 72 (1982) 164–169.

Bailey, K. E. *Poet and Peasant.* Grand Rapids: Eerdmans, 1976.

Balch, D. L. "Household Codes". *Greco-Roman Literature and the New Testament: Selected Forms and Genres.* Ed. D. E. Aune. Atlanta: Scholars Press, 1988, pp. 25–50.

Baldwin, Barry. *Studies in Lucian.* Toronto: Hakkert, 1973.

——. "Testamentum Porcelli". *Studies on Late Roman and Byzantine History, Literature and Language.* Amsterdam: J. C. Gieben, 1984, pp. 137–148.

——. "The Philogelos: An Ancient Joke Book". *Roman and Byzantine Papers.* Amsterdam: J. C. Gieben, 1989, pp. 624–637.

Baldwin, F. E. *Sumptuary Legislation and Personal Regulation in England.* Baltimore: Johns Hopkins University Press, 1926.

Ball, W. E. B. *St Paul and Roman Law.* Edinburgh: T. & T. Clark, 1901.

Bammel, E. "Ein Beitrag zur paulischen Staatsanschauung". *Theologische Literaturzeitung* 85 (1960) 838–839.

——. "πτωχός". *Theological Dictionary of the New Testament* 6. Ed. G. Kittel. Grand Rapids: Eerdmans, 1976, pp. 885–915.

——. "Romans 13". *Jesus and the Politics of His Day*. Ed. E. Bammel and C. Moule. Cambridge: Cambridge University Press, 1984, pp. 365–383.

Barb, A. A. "The Survival of the Magic Arts". *Conflict Between Paganism and Christianity in the Fourth Century*. Ed. A. Momigliano. Oxford: Oxford University Press, 1963, pp. 100–125.

Barclay, Harold. *People Without Government: An Anthropology of Anarchy*. Second Edition. London: Kahn & Averill, 1990.

Barclay, J. M. G. "Paul, Philemon, and the Dilemma of Christian Slave Ownership". *New Testament Studies* 37 (1991) 161–186.

——. "Thessalonica and Corinth: Social Contrasts in Pauline Christianity". *Journal for the Study of the New Testament* 47 (1992) 49–74.

Barrett, C. K. *A Commentary on the Epistle to the Romans*. London: A. & C. Black, 1957.

——. "Things Sacrificed to Idols". *New Testament Studies* 11 (1963) 138–153.

——. *A Commentary on the First Epistle to the Corinthians*. Second edition. London: A. & C. Black, 1971.

——. *A Commentary on the Second Epistle to the Corinthians*. London: A. & C. Black, 1973.

Bartchy, S. Scott. *ΜΑΛΛΟΝ ΧΡΕΣΑΙ: First Century Slavery and the Interpretation of First Corinthians 7:21*. Missoula: Scholars Press, 1973.

——. "Community of Goods in Acts: Idealization or Social Reality?" *The Future of Early Christianity*. Ed. B. A. Pearson. Minneapolis: Fortress Press, 1991, pp. 309–318.

Barth, K. *The Epistle to the Romans*. Oxford: Oxford University Press, 1933.

——. *A Shorter Commentary*. London: SCM, 1959

Barton, Ian M. "Introduction". *Roman Domestic Buildings*. Ed. Ian M. Barton. Exeter: Exeter University Press, 1996, pp. 1–5.

Barton, S. C. "Paul and the Cross: A Sociological Approach". *Theology*. 85 (1982) 13–19.

Batiffol, Pierre. *Études d'Histoire et de Theologie Positive*. Third edition. Paris: Librairie Victor Lecoffre, 1904.

Baunstein, O. *Die politische Wirksamkeit der grieschischen Frau: eine Nachwirkung urgrieschischen Mutterrechts.* Unpublished dissertation: Leipzig, 1911.

Baxter, A. G. and J. A. Ziesler. "Paul and Arboriculture: Romans 11:17–24". *Journal for the Study of the New Testament* 24 (1985) 24–32.

Beacham, Richard. *The Roman Theatre and Its Audience.* London: Routledge, 1991.

Beard, Mary. "Writing and Religion: Ancient Literacy and the Function of the Written Word in Roman Religion". *Literacy in the Roman World.* Ed. J. H. Humphrey. Ann Arbor: Journal of Roman Archaeology, 1991, pp. 35–58.

Beaudry, Mary, L. Cook and S. Mrozowski. "Artifacts and Active Voices: Material Culture as Social Discourse". *The Archaeology of Inequality.* Ed. R. McGuire and R. Paynter. Oxford: Blackwell, 1991, pp. 150–191.

Becker, Jürgen. "Paul and His Churches". *Christian Beginnings: Word and Community from Jesus to Post-Apostolic Times.* Ed. Jürgen Becker. Louisville: Westminster/John Knox Press, 1993, pp. 132–210.

Beik, W. H. "Searching for Popular Culture in Early Modern France". *Journal of Modern History* 49 (1977) 266–281.

Bellen, H. "Antike Staatsräson: Die Hinrichtung der 400 Sklaven des römischen Stadtpräfekten L. Pedanius Secundus im Jahre 61 n. Chr". *Gymnasium* 89 (1982) 449–467.

Belo, F. *A Materialist Reading of the Gospel of Mark.* New York: Orbis, 1981.

Benko, Stephen. *Pagan Rome and the Early Christians.* London: B. T. Batsford, 1985.

Bennett, Tony, C. Mercer and J. Woollacott, *Popular Culture and Social Relations.* Milton Keynes: Open University Press, 1986.

Berger, Peter and Thomas Luckmann. *The Social Construction of Reality: A Treatise in the Sociology of Knowledge.* London: Allen Lane, 1971.

Best, E. E. "Attitudes Towards Literacy in Petronius". *Classical Journal* 61 (1965) 72–76.

———. "The Literate Roman Soldier". *Classical Journal* 62 (1966) 122–127.

———. "Martial's Readers in the Roman World". *Classical Journal* 64 (1969) 208–212.

Best, Ernest. *A Commentary on the First and Second Epistles to the Thessalonians.* London: A. & C. Black, 1972.

Best, Ernest. "Paul's Apostolic Authority?" *Journal for the Study of the New Testament* 27 (1986) 3–25.

———. *Paul and His Converts.* Edinburgh: T. & T. Clark, 1988.

Betz, H. D. "The Literary Composition and Function of Paul's Letter to the Galatians". *New Testament Studies* 21 (1975) 353–379.

———. *2 Corinthians 8 and 9: A Commentary on Two Adminstrative Letters of the Apostle Paul.* Philadelphia: Fortress Press, 1985.

Bickerman, Elias. *The Jews in the Greek World.* Cambridge MA: Harvard University Press, 1988.

Biezunska-Malowist, I. "Les enfants-esclaves à la lumière des papyrus". *Collection Latomus* 102 (1969) 91–96.

———. *L'Esclavage dans l'Egypte Gréco-Romaine: Période Romaine.* Warsaw: Zakkadnarodowy Imienia Osslínskich, 1977.

Black, M. *Romans.* London: Oliphants, 1973.

Boak, A. E. R. "The Organization of Gilds in Greco-Roman Egypt". *Transactions of the American Philological Association* 68 (1937) 212–220.

Boatwright, Mary T. "Plancia Magna of Perge: Women's Roles and Status in Asia Minor". *Women's History and Ancient History.* Ed. S. Pomeroy. Chapel Hill: University of North Carolina Press, 1991, pp. 249–272.

Boer, W. Den. "Demography in Roman History: Facts and Impressions". *Mnemosyne* 26 (1973) 29–46.

Bolchazy, Ladislaus J. *Hospitality in Early Rome: Livy's Concept of Its Humanising Force.* Chicago: Ares Pub Inc, 1977.

Bolkestein, H. *Wohltätigkeit und Armenpflege im vorchristlichen Altertum.* Utrecht: Oosthoek, 1939.

Bonner, C. "Witchcraft in the Lecture Room of Libanius". *Transactions of the American Philological Association* 63 (1932) 34–44.

Bonner, Stanley F. *Education in Ancient Rome: From the Elder Cato to the Younger Pliny.* London: Methuen & Co., 1977.

Bookidis, N. and R. S. Stroud. *Demeter and Persephone in Ancient Corinth.* Princeton: American School of Classical Studies at Athens, 1989.

Booth, A. "The Schooling of Slaves in First Century Rome". *Transactions of the American Philological Association* 109 (1979) 11–19.

Bornkamm, G. "The History of the Origin of the So-Called Second Letter to the Corinthians". *The Authority and Integrity of the New Testament.* London: SPCK, 1965, pp. 73–81.

Bornkamm, G. "Der Römerbrief als Testament des Paulus". *Geschichte und Glaube*. Volume 2. München: Chr. Kaiser, 1971, pp. 120–139.

Bouman, F. J. A. "Indigenous Savings and Credit Associations in the Third World: A Message". *Savings and Development Quarterly Review* 4 (1977) 181–214.

Bouyer, Louis. *Eucharist: Theology and the Spirituality of the Eucharist Prayer*. Notre Dame: University of Notre Dame Press, 1968.

Bowersock, Glen W. *Augustus and the Greek World*. Oxford: Clarendon Press, 1965.

Bowie, E. L. "The Importance of Sophists". *Yale Classical Studies* 27 (1982) 29–59.

Bowker, John. *Jesus and the Pharisees*. Cambridge: Cambridge University Press, 1973.

Bowman, Alan K. "Literacy in the Roman Empire: Mass and Mode". *Literacy in the Roman World*. Ed. J. H. Humphrey. Ann Arbor: Journal of Roman Archaeology, 1991, pp. 119–131.

———. *Life and Letters on the Roman Frontier*. London: British Museum Press, 1994.

Bradley, K. R. "The Age at Time of Sale of Female Slaves". *Arethusa* 11 (1978) 243–252.

———. "Child Labour in the Roman World". *Historical Reflections/ Réflexions Historiques* 12 (1985) 311–330.

———. "Wet-nursing at Rome". *The Family in Ancient Rome*. Ed. Beryl Rawson. Ithaca: Cornell, 1986, pp. 201–229.

———. *Slaves and Masters in the Roman Empire*. Oxford: Oxford University Press, 1987.

———. "Dislocation in the Roman Family". *Historical Reflections/ Réflexions Historiques* 14 (1987) 33–62.

———. *Slavery and Rebellion in the Roman World, 140 B.C.–70 B.C.* Bloomington: Indiana University Press, 1989.

———. *Slavery and Society At Rome*. Cambridge: Cambridge University Press, 1994.

Braudel, F. *Capitalism and Material Life*. London: Fontana, 1974.

Braun, F. *Terms of Address: Problems of Patterns and Usage in Various Languages and Cultures*. Berlin: Mouton de Gruyter, 1988.

Braund, D. "Function and Dysfunction: Personal Patronage in Roman Imperialism". *Patronage in Ancient Society*. Ed. A. Wallace-Hadrill. London: Routledge, 1990, pp. 137–152.

Broneer, O. "Excavations in the Agora at Corinth". *American Journal of Archaeology* 37 (1933) 554–572.

——. "Corinth, Center of St Paul's Missionary Work in Greece". *Biblical Archaeologist* 14 (1951) 78–96.

Brooten, Bernadette. *Women Leaders in the Ancient Synagogue.* Chico, CA: Scholars Press, 1982.

Brothers, A. J. "Urban Housing". *Roman Domestic Buildings.* Ed. Ian M. Barton. Exeter: Exeter University Press, 1996, pp. 33–63.

Broughton, T. R. S. "Roman Asia Minor". *An Economic Survey of Ancient Rome.* Ed. Tenney Frank. New York: Octagon Books, 1975, pp. 627–648.

Brown, Peter. "Sorcery, Demons and the Rise of Christianity". *Religion and Society in the Age of Augustine.* London: Faber & Faber, 1972, pp. 119–146.

Bruce, F. F. *1 and 2 Corinthians.* London: Oliphants, 1971.

——. *1 and 2 Thessalonians.* Waco: Word Books, 1982.

——. *The Letter of Paul to the Romans.* Leicester: InterVarsity Press, 1985.

——. "Paul in Acts and Letters". *Dictionary of Paul and His Letters.* Ed. G. Hawthorne. Leicester: InterVarsity Press, 1993, pp. 679–692.

Brunt, P. A. "Review of W. L. Westerman, *The Slaves Systems of Greek and Roman Antiquity*". *Journal of Roman Studies* 48 (1958) 164–170.

——. *Italian Manpower.* Oxford: Clarendon Press, 1971.

——. "Aspects of the Social Thought of Dio Chrysostom and of the Stoics". *Proceedings of the Cambridge Philological Society* 19 (1973) 9–34.

——. "The Romanisation of the Local Ruling Classes in the Roman Empire". *Assimilation et résistance à la culture Gréco-Romaine dans le monde ancien.* Ed. D. M. Pippidi. Paris: La Société d'Édition Les Belles Lettres, 1976, pp. 161–173.

——. "Josephus on Social Conflicts in Roman Judaea". *Klio* 59 (1977) 149–153.

——. *Social Conflict in the Roman Republic.* London: Hogarth Press, 1978.

——. "A Marxist View of Roman History". (Review of de Ste Croix, *The Class Struggle in the Ancient Greek World*). *Journal of Roman Studies* 72 (1982) 158–163.

——. *The Fall of the Roman Republic.* Oxford: Clarendon Press, 1988.

Buchanan, G. W. "Jesus and the Upper Class". *Novum Testamentum* 7 (1965) 195–209.

Bücher, Karl. *Industrial Evolution*. New York: Franklin, 1901.

Buck, Chas H. "The Collection for the Saints". *Harvard Theological Review* 43 (1950) 3–9.

Buckland, W. W. *The Roman Law of Slavery*. Cambridge: Cambridge University Press, 1908.

Buckler, W. H. "Labour Disputes in the Province of Asia". *Anatolian Studies Presented to Sir Michael Ramsay*. Ed. W. H. Buckler. Manchester: Manchester University Press, 1923, pp. 27–50.

Burford, Alison. *Craftsmen in Greek and Roman Society*. Ithaca: Cornell University Press, 1972.

Burke, Peter. *Popular Culture in Early Modern Europe*. London: Temple Smith, 1978.

———. "Introduction". *Social History of Language*. Ed. P. Burke and R. Porter. Cambridge: Cambridge University Press, 1987, pp. 1–20.

———. "Overture: The New History". *New Perspectives on Historical Writing*. Ed. Peter Burke. Cambridge: Polity Press, 1991, pp. 1–23.

———. *History and Social Theory*. Cambridge: Polity Press, 1992.

Burkert, W. *Greek Religion*. Oxford: Basil Blackwell, 1985.

———. *Ancient Mystery Cults*. Cambridge, MA: Harvard University Press, 1987.

Burling, Robbins. "Maximization Theories and the Study of Economic Anthropology". *Economic Anthropology: Readings in Theory and Analysis*. Ed. Edward E. LeClair and Harold K. Schneider. New York: Holt, Rinehart & Winston Inc., 1968, pp. 168–187.

Burridge, Kenelm. *New Heaven, New Earth: A Study of Millinarian Activities*. Oxford: Basil Blackwell, 1969.

Cabaniss, Allen. *Patterns in Early Christian Worship*. Macon: Mercer University Press, 1989.

Cadbury, Henry J. "Luke's Interest in Lodging". *Journal of Biblical Literature* 45 (1926) 305–322.

———. "Erastus of Corinth". *Journal of Biblical Literature* 50 (1931) 42–58.

——— and Kirsopp Lake. *Beginnings of Christianity*. Volume 5. London: Macmillan & Co., 1933.

Callander, T. "The Tarsian Orations of Dio Chrysostom". *Journal of Hellenic Studies* 24 (1904) 58–69.

Camarmond, P. de. and D. Soen. "Saving Associations Among the Bamileke: Traditional and Modern Cooperatives in South Western Cameroon". *American Anthropologist* 74 (1972) 1170–1179.

Cameron, Averil. "Neither Male Nor Female". *Greece and Rome* 27 (1980) 60–68.

Campbell, J. Y. "Κοινωνία and its Cognates in the New Testament". *Journal of Biblical Literature* 51 (1932) 352–380.

Campenhausen, H. von. *Ecclesiastical Authority and Spiritual Authority in the Church of the First Three Centuries.* London: A. & C. Black, 1969.

Cantarella, Eva. *Pandora's Daughters: The Role and Status of Women in Greek and Roman Antiquity.* Baltimore: Johns Hopkins University Press, 1987, pp. 135–170.

Capper, Brian. "The Palestinian Cultural Context of Earliest Christian Community of Goods". *The Book of Acts in its First Century Setting. Volume 4: The Book of Acts in its Palestinian Setting.* Ed. R. Bauckham. Carlisle: Paternoster Press, 1995, pp. 323–356.

Carandini, A. "Il mondo della tarda antichità visto attraverso le merci". *Società romana e impero tardoantico III.* Ed. A. Giardina. Rome: Editori Laterza, 1986, pp. 3–19.

———. "Italian Wine and African Oil: Commerce in a World Empire". *The Birth of Europe. Archaeology and Social Development in the First Millenium AD.* Ed. K. Randsborg. Rome: L'Erma di Bretschneider, 1989, pp. 16–24.

Carney, T. F. *The Shape of the Past: Models and Antiquity.* Lawrence: Coronado Press, 1975.

Carr, W. *Angels and Principalities.* Cambridge: Cambridge University Press, 1981.

Case, Shirley Jackson. *The Social Triumph of the Early Church.* New York: Books for Libraries, 1971.

Casson, Lionel. *Ships and Seamanship in the Ancient World.* Princeton: Princeton University Press, 1971.

———. *Travel in the Ancient World.* London: Allen & Unwin, 1974.

———. *Ancient Trade and Society.* Detroit: Wayne State University Press, 1984.

———. "Egypt, Africa, Arabia and India: Patterns of Seaborne Trade in the First Century AD". *Bulletin of the American Society of Papyrologists* 21 (1984) 39–47.

Cervin, Richard S. "A Note Regarding The Name 'Junia(s)' in Romans 16.7". *New Testament Studies* 40 (1994) 464–470.

Cha, Y. "The Function of Peculium in Roman Slavery During the First Two Centuries AD". *Forms of Control and Subordination in Antiquity*. Ed. Toru Yuge and Masaoki Doi. Leiden: E. J. Brill, 1988, pp. 433–436.

Chadwick, Henry. *The Sentences of Sextus: A Contribution to the History of Early Christian Ethics*. Cambridge: Cambridge University Press, 1959.

Champlin, E. *Final Judgments: Duty and Emotion in Roman Wills, 200 BC – AD 250*. Oxford: University of California Press, 1991.

Charlesworth, J. H. "Archaeology, Jesus, and the Christian Faith". *What Has Archaeology To Do With Faith?* Ed. J. H. Charlesworth and W. P. Weaver. Philadelphia: Trinity Press, 1992, pp. 1–22.

Charlesworth, M. P. *Trade Routes and Commerce in the Roman Empire*. Cambridge: Cambridge University Press, 1926.

Chesnutt, Randall D. "The Social Setting and Purpose of Joseph and Aseneth". *Journal for the Study of the Pseudepigrapha* 2 (1988) 21–48.

Chow, J. K. *Patronage and Power*. Sheffield: JSOT Press, 1992.

Cilliers, Louise. "Public Health in Roman Legislation". *Acta Classica* 36 (1993) 1–10.

Cirlot, Felix L. *The Early Eucharist*. London: SPCK, 1939.

Clark, Gillian. "The Social Status of Paul". *Expository Times* 96 (1985) 110–111.

——. *Women in the Ancient Greek World*. Oxford: Oxford University Press, 1989.

Clarke, Andrew D. "Another Corinthian Erastus Inscription". *Tyndale Bulletin* 42 (1991) 146–151.

——. *Secular and Christian Leadership in Corinth: A Socio-Historical and Exegetical Study of 1 Corinthians 1–6*. Leiden: E. J. Brill, 1993.

Clastres, Pierre. *Society Against the State*. Oxford: Basil Blackwell, 1977.

Cloud, D. "The Client-Patron Relationship: Emblem and Reality in Juvenal's First Book". *Patronage in Ancient Society*. Ed. A. Wallace-Hadrill. London: Routledge, 1990, pp. 205–218.

Cohen, Anthony P. *The Symbolic Construction of Community*. London: Routledge, 1985.

Colson, E. *Tradition and Contract: The Problem of Order*. London: Heinemann, 1975.

Conzelmann, H. *A Commentary on the First Epistle to the Corinthians.* Philadelphia: Fortress Press, 1975.

Corbier, Mireille, "Fiscus and Patromonium: The Saepium Inscription and Transhumance in the Abruzzi". *Journal of Roman Studies* 73 (1983) 126–131.

———. "The Ambiguous Status of Meat in Ancient Rome". *Food and Foodways* 3 (1989) 223–264.

———. "City, Territory, Tax". *City and Country in the Ancient World.* Ed. J. Rich and A. Wallace-Hadrill. London: Routledge, 1991, pp. 211–239.

Cormack, J. M. "A Tabella Defixionis in the Museum of the University of Reading, England". *Harvard Theological Review* 44 (1951) 25–34.

Cotter, W. "Women's Authority Role in Paul's Churches: Counter-cultural or Conventional?" *Novum Testamentum* 36 (1994) 350–372.

———. "The Collegia and Roman Law: State Restrictions on Voluntary Associations, 64 BCE – 200 CE". *Voluntary Associations in the Graeco-Roman World.* Ed. John S. Kloppenborg and Stephen G. Wilson. London: Routledge, 1996, pp. 74–89.

Coulter, C. C. "Further Notes on the Ritual of the Bithynian Christians". *Classical Philology* 35 (1940) 60–63.

Countryman, L. W. "Welfare in the Churches of Asia Minor". *SBL 1979 Seminar Papers.* Ed. J. Achtemeier. Missoula, MT: Scholars Press, 1979, pp. 131–146.

———. *The Rich Christians in the Church of the Early Empire: Contradictions and Accommodations.* New York: Edwin Mellen Press, 1980.

Cranfield, C. E. B. "Some Observations on Romans XIII. 1–7". *New Testament Studies* 6 (1960) 241–249.

———. *The Epistle to the Romans.* 2 vols. Edinburgh: T. & T. Clark, 1975, 1979.

Crawford, M. H. "Money and Exchange in the Roman World". *Journal of Roman Studies* 60 (1970) 40–48.

———. "Republican Denarii in Romania: The Suppression of Piracy and the Slave Trade". *Journal of Roman Studies* 67 (1977) 117–124.

——— and J. M. Reynolds. "The Aezani Copy of the Prices Edict". *Zeitschrift für Papyrologie und Epigraphik* 34 (1979) 163–210.

Crone, P. *Pre-Industrial Societies.* Oxford: Basil Blackwell, 1989.

Crook, J. A. *Law and Life of Rome*. London: Thames & Hudson, 1967.

——. "Patria Potestas". *Classical Quarterly* 17 (1967) 113–122.

Crosby, Michael H. *The House of Disciples: Church, Economics and Justice in Matthew*. Maryknoll: Orbis, 1988.

Crossan, J. D. *The Historical Jesus: The Life of a Mediterranean Jewish Peasant*. Edinburgh: T. & T. Clark, 1991.

Csillag, Pál. *The Augustan Laws on Family Relations*. Budapest: Akadémiai Kiadó, 1976.

Cullman, O. *Early Christian Worship*. London: SCM, 1954.

——. *The State in the New Testament*. London: SCM, 1963.

Cumont, F. "La Grande Inscription Bachique Du Metropolitan Museum". *American Journal of Archaeology* 37 (1933) 232–270.

Cyert R. and J. March. *A Behavioural Theory of the Firm*. Englewood Cliffs: Prentice Hall, 1963.

Dahl, Nils Alstrup. "Paul and Possessions". *Studies in Paul*. Minneapolis: Ausburg, 1977, pp. 22–39.

Dalton, G. "Theoretical Issues in Economic Anthropology". *Current Anthropology* 10 (1969) 63–80.

——. "Peasantries in Anthropology and History". *Current Anthropology* 13 (1972) 385–407.

Danker, Frederick W. *Benefactor: Epigraphic Study of a Graeco-Roman and New Testament Semantic Field*. St Louis: Clayton, 1982.

——. *II Corinthians*. Minneapolis: Augsburg, 1989.

D'Arms, J. "The Status of Traders in the Roman World". *Ancient and Modern: Essays in Honour of G. F. Else*. Ed. J. D'Arms and J. W. Eadie. Ann Arbor: University of Michigan Press, 1977, pp. 159–179.

——. *Commerce and Social Standing in Ancient Rome*. Cambridge, MA: Harvard University Press, 1981.

——. "Control, Companionship, and Clientela: Some Social Functions of the Roman Communal Meal". *Echos du Monde Classique/ Classical Views* 28 (1984) 327–328.

——. "Heavy Drinking and Drunkenness in the Roman World: Four Questions for Historians". *In Vino Veritas*. Ed. Oswyn Murray and Manuela Tecusan. London: The British School at Rome, 1995, pp. 304–317.

—— and E. C. Kopff (Eds). *The Seaborne Commerce of Ancient Rome: Studies in Archaeology and History*. Rome: American Academy at Rome, 1984.

Daube, D. "Slave Catching". *Juridical Review* 64 (1952) 12–28.

———. *Roman Law: Linguistic, Social and Philosophical Aspects.* Edinburgh: Edinburgh University Press, 1969.

Davies, J. "Cultural, Social and Economic Features of the Hellenistic World". *Cambridge Ancient History.* Volume 7. Second edition. Ed. F. W. Wallbank. Cambridge: Cambridge University Press, 1984, pp. 257–320.

Davies, R. W. "The Roman Military Diet". *Britannia* 2 (1971) 122–142.

Davies, W. D. *Paul and Rabbinic Judaism.* Philadelphia: Fortress Press, 1980.

Davis, John. *Exchange.* Buckingham: Open University Press, 1992.

Davis, Natalie Z. *Society and Culture in Early Modern France.* Cambridge: Polity Press, 1975.

Deetz, James. *In Small Things Forgotten: The Archaeology of Early American Life.* New York: Anchor Press, 1977.

———. "Historical Archaeology as the Science of Material Culture". *Historical Archaeology and the Importance of Material Things.* Ed. Leland G. Ferguson. Tucson: Society for Historical Archaeology, 1977, pp. 9–12.

———. "Archaeography, Archaeology, or Archeology?" *American Journal of Archaeology* 93 (1989) 429–435.

Deissmann, Adolf. *Paul: A Study in Social and Religious History.* New York: Harper & Row, 1957.

———. *Light From the Ancient East: The New Testament Illustrated by Recently Discovered Texts of the Graeco-Roman World.* Fourth Edition. London: Hodder & Stoughton, 1922.

Derrett, J. D. M. "'Handing Over to Satan': An Explanation of 1 Corinthians 5:1–7". *Studies in the New Testament.* Leiden: E. J. Brill, 1986, pp. 167–186.

Detienne, M. and J. P. Vernant. *La Cuisine du sacrifice en pays grec.* Paris: Gallimard, 1979.

Digby, Margaret. *The World Co-operative Movement.* London: Hutchinson's University Library, 1948.

Dirks, R. *The Black Saturnalia: Conflict and its Ritual Expression On British West Indian Slave Plantations.* Gainsville: University Presses of Florida, 1987.

Dixon, D. "Polybius on Roman Women and Property". *American Journal of Philology* 106 (1985) 147–170.

Dixon, Suzanne. *The Roman Mother*. London: Croom Helm, 1988.

Dobschütz, E. von. *Christian Life in the Primitive Church*. New York: G. Putman's Sons, 1904.

Dodd, C. H. "The Mind of Paul: A Psychological Approach". *Bulletin of the John Rylands Library* 17 (1933) 91–105.

——. *The Epistle to the Romans*. London: Hodder & Stoughton, 1942.

Doi, Masaoki. "Methods for Viewing World History from the Perspective of the Ruled". *Forms of Control and Subordination in Antiquity*. Ed. Toru Yuge and Masaoki Doi. Leiden: E. J. Brill, 1988, pp. 3–8.

Donfried, K. P. *The Romans Debate*. Second Edition. Edinburgh: T. & T. Clark, 1991.

Doty, W. G. *Letters in Primitive Christianity*. Philadelphia: Fortress Press, 1973.

Douglas, Dorothy. "P. J. Proudhon: A Prophet of 1848. Part 1: Life and Works". *American Journal of Sociology* 34 (1929) 781–803 and "P. J. Proudhon. Part 2", 35 (1930) 35–59.

Douglas, Mary. *Constructive Drinking: Perspectives on Drink from Anthropology*. Cambridge: Cambridge University Press, 1987.

Dover, K. J. *Greek Popular Morality in the Time of Plato and Aristotle*. Oxford: Blackwell, 1974.

Downing, F. G. *Christ and the Cynics*. Sheffield: JSOT Press, 1988.

——. *Cynics and Christian Origins*. Edinburgh: T. & T. Clark, 1992.

Drew-Bear, T. Review of H. J. Mason, *Greek Terms for Roman Institutions*. *Classical Philology* 71 (1976) 349–355.

Drinkwater, John. "Peasants and Bagaudae in Roman Gaul". *Classical Views* 3 (1984) 349–371.

——. "Patronage in Roman Gaul and the problem of the Bagaudae". *Patronage in Ancient Society*. Ed. A. Wallace-Hadrill. London: Routledge, 1990, pp. 189–203.

Duckworth, George E. "Wealth and Poverty in Roman Comedy". *Studies in Roman Economic and Social History*. Ed. P. R. Coleman-Norton. New Jersey: Princeton University Press, 1951, pp. 35–48.

Duff, A. M. *Freedmen in the Early Roman Empire*. Oxford: Oxford University Press, 1928.

Duff, J. W. *A Literary History of Rome in the Silver Age*. Third Edition. London: Ernest Benn Ltd., 1964.

——. *Roman Satire*. Cambridge: Cambridge University Press, 1936.

Duncan-Jones, Richard. "Wealth and Munificence in Roman Africa". *Papers of the British School at Rome* 18 (1963) 160–177.

———. "An Epigraphic Survey of Costs in Roman Italy". *Papers of the British School at Rome* 20 (1965) 189–206.

———. *The Economy of the Roman Empire.* Cambridge: Cambridge University Press, 1974.

———. "Age-Rounding, Illiteracy and Social Differentiation in the Roman Empire". *Chiron* 7 (1977) 332–353.

———. "Problems of the Delphic Manumission Payments 220–1 BC". *Zeitschrift für Papyrologie und Epigraphik* 57 (1984) 203–209.

———. *Structure and Scale in the Roman Economy.* Cambridge: Cambridge University Press, 1990.

Dungan, David L. *The Sayings of Jesus in the Churches of Paul.* Oxford: Basil Blackwell, 1971.

Dunkin, P. S. *Post-Aristophanic Comedy: Studies in the Social Outlook of Middle and New Comedy at Both Athens and Rome.* Urbana: Illinois University, 1936.

Dunn, J. D. G. *Romans 9–16.* Waco: Word Books, 1988.

———. *1 Corinthians.* Sheffield: Sheffield Academic Press, 1995.

Dyson, S. L. *Community and Society in Roman Italy.* London: Johns Hopkins University Press, 1992.

Easton, B. S. "New Testament Ethical Lists". *Journal of Biblical Literature* 51 (1932) 1–12.

Edwards, Catherine. *The Politics of Immorality.* Cambridge: Cambridge University Press, 1993.

Ehrhardt, A. A. T. "Jesus Christ and Alexander the Great". *Journal of Theological Studies* 46 (1945) 45–51.

Eisenstadt, S. N. *Patrons, Clients and Friends: Interpersonal Relations and the Structure of Trust in Society.* Cambridge: Cambridge University Press, 1984

——— and Louis Roniger. "The Study of Patron-Client Relations and Recent Developments in Sociological Theory". *Political Clientism: Patronage and Development.* Ed. S. N. Eisenstadt and René Lemarchand, London: Sage Publications, 1981, pp. 271–295.

Elliot, John H. "Social Scientific Criticisms of the New Testament: More on Methods and Models". *Semeia* 35 (1986) 1–34.

Elliott, Neil. *Liberating Paul: The Justice of God and the Politics of the Apostle.* Sheffield: Sheffield Academic Press, 1995.

Ellis, E. Earle. *Pauline Theology: Ministry and Society*. Grand Rapids: Eerdmans, 1989.

——. "Paul and His Co-Workers". *New Testament Studies* 17 (1977) 437–452.

Engels, D. "The Problem of Female Infanticide in the Greco-Roman World". *Classical Philology* 75 (1980) 112–120.

——. *Roman Corinth: An Alternative Model for a Classical City*. Chicago: University of Chicago Press, 1990.

Engels, F. "On the History of Early Christianity". *On Religion*. Ed. K. Marx and F. Engels. London: Lawrence & Wishart, 1959, pp. 313–343.

Epp, Erman N. *Servus vicarius: L'esclave de l'esclave romain*. Lausanne: F. Rouge, 1896.

Esler, P. *Community and Gospel in Luke-Acts*. Cambridge: Cambridge University Press, 1987.

——. *The First Christians in Their Social World: Social-Scientific Approaches to New Testament Interpretation*. London: Routledge, 1994.

Evans, John K. *War, Women and Children in Ancient Rome*. London: Routledge, 1991.

Eyben, E. "Family Planning in Graeco-Roman Antiquity". *Ancient Society* 11 (1980) 5–82.

——. *Restless Youth in Ancient Rome*. London: Routledge, 1993.

Falkner, Thomas and Judith De Luce. *Old Age in Greek and Latin Literature*. Albany: State University of New York Press, 1989.

Faraone, Christopher. "The Agonistic Context of Early Greek Binding Spells". *Magika Hiera Sine Lege: Ancient Greek Magic and Religion*. Ed. Christopher A. Faraone and Dirk Obbink. Oxford: Oxford University Press, 1991, pp. 3–32.

——. *Talismans and Trojan Horses*. Oxford: Oxford University Press, 1992.

Fee, G. D. *The First Epistle to the Corinthians*. Grand Rapids: Eerdmans, 1987.

Filoramo, Giovanni. *A History of Gnosticism*. Oxford: Basil Blackwell, 1990.

Filson, F. V. "The Significance of the Early House Churches". *Journal of Biblical Literature* 58 (1939) 105–112.

Finley, M. I. "The Trojan War". *Journal of Hellenic Studies* 84 (1964) 1–9.

Finley, M. I. *The Ancient Economy*. London: Chatto & Windus, 1973.

———. "Aristotle and Economic Analysis". *Studies in Ancient Society*. Ed. M. I. Finley. London: Routledge, 1974, pp. 26–52.

———. *Ancient Slavery and Modern Ideology*. London: Chatto & Windus, 1980.

———. "The Elderly in Classical Antiquity". *Greece and Rome* 28 (1981) 156–171

Fiore, B. "'Covert Allusion' in 1 Corinthians 1–4". *Catholic Biblical Quarterly* 47 (1985) 85–102.

Fiorenza, E. Schüssler. *In Memory of Her: A Feminist Reconstruction of Christian Origins*. London: SCM, 1983.

Fishman, Joshua A. "The Sociology of Language: An Interdisciplinary Social Science Approach to Language in Society". *Advances in the Sociology of Language*. Ed. Joshua A. Fishman. The Hague: Moulton, 1971, pp. 217–404.

———. "Domains and the Relationship Between Micro- and Macro-sociolinguistics". *Directions in Sociolinguistics: The Ethnography of Communication*. Ed. J. J. Gumperz and Dell Hymes. Oxford: Basil Blackwell, 1972, pp. 435–453.

Flory, M. B. "Family in *Familia*: Kinship and Community in Slavery". *American Journal of Ancient History* 3 (1978) 78–95.

Food and Agriculture Organisation of the United Nations, *Handbook on Nutritional Requirements*. Rome: FAO and WHO, 1974.

Foraboschi, D. *Onomasticon alterum papyrologicum*. Milano: Istituto Editoriale Cisapino, 1971.

Forbes, C. "Comparison, Self-Praise, and Irony: Paul's Boasting and the Convention of Hellenistic Rhetoric". *New Testament Studies* 32 (1986) 1–30.

Forbes, Clarence A. "The Education and Training of Slaves in Antiquity". *Transactions of the American Philological Association* 86 (1955) 321–360.

Ford, J. M. "Three Ancient Jewish Attitudes Towards Poverty". *The New Way of Jesus*. Ed. W. Klassen. Kansas: Faith and Life Press, 1980, pp. 39–55.

Forgacs, D. and G. Nowell. *A. Gramsci: Selections From Cultural Writings*. London: Lawrence & Wishart, 1985.

Fox, Robin Lane. *Pagans and Christians*. Harmondsworth: Penguin, 1986.

Fraade, Steven. "The Nazirite in Ancient Judaism". *Ascetic Behaviour in Greco-Roman Antiquity*. Ed. Vincent L. Wimbush. Minneapolis: Fortress Press, 1990, pp. 213–223.

Frame, James Everett. *A Critical and Exegetical Commentary on the Epistles of St Paul to the Thessalonians*. Edinburgh: T. & T. Clark, 1912.

Frank, Richard I. "Augustus' Legislation on Marriage and Children". *California Studies in Classical Antiquity* 8 (1975) 41–52.

Frank, T. "Race Mixture in the Roman Empire". *American History Review* 21 (1915–1916) 689–708.

——. *An Economic History of Rome*. London: Jonathon Cape, 1927.

Franklin, James L. "Literacy and Parietal Inscriptions of Pompeii". *Literacy in the Roman World*. Ed. J. H. Humphrey. Ann Arbor: Journal of Roman Archaeology, 1991, pp. 77–98.

Fraser, P. and E. Matthews (Eds). *Lexicon of Greek Personal Names (Volume 1, Aegean Islands, Cyprus, Cyrenaica)*. Oxford: Clarendon Press, 1987.

—— (Eds). *Lexicon of Greek Personal Names (Volume 2, Attica)*. Oxford: Clarendon Press, 1994.

Frayn, Joan M. *Markets and Fairs in Roman Italy*. Oxford: Clarendon Press, 1993.

Friedländer, Ludwig. *Roman Life and Manners Under the Early Empire*. 4 vols. London: George Routledge & Sons, 1913.

Frier, Bruce W. "The Rental Market in Early Imperial Rome". *Journal of Roman Studies* 67 (1977) 27–37.

——. *Landlords and Tenants in Imperial Rome*. Princeton: Princeton University Press, 1980.

——. "Roman Life Expectancy". *Harvard Studies in Classical Philology* 86 (1982) 213–251.

——. "Natural Fertility and Family Limitation in Roman Marriage". *Classical Philology* 89 (1994) 318–333.

Fulford, M. "Economic Interdependence Among the Urban Communities of the Roman Empire". *World Archaeology* 19 (1987) 58–75.

——. "Territorial Expansion and the Roman Empire". *World Archaeology* 23 (1992) 294–305.

Furnish, V. P. "Corinth in Paul's Time. What Can Archaeology Tell Us?" *Biblical Archaeology Review* 15 (1988) 14–27.

Gager, John C. *Kingdom and Community: The Social World of Early Christianity*. Englewood Cliffs: Prentice Hall, 1975.

Gager, John C. "Review of Grant, Malherbe, Theissen". *Religious Studies Review* 5 (1979) 174–180.

——. "Shall We Marry Our Enemies? Sociology and the New Testament". *Interpretation* 36 (1986) 256–265.

Gager, John G. *Curse Tablets and Binding Spells From the Ancient World*. Oxford: Oxford University Press, 1992.

Gallagher, Eugene V. "The Social World of Saint Paul". *Religion* 14 (1984) 91–99.

Gallant, Thomas W. "Crisis and Response: Risk-Buffering Behaviour in Ancient Greek Communities". *Journal of Interdisciplinary History* 19 (1989) 393–413.

——. *Risk and Survival in Ancient Greece*. Cambridge: Polity Press, 1991.

Gamble, H. *The Textual History of the Letter to the Romans*. Grand Rapids: Eerdmans, 1977.

——. *Books and Readers in the Early Church: A History of Early Christian Texts*. New Haven: Yale University Press, 1995.

Gardner, Jane F. "Proofs of Status in the Roman World". *Bulletin of the Institute of Classical Studies* 33 (1986) 1–14.

——. "The Adoption of Freedmen". *Phoenix* 43 (1989) 236–257.

——. *Women in Roman Law and Society*. London: Routledge, 1991.

—— and Thomas Wiedemann. *The Roman Household*. London: Routledge, 1991.

Garland, Robert. *The Eye of the Beholder*. London: Duckworth, 1995.

Garnsey, Peter. "The Lex Iulia and Appeal under the Empire". *Journal of Roman Studies* 56 (1966) 167–189.

——. "The Criminal Jurisdiction of Governors". *Journal of Roman Studies* 58 (1968) 51–59.

——. *Social Status and Legal Privilege*. Oxford: Oxford University Press, 1970.

——. "Legal Privilege in the Roman Empire". *The Social Organization of the Law*. Ed. D. Black and M. Mileski. London: Seminar Press, 1973, pp. 146–166.

——. "Aspects of the Decline of the Urban Aristocracy in the Empire". *Aufstieg und Niedergang der römischen Welt*. Volume 2.1. Ed. H. Temporini. Berlin: Walter De Gruyter, 1974, pp. 229–252.

——. "Urban Property Investment". *Studies in Roman Property*. Ed. M. Finley. Cambridge: Cambridge University Press, 1976, pp. 123–136.

Garnsey, Peter (Ed.) *Non-Slave Labour in the Greco-Roman World.* Cambridge: Cambridge Philological Society, 1980.

———. "Grain For Rome". *Trade in the Ancient Economy.* Ed. P. Garnsey, K. Hopkins, and C. R. Whittaker. London: Chatto & Windus, 1983, pp. 118–130.

———. *Famine and Food Supply in the Graeco-Roman World: Responses to Risk and Crisis.* Cambridge: Cambridge University Press, 1988.

———. "Food Consumption in Antiquity: Towards a Quantitative Account". *Food, Health and Culture in Classical Antiquity.* Ed. P. Garnsey. Cambridge: Classical Department Working Papers, 1989, pp. 36–49.

———. "Mass Diet and Nutrition in the City of Rome". *Nourrir la Plèbe.* Ed. A. Giovannini and D. Berchem. Basel: Reinhardt, 1991, pp. 67–102.

———. "Child Rearing in Ancient Italy". *The Family in Italy From Antiquity to the Present.* Ed. D. Kertzer and R. Saller. New Haven: Yale University Press, 1991, pp. 48–65.

——— and R. Saller. *The Roman Empire: Economy, Society, and Culture.* London: Duckworth, 1987.

——— and Greg Woolf. "Patronage of the rural poor in the Roman world". *Patronage in Ancient Society.* Ed. Andrew Wallace-Hadrill. Routledge: London, 1990, pp. 153–170.

Garrison, Roman. *Redemptive Almsgiving in Early Christianity.* Sheffield: Sheffield Academic Press, 1993.

Geertz, C. "Ideology as a Cultural System". *Ideology and Discontent.* Ed. D. Apter. London: Macmillan, 1964, pp. 47–78.

———. *The Interpretation of Culture.* New York: Basic Books, 1973.

Geertz, H. and Keith Thomas. "An Anthropology of Religion and Magic: Two Views". *Journal of Interdisciplinary History* 6 (1975) 71–109.

Genovese, E. *Roll, Jordan, Roll: The World The Slaves Made.* New York: Vintage, 1976.

Gellner, E. "Patrons and Clients". *Patrons and Clients in Mediterranean Societies.* Ed. E. Gellner and J. Waterbury. London: Duckworth, 1977.

Georgi, Dieter. *Remembering the Poor: The History of Paul's Collection for Jerusalem.* Second Edition. Nashville: Abingdon Press, 1992.

Giddens, A. *The Constitution of Society.* Cambridge: Polity Press, 1984.

Gill, David W. J. "Erastus the Aedile". *Tyndale Bulletin* 40 (1989) 293–301.

Gill, David W. J. "The Importance of Roman Portraiture for Head-coverings in 1 Corinthians 11:2–16". *Tyndale Bulletin* 41 (1990) 245–260.

———. "In Search of the Social Élite in the Corinthian Church". *Tyndale Bulletin* 44 (1993) 323–337.

———. "Acts and the Urban Élites". *The Book of Acts in Its First Century Setting: Graeco-Roman Setting.* Ed. David Gill and Conrad Gempf. Carlisle: Paternoster Press, 1994, pp. 105–118.

Gilliam, S. F. "The Plague Under Marcus Aurelius". *American Journal of Philology* 82 (1961) 225–251.

Gilsenan, M. "Against Patron-Client Relations". *Patrons and Clients in Mediterranean Society.* Ed. E. Gellner and J. Waterbury. London: Duckworth, 1977, pp. 167–183.

Ginzburg, Carlo. *The Cheese and the Worms: The Cosmos of a Sixteenth Century Miller.* London: Routledge, 1980.

Goguel, M. *The Primitive Church.* London: Allen & Unwin, 1964.

Goldsmith, Raymond. "An Estimate of the Size and Structure of the National Product of the Early Roman Empire". *Review of Income and Wealth* 30 (1984) 263–288.

Gonzalez, Justo L. *Faith and Wealth: A History of Early Christian Ideas on the Origin, Significance and Use of Money.* San Francisco: Harper & Row, 1990.

Gooch, Peter D. *Dangerous Food: 1 Corinthians 8–10 in Context.* Waterloo: Wilfrid Laurier University Press, 1994.

Goodman, M. *The Ruling Class of Judaea.* Cambridge: Cambridge University Press, 1987.

Goodspeed, E. J. "Phoebe's Letter of Introduction". *Harvard Theology Review* 44 (1951) 55–57.

Gorday, Peter. "Paul in Eusebius and Other Early Christian Literature". *Eusebius, Christianity and Judaism.* Ed. Harold W. Attridge and Gohei Hata. Detroit: Wayne State University Press, 1992, pp. 139–165.

Gordon, Arthur E. *Illustrated Introduction to Latin Epigraphy.* Berkeley: University of California Press, 1983.

Gordon, M. L. "The Nationality of Slaves Under the Early Roman Empire". *Journal of Roman Studies* 14 (1924) 89–111.

Gordon, Richard, M. Beard, J. Reynolds and C. Roueché. "Roman Inscriptions 1986–1990". *Journal of Roman Studies* 83 (1993) 131–158.

Gosden, P. H. *The Friendly Societies in England 1815–1875*. Manchester: Manchester University Press, 1961.

——. *Self-Help: Voluntary Associations in the 19th Century*. London: B. T. Batsford, 1973.

Gotoh, A. "Circumcelliones: The Ideology Behind Their Activities". *Forms of Control and Subordination in Antiquity*. Ed. Toru Yuge and Masaoki Doi. Leiden: E. J. Brill, 1988, pp. 303–311.

Gowers, E. *The Loaded Table*. Oxford: Clarendon Press, 1993.

Grant, Michael. *Saint Paul*. London: Weidenfeld & Nicolson, 1976.

Gratwick, A. S. "Free or Not so Free? Wives and Daughters in the Late Roman Republic". *Marriage and Property*. Ed. E. M. Craik. Aberdeen: Aberdeen University Press, 1984, pp. 30–53.

Green, Henry A. *The Economic and Social Origins of Gnosticism*. Atlanta: Scholars Press, 1985.

Greene, K. *The Archaeology of the Roman Economy*. London: B. T. Batsford, 1986.

——. "Technology and Innovation in Context". *Journal of Roman Archaeology* 7 (1994) 22–33.

Griffin, M. "Urbs Roma, Plebs and Princeps". *Images of Empire*. Ed. L. Alexander. Sheffield: JSOT, 1991, pp. 19–46.

Griffiths, D. R. *The New Testament and the Roman State*. Swansea: John Penry Press, 1976.

Grosheide, F. W. *Commentary on the First Epistle to the Corinthians*. Grand Rapids: Eerdmans, 1972.

Gruen, Erich S. *Studies in Greek Culture and Roman Policy*. Leiden: E. J. Brill, 1990.

Gudeman, S. *Economics as Culture: Models and Metaphors of Livelihood*. London: Routledge & Kegan Paul, 1986.

Guinan, Michael D. *Gospel Poverty: Witness to the Risen Christ*. Ramsey: Paulist Press, 1981.

Gumperz, John H. *Discourse Strategies*. Cambridge: Cambridge University Press, 1982.

Gusfield, J. R. "Moral Passage: The Symbolic Process in Public Designation of Deviance". *Social Problems* 15 (1967) 175–188.

Hadas, M. *Hellenistic Culture*. New York: Columbia University Press, 1969.

Haenchen, E. *The Acts of the Apostles*. Oxford: Basil Blackwell, 1971.

Hahn, F. *The Worship of the Early Church*. Philadelphia: Fortress Press, 1975.

Hall, J. *Lucian's Satire*. New York: Arno Press, 1981.

Halliday, M. A. K. *Language as Social Semiotic: The Social Interpretation of Language and Meaning*. London: Edward Arnold, 1978.

Halperin, R. "Conclusion: A Substantivist Approach to Livelihood". *Peasant Livelihood*. Ed. R. Halperin and J. Dow. New York: St Martin's Press, 1977, pp. 267–297.

Hamel, Gildas. *Poverty and Charity in Roman Palestine, First Three Centuries C.E.* Berkeley: University of California Press, 1990.

Hands, A. R. *Charities and Social Aid in Greece and Rome*. London: Thames & Hudson, 1968.

Hanfmann, G. (Ed.) *Sardis From Prehistory to Roman Times: Results of the Archaeological Excavation of Sardis 1958–1975*. Cambridge, MA: Harvard University Press, 1983.

Hanson, Paul. *The Dawn of Apocalyptic: Historical and Sociological Roots of Jewish Apocalyptic*. Philadelphia: Fortress Press, 1979.

Hardie, A. *Statius and the Silvae: Poets, Patrons and Epideixis in the Graeco-Roman World*. Liverpool: Francis Cairns, 1983.

Harrill, J. Albert. *The Manumission of Slaves in Early Christianity*. Tübingen: J. C. B. Mohr, 1995.

Harris, Gerald. "The Beginnings of Church Discipline: 1 Corinthians 5". *New Testament Studies* 37 (1991) 1-21.

Harris, M. "History and Significance of the Emic/Etic Distinction". *Annual Review of Anthropology* 5 (1976) 329–350.

Harris, William V. "Towards a Study of the Roman Slave Trade". *Seaborne Commerce of Ancient Rome*. Ed. J. D'Arms and E. Kopff. Rome: American Academy in Rome, 1980, pp. 117–140.

———. *Ancient Literacy*. Cambridge, MA: Harvard University Press, 1989.

———. "Between Archaic and Modern: Some Current Problems in the History of the Roman Economy". *The Inscribed Economy: Production and Distribution in the Roman Empire in the Light of Instrumentum Domesticum*. Ed. W. V. Harris. Ann Arbor: University of Michigan Press, 1993, pp. 11–29.

Harrison, John. "The Crisis in Economics and the Economics of Crisis". *New Movements in the Social Sciences and Humanities*. Ed. B. Dufour. London: Maurice Temple Smith, 1982, pp. 32–48.

Hasebroek, J. *Trade and Politics in Ancient Greece*. New York: Biblo & Tannen, 1965.

Hawthorne, Gerald F. *Philippians*. Waco: Word Books, 1983.

Heal, Felicity. *Hospitality in Early Modern England*. Oxford: Clarendon Press, 1990.

Heine, Susan. *Women and Early Christianity*. London: SCM, 1987.

Hemer, Colin J. *The Book of Acts in the Setting of Hellenistic History*. Tübingen: J. C. B Mohr, 1989.

Hendrix, Holland Lee. "Archaeology and Eschatology at Thessalonica". *The Future of Early Christianity*. Ed. Birger A. Pearson. Minneapolis: Fortress Press, 1991, pp. 107–118.

Hengel, Martin. *Property and Riches in the Early Church*. Philadelphia: Fortress Press, 1974.

——. *Judaism and Hellenism*. 2 vols. London: SCM, 1974.

——. *Crucifixion*. London: SCM, 1977.

——. *The Pre-Christian Paul*. London: SCM, 1991.

Hennecke, E. *New Testament Apocrypha*. 2 vols. London: SCM, 1971.

Henretta, J. "Social History as Lived and Written". *American Historical Review* 84 (1979) 1293–1322.

Hermansen, G. "The Population of Imperial Rome". *Historia* 27 (1978) 129–168.

——. *Ostia: Aspects of Roman City Life*. Edmonton: University of Alberta Press, 1981.

Hernandez, Jose Amaro. *Mutual Aid for Survival: The Case of the Mexican American*. Malabar, FL: Robert E. Kreiger, 1983.

Highet, G. *Juvenal the Satirist*. Oxford: Clarendon Press, 1954.

Hill, Clifford. *The Sociology of the New Testament*. Unpublished PhD dissertation: Nottingham University, 1972.

Hill, David. *New Testament Prophecy*. London: Marshall, 1979.

Hill, H. "Roman Revenues from Greece After 146 BC". *Classical Philology* 41 (1946) 38–45.

——. *The Roman Middle-Class in the Republican Period*. Oxford: Basil Blackwell, 1952.

Hill, Michael. *A Sociology of Religion*. London: Heinemann Educational Books, 1973.

Hills, S. L. *Crime, Power and Morality*. London: Chandler, 1971.

Hobsbawm, E. "Friendly Societies". *Amateur Historian* 3 (1957) 98–99.

——. *Primitive Rebels*. Manchester: Manchester University Press, 1959.

—— and G. Rudé. *Captain Swing*. Harmondsworth: Penguin, 1973.

Hobson, Deborah. "Women as Property Owners in Roman Egypt". *Transactions of the American Philological Association* 113 (1983) 311–321.

———. "The Role of Women in the Economic Life of Roman Egypt: A Case Study from First Century Tebtunis". *Echos du monde classique/ Classical Views* 28 (1984) 373–390.

———. "House and Household in Roman Egypt". *Yale Classical Studies* 28 (1984) 211–229.

———. "Towards a Broader Context for the Study of Graeco-Roman Egypt". *Echos du monde classique/Classical Views* 32 (1988) 353–363.

———. "The Impact of Law on Village Life in Roman Egypt". *Law, Politics and Society in the Ancient Mediterranean.* Ed. Baruch Halpern and Deborah Hobson. Sheffield: Sheffield Academic Press, 1993, pp. 193–219.

Hock, R. F. "Simon the Shoemaker as an Ideal Cynic". *Greek, Roman and Byzantine Studies* 17 (1976) 41–53.

———. "Paul's Tentmaking and the Problem of his Social Class". *Journal of Biblical Literature* 97 (1978) 555–564.

———. "The Workshop as a Social Setting for Paul's Missionary Preaching". *Catholic Biblical Quarterly* 41 (1979) 438–450.

———. *The Social Context of Paul's Ministry: Tentmaking and Apostleship.* Philadelphia: Fortress, 1980.

———. "Lazarus and Micyllus: Greco-Roman Backgrounds to Luke 16:19–31". *Journal of Biblical Literature* 106 (1987) 447–463.

Hohlfelder, R. L. "Kenchreai on the Saronic Gulf: Aspects of its Imperial History". *Classical Journal* 76 (1980–1981) 217–226.

———. *Kenchreai, Eastern Port of Corinth, III: Coins.* Leiden: E. J. Brill, 1978.

Holmberg, Bengt. *Paul and Power: The Structure of Authority in the Primitive Church as Reflected in the Pauline Epistles.* Philadelphia: Fortress Press, 1980.

———. *Sociology and the New Testament: An Appraisal.* Philadelphia: Fortress, 1990.

Hopkins, Eric. *Working-Class Self-Help in Nineteenth-Century England.* London: UCL Press, 1995.

Hopkins, Keith. "Élite Mobility in the Roman Empire". *Past and Present* 32 (1965) 12–26.

Hopkins, Keith. "Contraception in the Roman Empire". *Comparative Studies in Society and History* 8 (1966) 124–151.

——. "On the Probable Age Structure of the Roman Population". *Population Studies* 20 (1966) 245–264.

——. *Conquerors and Slaves.* Cambridge: Cambridge University Press, 1978.

——. "Economic Growth of Towns in Classical Antiquity". *Towns in Societies.* Ed. P. Abrams and E. Wrigley. Cambridge: Cambridge University Press, 1978, pp. 35–77.

——. "Rules of Evidence". *Journal of Roman Studies* 68 (1978) 178–186.

——. "Taxes and Trade in the Roman Empire (200 BC – AD 400)". *Journal of Roman Studies* 70 (1980) 101–125.

——. "The Transport of Staples in the Roman Empire". *Trade in Staples in Antiquity.* Ed. P. Garnsey and C. Whittaker. Budapest: Akadémia Kiadó, 1982, pp. 80–87

——. "Introduction". *Trade in the Ancient Economy.* Ed. P. Garnsey, K. Hopkins, and C. R. Whittaker. London: Chatto & Windus, 1983, pp. i-xxv.

——. *Death and Renewal: Sociological Studies in Roman History 2.* Cambridge: Cambridge University Press, 1983.

——. "Graveyard for Historians". *La Mort, Les Morts et L'Au-Delà Dans Le Monde Romain.* Ed. F. Hinard. Caen: Centre de Publications, 1987, pp. 113–126.

——. "Conquest by the Book". *Literacy in the Roman World.* Ed. J. H. Humphrey. Ann Arbor: Journal of Roman Archaeology, 1991, pp. 133–158.

——. "Novel Evidence for Roman Slavery". *Past and Present* 138 (1993) 3–27.

Hopwood, K. "Policing the Hinterland: Rough Cilicia and Isauria". *Armies and Frontiers in Roman and Byzantine Anatolia.* Ed. S. Mitchell. London: B. A. R., 1983, pp. 173–187.

——. "Bandits, Élites and Roman Order". *Patronage in Ancient Society.* Ed. A. Wallace-Hadrill. London: Routledge, 1990, pp. 171–187.

Horbury, William and David Noy (Eds). *Jewish Inscriptions of Graeco-Roman Egypt.* Cambridge: Cambridge University Press, 1992.

Hornsby, H. M. "The Cynicism of Peregrinus Proteus". *Hermathema* 48 (1933) 65–84.

Horrell, David. "Paul's Collection: Resources for a Materialist Theology". *Epworth Review* 22 (1995) 74–83.

Horrell, David. *The Social Ethos of the Corinthian Correspondence: Interests and Ideology from 1 Corinthians to 1 Clement*. Edinburgh: T. & T. Clark, 1996.

Horsfall, N. "Statistics or State of Mind". *Literacy in the Roman World*. Ed. J. H. Humphrey. Ann Arbor: Journal of Roman Archaeology, 1991, pp. 59–76.

Horsley, G. H. R. (Ed.). *New Documents Illustrating Early Christianity*. Volume 4. North Ryde: Macquarrie University Press, 1987.

———. "'How can some of you say that there is no resurrection of the dead?' Spiritual Elitism in Corinth". *Novum Testamentum* 20 (1978) 203–231.

———. "The Sicarii: Ancient Jewish 'Terrorists'". *Journal of Religion* 59 (1979) 435–458.

Horsley,. R. "The Zealots: Their Origin, Relationships, and Importance in the Jewish Revolt". *Novum Testamentum* 27 (1986) 159–192

——— and J. Hanson. *Bandits, Prophets and Messiahs*. Minneapolis: Winston, 1985.

Howell, N. "Toward a Uniformitarian Theory of Human Palaeodemography". *The Demographic Evolution of Human Populations*. Ed. R. H. Ward and K. M. Weiss. London: Academic Press, 1976, pp. 25–40.

Howgego, C. "The Supply and Use of Money in the Roman World 200 BC to AD 300". *Journal of Roman Studies* 82 (1992) 1–31.

———. *Ancient History From Coins*. London: Routledge, 1995.

Hudson, N. A. "Food in Roman Satire". *Satire and Society in Ancient Rome*. Ed. S. Braund. Exeter: Exeter University Press, 1989, pp. 57–76.

Hughes, F. W. *Second Thessalonians as a Document of Early Christian Rhetoric*. Unpublished PhD dissertation: Northwestern University, 1984.

Hull, J. M. *Hellenistic Magic and the Synoptic Tradition*. London: SCM, 1974.

Hunt, E. D. "Travel, Tourism and Piety in the Roman Empire: A Context for the Beginnings of Christian Pilgrimage". *Echos du monde classique/Classical Views* 28 (1984) 391–417.

Hurd, J. C. *The Origins of First Corinthians*. London: SPCK, 1965.

Hyden, G. *Beyond Ujama in Tanzania: Underdevelopment and an Uncaptured Peasantry*. London: Heinemann, 1980.

Isaac, B. "Bandits in Judaea and Arabia". *Harvard Studies in Classical Philology* 88 (1984) 169–203.

Jackson, R. *Doctors and Diseases in the Roman Empire*. London: British Museum Press, 1988.

Jaeger, W. *Christianity and the Greek Paideia*. Cambridge, MA: Harvard University Press, 1961.

Jashemski, W. F. *The Gardens of Pompeii, Herculaneum and the Villas Destroyed by Vesuvius*. New York: Caratzas Bros., 1979.

Jellinek, E. M. "Drinkers and Alcoholics in Ancient Rome". *Journal of Studies on Alcohol* 37 (1976) 1718–1741.

Jeremias, Joachim. *Jerusalem in the Time of Jesus*. London: SCM, 1969.

Jewett, R. "Tenement Churches and Communal Meals in the Early Church: The Implications of a Form-Critical Analysis of 2 Thessalonians 3:10". *Biblical Research* 38 (1993) 23–43.

Johnson, Luke T. *Sharing Possessions: Mandate and Symbol of Faith*. Philadelphia: Fortress Press, 1981.

———. *The Acts of the Apostles*. Collegeville, MN: The Liturgical Press, 1992

Johnson T. and C. Dandeker. "Patronage: Relation and System". *Patronage in Ancient Society*. Ed. A. Wallace-Hadrill. London: Routledge, 1989, pp. 219–242.

Jones, A. H. M. *The Cities of the Eastern Provinces*. Oxford: Clarendon Press, 1937.

———. *The Social and Economic History of the Hellenistic World*. Oxford: Clarendon Press, 1941.

———. "Slavery in the Ancient World". *Slavery in Classical Antiquity*. Ed. M. I. Finley. Cambridge: Heffer and Sons Ltd, 1960, pp. 1–15.

———. *The Greek City From Alexander to Justinian*. Oxford: Clarendon Press, 1966.

———. "The Economic Life of the Towns of the Roman Empire". *The Roman Economy: Studies in Ancient Economic and Administrative History*. Ed. P. A. Brunt. Oxford: Basil Blackwell, 1974.

Jones, Philip. *Studying Society*. London: Collins Educational, 1993.

Jongman, W. *The Economy and Society of Pompeii*. Amsterdam: J. C. Gieben, 1988.

——— and R. Dekker. "Public Intervention in the Food Supply in Pre-Industrial Europe". *Bad Year Economics: Cultural Responses to Risk and Uncertainty*. Ed. P. Halstead and J. O'Shea. Cambridge: Cambridge University Press, 1989, pp. 114–122.

Jory, E. J. "The Early Pantomime Riots". *Maistor: Classical, Byzantine and Renaissance Studies for Robert Browning*. Ed. Ann Moffatt. Canberra: The Australian Association For Byzantine Studies, 1984, pp. 57–66.

Joshel, Sandra P. *Work, Identity and Legal Status at Rome: A Study of the Occupational Inscriptions*. Norman: University of Oklahoma Press, 1992.

Judge, Edwin A. *The Social Pattern of Christian Groups in the First Century*. London: Tyndale Press, 1960.

——. "The Early Christians as a Scholastic Community". *Journal of Religious History* 1 (1960) 4–15 and 125–137.

——. "St Paul and Classical Society". *Jahrbuch für antike und christentum* 15 (1972) 19–36.

——. "Paul as Radical Critic of Society". *Interchange* 16 (1974) 191–203.

——. "The Social Identity of the First Christians: A Question of Method in Religious History". *Journal of Religious History* 11 (1980) 201–217.

——. "Cultural Conformity and Innovation in Paul: Some Clues from Contemporary Documents". *Tyndale Bulletin* 35 (1984) 3–24.

Kampen, Natalie. *Image and Status: Roman Working Women in Ostia*. Berlin: Gebr. Mann, 1981.

Kaplan, D. "The Formal-Substantive Controversy in Economic Anthropology". *Southwestern Journal of Anthropology* 24 (1968) 226–255.

Kaplan, Steven L. (Ed.). *Understanding Popular Culture: Europe from the Middle Ages to the Nineteenth Century*. New York: Moulton Publishers, 1984.

Kautsky, Karl. *Der Ursprung des Christentus*. Hannover: J. H. W. Dietz, 1910.

——. *The Foundations of Christianity*. New York: Russell & Russell, 1953.

Kearsley, R. A. "Asiarchs, Archiereis and Archieriai of Asia: New Evidence From Amorium in Phrygia". *Epigraphica Anatolica* 16 (1990) 69–80.

——. "Women in Public Life". *New Documents Illustrating Early Christianity*. Volume 6. Ed. S. Llewelyn and R. A. Kearsley. North Ryde: Macquarrie University Press, 1992, pp. 24–27.

Keating, J. *The Agape and the Eucharist in the Early Church: Studies in the History of the Christian Love Feasts*. London: Methuen & Co., 1901.

Keck, L. E. "The Poor Among the Saints in the New Testament". *Zeitschrift für neutestamentalich Wissenschaft* 56 (1965) 100–125.

Kee, Howard C. *Christian Origins in Sociological Perspective*. London: SCM, 1980.

——. *Medicine, Miracle, and Magic in New Testament Times*. Cambridge: Cambridge University Press, 1986.

Keenan, James. "Pastoralism in Roman Egypt". *Bulletin of the American Society of Papyrology* 26 (1989) 175–200.

——. "Ancient Literacy". *Ancient History Bulletin* 5 (1991) 101–106.

Keener, C. S. "Man and Woman". *Dictionary of Paul and His Letters*. Ed. G. Hawthorne. Leicester: InterVarsity Press, 1993, pp. 583–592.

Kehoe, Dennis P. "Comparative Approaches to the Social History of Roman Egypt". *Bulletin of the American Society of Papyrologists* 26 (1989) 153–156.

Kelly, C. M. *Corruption and Bureaucracy in the Later Roman Empire*. Unpublished PhD dissertation: Cambridge University, 1993.

Kelly, J. M. *Roman Litigation*. Oxford: Clarendon Press, 1966.

Kennedy, George A. *New Testament Interpretation Through Rhetorical Criticism*. London: University of North Carolina Press, 1984.

Kent, J. H. *Inscriptions 1926–1950: Corinth viii. Part Three*. Princeton: The American School of Classical Studies at Athens, 1966.

Klassen, P. J. *The Economics of Anabaptism 1525–1560*. The Hague: Mouton & Co., 1964.

Klassen, W. "Musonius Rufus, Jesus and Paul: Three First Century Feminists". *From Jesus to Paul*. Ed. Peter Richardson and John Hurd. Waterloo: Wilfrid Laurier University Press, 1984, pp. 185–206.

——. "The Sacred Kiss in the New Testament: An Example of a Social Boundary Line". *New Testament Studies* 39 (1993) 122–135.

Kleberg, T. *Hôtels, Restaurants et Cabarets dans L'Antiquité Romaine*. Uppsala: Almqvist & Wiksells, 1957.

Kleiner, D. E. E. *Roman Group Portraiture: The Funerary Reliefs of the Late Republic and Early Empire*. London: Garland, 1977.

Kloppenborg, John S. "Collegia and *Thiasoi*: Issues in Function, Taxonomy and Membership". *Voluntary Associations in the Greco-Roman World*. Ed. John S. Kloppenborg and Stephen G. Wilson. London: Routledge, 1996, pp. 16–30.

Kluckholn, Richard (Ed.). *Culture and Behavior: Collected Essays of Clyde Kluckholn*. New York: Free Press, 1965.

Knox, J. *Philemon Among the Letters of Paul*. London: Collins, 1960.

Knox, W. L. *Saint Paul and the Church of Jerusalem*. Cambridge: Cambridge University Press, 1925.

Koenig, John. *New Testament Hospitality: Partnership with Strangers as Promise and Mission*. Philadelphia: Fortress Press, 1985.

Koester, H. *History and Literature of Early Christianity*. Volume 2. Philadelphia: Fortress Press, 1982.

—— (Ed.). *Ephesos: Metropolis of Asia. An Interdisciplinary Approach to Its Archaeology, Religion and Culture*. Valley Forge: Trinity Press Int., 1995.

Kraabel, A. "Paganism and Judaism: The Sardis Evidence". *Paganisme, Judaïsme, Christianisme: Influences et affrontements dans le monde antique*. Ed. A. Benoit, et al. Paris: Boccard, 1978, pp. 13–33.

Kraemer, Ross S. *Maenads, Martyrs, Matrons, Monastics: A Sourcebook on Women's Religion in the Greco-Roman World*. Philadelphia: Fortress, 1988.

——. *Her Share of the Blessings: Women's Religions Among Pagans, Jews and Christians in the Greco-Roman World*. Oxford: Oxford University Press, 1992.

Krantz, F. *History From Below: Studies in Popular Protest and Popular Ideology in Honour of George Rudé*. Montreal: Concordia University, 1985.

Kropotkin, Peter. *Mutual Aid*. London: Freedom Press, 1987.

Kuhn, K. G. "The Lord's Supper and the Communal Meal at Qumran", *The Scrolls and the New Testament*. Ed. K. Stendahl. New York: Harper & Brothers, 1958, pp. 65–93.

Kummel, W. G. *Introduction to the New Testament*. London: SCM, 1975.

Kunkel, W. *An Introduction to Roman Legal and Constitutional History*. Oxford: Clarendon Press, 1973.

Kyrtatas, Dimitris J. "Review of W. Meeks, *First Urban Christians*". *Journal of Roman Studies* 75 (1985) 265–267.

Kyrtatas, Dimitris J. *The Social Structure of the Early Christian Communities*. London: Verso, 1987.

Lacey, W. K. *The Family in Classical Greece*. London: Thames & Hudson, 1968.

Lagrange, M.-J. *Saint Paul Épitre Aux Romains*. Paris: J. Gabalda, 1950.

Lampe, P. *Die stadtrömischen Christen in den ersten beiden Jahrhunderten*. Tübingen: J. C. B. Mohr, 1987.

———. "The Roman Christians of Romans 16". *The Romans Debate*. Ed. K. Donfried. Second edition. Edinburgh: T. & T. Clark, 1991, pp. 216–230.

Lange, N. de. "Jewish Attitudes to the Roman Empire". *Imperialism in the Ancient World*. Ed. P. Garnsey and C. Whittaker. Cambridge: Cambridge University Press, 1978, pp. 255–281.

Laslett, P and R. Wall. *Household and Family in Past Time*. Cambridge: Cambridge University Press, 1972.

Lassèr, J. M. *Ubique Populus*. Paris: Centre National de la Recherche et de Scientifique, 1977.

Lattimore, Richmond. *Themes in Greek and Latin Epitaphs*. Urbana: The University of Illinois Press, 1942.

Laurence, Ray. *Roman Pompeii: Space and Society*, London: Routledge, 1994.

———. "The Organization of Space in Pompeii". *Urban Society in Roman Italy*. Ed. T. Cornell and K. Lomas. London: UCL Press, 1995, pp. 63–78.

Lefkowitz, Mary R. and M. B. Fant. *Women's Life in Greece and Rome*. London: Duckworth, 1982.

Leon, Harry J. *The Jews of Ancient Rome*. Philadelphia: The Jewish Publications Society, 1960.

Lenski, G. *Power and Privilege: A Theory of Social Stratification*. New York: McGraw Hill, 1966.

Lentz, John C. *Luke's Portrait of Paul*. Cambridge: Cambridge University Press, 1993.

Levick, Barbara. *Roman Colonies in Southern Asia Minor*. Oxford: Clarendon Press, 1967.

Lewis, Naphtali. *The Interpretation of Dreams and Portents*. Toronto: Samuel Stevens, 1976.

———. *Life in Egypt Under Roman Rule*. Oxford: Clarendon Press, 1983.

Lewis, Naphtali. "The Romanity of Roman Egypt: A Growing Consensus". *Atti del XVII Congresso Internazionale di Papirologia*. Naples: Centro Internazionale per lo studio dei papiri Ercolanesi, 1984, pp. 1077–84.

Lieberman, Saul. *Hellenism in Jewish Palestine*. New York: Jewish Theological Seminary of America, 1950.

Lietzmann, Hans. *A History of the Early Church*. London: Lutterworth, 1963.

——. *Mass and the Lord's Supper: A Study in the History of Liturgy*. Leiden: E. J. Brill, 1979.

Lieu, S. N. C. *Manichaeism in the Later Roman Empire and Medieval China*. Second Edition. Tübingen: J. C. B. Mohr, 1992.

Lightfoot, J. B. *St Paul's Epistle to the Philippians*. London: Macmillan & Co., 1879.

Ligt, L. de. *Fairs and Markets in the Roman Empire*. Amsterdam: J. C. Gieben, 1993.

Lintott, A. *Imperium Romanum*. London: Routledge, 1993.

Llewelyn, S. R. and R. A. Kearsley (Eds). *New Documents Illustrating Early Christianity*. Volume 6. North Ryde: Macquarrie University Press, 1992.

Loane, H. *Industry and Commerce in the City of Rome (50 BC–200 AD)*. Baltimore: Johns Hopkins University Press, 1938.

Lohfink, Gerhard. *Jesus and Community*. London: SPCK, 1985.

Lohse, Eduard. *Colossians and Philemon*. Philadelphia: Fortress Press, 1971.

Loisy, A. *L'Evangile: Selon Luc*. Paris: Nourry, 1924.

Longenecker, R. N. *The Ministry and Message of Paul*. Grand Rapids: Zondervan, 1971.

——. *Paul, Apostle of Liberty*. Grand Rapids: Baker, 1976.

Love, John R. *Antiquity and Capitalism: Max Weber and the Sociological Foundations of Roman Civilisation*. London: Routledge, 1991.

Lüdemann, Gerd. *Paul: Apostle to the Gentiles: Studies in Chronology*. London: SCM, 1984.

Luhmann, N. *The Differentiation of Society*. New York: Columbia University Press, 1982.

Lyall, F. L. "Roman Law in the Writings of Paul: Adoption". *Journal of Biblical Literature* 88 (1969) 458–466.

Lyons, George. *Pauline Autobiography: Toward a New Understanding*. Atlanta: Scholars Press, 1985.

MacCormack, G. "Reciprocity". *Man* 11 (1976) 89–104.

MacDonald, Denis. "Virgins, Widows and Paul in Second Century Asia-Minor". *Society of Biblical Literature 1979 Seminar Papers*. Ed. J. Achtemeier. Missoula, MT: Scholars Press, 1979.

MacDonald, Margaret. *The Pauline Churches: A Socio-Historical Study of Institutionalisation in the Pauline and Deutero-Pauline Writings*. Cambridge: Cambridge University Press, 1988.

MacLean, Guy. *The Sacred Identity of Ephesos*. London: Routledge, 1991.

MacMullen, Ramsey. "Roman Imperial Building in the Provinces". *Harvard Studies in Classical Philology* 64 (1959) 207–235.

——. *Enemies of the Roman Order: Treason, Unrest and Alienation in the Roman Empire*. Cambridge MA: Harvard University Press, 1967.

——. "Social History in Astrology". *Ancient Society* 2 (1971) 105–116.

——. *Roman Social Relations 50 BC to AD 284*. New Haven: Yale University Press, 1974.

——. "Women in Public in the Roman Empire". *Historia* 29 (1980) 208–218.

——. "The Epigraphic Habit in the Roman Empire". *American Journal of Philology* 103 (1982) 233–246.

——. *Corruption and the Decline of Rome*. New Haven: Yale University Press, 1988.

Malherbe, A. J. "The Beasts at Ephesus". *Journal of Biblical Literature* 87 (1968) 71–80.

——. "Gentle as a Nurse". *Novum Testamentum* 12 (1970) 203–217.

——. *Social Aspects of Early Christianity*. Baton Rouge: Louisiana State University Press, 1977.

——. *Ancient Epistolary Theorists*. Atlanta: Scholars Press, 1988.

——. *Paul and the Popular Philosophers*. Philadelphia: Fortress Press, 1989.

——. "Paul's Self-Sufficiency (Phil. 4:11)". *Friendship, Flattery, and Frankness of Speech: Studies on Friendship in the New Testament World*. Ed. J. Fitzgerald. Leiden: E. J. Brill, 1996, pp. 125–139.

Malina, Bruce J. *The New Testament World: Insights From Cultural Anthropology*. London: SCM, 1983.

——. "Wealth and Poverty in the New Testament and Its World". *Interpretation* 41 (1987) 354–381.

—— and Richard R. Rohrbaugh. *Social-Science Commentary on the Synoptic Gospels*. Minneapolis: Fortress Press, 1992.

Manganaro, G. "Graffiti e Iscrizioni Funerarie della Sicilla Orientale". *Helikon* 2 (1962) 485–501.

Mango, Cyril. "Daily Life in Byzantium". *Jahrbuch der Österreichischen Byzantinistik* 31 (1981) 337–353.

Marrou, H. I. *A History of Education in Antiquity*. London: Sheed & Ward, 1956.

Marsh, H. *The Rebel Jew*. London: Skilton & Shaw, 1980.

Marshall, A. J. "The Role of Women in the Roman Civil Courts". *Studies in Latin Literature and Roman History V*. Ed. C. Deroux. Bruxelles: Latomus, 1989, pp. 35–54.

Marshall, I. H. *1 and 2 Thessalonians*. London: Marshall, Morgan & Scott, 1983.

Marshall, P. *Enmity in Corinth: Social Conventions in Paul's Relations with the Corinthians*. Tübingen: J. C. B. Mohr, 1987.

Martin, C. F. "The Rhetorical Function of Commercial Language in Paul's Letter to Philemon (Verse 18)". *Persuasive Artistry*. Ed. D. F. Watson. Sheffield: JSOT Press, 1991, pp. 321–337.

Martin, Dale. *Slavery as Salvation*. New Haven: Yale University Press, 1990.

———. *The Corinthian Body*. New Haven: Yale University Press, 1995.

Martin, R. P. *Worship in the Early Church*. London: Marshall, Morgan, & Scott, 1975.

——— *Colossians and Philemon*. Grand Rapids: Eerdmans, 1981.

———. *2 Corinthians*. Waco: Word Books, 1986.

Marx, Karl. *The German Ideology*. London: Lawrence & Wishart, 1970.

Mason, H. J. *Greek Terms for Roman Institutions*. Toronto: Hakkert, 1974.

Matthews, K. D. "Roman Aqueducts: Technical Aspects of Their Construction". *Expedition* 13 (1970) 2–16.

Mauss, Marcel. *The Gift. Forms and Functions of Exchange in Archaic Societies*. London: Cohen & West, 1954.

Maxey, Mima. *Occupations of the Lower Classes in Roman Society*. Chicago: Chicago University Press, 1938.

Mayer, D. *Playing Out the Empire: Ben-Hur and Other Toga Plays and Films*. Oxford: Oxford University Press, 1994.

Mayerhoff, E. *Der Brief an die Colosser*. Berlin: H. Schultze, 1838.

McCullagh, C. Behan. *Justifying Historical Descriptions*. Cambridge: Cambridge University Press, 1984.

McGinn, T. "The Taxation of Roman Prostitutes". *Helios* 16 (1989) 79–110.

McIntosh, J. *The Woman and the Lyre: Classical Writers in Classical Greece and Rome.* Carbondale: Southern Illinois University Press, 1989.

McKay, A. G. *Houses, Villas and Palaces in the Roman World.* London: Thames & Hudson, 1975.

McLellan, D. *Ideology.* Milton Keynes: Open University Press, 1986.

McNeill, W. H. *Plagues and Peoples.* Harmondsworth: Penguin, 1976.

Mealand, D. L. "Community of Goods and Utopian Allusions in Acts II-IV". *Journal of Theological Studies* 28 (1977) 96–99.

———. *Poverty and Expectation in the Gospels.* London: SPCK, 1980.

———. "The Close of Acts and Its Hellenistic Greek Vocabulary". *New Testament Studies* 36 (1990) 584–587.

Meeks, Wayne. "The Social Context of Pauline Theology". *Interpretation* 36 (1982) 266–277.

———. *The First Urban Christians.* New Haven: Yale University Press, 1983.

———. *The Moral World of the First Christians.* Philadelphia: Westminster Press, 1986.

———. "The Circle of Reference in Pauline Morality". *Greeks, Romans and Christians.* Ed. D. L. Balch et al. Minneapolis: Fortress Press, 1990, pp. 305–317.

——— and Robert L Wilken. *Jews and Christians in Antioch in the First Four Centuries of the Common Era.* Missoula: Scholars Press, 1978.

Meggitt, J. J. "Meat Consumption and Social Conflict in Corinth". *Journal of Theological Studies* 42 (1994) 137–141.

———. "The Social Status of Erastus (Rom. 16:23)". *Novum Testamentum* 38 (1996) 218–223.

———. "Laughing and Dreaming at the Foot of the Cross: Context and Reception of a Religious Symbol". *Journal for the Critical Study of Religion, Ethics and Society* 1 (1996) 9–14.

Meiggs, R. *Roman Ostia.* Oxford: Clarendon Press, 1960.

Meijer, Fik. *A History of Seafaring in the Classical World.* London: Croom Helm, 1986.

——— and Onno van Nijf. *Trade, Transport and Society in the Ancient World: A Sourcebook.* London: Routledge, 1992.

Meikle, Scott. "Modernism, Economics and the Ancient Economy". *Proceedings of the Cambridge Philological Society* 41 (1995) 174–191.

Meinardus, Otto F. A. *St. Paul in Greece*. Sixth edition. Athens: Lycabettus Press, 1992.

Melnyk, George. *The Search For Community: From Utopia to Co-operative Society*. Toronto: Black Rose Books, 1985.

Menken, M. J. J. *2 Thessalonians*. London: Routledge, 1994.

Merton, R. K. *Social Theory and Social Structure*. London: The Free Press, 1957.

Meyer, E. "Explaining the Epigraphic Habit in the Roman Empire". *Journal of Roman Studies* 80 (1990) 74–96.

Mickwitz, G. "Economic Rationalisation in Graeco-Roman Agriculture". *English Historical Review* 52 (1937) 577–589.

Migeotte, Léopold. *L'emprunt public dans les cités Grecques: Recueil des documents et analys critique*. Quebec: Les Éditions du Sphinx, 1984.

Millar, F. "The World of the Golden Ass". *Journal of Roman Studies* 71 (1981) 63–75.

——. "Epigraphy". *Sources for the Study of Ancient History*. Ed. M. Crawford. Cambridge: Cambridge University Press, 1983, pp. 80–135.

——. *The Emperor in the Roman World*. Second edition. London: Duckworth, 1992.

Millet, P. "Patronage and its Avoidance in Classical Athens". *Patronage in Ancient Society*. Ed. Andrew Wallace-Hadrill. London: Routledge, 1989, pp. 15–27.

Mitchell, A. J. "Rich and Poor in the Courts of Corinth: Litigiousness and Status in 1 Corinthians 6.1–11". *New Testament Studies* 39 (1993) 562–586.

Moeller, O. *The Wool Trade of Ancient Pompeii*. Leiden: E. J. Brill, 1976.

Momigliano, A. D. "Greek Culture and the Jews". *The Legacy of Greece*. Ed. M. I. Finley. Oxford: Clarendon Press, 1981, pp. 325–346.

Montgomery, Hugo. "Women and Status in the Greco-Roman World". *Studia Theologica* 43 (1989) 115–124.

Moore, George. *Judaism in the First Centuries of the Christian Era*. Cambridge, MA: Harvard University Press, 1962.

Moretti, L. *Inscriptiones Graecae Urbis Romae I-III*. Roma: Istit. Ital per la Storia Antica, 1968–1979.

Morris, Ian. *Death Ritual and Social Structure in Classical Antiquity.* Cambridge: Cambridge University Press, 1992.

Mossé, Claude. *The Ancient World of Work.* London: Chatto & Windus, 1969.

Motomura, R. "The Practice of Exposing Infants and its Effects on the Development of Slavery in the Ancient World". *Forms of Control and Subordination in Antiquity.* Ed. T. Yuge and M. Doi, Leiden: E. J. Brill, 1988. pp. 410–415.

Mott, Stephen. "The Power of Giving and Receiving: Reciprocity in Hellenistic Benevolence". *Current Issues in Biblical and Patristic Interpretation.* Ed. G. F. Hawthorne. Grand Rapids: Eerdmans, 1975, pp. 60–72.

Moule, C. F. D. *The Birth of the New Testament.* London: A. & C. Black, 1966.

Moxnes, Halvor. *The Economy of the Kingdom.* Philadelphia: Fortress Press, 1988.

Mullins, Terence Y. "Greeting as a New Testament Form". *Journal of Biblical Literature* 87 (1968) 418–426.

Munck, J. *Paul and the Salvation of Mankind.* London: SCM, 1959.

Murchie, D. "The New Testament View of Wealth Accumulation". *Journal of Theological Studies* 21 (1978) 335–344.

Murphy-O'Connor, J. *Paul on Preaching.* London: Sheed & Ward, 1964.

——. *St Paul's Corinth: Texts and Archaeology.* Wilmington, DE: Michael Glazier, 1983.

——. "Interpolations in 1 Corinthians". *Catholic Biblical Quarterly* 48 (1986) 81–94.

——. *Paul: A Critical Life.* Oxford: Clarendon Press, 1996.

Murray, Oswyn. "Introduction". *Bread and Circuses.* By Paul Veyne. London: Penguin, 1990, pp. vii–xxii.

Neave, David. *Mutual Aid in the Victorian Countryside, 1830–1914.* Hull: University of Hull Press, 1991.

Neeve, P. W. "A Roman Landowner and His Estates: Pliny the Younger". *Athenaeum* 68 (1990) 363–402

Neusner, J. *The Rabbinic Traditions about the Pharisees before 70.* 3 vols. Leiden: E. J. Brill, 1971.

——. *The Economics of the Mishnah.* Chicago: The University of Chicago Press, 1990.

Newbold, R. F. "Social Tension at Rome in the Early Years of Tiberius' Reign". *Athenaeum* 52 (1974) 110–143.

Neyrey, Jerome H. *Paul in Other Words: A Cultural Reading of His Letters.* Louisville: Westminster/John Knox Press, 1990.

Nicholas, Barry. *An Introduction to Roman Law.* Oxford: Oxford University Press, 1962.

Nickle, Keith F. *The Collection: A Study in Paul's Strategy.* London: SCM Press, 1966.

Nielsen, T. H., L. Bjertrup, M. Hansen, L. Rubinstein and T. Vestergaard. "Athenian Grave Monuments and Social Class". *Greek, Roman and Byzantine Studies* 30 (1989) 411–420.

Nippel, W. "Policing Rome". *Journal of Roman Studies* 74 (1984) 20–29.

——. *Public Order in Ancient Rome.* Cambridge: Cambridge University Press, 1995.

Nisbet, Robert. "Kinship and Political Power in First Century Rome". *The Social Organization of the Law.* Ed. D. Black and M. Mileski. London: Seminar Press, 1973, pp. 262–272.

Nock, A. D. "The Vocabulary of the New Testament". *Journal of Biblical Literature* 52 (1933) 131–139.

Nording, J. G. "Onesimus Fugitivus: A Defense of the Runaway Slave Hypothesis in Philemon". *Journal for the Study of the New Testament* 41 (1991) 97–119.

North, J. A. "Religion and Rusticity". *Urban Society in Roman Italy.* Ed. T. Cornell and K. Lomas. London: UCL Press, 1995, pp. 135–152.

Nutton, Vivian (Ed.). *Galen: Problems and Prospects.* London: Wellcome Institute for the History of Medicine, 1981.

——. "Galen and the Traveller's Fare". *Food in Antiquity.* Ed. J. Wilkins, D. Harvey and M. Dobson. Exeter: Exeter University Press, 1995, pp. 359–369.

Ober, J. *Mass and Élite in Democratic Athens: Rhetoric, Ideology and the Power of the People.* Princeton: Princeton University Press, 1989.

O'Brien, P. T. *Colossians, Philemon.* Waco: Word Books, 1982.

——. "Letter to the Colossians". *Dictionary of Paul and His Letters.* Ed. G. Hawthorne. Leicester: InterVarsity Press, 1993, pp. 147–153.

Oertel, F. "The Economic Unification of the Mediterranean Region: Industry, Trade and Commerce". *The Cambridge Ancient History.* Volume 10. Ed. S. Cook, F. Adcock, M. Charlesworth. Cambridge: Cambridge University Press, 1971, pp. 382–424.

Ohrenstein, A and Barry Gordon. *Economic Analysis in Talmudic Literature: Rabbinic Thought in the Light of Modern Economics.* Leiden: E. J. Brill, 1992.

Okamura, L. "Social Disturbances in Late Roman Gaul: Deserters, Rebels and Baguadae". *Forms of Control and Subordination in Antiquity.* Ed. Toru Yuge and Masaoki Doi. Leiden: E. J. Brill, 1988, pp. 288–302.

Okorie, A. and M. E. Obeta. "Nigerian Traditional Mutual Aid Societies and Their Compatibility with Modern Cooperatives". *Journal of Rural Cooperation* 14 (1986) 107–118.

Oleson, J. P. *Greek and Roman Mechanical Water-Lifting Devices: The History of a Technology.* Toronto: Unversity of Toronto Press, 1984.

Omanson, R. "Acknowledging Paul's Quotations". *The Bible Translator* 43 (1992) 201–213.

O'Neill, J. C. *Paul's Letter to the Romans.* Harmondsworth: Penguin, 1975.

Orr, D. G. "Roman Domestic Religion: The Evidence of Household Shrines". *Aufstieg und Niedergang der römischen Welt.* Volume 2.16.2. Ed. H. Temporini and W. Haase. Berlin: Walter de Gruyter, 1978, pp. 1557–1591.

Orr, W. F. and J. A. Walther. *1 Corinthians.* New York: Doubleday, 1976.

Osborne, C. "Ancient Vegetarianism". *Food in Antiquity.* Ed. J. Wilkins, D. Harvey and M. Dobson. Exeter: Exeter University Press, 1995, pp. 214–224.

Osiek, Carolyn. *Rich and Poor in the Shepherd of Hermas.* Washington: Catholic Biblical Association of America, 1983.

——. *What Are They Saying about the Social Setting of the New Testament?* New York: Paulist Press, 1984.

Oster, R. E. "When Men Wore Veils to Worship: The Historical Contexts of 1 Corinthians 11:4". *New Testament Studies* 34 (1988) 481–505.

——. "Use, Misuse and Neglect of Archaeological Evidence in Some Modern Works on 1 Corinthians". *Zeitschrift für neutestamentalich Wissenschaft* 83 (1992) 52–73.

Ostrow, S. E. "The *Augustales* in the Augustan Scheme". *Between Republic and Empire: Interpretations of Augustus and His Principate.* Ed. K. A. Raaflaub and M. Toher. Berkeley: University of California Press, 1990, pp. 364–379.

Overman, J. A. "Who Were the First Urban Christians? Urbanization in Galilee in the First Century". *Society of Biblical Literature Seminar Papers 1988*. Ed. D. Lull. Atlanta: Scholars Press, 1988, pp. 160–168.

———. "Recent Advances in the Archaeology of Galilee in the Roman Period". *Currents in Research: Biblical Studies* 1 (1993) 35–57.

Owens, E. J. "Residential Districts". *Roman Domestic Buildings*. Ed. Ian M. Barton. Exeter: Exeter University Press, pp. 7–32.

Packer, J. E. "Housing and Population in Imperial Ostia and Rome". *Journal of Roman Studies* 57 (1967) 80–95.

———. "Middle and Lower Class Housing in Pompeii and Herculaneum: A Preliminary Survey". *Neue Forschungen in Pompeji*. Ed. B. Andreae and H. Kyrieleis. Recklinghausen: Anurel Bongers, 1975, pp. 133–142.

Pagels, Elaine. "Christian Apologists and 'The Fall of the Angels': An Attack on Roman Imperial Power". *Harvard Theological Review* 78 (1985) 301–325.

Pallas, D. I., S. Charitonidis, and J. Venencie. "Inscription Lyciennes Trouvées à Solômos près de Corinth". *Bulletin de correspondance héllenique* 83 (1959) 496–508.

Parkin, T. *Demography and Roman Society*. Baltimore: Johns Hopkins University Press, 1992.

Parry, Reginald St John. *The First Epistle of Paul the Apostle to the Corinthians*. Cambridge: Cambridge University Press, 1926.

Parsons, T. and N. Smelser. *Economy and Society*. Glencoe, NY: The Free Press, 1964.

Paynter, R. and R. McGuire, "The Archaeology of Inequality: Material Culture, Domination and Resistance". *The Archaeology of Inequality*. Ed. R. McGuire and R. Paynter. Oxford: Blackwell, 1991, pp. 1–27.

Peacock, D. P. and D. F. Williams. *Amphorae and the Roman Economy: An Introductory Guide*. London: Longman, 1986.

Pearse, J. L. *The Organisation of Roman Building During the Late Republic and Early Empire*. Unpublished PhD dissertation: Cambridge University, 1974.

Penn, R. G. *Medicine on Ancient Greek and Roman Coins*. London: Seaby, 1994.

Pestman, P. W. *The Papyrological Primer*. Sixth edition. Leiden: E. J. Brill, 1990.

Philips, C. R. "Nullum Crimen Sine Lege: Socioreligious Sanctions on Magic". *Magika Hiera: Ancient Greek Magic and Religion*. Ed. Christopher A. Faraone and Dirk Obbink. Oxford: Oxford University Press, 260–276.

Piggott, Stuart. *Wagon, Chariot and Carriage: Symbol and Status in the History of Transport*. London: Thames & Hudson, 1992.

Pitt-Rivers, J. "The Law of Hospitality". *The Fate of Shechem*. Cambridge: Cambridge University Press, 1977, pp. 94–112.

Plank, K. A. *Paul and the Irony of Affliction*. Atlanta: Scholars Press, 1987.

Plassard, J. *Le concubinat romain sous le Haut Empire*, Paris: Librairie de la Société du Recueil Sirey, 1921.

Pleket, H. W. *Epigraphica II: Texts on the Social History of the Greek World*. Leiden: E. J. Brill, 1968.

——. "Greek Epigraphy and Comparative History: Two Case Studies". *Epigraphica Anatolica* 12 (1982) 25–37.

——. "Urban Élites and Business". *Trade in the Ancient Economy*. Ed. P. Garnsey, K. Hopkins, and C. R. Whittaker. London: Chatto & Windus, 1983, pp. 131–144.

——. "Labour and Unemployment in the Roman Empire: Some Preliminary Remarks". *Soziale Randgruppen und Außenseiter im Altertum*. Ed. I. Weiler. Graz: Leykam, 1988. pp. 267–276.

Plummer, Alfred. *A Critical and Exegetical Commentary on the Second Epistle of St Paul to the Corinthians*. Edinburgh: T. & T. Clark, 1915.

Polanyi, Karl. *The Great Transformation*. Boston: Beacon Press, 1944.

——. "The Economy as Instituted Process". *Trade and Markets in the Early Empires*. Ed. Karl Polanyi, Conrad Arensberg and Harry W. Pearson. Glencoe, NY: The Free Press, 1958, pp. 243–270.

——. *Primitive, Archaic and Modern Economies: Essays of Karl Polanyi*. Ed. G. Dalton. Boston: Beacon Press, 1968.

——. *The Livelihood of Man*. Ed. H. W. Pearson. London: Academic Press, 1977.

Polhill, John B. *The New American Commentary: Acts*. Nashville: Broadman Press, 1992.

Pollard, Sidney. "Nineteenth-Century Co-operation: From Community Building to Shopkeeping". *Essays in Labour History*. Ed. Asa Briggs and John Saville. London: Macmillan, 1967, pp. 74–112.

Pomeroy, A. J. "Status and Status-Concern in the Greco-Roman Dream Books". *Ancient Society* 22 (1991) 51–74.

Pomeroy, Sarah. *Goddesses, Whores, Wives and Slaves*. London: Robert Hale, 1976.

Porter, Stanley E. *Idioms of the Greek New Testament*. Sheffield: JSOT Press, 1992.

———. "The Theoretical Justification for Application of Rhetorical Categories to Pauline Epistolary Literature". *Rhetoric and the New Testament*. Ed. S. Porter and T. Olbricht. Sheffield: JSOT Press, 1994, pp. 100–122.

Prattis, J. "Alternative Views of Economy in Economic Anthropology". *Beyond the New Economic Anthropology*. Ed. J. Clammer. London: Macmillan, 1987, pp. 8–44.

Preisigke, F. *Namenbuch*. Heidelberg: Herausgebers, 1922.

Price, S. R. F. "From Noble Funerals to Divine Cult: The Consecration of the Roman Emperor". *Rituals of Royalty, Power, and Ceremonial in Traditional Societies*. Ed. D. Cannadine and S. Price. Cambridge: Cambridge University Press, 1987, pp. 56–105.

Proudhon, P. J. *Qu'est-ce que la propriété?* Paris: Garnier Flammarion, 1940.

Pryer, Jane and N. Cook. *Cities of Hunger. Urban Malnutrition in Developing Countries*. Oxford: Oxfam, 1988.

Purcell, Nicholas. "The Roman Garden as a Domestic Building". *Roman Domestic Buildings*. Ed. Ian M. Barton. Exeter: Exeter University Press, 1996, pp. 121–151.

Rainbird, J. S. "The Fire Stations of Imperial Rome". *Papers of the British School at Rome* 54 (1986) 147–169.

Rajak, Tessa and David Noy. "Archisynagogoi: Office, Title and Social Status in the Greco-Jewish Synagogue". *Journal of Roman Studies* 83 (1993) 75–93.

Ramsay, W. M. *St Paul the Traveller and the Roman Citizen*. London: Hodder & Stoughton, 1895.

———. *The Church in the Roman Empire Before AD 170*. London: Hodder & Stoughton, 1907.

Raper, R. A. "The Analysis of the Urban Structure of Pompeii: a Sociological Examination of Land Use (Semi-Micro)". *Spatial Archaeology*. Ed. D. L. Clarke. London: Academic Press, 1977, pp. 189–221.

———. "Pompeii: Planning and Social Implications". *Space, Hierarchy. and Society: Interdisciplinary Studies in Social Area Analysis*. Ed. B. C. Burnham and J. Kingsbury. Oxford: BAR, 1979, pp. 137–148.

Rapske, Brian. *The Book of Acts in its First Century Setting. Volume 3: Paul in Roman Custody*. Carlisle: Paternoster Press, 1994.

Rawson, Beryl. "Family Life Among the Lower Classes at Rome in the First Two Centuries of the Empire". *Classical Philology* 61 (1966) 75–83.

———. "Roman Concubinage and Other De Facto Marriages". *Transactions of the American Philological Association* 104 (1974) 279–305.

———. *The Family in Ancient Rome*. London: Croom Helm, 1986.

Reale, Giovanni. *The Systems of the Hellenistic Age*. Albany: State University of New York, 1985.

Reed, Mick. "'The Lord Does Combination Love': Religion and Co-operation Amongst a Peculiar People". *New Views of Co-operation*. Ed. S. Yeo. London: Routledge, 1988, pp. 73–87.

Reekmans, T. "Prosperity and Security in the Historia Augusta". *Ancient Society* 10 (1979) 239–270.

Rees, B. R. *The Letters of Pelagius and His Followers*. Woodbridge: Boydell Press, 1991.

Reimer, Ivoni Richter. *Women in the Acts of the Apostles: A Feminist Liberation Perspective*. Philadelphia: Fortress, 1995.

Reinhold, M. "On Status Symbols in the Ancient World". *Classical Journal* 64 (1969) 300–304.

———. *History of Purple as a Status Symbol in Antiquity*. Bruxelles: Latomus, 1970.

———. "The Usurpation of Status and Status Symbols in the Roman Empire". *Historia* 20 (1971) 275–302.

Rex, J. *Race Relations and Social Theory*. London: Wiedenfeld & Nicolson, 1970.

Reynolds, J. "Cities". *The Administration of the Roman Empire*. Ed. D. Braund. Exeter: Exeter University Press, 1988, pp. 15–51.

———. "Roman Inscriptions 1981–1985". *Journal of Roman Studies* 76 (1986) 124–145.

——— and R. Tannenbaum. *Jews and Godfearers at Aphrodisias*. Cambridge: Cambridge Philological Society, 1986.

Reynolds, P. K. *The Vigiles of Imperial Rome*. Oxford: Oxford University Press, 1926.

Rich, A. N. "The Cynic Conception of AUTARKEIA". *Mnemsoyne* 9 (1956) 23–29.

Richards, E. R. *The Secretary in the Letters of Paul*. Tübingen: J. C. B. Mohr, 1991.

Richter, Philip J. "Recent Sociological Approaches to the Study of the New Testament". *Religion* 14 (1984) 77–90.

Rigaux, B. *Saint Paul, Les Épîtres aux Thessaloniciens*. Paris: J. Gabalda, 1956.

Riggs, John W. "From Gracious Table to Sacramental Elements: The Tradition History of Didache 9 and 10". *Second Century* 4 (1984) 83–101.

Robbins, Lionel. "The Subject Matter of Economics". *An Essay on the Nature and Significance of Economic Science*. Second edition. London: Macmillan, 1935, pp. 1–23.

Robert, Louis. "De Cilicie à Messine et à Plymouth". *Journal des Savants* Jul-Sep (1972) 161–211.

Robertson, A. and A. Plummer. *The First Epistle of St Paul to the Corinthians*. New York: Scribners & Sons, 1911.

Robinson, J. A. T. *The Body: A Study in Pauline Theology*. London: SCM Press, 1953.

Robinson, O. "The Water Supply of Rome". *Studia et Documenta Historiae et Iuris* 46 (1980) 207–235.

———. *Ancient Rome: City Planning and Administration*. London: Routledge, 1994.

———. *Roman Criminal Law*. London: Duckworth, 1995.

Rodd, Cyril S. "Sociology and Social Anthropology". *A Dictionary of Biblical Interpretation*. Ed. R. J. Coggins and J. L. Houlden. London: SCM Press, 1990, pp. 635–639.

Rogers, Guy MacLean. *The Sacred Identity of Ephesos: Foundation Myths of a Roman City*. London: Routledge, 1991.

Rohrbaugh, R. L. "The Pre-Industrial City in Luke Acts: Urban Social Relations". *The Social World of Luke Acts: Models for Interpretation*. Ed. J. H. Neyrey, Peabody, MA: Hendrickson, 1991, pp. 125–149.

Romaine, Suzanne. *Language in Society: An Introduction to Socio-linguistics*. Oxford: Oxford University Press, 1994.

Romaniuk, K. "Was Phoebe in Romans 16:1 a Deaconess?" *Zeitschrift für die neuetestamentliche Wissenschaft* 81 (1990) 132–134.

Röring, C. W. *Untersuchungen zu römischen Reisewagen*. Koblenz: Numismatischer Verlag Forneck, 1983.

Rosner, Brian. *Paul, Scripture and Ethics: A Study of 1 Corinthians 5–7*. Leiden: E. J. Brill, 1994.

Rostovtzeff, M. *The Social and Economic History of the Roman Empire*. 2 vols. Oxford: Oxford University Press, 1957.

Roueché, Charlotte. *Performers and Partisans at Aphrodisias in the Roman and Late Roman Periods*. London: The Society for the Promotion of Roman Studies, 1993.

Rowland, Christopher. "Reading the New Testament Sociologically: An Introduction". *Theology* 88 (1985) 358–364.

——. *Christian Origins*. London: SPCK, 1985.

——. *Radical Christianity*. Cambridge: Polity Press, 1988.

Royden, H. L. *The Magistrates of The Roman Professional Collegia in Italy From the First to the Third Century A. D.* Pisa: Giardini, 1988.

Rubin, Zeev. "Mass Movements in Late Antiquity". *Leaders and Masses in the Roman World*. Ed. I. Malkin and Z. W. Rubinsohn. Leiden: E. J. Brill, 1995, pp. 129–187.

Rudd, N. *Themes in Roman Satire*. London: University of Oklahoma Press, 1986.

Rudé, G. *The Crowd in History: A Study of Popular Disturbances in England and France*. London: Lawrence & Wishart, 1964

——. *Ideology and Popular Protest*. London: Lawrence & Wishart, 1980.

Ruef, John. *Paul's First Letter to Corinth*. Harmondsworth: Penguin, 1971.

Ruether, R. R. *Faith and Fratricide*. New York: The Seabury Press, 1979.

Runciman, Steven. *The Medieval Manichee*. Cambridge: Cambridge University Press, 1947.

Runciman, W. *A Treatise on Social Theory 1: The Methodology of Social Theory*. Cambridge: Cambridge University Press, 1983.

Russell, R. "The Idle in 2 Thes 3: 6–12: An Eschatological or a Social Problem". *New Testament Studies* 34 (1988) 105–119.

Safrai, S. and M. Stern. *Compendium Rerum Iudaicarum Ad Novum Testamentum*. Assen: Van Gorcum, 1974.

Sahlins, Marshall. *Stone Age Economics*. London: Tavistock Publications, 1974.

Saldarini, A. J. "The Social Class of Pharisees in Mark". *The Social World of Formative Christianity and Judaism*. Ed. J. Neusner. Philadelphia: Fortress, 1988, pp. 69–77.

——. *Pharisees, Scribes and Sadducees*. Edinburgh: T. & T. Clark, 1989.

Saller, Richard P. "Anecdotes as Historical Evidence for the Principate". *Greece and Rome* 27 (1980) 69–83.

—— *Personal Patronage under the Roman Empire*. Cambridge: Cambridge University Press, 1982.

Saller, Richard P. "Familia, Domus, and the Roman Conception of the Family". *Phoenix* 38 (1984) 336–355.

———. "Patria Potestas and the Stereotype of the Roman Family". *Continuity and Change* 1 (1986) 7–22.

———. "Slavery and Roman Family". *Slavery and Abolition* 8 (1987) 65–87.

———. "Men's Age at Marriage and Its Consequences in the Roman Family". *Classical Philology* 82 (1987) 21–34.

———. "Patronage and Friendship in Early Imperial Rome". *Patronage in Ancient Society*. Ed. A. Wallace-Hadrill. London: Routledge, 1990, pp. 49–62.

———. Review of Donald Engels, *Roman Corinth: An Alternative Model for the Classical City*. *Classical Philology* 86 (1991) 351–357.

———. "Roman Heirship Strategies in Principle and in Practice". *The Family in Italy from Antiquity to the Present*. Ed. D. Kertzer and R. Saller. New Haven: Yale University Press, 1991, pp. 26–47.

——— and Shaw, B. "Tombstones and Roman Family Relations in the Principate: Civilians, Soldiers and Slaves". *Journal of Roman Studies* 74 (1984) 124–156.

Sampley, J. P. "Societas Christi: Roman Law and Paul's Conception of Christian Community". *God's Christ and His People*. Ed. W. Meeks and J. Jervell. Oslo: Oslo University Press, 1977, pp. 158–174.

———. *Pauline Partnership in Christ: Christian Community and Commitment in the Light of Roman Law*. Philadelphia: Fortress, 1980.

Sanders, E. P. *Paul and Palestinian Judaism*. London: SCM Press, 1977.

———. *Paul*. Oxford: Oxford University Press, 1991.

———. *Judaism: Practice and Belief 63 BCE–66 CE*. London: SCM Press, 1992.

Sänger, D. "Die dynatoi in 1 Kor 1,26". *Zeitschrift für die neutestamentliche Wissenschaft* 76 (1985) 285–291.

Scarborough, John. *Roman Medicine*. Ithaca, NY: Cornell University Press, 1969.

Schaps, David. *Economic Rights of Women in Ancient Greece*. Edinburgh: Edinburgh University Press, 1979.

Schmidt, Thomas E. *Hostility to Wealth in the Synoptic Gospels*. Sheffield: JSOT Press, 1987.

Schneider, H. K. *Economic Man*. New York: The Free Press, 1974.

———. *Livestock and Equality in East Africa: The Economic Basis for Social Structure*. Bloomington: Indiana University Press, 1979.

Schöllgen, Georg. "Was wissen wir über die Sozialstruktur der paulinschen Gemeinden?" *New Testament Studies* 34 (1988) 71–82.

Schottroff, Luise. "Human Solidarity and the Goodness of God: The Parable of the Workers in the Vineyard". *God of the Lowly*. Ed. W. Schottroff and W. Stegemann, Maryknoll: Orbis, 1984, pp. 129–147.

———. *Befreiungserfahrungen: Studien zur Sozialgeschichte des Neuen Testaments*. München: Ch. Kaiser, 1990, pp. 247–256.

Schrage, W. *Der erste Brief an die Korinther*. Zurich: Benzinger, 1991.

Schreiner, K. "Zur biblischen Legitimation des Adels: Auslegungsgeschichtliche Studien zum 1. Kor 1,26–29". *Zeitschrift für Kirkengeschichte* 85 (1974) 317–347.

Schulz, D. "Einleitung in das neue Testament". *Theologische Studien und Kritiken* 2 (1829) 563–636.

Schürer, Emil. *The History of the Jewish People in the Age of Jesus Christ*. Volume 2. Revised edition. Ed. G. Vermes, F. Millar, and M. Black. Edinburgh: T. & T. Clark, 1979.

Schweitzer, A. *The Mysticism of Paul the Apostle*. New York: H. Holt, 1931.

Schweizer, E. *Church Order in the New Testament*. London: SCM Press, 1961.

Scobie, A. "Slums, sanitation, and mortality in the Roman World". *Klio* 68 (1986) 399–433.

Scott, James. "Patronage or Exploitation?" *Patrons and Clients*. Ed. E. Gellner and J. Waterbury. London: Duckworth, 1977, pp. 21–39.

Scroggs, Robin. "The Sociological Interpretation of the New Testament: The Present State of Research". *New Testament Studies* 26 (1980) 164–179.

Seccombe, D. "Was There Organized Charity in Jerusalem Before the Christians?" *Journal of Theological Studies* 29 (1978) 140–143.

Seeley, David. "The Background of the Philippians Hymn (2:6–11)". *Journal of Higher Criticism* 1 (1994) 49–72.

Segal, Alan F. *Paul the Convert: The Apostolate and Apostasy of Saul the Pharisee*. New Haven: Yale University Press, 1990.

Segal, Erich. *Roman Laughter: The Comedy of Plautus*. Second edition. Oxford: Oxford University Press, 1987.

Sen, Amartya. *Poverty and Famines: An Essay On Entitlement*. Oxford: Oxford University Press, 1981.

Sharpe, J. "History From Below". *New Perspectives on Historical Writing*. Ed. Peter Burke. Cambridge: Polity Press, 1991, pp. 24–41.

Shaw, B. D. "Social Sciences and Ancient History". *Helios* 9 (1982) 17–57.

———. "Among the Believers". *Echos du monde classique/Classical Views* 28 (1984) 453–479.

———. "Latin Funerary Epigraphy and Family Life in the Later Roman Empire". *Historia* 33 (1984) 457–497.

———. "The Age of Roman Girls at Marriage: Some Reconsiderations". *Journal of Roman Studies* 77 (1987) 30–46.

———. "The Cultural Meaning of Death. Age and Gender in the Roman Family". *The Family in Italy from Antiquity to the Present*. Ed. D. Kertzer and R. Saller. New Haven: Yale University Press, 1991, pp. 66–90.

Shear, T. L. "Excavations in the Theatre District and Tombs of Corinth in 1929". *American Journal of Archaeology* 33 (1929) 515–546

Shelton, J. *As the Romans Did: A Sourcebook in Roman Social History*. Oxford: Oxford University Press, 1988.

Sherwin-White, A. N. *Roman Society and Roman Law in the New Testament*. Oxford: Clarendon Press, 1963.

———. *The Roman Citizenship*. Oxford: Oxford University Press, 1974.

———. *Racial Prejudice in Imperial Rome*. Cambridge: Cambridge University Press, 1976.

Silverman, S. "Patronage as Myth". *Patrons and Clients in Mediterranean Societies*. Ed. E. Gellner and J. Waterbury, London: Duckworth, 1977, 7–19.

Simon, H. A. *Adminstrative Behaviour*. Third edition. New York: Free Press, 1976.

Sippel, D. V. "Dietary Deficiency Among the Lower Classes of Late Republican and Early Imperial Rome". *The Ancient World* 16 (1987) 47–54.

Sjoberg, G. *The Pre-Industrial City*. Glencoe, NY: The Free Press, 1960.

Slim, Hédi. "Les Amphithéâtres d'El-Jem". *Académie des Inscriptions & Belles-Lettres* 3 (1986) 440–469.

———. *El-Jem: Ancient Thysdrus*. Tunis: Alif, 1996.

Smallwood, Mary E. *The Jews Under Roman Rule: From Pompey to Diocletian.* Leiden: E. J. Brill, 1979.

Smith, J. Z. "The Social Description of Early Christianity". *Religious Studies Review* 1 (1975) 19–25.

Smith, M. "Pauline Worship as Seen by Pagans". *Harvard Theological Review* 73 (1980) 245–249.

Snowden, Frank M. *Blacks in Antiquity.* Cambridge MA: Belknap Press, 1976.

———. *Before Color Prejudice: The Ancient View of Blacks.* Cambridge, MA: Harvard University Press, 1983.

Soler, Jean. "The Semiotics of Food in the Bible". *Food and Drink in History.* Ed. Robert Foster and Orest Ranum. Baltimore: Johns Hopkins University Press, 1979.

Solin, Heikki. *Die greichischen Personennamen in Rom: Ein Namenbuch.* 3 vols. Berlin: Walter De Gruyter and Co., 1982.

South, James T. *Disciplinary Practices in Pauline Texts.* Lewiston: Edwin Mellen Press, 1992.

Spawforth, A. J. "Agonistic Festivals in Roman Greece". *The Greek Renaissance in the Roman Empire.* Ed. S. Walker and A. Cameron. London: Institute of Classical Studies, 1989, pp. 193–197.

———. "Roman Corinth and the Ancient Urban Economy". *Classical Review* 42 (1992) 119–120.

Speidel, M. P. "The Soldier's Servants". *Ancient Society* 20 (1989) 239–247.

———. "The Police Officer, a Hero. An Inscribed Relief From Near Ephesos". *Epigraphica Anatolica* 5 (1985) 159–160.

Stählin, Gustav. "ἴσος, ἰσότης, ἰσότιμος". *Theological Dictionary of the New Testament.* Volume 3. Ed. G. Kittel and G. Friedrich. Grand Rapids: Eerdmans, 1965, pp. 345–483.

———. "χήρα". *Theological Dictionary of the New Testament.* Volume 9. Ed. G. Kittel and G. Friedrich. Grand Rapids: Eerdmans, 1974, pp. 440–465.

Stambaugh John and D. Balch, *The Social World of the First Christians.* London: SPCK, 1986.

———. *The Ancient Roman City.* Baltimore: Johns Hopkins University Press, 1989.

Stanfield, J. R. *The Economic Thought of Karl Polanyi: Lives and Livelihood.* London: Macmillan, 1986.

Stark, Rodney. *The Rise of Christianity: A Sociologist Reconsiders History*. Princeton: Princeton University Press, 1996.

Stayer, J. M. *The German Peasants War and Anabaptist Community of Goods*. Montreal: McGill-Queen's University Press, 1991.

Ste. Croix, G. E. M. de. "Suffragium: from Vote to Patronage". *British Journal of Sociology* 5 (1954) 33–40.

———. "Early Christian Attitudes to Property and Slavery". *Church, Society and Politics*. Oxford: Basil Blackwell, 1975, pp. 1–38.

———. *Class Struggle in the Ancient Greek World*. London: Duckworth, 1981.

Stegemann, W. "War der Apostel Paulus ein römischen Bürger?" *Zeitschrift für die neutestamentliche Wissenschaft* 78 (1987) 200–229.

Steinem, Gloria. *If Women Counted: A New Feminist Economics*. San Francisco: Harper & Row, 1988.

Stephens, Susan and John J. Winkler (Eds) *Ancient Greek Novels: The Fragments*. Princeton: Princeton University Press, 1995.

Stern, Menahem. *Greek and Latin Authors on Jews and Judaism. Part One: From Herodotus to Plutarch*. Leiden: E. J. Brill, 1974.

———. "The Jews in Greek and Latin Literature". *Compendum Rerum Iudaicarum ad Novum Testamentum*. Ed. S. Safrai and M. Stern. Philadelphia: Fortress Press, 1976, pp. 1101–1159.

Stevenson, John. *Popular Disturbances in England 1700–1870*. London: Longman, 1979.

Stevenson, T. R. "The Ideal Benefactor and Father Analogy in Greek and Roman Thought". *Classical Quarterly* 42 (1992) 421–436.

Stillwell, R. *The Theatre: Corinth ii*. Princeton: The American School of Classical Studies at Athens, 1962.

Storey, John. *An Introductory Guide to Cultural Theory and Popular Culture*. London: Harvester Wheatsheaf, 1993.

Stowers, Stanley K. *The Diatribe and Paul's Letter to the Romans*. Atlanta: Scholars Press, 1981.

———. "Social Status, Public Speaking and Private Teaching: The Circumstances of Paul's Preaching Activity". *Novum Testamentum* 26 (1984) 59–82.

———. "Diatribe". *Greco-Roman Literature and the New Testament*. Ed. D. E. Aune. Atlanta: Scholars Press, 1988, pp. 71–84.

———. *Letter Writing in Greco-Roman Antiquity*. Philadelphia: Fortress Press, 1989.

Strange, J. F. "Some Implications of Archaeology for New Testament Studies". *What Has Archaeology To Do With Faith?* Ed. J. H. Charlesworth and W. P. Weaver. Philadelphia: Fortress Press, 1992, pp. 23–59.

Stray, C. *Culture and Discipline: The Transformation of Classics in England 1830–1900.* Oxford: Oxford University Press, 1996.

Strobel, A. "Der Begriff des 'Hauses' im griechischen und römischen Privatrecht". *Zeitschrift für die neutestamentliche Wissenschaft.* 56 (1965) 91–100.

Susini, G. C. *The Roman Stonecutter: An Introduction to Latin Epigraphy.* Oxford: Basil Blackwell, 1973.

Tajra, H. W. *The Trial of St Paul.* Tübingen: J. C. B. Mohr, 1989.

Tanzer, H. H. *The Common People of Pompeii. A Study of the Graffiti.* Baltimore: Johns Hopkins University Press, 1939.

Taubenschlag, R. *The Law of Greco-Roman Egypt in the Light of the Papyri.* Second edition. Warsaw: Panstwowe Wydawnictwo Naukowe, 1958.

Taylor, A. "A Roman Lead Coffin with Pipeclay Figurines from Arrington, Cambridgeshire". *Britannia* 24 (1993) 191–225.

Taylor, Michael. *Community, Anarchy and Liberty.* Cambridge: Cambridge University Press, 1982.

Tellegen-Couperus, Olga. *A Short History of Roman Law.* London: Routledge, 1990.

Theissen, Gerd. *The Social Setting of Pauline Christianity.* Philadelphia: Fortress Press, 1982.

——. *Social Reality and the Early Christians: Theology, Ethics and the World of the New Testament.* Edinburgh: T. & T. Clark, 1993.

Thiselton, A. C. "Realized Eschatology at Corinth". *New Testament Studies* 24 (1977) 510–526.

Thomas, J. A. C. *Textbook of Roman Law.* Oxford: North Holland Publishing Company, 1976.

Thomas, Keith. *Religion and the Decline of Magic.* London: Weidenfeld & Nicolson, 1971.

Thompson, Cynthia L. "Hairstyles, Headcoverings and St Paul". *Biblical Archaeologist* 51 (1988) 99–115.

Thompson, E. A. "Peasant Revolts in Late Roman Gaul and Spain". *Studies in Ancient Roman Society.* Ed. M. I. Finley. London: Routledge, 1974, pp. 304–320.

Thompson, E. A. *Romans and Barbarians*. Madison: University of Wisconsin Press, 1982.

Thompson, E. P. *The Making of the English Working Class*. London: Victor Gollancz, 1963.

———. "Eighteenth-century English Society: Class Struggle Without Class?" *Journal of Social History* 3 (1978) 133–165.

Thompson, Lloyd A. *Romans and Blacks*. London: Routledge, 1989.

Thorley, John. "Junia, A Woman Apostle". *Novum Testamentum* 38 (1996) 18–29.

Tidball, D. *An Introduction to the Sociology of the New Testament*. Exeter: Paternoster Press, 1983.

Toner, J. P. *Leisure and Ancient Rome*. Cambridge: Polity Press, 1995.

Townsend, J. T. "Ancient Education in the Time of the Roman Empire". *Early Church History: The Roman Empire as the Setting of Primitive Christianity*. Ed. S. Benko and J. O'Rourke. London: Oliphants, 1971, pp. 139–163.

Townsend, P. "Measures and Explanations of Poverty in High Income and Low Income Countries: The Problem of Operationalizing the Concepts of Development, Class and Poverty". *The Concept of Poverty*. Ed. P. Townsend. London: Heinemann, 1970, pp. 1–45.

Toynbee, A. J. *Hannibal's Legacy*. Oxford: Oxford University Press, 1965.

Trebilco, Paul. *Jewish Communities in Asia Minor*. Cambridge: Cambridge University Press, 1991.

Treggiari, Susan. *Roman Freedmen During the Late Republic*. Oxford: Clarendon Press, 1969.

———. "Urban Labour In Rome: Mercennarii and Tabernarii". *Non-Slave Labour in the Graeco-Roman World*. Ed. P. Garnsey. Cambridge: Cambridge Philological Society, 1980, pp. 48–64.

———. "Divorce Roman Style: How Easy and How Frequent was it?" *Marriage, Divorce and Children in Ancient Rome*. Ed. Beryl Rawson. Oxford: Clarendon Press, 1991, pp. 31–46.

———. *Roman Marriage*. Oxford: Oxford University Press, 1991.

Trilling, W. *Der zweite Brief an die Thessalonicher*. Zürich: Benziger, 1980.

Tuarnø, Henrik. "Roman Social Structure: Different Approaches for Different Purposes". *Studies in History and Numismatics*. Ed. Rudi Thomsen et al. Aarhus: Aarhus University Press, 1988, pp. 114–123.

Turner, Nigel. *A Grammar of New Testament Greek. III: Syntax.* Edinburgh: T. & T. Clark, 1963.

——. "Second Thoughts: Papyrus Finds". *Expository Times* 76 (1974) 44–48.

Unnik, C. van. *Tarsus or Jerusalem?* London: Epworth Press, 1962.

Urbach, E. E. "Class-Status and Leadership in the World of the Palestinian Sages". *Proceedings of the Israel Academy of Sciences and Humanities* 2 (1968) 38–74.

Vaage, Leif E. "The Cynic Epistles". *Ascetic Behaviour in Greco-Roman Antiquity.* Ed. Vincent L. Wimbush. Minneapolis: Fortress Press, 1990, pp. 117–128

——. "Musonius Rufus". *Ascetic Behaviour in Greco-Roman Antiquity.* Minneapolis: Fortress Press, 1990, pp. 129–133.

Van Dam, R. *Leadership and Community in Late Antique Gaul.* Berkeley: University of California Press, 1985.

Vassiliadis, P. "Equality and Justice in Classical Antiquity and in Paul: The Social Implications of the Pauline Collection". *St Vladimir's Theological Quarterly* 36 (1992) 51–59.

Verhagen, Koenraad. *Co-operation for Survival: An Analysis of an Experiment in Participatory Research and Planning with Small Farmers in Sri Lanka and Thailand.* Amsterdam: Royal Tropical Institute, 1984.

Verhey, A. *The Great Reversal.* Grand Rapids: Eerdmans, 1984.

Veyne, Paul. "Vie de Trimalchion". *Annales: économies, sociétés, civilisations* 16 (1961) 213–247.

——. "Titulus Praelatus". *Revue Archéologique.* (1983) 281–300

——. *Bread and Circuses.* Harmondsworth: Penguin, 1990.

Virlouvet, Catherine. "La plèbe frumentaire à l'époque d'Auguste". *Nourrir la Plèbe.* Ed. A. Giovannini. Basel: Friedrich Reinhardt, 1991, pp. 43–65.

Waele, F. J. de. "Erastus, Oikonoom van Korinthe en Vriend van St. Paulus". *Mededelingen van het Nederlandsch historisch Instituut te Rome* 9 (1929) 40–88.

Waldron, T. "The Effects of Urbanisation on Human Health: The Evidence From Skeletal Remains". *Diet and Crafts in Towns: The Evidence of Animal Remains From the Roman to the Post-Medieval Periods.* Oxford: B. A. R., 1989, pp. 55–73.

Wallace, R. and W. Williams. *The Acts of the Apostles.* London: Bristol Classical Press, 1993.

Wallace-Hadrill, A. "Family and Inheritance in the Augustan Marriage Laws". *Proceedings of the Cambridge Philological Society* 27 (1981) 58–80.

——. "Introduction". *Patronage in Ancient Society.* Ed. A. Wallace-Hadrill. London: Routledge, 1990, pp. 1–13.

——. "Patronage in Roman Society: From Republic to Empire". *Patronage in Ancient Society.* Ed. A. Wallace-Hadrill. London: Routledge, 1990, pp. 63–87.

——. "Roman Arches and Greek Honours". *Proceedings of the Cambridge Philological Society* 36 (1990) 143–181.

——. "Houses and Households: Sampling Pompei and Herculaneum". *Marriage, Divorce and Children in Ancient Rome.* Ed. Beryl Rawson. Oxford: Oxford University Press, 1991, pp. 191–227.

——. "Élites and Trade in the Roman Town". *City and Country.* Ed. J. Rich and A. Wallace-Hadrill, London: Routledge, 1991, pp. 241–269.

——. *Augustan Rome.* London: Bristol Classical Press, 1993.

——. *Houses and Society in Pompeii and Herculaneum.* Princeton: Princeton University Press, 1994.

——. "Public Honour and Private Shame: The Urban Texture of Pompeii". *Urban Society in Roman Italy.* Ed. T. Cornell and K. Lomas. London: UCL Press, 1995, pp. 39–62.

Waltzing, J. P. *Étude historique sur les corporations professionelles chez les Romains depuis les origines jusqu'à la chute de l'Empire d'Occident.* 4 vols. Louvain: Charles Peteri, 1900.

Wansink, Craig S. *Chained in Christ: The Experience and Rhetoric of Paul's Imprisonment.* Sheffield: Sheffield Academic Press, 1996.

Waterbury, J. "An Attempt to Put Patrons and Clients in their Place". *Patrons and Clients in Mediterranean Society.* Ed. E. Gellner and J. Waterbury. London: Duckworth, 1977, pp. 329–343.

Watson, Alan. *The Evolution of the Law.* Oxford: Basil Blackwell, 1985.

——. *Roman Slave Law.* Baltimore: Johns Hopkins University Press, 1987.

Watson, D. F. and A. J. Hauser, *Rhetorical Criticism of the Bible: A Comprehensive Bibliography with Notes on History and Method.* Leiden: E. J. Brill, 1994.

——. "Rhetorical Criticism of the Pauline Epistles Since 1975". *Currents in Research: Biblical Studies. Forthcoming.*

Watson, Francis. *Paul, Judaism and the Gentiles*. Cambridge: Cambridge University Press, 1986.

Watson, Patricia. *Ancient Stepmothers: Myth, Mysogyny and Reality*. Leiden: E. J. Brill, 1995.

Weaver, P. R. C. *Familia Caesaris*. Cambridge: Cambridge University Press, 1972.

——. "Where have all the Junian Latins Gone? Nomenclature and Status in the Early Empire". *Chiron* 20 (1990) 276–304.

Weber, M. *The Protestant Ethic and the Spirit of Capitalism*. London: HarperCollins Academic, 1991.

——. *General Economic History*. New York: Collier, 1961.

——. *The Sociology of Religion*. London: Methuen & Co., 1963.

——. *The City*. New York: The Free Press, 1966.

——. *Economy and Society*. New York: Bedminster Press, 1968.

Weerd, H. van de. "Een Nieuw Opschrift van Korinthe". *Revue belge de philologie et d'histoire* 10 (1931) 87–95.

Weinfeld, Moshe. *The Organisational Pattern and the Penal Code of The Qumran Sect*. Göttingen: Vandenhoeck & Ruprecht, 1986.

Welborn, L. L. "On the Discord in Corinth". *Journal of Biblical Literature* 106 (1987) 85–111.

Welles, C. B. (Ed.). *The Excavation at Dura-Europos. The Final Report VIII: Part 1. The Synagogue*. New Haven: Yale University Press, 1956.

Wells, C. *Bones, Bodies and Disease*. London: Thames & Hudson, 1964.

Wengst, K. *Pax Romana and the Peace of Jesus Christ*. London: SCM Press, 1987.

Westermann, W. L. *The Slave Systems of Greek and Roman Antiquity*. Philadelphia: The American Philosophical Society, 1955.

Whelan, Caroline F. "Amica Pauli: The Role of Phoebe in the Early Church". *Journal for the Study of the New Testament* 49 (1993) 67–85.

White, John L. *Light From Ancient Letters*. Philadelphia: Fortress, 1986.

White, K. D. "Latifundia". *Institute of Classical Studies Bulletin* 14 (1967) 62–79.

——. "Cereals, Bread and Milling in the Roman World". *Food in Antiquity*. Ed. J. Wilkins, D. Harvey and M. Dobson. Exeter: Exeter University Press, 1995, pp. 38–43.

White, L. M. *Building God's House in the Roman World*. London: Johns Hopkins University Press, 1990.

Whittaker, C. R. "The Consumer City Revisited: The Vicus and the City". *Journal of Roman Archaeology* 3 (1990) 110–118.

——. "Studying The Poor in the City of Rome". *Land, City and Trade in the Roman Empire*. Aldershot: Variorum, 1993, pp. 1–25.

——. "Do Theories of the Ancient City Matter?" *Urban Society in Roman Italy*. Ed. T. Cornell and K. Lomas. London: UCL Press, 1995, pp. 9–26.

Wiedemann, T. *Greek and Roman Slavery*. London: Croom Helm, 1981.

——. *Emperors and Gladiators*. London: Routledge, 1992.

Wikander, Ö. *Exploitation of Water-Power or Technological Stagnation?* Lund: Scripta Minora, 1984.

Wilder, Amos. *Early Christian Rhetoric*. Cambridge, MA: Harvard University Press, 1971.

Wilken, R. L. "Collegia, Philosophical Schools and Theology". *Early Church History: The Roman Empire as the Setting of Primitive Christianity*. Ed. S. Benko and J. O'Rourke. London: Oliphants, 1971, pp. 268–291.

——. *John Chrysostom and the Jews*. Berkeley: University of California Press, 1983.

——. *The Christians as the Romans Saw Them*. New Haven: Yale University Press, 1984.

Williams, C. K. and O. H. Zervos. "Corinth 1985: East of the Theatre". *Hesperia* 55 (1986) 129–187.

Williams, Raymond. *Keywords*. London: Fontana, 1983.

Willis, W. L. *Idol Meat at Corinth*. Chico, CA: Scholars Press, 1985.

Wilson, A. "Water-Power in North Africa and the Development of the Horizontal Water-Wheel". *Journal of Roman Archaeology* 8 (1995) 499–510.

——. "Drainage and Sanitation". *Ancient Water Technology*. Ed. Örjan Wikander. Leiden: E. J. Brill, *forthcoming*.

Wilson, Lillian M. *The Clothing of the Ancient Romans*. Baltimore: The Johns Hopkins University Press, 1938.

Wilson, R. McL. "Slippery Words II: Gnosis, Gnostic, Gnosticism". *Expository Times* 89 (1978) 296–300.

Wimbush, Vincent L. *The Worldly Ascetic*. Macon, GA: Mercer University Press, 1987.

Winkler, John J. *The Constraints of Desire: The Anthropology of Sex and Gender in Ancient Greece*. New York: Routledge, 1990.

Winter, B. W. "The Lord's Supper at Corinth: An Alternative Reconstruction". *Reformed Theological Review* 37 (1978) 73–82.

———. "The Public Honouring of Christian Benefactors, Romans 13:3–4 and 1 Peter 2:14–15". *Journal for the Study of the New Testament* 34 (1988) 87–103.

———. "'If a man does not work . . . ,' A Cultural and Historical Setting for II Thessalonians 3:6". *Tyndale Bulletin* 40 (1989) 303–315.

———. "Secular and Christian Responses to Corinthian Famines". *Tyndale Bulletin* 40 (1989) 88–106.

———. "Civil Litigation in Secular Corinth and the Church: The Forensic Background to 1 Corinthians 6:1–8". *New Testament Studies* 37 (1991) 559–572.

———. *Seek the Welfare of the City: Christians as Benefactors and Citizens*. Carlisle: Paternoster Press, 1994.

———. "Acts and Food Shortages". *The Book of Acts in its First Century Setting: Volume 2: Graeco-Roman Setting*. Ed. David W. J. Gill and Conrad Gempf. Carlisle: Paternoster Press, 1994, pp. 59–78.

Winter, Sara. "Methodological Observations on a New Interpretation of Paul's Letter to Philemon". *Union Seminary Quarterly Review* 39 (1984) 203–212.

———. "Paul's Letter to Philemon". *New Testament Studies* 33 (1987) 1–15.

Wire, Antoinette Clark. *The Corinthian Women Prophets*. Minneapolis: Fortress, 1990.

Wiseman, J. "Corinth and Rome I: 228 BC – AD 267". *Aufstieg und Niedergang der römischen Welt*. Volume 2.7.1. Ed. H. Temporini and W. Haase. Berlin: Walter de Gruyter, 1979, pp. 438–548.

Wistrand, Magnus. *Entertainment and Violence in Ancient Rome: The Attitudes of Roman Writers of the First Century AD*. Göteborg: Acta Universitatis Gothoburgensis, 1992.

Witherington, B. *Conflict and Community in Corinth: A Socio-Rhetorical Commentary on 1 and 2 Corinthians*. Carlisle: Paternoster Press, 1995.

Witke, E. C. "Juvenal III. Eclogue for the Urban Poor". *Hermes* 90 (1962) 244–248.

Wood, N. "African Peasant Terrorism". *History From Below: Studies in Popular Protest and Popular Ideology in Honour of George Rudé*. Ed. F. Krantz. Montreal: Concordia University, 1985, pp. 279–299.

Woodhead, A. G. *The Study of Greek Inscriptions*. Second edition. Bristol: Bristol Classical Press, 1992.

Woolf, G. "World-Systems Analysis and the Roman Empire". *Journal of Roman Archaeology* 3 (1990) 43–58.

——. "Imperialism, Empire and the Integration of the Roman Economy". *World Archaeology* 23 (1992) 283–293.

—— and A. K. Bowman (Ed.) *Literacy and Power in the Ancient World*. London: Routledge, 1995.

Wuellner, W. H. "The Sociological Implications of 1 Corinthians 1:26–28 Reconsidered". *Studia Evangelica IV*. Ed. E. A. Livingstone. Berlin: Akademie, 1973, pp. 666–672.

——. "Traditions and Interpretation of the "Wise – Powerful – Noble" Triad in 1 Cor 1,26". *Studia Evangelica VII*. Ed. E. A. Livingstone. Berlin: Akademie, 1982, pp. 557–562.

Wyke, Maria. "Make Like Nero! The Appeal of a Cinematic Emperor". *Reflections of Nero: Culture, History and Representation*. Ed. J. Elsner and J. Masters. London: Duckworth, 1994, pp. 11–28.

Yamauchi, Edwin. *Pre-Christian Gnosticism*. London: Tyndale Press, 1973.

——. *The Archaeology of the New Testament Cities in Western Asia Minor*. London: Pickering & Inglis, 1980.

Yavetz, Z. "The Living Conditions of the Urban Plebs in Republican Rome". *Crisis in the Roman Republic*. Ed. R. Seager, Cambridge: W. Heffer & Sons, 1969, pp. 162–179.

Yeo, Stephen. "Introduction: Rival Clusters of Potential: Ways of Seeing Co-operation". *New Views of Co-operation*. Ed. Stephen Yeo. London: Routledge, 1988, pp. 1–9.

Yoder, John H. *The Politics of Jesus*. First edition. Grand Rapids: Eerdmans, 1972.

Yorke, Gosnell. *The Church as the Body of Christ in the Pauline Corpus: A Re-examination*. Lanham: University Press of America, 1991.

Zahn, T. *Apostelgeschichte des Lucas*. Leipzig: A. Deichertsche, 1919.

Zanker, Paul. *The Power of Images in the Age of Augustus*. Ann Arbor: The University of Michigan Press, 1990.

Ziesler, J. *Christian Asceticism*. Grand Rapids: Eerdmans, 1973.

——. *Paul's Letter to the Romans*. London: SCM Press, 1989.

——. *Pauline Christianity*. Second edition. Oxford: Oxford University Press, 1991.

Zimmerman, A. F. *Die urchristlichen Lehrer*. Tübingen: J. C. B. Mohr, 1988.

Zivanovic, S. *Ancient Diseases: The Elements of Palaeopathology*. London: Methuen & Co., 1982.

Index of New Testament References

Index of Ancient Authors

(and multi-authored, anonymous and pseudepigraphical works)

Index of Modern Authors

(Selected)

Index of Subjects